Dr. Yang Jianli's extraordinary [illegible] ment we need for both our spirits and intellects [illegible] and doubt. The clarity of Dr. Yang's moral vision is compelling but it is the compassion and humility of this brave man that wins our hearts. He speaks with great moral authority born out of decades of courageous leadership and sacrifice that has taken him from the terror of Tiananmen Square to the brutality of imprisonment in solitary confinement. In his words we find wisdom and a call to be our brother's keepers. It is fitting that this powerful collection takes its title from Abraham Lincoln's Gettysburg Address because like the Great Emancipator, himself, Dr. Yang Jianli calls forth "the better angels of our nature".

—Dr. Katrina Lantos Swett,
President of Lantos Foundation for Human Rights and Justice, Former Chair of US Commission on International Religious Freedom

Jianli Yang's voice has been prescient and prophetic, frequently warning the world to wake up to the dangers posed by the Chinese Communist Party. His authoritative book should be read by anyone in doubt about the seriousness of the threat posed to our fundamental freedoms and human rights by the CCP and its ideology.

—David (Lord) Alton

Dr Yang Jianli is a truly courageous voice for truth, justice, liberty and human dignity for the peoples of China and beyond, and has shown inspirational, visionary leadership in fighting for the rights of China's diverse ethnic and religious communities and building unity among them, as well as struggling for freedom and democracy itself. This powerful collection of his thoughts and ideas is a testimony to his tireless work and provides essential insights into the nature of the Chinese Communist Party regime, which is without doubt the major global challenge of our times. Anyone who wants to understand the fight for freedom against tyranny, truth against lies and justice against repression should read this book.

—Benedict Rogers
co-founder and Chief Executive, Hong Kong Watch

Yang Jianli has dedicated his life to the freedom and rights of Chinese people. Yet he speaks for the freedom and rights of all of us, everywhere. Morally and intellectually, he is one of the most impressive people in the world. Also, he's got guts.

—Jay Nordlinger
Senior Editor of National Review

Yang Jianli's brilliant and inspiring speeches take us on a compelling journey through his struggle to free the people of China, and are a must-read for anyone interested in the universal cause of defending democracy against tyranny. Read this book — and learn from one of the most articulate, brave and dedicated human rights dissidents of our time.

— Hillel Neuer
Executive Director of United Nations Watch

This is necessary reading. The words of Dr. Yang Jianli provide a clarity and reason as the world crisis concerning totalitarian China becomes greater each day. Here lies hope for the people who live under CCP oppression or, as is the case of Taiwan, are threatened by it.

—Dr. Orlando Gutierrez Boronat
Cuban American author and democracy advocate

As the Communist Party of China has rapidly become the greatest threat to all of humanity, For Us, The Living is a most timely and vital source of history, vision, and hope that this evil menace can be defeated so that those living under the CCP's oppression will no longer be slaves. An eyewitness to China's history, Dr. Yang Jianli was first dubbed a counter revolutionary by his own father, a local Party official, for questioning whether communism was a system that could truly help the Chinese people. He started his activism at age 12 trying to protect Chinese farmers from the CCP's tyranny and as a graduate student participated in the Tiananmen Square demonstrations. Despite 5 years of jail in China and numerous death threats, Yang has never stopped being an activist for the freedom of his homeland and a voice for all those who have suffered whether Tibetans or Uyghurs from the CCP's tyranny. He has been a source of inspiration and hope to so many, myself included, and anyone who believes that no one should be a slave, should read this book and take action before it is too late.

—Suzanne Scholte Seoul Peace Prize Laureate

Over decades, Yang Jianli has maintained moral clarity in his tireless advocacy for freedom, democracy and human rights in China. These documents offer information and inspiration on how to deal with the greatest challenge facing the international community today.

—Dr. Aaron Rhodes, President,
Forum for Religious Freedom-Europe and former Executive Director
of the International Helsinki Federation for Human Rights

Dr. Jianli Yang is a courageous visionary and voice in the pursuit of justice. "For Us, The Living"- a compelling compendium of speeches and essays- is a testament to his inspired vision and values- of speaking truth to power; and is at one and the same time an elegy to the fallen heroes of the struggle for freedom, and a roadmap for how this quest for freedom can be realized. "For Us, The Living" is as timely as it is necessary.

—Irwin Cotler
Lawyer, law professor, Founder and
Chair of the Raul Wallenberg Centre for Human Rights
Former Minister of Justice and Attorney General
of Canada and Canadian MP

When I think about Yang Jianli, my friend, collaborator, and former client – who I've now known for almost a quarter century – there are many words that immediately come to mind: brilliant, compassionate, courageous, indefatigable, and a committed Christian. But these only scratch the surface. More than anyone else, it was Yang who changed the course of my life and inspired me to become an international human rights lawyer, after we met as graduate students at Harvard University and planned the protests against

Chinese President Jiang Zemin's visit to campus in Fall 1997. Later, I served as Yang's pro bono counsel when he served five years as a political prisoner in China. And when he came home, we worked together to advocate on behalf of numerous persecuted Chinese dissidents such as Liu Xiaobo and his wife Liu Xia, Gao Zhisheng, and Chen Kegui. But Yang's remarkable volume For Us, The Living does something truly extraordinary. In a single book, he brings into focus through his own work the narrative arc the Chinese's people's struggle, against all odds, to persevere and achieve something they and the world deserve – a peaceful and democratic China, whose government respects the fundamental human rights of all its diverse ethnic and religious peoples, whose cause has always been Yang's own. It also shows, importantly, that as hard as the Chinese Communist Party might try, with more than 1.4 billion Chinese, it will either need to fulfill its people's yearning for freedom or find itself swept away by the tide of history.

—Jared Genser
International Human Rights Lawyer

The speeches and essays you find in this book will inspire commitment to the work of justice, an everlasting struggle calling all those who can see a fairer future and are not afraid to help bring it in. As activist scholars, and all those who follow in the footsteps of the Tiananmen Square generation, encounter the words and work of Dr. Yang Jianli, they will be encouraged to mirror his courageous commitment.

—The Reverend Gordon J. Schultz taught philosophy
and ethics at Mt. Ida College in Newton, Massachusetts (ret.).
He also served as pastor and theologian for the
Episcopal and Lutheran churches in the US.

FOR US,
the
LIVING

Collected Speeches From 2000-2020

FOR US,

the

LIVING

A Journey to Shine the Light on Truth

Dr. YANG Jianli

Redwood Publishing, LLC
Orange County, California
(949) 829-BOOK (2665)
www.redwooddigitalpublishing.com

Printed in the United States of America

First Printing, 2021

ISBN 978-1-952106-83-5 (paperback)
ISBN 978-1-952106-84-2 (ebook)
Library of Congress Control Number: 2021908533

To contact the author, Dr. YANG Jianli - 楊建利, directly:
President & Founder - 發起人
Citizen Power Initiatives for China - 公民力量
Office: 202-827-5762
Direct: 857-472-9039
Address: 533 5th Street NE. Washington, D.C. 20002
www.citizenpowerforchina.org

I would like to dedicate this book to Liu Xiaobo, the 2010 Nobel Peace Prize laureate who died in 2017 as a political prisoner (I represented him at the 2010 Nobel Peace Prize award ceremony); to the two nameless Tiananmen "Tank Men"—a young man who risked his life by standing courageously in front of an array of tanks and the front tank's driver who took the moral high ground by refusing to slay his compatriot; and to the more than 150 Tibetans who have resorted to self-immolation as a means of protest to free Tibet from the CCP's oppressive rule. I have mentioned these heroes many times in my speeches, and I will continue to hold them in my heart and look to them for moral guidance.

Table of Contents

SECTION IV—INTERETHNIC/INTERFAITH CONFERENCES: UNIFIED IN A COMMON BELIEF *November 2008–October 2009*

Chapter 26 Our Strive for Freedom Is an Integrated One and Cannot Be Separately Carried Out. 147
Fourth Interethnic/Interfaith Leadership Conference
Harvard University, Cambridge, MA

Chapter 27 Reciprocity Should Be US China Policy Platform . . . 152
Eastern Kentucky University
Richmond, KY

Chapter 28 Charter 08: A Wake-Up Call for America and China. . 162
Congressional Defense and Foreign Policy Forum
Washington, DC

Chapter 29 Massacre, Miracle and Model. 172
Gustavus Adolphus College
St Peter, MN

Chapter 30 The Pain of Victims and Their Families of Tiananmen Massacre Will Endure until This Justice Is Served. . . . 182
Boston, MA

Chapter 31 Key to Reconciliation Is the Growth of the Democratic Forces 184
Congressional-Executive Commission on China Hearing
Washington, DC

Chapter 32 You Shall Know the Truth and the Truth Will Make You Free. 189
Rally Commemorating the Twentieth Anniversary of Tiananmen
Washington, DC

Chapter 33 The Nonviolent Tiananmen Democracy Movement 191
ICNC Summer Institute for the Advanced Study of Nonviolent Conflict
Tufts University, Medford, MA

Chapter 34 Statement Regarding the Continued Violence in Xinjiang Region of China 198
Rally Supporting Uyghurs' Peaceful Resistance
Washington, DC

SECTION VI—THE LIU XIAOBO STORY: THE UNIVERSAL HUMAN DESIRE FOR FREEDOM *December 2010—February 2012*

Chapter 43 If Liu Xiaobo Is Guilty, Then We Are All Guilty 247
Event Supporting Liu Xiaobo, Hosted by the Visual Artists Guild, PEN America, and Reporters Without Borders
Columbia University, New York, NY

Chapter 44 To You, Xiaobo and Liu Xia, to the People of China, to Freedom! 250
Banquet for Liu Xiaobo on the Eve of the 2010 Nobel Peace Prize Award Ceremony
Oslo, Norway

Chapter 45 I, Too, Have No Enemies. 253
Exhibition Honoring Liu Xiaobo
Nobel Center, Oslo, Norway

Chapter 46 It Is the Matter of How Chinese Government Treats Its Own Citizens. 255
Hearing Hosted by Chairwoman Ros-Lehtinen of the Committee on Foreign Affairs of US House of Representatives
Washington, DC

Chapter 47 The Time Has Come to Realize That Tolerance for Tyrannies Does Not Promote Security 258
Third Annual Geneva Summit for Human Rights and Democracy
Geneva, Switzerland

Chapter 48 We Must Prepare Ourselves to Seize That Torch 264
Amnesty International Meeting
Seattle, WA

Chapter 49 Cultural and Religious Identities Are Allies of Democracy 269
Sixth Interethnic/Interfaith Leadership Conference
Los Angeles, CA

Chapter 50 The Myth of Han China 273
Oslo Freedom Forum
Oslo, Norway

Chapter 96 Your Slavery Is My Servitude, Your Fight Is My Struggle, and Your Liberty Will Be My Freedom 460
Presenting the 2015 Pedro Luis Boitel Freedom Award at Summit of Generations
Institute for Cuban and Cuban American Studies, University of Miami, Miami, FL

SECTION XII—WHAT IS THE WEST'S RECORD ON DEFENDING HUMAN RIGHTS? *November 2015—March 2017*

Chapter 97 Propose an Index Ranking Democracies on the Basis of What Efforts They Make to Help Promote Human Rights in Autocracies. 465
Victims of Communism Memorial Foundation's Truman-Reagan Medal of Freedom Award Ceremony
Washington, DC

Chapter 98 Campaign to Inscribe the Tiananmen Massacre on the UNESCO's Memory of the World Register, and Seek Truth about the Two Tiananmen Tank Men. 468
CECC Press Conference Commemorating the Fifth Anniversary of Liu Xiaobo's Winning the Nobel Peace Prize
Washington, DC
Appendix. Announcement of the Launching of Two Worldwide Campaigns

Chapter 99 That Day Will Come Sooner with Our United Effort . . 473
March 10 Tibetan Rally in Front of the Chinese Embassy
Washington, DC

Chapter 100 The Best Use of Power Is to Help the Powerless 476
March 10 Tibetan Rally in Front of the White House
Washington, DC

Chapter 101 Follow Dolkun Isa's Example to Continue Our United Effort 478
Victims of Communism Memorial Foundation's Human Rights Award Ceremony
Washington, DC

Chapter 102 Democracy for China: Missed Opportunities and Opportunities Ahead. 480
Congressional Defense and Foreign Policy Forum Hosted by Defense Forum Foundation
Washington, DC

Chapter 103 Report about China at the 2016 National Captive Nations Week Luncheon. 492
Luncheon at Heritage Foundation Hosted by Victims of Communism Memorial Foundation
Washington, DC

Chapter 104 Steps to Make the United Nations Address China's Human Rights Situation More Effectively 495
Forum Hosted by Freedom House and the United Nations Association
Washington, DC

Chapter 105 Never Give Up 499
Tibetan Rally in Front of the Chinese Embassy
Washington, DC

SECTION XIII—THE DEATH OF LIU XIAOBO: HIS SEED WILL GROW *July 2017—October 2017*

Chapter 106 Preserve the Legacy of Liu Xiaobo's Struggle for a Democratic Free China 505
Hearing Hosted by the House Foreign Affairs Subcommittee on Africa, Global Health, Global Human Rights, and International Organizations
Washington, DC

Chapter 107 Additional Remarks at Hearing on "The Tragic Case of Liu Xiaobo" 508
Hearing Hosted by the House Foreign Affairs Subcommittee on Africa, Global Health, Global Human Rights, and International Organizations
Washington, DC

Chapter 108 He Represents the Best of What China Can Ever Be . 511
"Remembering the Legacy of Liu Xiaobo" Hosted by Victims of Communism Memorial Foundation
Washington, DC
Chapter 109 Taiwan Out of the UN: Unfair to Taiwan and Harmful to Global Interests 513
Rally "Taiwan Membership for the UN"
New York, NY
Chapter 110 Liu Xiaobo's Shining Example and Stern Warning 516
Forum 2000
Prague, Czech Republic
Chapter 111 People of China, Too, Want Human Rights. 520
The 2017 Convention of the Nonviolent Radical Party Transnational Transparency
Rome, Italy

SECTION XIV—SETBACKS TO FREEDOM: A CLEAR AND PRESENT DANGER *November 2017—April 2019*

Chapter 112 Overcoming Setbacks to the Advance of Democracy . . 527
Twelfth Interethnic/Interfaith Leadership Conference
Tokyo, Japan
Chapter 113 Let's Redouble Our Efforts for a Free Tibet 531
Human Rights Day Tibetans Rally in New York
New York, NY
Chapter 114 Tyranny's Desperate Wars Against Fundamental Human Dignity Are Bound to Fail 534
Opening Session of Tenth Geneva Summit for Human Rights and Democracy
Geneva, Switzerland
Chapter 115 Human Rights Defenders Wang Quanzhang and Yu Wensheng. 536
Tenth Geneva Summit for Human Rights and Democracy
Geneva, Switzerland

Chapter 116 The Two Tank Men 541
TEDx Talk at Carnegie Mellon University
Pittsburgh, PA
Chapter 117 Red China and Red Notices. 545
Twelfth International Journalism Festival
Perugia, Italy
Chapter 118 The Spirit of Tiananmen Continues to Change China . 550
Candlelight Vigil Commemorating the Twenty-Ninth Anniversary of 1989 Tiananmen Square Massacre
Washington, DC
Chapter 119 Jointly Counter Fascism with Chinese Characteristics 552
Thirteenth Interethnic/Interfaith Leadership Conference
Washington, DC
Chapter 120 To Tibetan Brothers and Sisters 555
Rally Commemorating the Sixtieth Anniversary of the Tibetan National Uprising
Dharamsala, India
Chapter 121 Presentation Speech for Courage Award to Dhondup Wangchen. 557
Geneva Summit 2019
Geneva, Switzerland
Chapter 122 Supporting the Uyghur Human Rights Policy Act and UIGHUR Act. 560
Rally Supporting Human Rights for Uyghurs
Washington, DC

SECTION XV—CALLING ON AMERICA: SHINE THE LIGHT OF FREEDOM *May 2019—September 2019*

Chapter 123 To Make America Great Again: Lincoln and Reagan Standing as Shining Examples for President Trump and the American People to Follow 565
Skagit County Republican Party Lincoln/Reagan Dinner
Skagit, WA

Chapter 124 Xi Jinping's Grave Threat to China and the World . . 571
#RightsCity Montreal 2019
Concordia University, Montreal, Canada
Chapter 125 Every Day, We Must Be Vigilant 574
Candlelight Vigil Commemorating the Thirtieth Anniversary of Tiananmen Massacre
Victims of Communism Memorial Park; Washington, DC
Chapter 126 "Go to Hell. I'm in America Now." 576
Accepting Honorary Citizenship of Skagit County of Washington State
Washington, DC
Chapter 127 Your Liberty Will Be My Freedom 578
Acceptance Speech for Order of Merit of Human Solidarity Bestowed by the Assembly of the Cuban Resistance
Miami, FL
Chapter 128 Washington Declaration on the Thirtieth Anniversary of the Tiananmen Massacre 580
Washington, DC
Chapter 129 Human Chain Against China. 588
Global Anti-Chinazi Rally
Chinese Embassy, Washington, DC

SECTION XVI—WHY WE NEED A HUMAN RIGHTS NATO: THE NEW COLD WAR WITH CHINA *October 2019—November 2020*

Chapter 130 A Human Rights NATO 593
Forum 2000 Panel: "China: Human Rights in the Twenty-First Century Digital Surveillance State"
Prague, Czech Republic
Chapter 131 Defeat Chinazi and Ensure Freedom for the People of Hong Kong and Us All. 595
Rally Standing with Hong Kong
Catholic University, Washington, DC

Foreword

By His Holiness the Dalai Lama

One of the reasons that has been giving me hope in finding a resolution to the Tibetan issue is the positive response from Chinese students and the scholar community when they come to learn the truth of our issue. Dr. Yang Jianli is one such Chinese individual, and I have known him for over two decades now. I have appreciated the opportunity to exchange views with ethnic Chinese friends like him and others about our common struggle for freedom and dignity.

He has been continuing his campaign for freedom, democracy, and rule of law in the People's Republic of China. In the process, he has taken his campaign to different fora, internationally. I am pleased to see that he has now compiled his speeches and remarks at different times into a book.

China, with a quarter of the world's population, can play a positive role in the comity of nations; for this it will have to be a more open society, and its leadership will have to work toward fulfilling the hopes and aspirations of its people. Dr. Yang Jianli has his perspective on how China can be transformed, and I am hopeful readers will find his book interesting and useful.

Foreword

By Natan Sharansky

Yang Jianli became a free man in 1989 at Tiananmen Square, where he crossed the red line between the world of doublethink (in which hundreds of millions of Chinese live) to the dissident world. Since then, over thirty years, he has continued the life of a free man despite persecutions, threats, and long years of imprisonment.

During this time, the Western leaders have changed their policy toward China many times—from flirting to confrontations, from condemnations of the regime to self-persuasion that this is the regime that Chinese people love and want.

But the position of free man Yang Jianli remained unchanged. He exposed the policy of violation of individual human rights as well as the national rights of Tibetans, Uyghurs, and many other nationalities, showing the Chinese regime's real face.

Why is it essential for the free world to hear Yang Jianli and other democratic dissidents' voices? Dissidents play a double role. First, they understand and see the real face and inner weakness of a regime trying to control its citizens and hiding behind the facade of a demonstration of strength and solidarity. Secondly—as another great dissident and Soviet scientist, Andrei Sakharov, used to say, "Never trust the regime more than it trusts its citizens." The free world should build their policy toward the dictatorships by listening to their dissidents. Listen to Yang Jianli's voice!

Natan Sharansky
Chair of ISGAP (The Institute for the Study
of Global Antisemitism and Policy)
Former Political Prisoner of the Soviet Union

Introduction

It was the afternoon of March 20, 2018. I was sitting in the meeting hall of the United Nations Human Rights Council (UNHRC) in Geneva, waiting my turn to address the Council. I was well aware that my home country, the People's Republic of China, was both a member of the forty-seven-nation Council and one of the world's worst abusers of human rights.

Seated in the back row reserved for speakers from non-governmental organizations (NGOs), I was busily trying to prepare. Each NGO speaker was allotted just ninety seconds to deliver their remarks. I had a lot to say, and fitting everything in would be challenging.

Finally, my turn came. Speaking in my native tongue of Mandarin, I introduced myself: "Mr. Chairman, my name is Yang Jianli, and I am a Chinese citizen."

Despite being abruptly interrupted three times by a Chinese diplomat in attendance, I still managed to get across most of what I wanted to say.

I began by posing a question to the delegates: Should the Chinese Communist Party (CCP)—a regime that utterly disregards the Universal Declaration of Human Rights—be eligible to represent China on the UN Human Rights Council?

I presented the following facts:

1. Ever since the CCP assumed power in 1949, it has committed countless human rights violations, directly causing the deaths of tens of millions of people and resulting in the false imprisonment of hundreds of millions of citizens. These human rights atrocities

include the Land Reform (1950–1953), the Anti-Rightist Campaign (1957–1959), the Great Leap Forward (1958–1962), the Cultural Revolution (1966–1976), the Tiananmen Square Massacre (1989), suppression of the Democracy Party of China (1998 to present), the crackdown on signatories of Charter 08 (2009 to present), as well as ongoing persecution of human rights defenders, activists, and lawyers.

2. Since Xi Jinping came to power in 2012, the narrow freedom that the Chinese people had achieved through decades of tireless struggle has been aggressively stamped out. From 2012 to 2017, the Chinese government committed round after round of brutal human rights crackdowns, including censorship of online speech, the illegal detainment of lawyers and activists, the implementation of suppressive policies in Tibet and Xinjiang, and the demolition of churches and mosques.
3. In 2017, Liu Xiaobo—a Chinese writer, human rights activist, and recipient of the 2010 Nobel Peace Prize—died while serving a lengthy prison term for the spurious charge of "inciting subversion of state power." The plight of Liu Xiaobo is not an isolated case. Over the years, China's top leader Xi Jinping has ruthlessly silenced anyone who threatens his personal political power and has made every effort to transform China from an authoritarian state into a personal dictatorship.

In conclusion, I asked the UN Human Rights Council to think about the following question: What does the continued reign of the CCP regime mean for the future of the world? I called on the countries represented at the Council to heed their consciences and take collective action to set China on a path toward rule of law, human rights, and individual freedom. I warned the Council that if the world sat by idly while the CCP continued to trample on human rights, it would not only be the Chinese people who get hurt; the CCP regime would ultimately become a giant malignant tumor threatening the future of all humanity.

About a week earlier, I had been in Geneva attending the Geneva Summit for Human Rights and Democracy. No sooner did I return to America than I learned that Xi Jinping had just removed the presidential term limit from the Chinese constitution, paving the path for him to become president for life. Setting term limits was one of the few positive changes China had made to its political system in the forty-some years since the end of the Cultural Revolution. My outrage at Xi's blatant power grab prompted me to return to Geneva right away to address the assembly of the UN Human Rights Council.

Until that moment, I had not thought another cultural revolution was possible. I wrongly believed that we the Chinese people, who'd experienced the ten years of disaster that was the first Cultural Revolution, must have learned our lesson.

* * *

I was just three years old when the Cultural Revolution was launched in 1966 by CCP chairman Mao Zedong. By that time, Mao—who had already been responsible for the genocide of approximately sixty million Chinese citizens since taking power in 1949—had come to believe that a large number of CCP officials and many ordinary citizens lacked a true understanding of communism. Mao's solution to this perceived crisis was to imprison people of all backgrounds and all walks of life in what became known as "re-education camps." In these camps, detainees were tortured and indoctrinated with a new and "purer" form of communism, known as "Maoism." At the time, many of Mao's comrades in the top leadership ranks were dissatisfied with him due to his string of disastrous policy failures (including the Great Leap Forward and the Great Famine). Mao launched the Cultural Revolution to incite the masses to rebel against officials who challenged his power and authority.

My father, Yang Fengshan, was a local party chief at the time. Like millions of other CCP officials whom Mao no longer trusted, my father was targeted and assaulted by rebels mobilized by Mao.

I was sitting in my house when I looked out the window and witnessed a group of men savagely punching and kicking my father for what seemed like an eternity. They beat him mercilessly, but apparently not to kill him, because he was still breathing when they hauled him away in their cart to a countryside detention camp.

Of course, as a three-year-old boy, I was unable to comprehend the circumstances surrounding the savage beating my father had endured. I was as terrified as I was indignant. I felt the urge to seek revenge on the perpetrators.

That feeling would be tested a few years later by a chance encounter I had with a small group of laborers. As a first or second grader, after school let out, I would often take short walks by myself outside the town. One day, I saw a group of construction laborers on a hillside using a huge hacksaw to cut a hole in the largest rock I had ever seen. I became even more interested as I heard them singing traditional Chinese workers' songs as they flexed their saws.

I walked over and introduced myself to the laborers and asked them some questions about their work. They were very friendly and seemed happy that a little boy like me had shown an interest in the work they were doing. As we started to talk, they told me that they were using the rocks they were cutting to build a new road and new houses. I was excited to learn something I had never known before.

But that feeling of excitement would soon turn to a feeling of unrest. Just to be friendly, they asked me what my name was, including my family name. As soon as I answered, they fell silent. Their sudden silence confused me. I became even more confused when, after they returned to their work, they once again started to sing songs. In their songs, I heard my father's name; the laborers were singing very unkind words about him. I felt shocked and embarrassed. It was beyond my comprehension why these laborers, who didn't seem like bad people, despised my father.

I later realized that the reason many people hated local officials like my father was because the CCP's oppressive policies were implemented from the top down by officials of various levels. During the Cultural Revolution, the local common people (known as the *laobaixing* in Chinese) who had suffered at the hands of local CCP officials like my father still harbored hatred toward them, even though the officials themselves were also brutalized by Mao.

In 1970, my father was reinstated as a local party chief, alongside many other officials. The rebels mobilized by Mao had done their job of helping Mao eliminate his immediate challenger—Liu Shaoqi, whom Mao referred to as "China's Khrushchev"—as well as Liu's followers, both real and perceived. Mao decided it was time for the rebels to go. They were no longer useful to him and were less trustworthy than the old cadres who had followed him in the revolution. Among the first things these reinstated officials did when they returned was to viciously seek revenge on those rebels who had brutalized them. Another round of bloodshed followed. It was "kill or be killed."

In the summer of 1975, there was a big flood in my native province of Shandong and adjacent areas. My father, as a top local government official, was tasked with organizing and overseeing relief efforts in the farm villages in our county. Perhaps as a fatherly gesture of love and respect for me (his youngest son), he took me with him on his relief trip to the countryside.

The flood was bad but manageable. What was unmanageable were the conditions of the people living there—which I learned had been going on for decades. I saw parents and their children trying to survive without enough food to eat, without running water to clean themselves, without electricity, coal, or fuel to keep themselves warm, without sufficient clothing to cover their bodies, and without beds to sleep in.

It was the opposite of what we learned in school, where we were taught that the Chinese were the luckiest and happiest people on earth thanks to the leadership of Chairman Mao and the Communist Party. I started to become suspicious and resentful.

When we returned home from the relief trip, I confronted my father about the things I had witnessed. I explained that, for the first time in my life, I understood the horrible human suffering caused by communist rule. For my father, though, such talk was unacceptable. After that, I often found myself arguing with my father across the dinner table. He even called me a "counter-revolutionary"—an accusation that (if made to government officials) would have resulted in my imprisonment.

I became even more vexed when I learned that three members of our nuclear family died of starvation during the Great Famine (1959–1961). How could my father still insist that Mao and the Communist Party were "great, glorious, and righteous?" Was my father a liar or a true believer?

I also felt guilty about the poor peasants I had just met in the countryside. To compensate, I removed my own mattress and began sleeping on a straw mat. My mother called me crazy for doing so. My older sister, with whom I discussed the need for a peasant uprising, warned that I would get in trouble.

Still, from the ages of 12 to 15, the fear of getting "in trouble" with the government did not prevent me from performing some acts of kindness to help ordinary people who were suffering under China's communist rule.

For example, I helped local farmers survive the communist government's prohibition against free trade. Starting from the Great Leap Forward, in which capital, natural resources, and means of production were all taken public, the communist government orchestrated police raids to capture and arrest farmers who dared to sell the crops they had harvested, items such as grains, peanuts, and fruit. The peasants wanted cash to buy essentials such as oil and salt. Before each raid was about to take place, I secretly informed the farmers about the police's plans.

My plans for initiating a covert "peasant revolution" turned out to be short-lived. With Mao's death in 1976, the Cultural Revolution came to an end. Of course, that end came too late for the millions of people who lost their lives and the hundreds of millions of families who were subjected to unspeakable suffering and fear during that tumultuous ten-year period. But with the end of the Cultural Revolution, life in China began to return to some semblance of normalcy. Schools and universities were reopened after a decade-long shutdown. Parents once again placed a primary emphasis on the education of their children.

In 1978, at the age of 15, I enrolled in Liaocheng Normal College (now known as Liaocheng University) to pursue a Bachelor of Science in Mathematics. For a time, I left my "peasant comrades" and my politics behind.

In 1982, after graduating from Liaocheng Normal College, I was accepted to the graduate mathematics program at Beijing Normal University. It was in 1983, during my studies there, that I faced another profound internal conflict. By the early 1980s, CCP officials from the 1949 Communist Revolution were gradually reaching retirement age. With a steep decline in the number of working-age and educated cadres, the CCP was in urgent need of fresh blood. China's "enlightenment faction" (represented by Hu Yaobang, then-general secretary of the CCP Central Committee) began recruiting young intellectuals to become Party members. When Hu Yaobang called on young intellectuals to "join the Party and change it from within," many young students—including me—believed he was sincere. With high hopes and an open mind, I joined the Party.

I soon came to regret that decision, despite being rapidly promoted to the middle ranks of the Party. It didn't take me long to realize it was wishful thinking to believe I could change the CCP from within. Indeed, it was the other way around—while the Party remained the same, it changed the young intellectuals who joined it in a negative and lasting way.

Three years later, in 1986, I abandoned what most people saw as a "bright future" in both academia and politics in China and came to the United States to pursue a PhD degree in Mathematics at the University of California. I breathed the fresh, beautiful air of freedom for the first time in my life.

For the next three years, my main focus was on my studies. Then history intervened. In the spring of 1989, tens of thousands of Chinese students staged a series of peaceful anti-government demonstrations in Tiananmen Square, located in the heart of Beijing. My hope was rekindled. I put my studies on hold and returned to China to join the protests.

I didn't realize that I was about to become both a participant in and a witness to an impending tragedy: the Tiananmen Massacre. On June 4th, ordered by the People's Liberation Army to show no restraint, government soldiers slaughtered thousands of demonstrators by firing at them with machine guns and rolling over them with tanks. I was among the fortunate protestors who survived the massacre. Still in possession of my US student visa, I was able to flee China and return to the United States before the CCP reasserted itself and launched mass arrests.

My memory of the tragedy I witnessed at Tiananmen Square will remain with me forever. I will never forget the sight of so many young men and women—mostly young college students with the rest of their lives ahead of them—lying dead in the street. I felt almost guilty to be among the lucky ones to survive. This experience refueled my commitment to fight the Chinese Communist Party and help achieve freedom for my native land.

Since then, my commitment has never wavered. As a student at UC Berkeley (from which I graduated with a PhD in Mathematics in 1991) and later as a student at Harvard University (from which I graduated with a PhD in Political Economy in 2001), I frequently testified before the US Congress, made appearances on television, and gave lectures on college campuses around the world. In addition, I established *Foundation for China in the 21st Century* (FC21C), a US-based, pro-democracy activism and research organization. As president of FC21C, I led a large-scale research project that produced a draft constitution for a future democratic China.

In 2000, I launched a series of annual "Interethnic/Interfaith Leadership Conferences." The conferences seek to advance mutual understanding, respect, and cooperation among the diverse ethnic, religious, and regional groups of the People's Republic of China. They also aim to explore universal values and establish common ground to advance democracy and human rights for all. The groups represented at the conferences include Han Chinese, Tibetans, Uyghurs, Mongolians, Christians, Muslims, Buddhists, Falun Gong practitioners, and people from Taiwan, Hong Kong, and Macau. In my opening speech at the inaugural conference on October 2, 2000, I said: "This is the first time in history that leaders from these ethnic, religious, and regional groups have come together—without coercion, fear, or hesitation—to fight for justice, liberty, and love."

I also actively engaged in discussions and consultations with the US Congress and American policymakers on US-China policy. In early 2000, for example, I gave a speech on Capitol Hill concerning whether the United States should grant Permanent Normal Trade Relations (PNTR) status to China. Echoing the sentiment expressed by William Safire in a *New York Times* op-ed published the prior year, I argued that "international trade that does not use its leverage to push for the freedom of the individual is unworthy of the name 'free trade.'"

In 2001, I took advantage of the internet and founded the online publication *Yibao* (a Chinese-language online magazine) to provide a forum for Chinese human rights and democracy activists both in China and abroad.

By then, in the eyes of the CCP leadership, I had turned from being an up-and-coming Communist Party member to a public enemy. I was deemed a traitor and was forbidden from entering China. But in the spring of 2002, I decided to defy the entry ban. That year, in China's industrial northeast, thousands of workers were taking to the streets to protest the government's exploitative policies. Sensing an opportunity to forge bonds between democracy advocates and grassroots activists, and to launch a democracy movement in China through nonviolent means, I reentered my native land using a borrowed passport and a forged ID card.

For two weeks, I met with exploited construction laborers, expropriated farmers, and striking workers. I documented their grievances and the hardship they were enduring and helped them conceive strategies to expand their rights and freedoms through nonviolent means. But as I attempted to slip out of China across the Burmese border, my fake ID was spotted, and I found myself in the hands of the Chinese security police.

I was detained in a Chinese prison for five years, much of that time in solitary confinement. My mental health deteriorated under the weight of prolonged isolation, repeated interrogations, and endless psychological and physical torture. I resorted to composing poems in my head and committing them to memory as a means of maintaining my sanity. On the edge of a nervous breakdown, I grasped my innermost resources of imagination, belief, and determination to find a reason to go on living. "Am I wrong?" I asked myself with an inkling of uncertainty.

I devised a thought experiment, which I would later draw upon frequently for strength: I imagined myself holding a copy of the Universal Declaration of Human Rights, arbitrarily choosing a street somewhere in China, showing the document to ordinary citizens, and asking them if they wanted the rights listed therein. Would anybody say "no"? Of course not. Nobody wants to be a slave. In this regard, the Chinese people are no different from any other people in the world. The yearning for freedom and dignity is, indeed, universal. I drew strength and inspiration from this fundamental truth.

I also thought of my fallen brothers and sisters in Tiananmen Square. I reassured myself that freedom is not free. Freedom must be fought for and earned. More determined than ever, I knew that I must never give up.

In 2007, thanks to overwhelming international support, I was freed and returned to the United States. After returning to the US, I founded another activist and research organization, Citizen Power Initiatives for China, and recommitted myself to the hard work of advancing human rights and democracy in China.

This book is a collection of 138 selected English speeches that I made between 2000 and 2020. In a sense, it is a record of the metaphorical footprints I have left behind on my journey of these past two decades. During this period, I gave nearly 200 speeches to world leaders, human rights advocates, students, politicians, and fellow activists across the globe. I have spoken in twenty different countries—at venues as varied as the United Nations Headquarters in New York City; the Nobel Peace Prize Ceremony in Oslo, Norway; Capitol Hill in Washington, DC; Harvard University in Cambridge, Massachusetts; Geneva, Switzerland; New Delhi, India; Brussels, Belgium; Rome, Italy; Taiwan; and many more. I have attended grassroots rallies, walked through corridors of power, traveled to remote villages, visited high schools and universities, attended NGO forums, spoken at churches, and delivered remarks to United Nations delegations.

Throughout these 138 speeches, I have exposed and documented the CCP's widespread human rights abuses and continued exploitation of the Chinese people. I have explained how the CCP's abuses of power threaten not only its own citizens, but also the rest of the world. I have called on the international community to stand up for human rights in China. I have laid out specific plans, initiatives, policies, laws, and approaches that I believe will most effectively produce meaningful change in China. And I have led a multi-ethnic, multi-faith international coalition of human rights activists who have personal stakes in the human rights abuses occurring in China.

As you will learn, human rights leaders from around the world have bravely fought for freedom in China throughout this period—for the sake of its 1.4 billion citizens and, indeed, for the security and well-being of the entire world. It is my hope that this book will serve as an invitation for readers to join us.

Seamus Heaney, the 1995 Nobel laureate in Literature, once wrote in his essay *The Government of the Tongue*: "In one sense, the efficacy of poetry is nil—no lyric has ever stopped a tank. In another sense, it is unlimited. It is like the writing in the sand in the face of which accusers and accused are left speechless and renewed."

To paraphrase Heaney, the efficacy of my speeches, in one sense, has been "nil." Under the oppressive regime of CCP leader Xi Jinping, human rights violations in China are at an all-time high, while personal and civic freedoms are at an all-time low. My work has failed to stop the juggernaut of communist tyranny in China. I cannot, on my own, dismantle the Chinese Communist Party, nor transform China into a democratic country that protects people's individual and civil liberties.

However, Heaney's quote is incomplete without the second sentence: "In another sense, it is unlimited." I am reminded of my favorite biblical story: the miracle of the five loaves and two fish, in which Jesus miraculously used five loaves of bread and two fish offered by a little boy to feed a multitude of hungry people. Like the little boy, all I can do is to faithfully present to God what I have, however meager it is. It is up to God to decide how much He will make of it. It is in this spirit that I present this book to you.

Each of us must do our part to bring about positive change in the world and leave it in a better state than that in which we found it. I hope this collection of speeches provides insight into my life, experiences, and endeavors and provides inspiration for continued action regarding this most pressing issue of our time. After all, continuing to add straws is the only way to know what the last straw on the camel's back will be.

SECTION I

AT THE BEGINNING OF A NEW CENTURY: LOOKING FOR A BETTER WAY

May 2000—September 2001

"It is my deep belief that there must be a better way, a better way to live together, a better way to cherish one another, a better way to honor our sacred potential, a better way to serve the life force, a better way to build justice and peace into the fabric of our lives. We may still not be clear about which way will work... but after experience with the Chinese communist one-party dominance, more and more of us are shaking our heads, saying 'That system doesn't work.'"

CHAPTER 1

It Is Unwise to Give Away the Leverage

Speech Made to a Group of Congressional Aides
Organized by Representative Nancy Pelosi's Office
Capitol Hill, Washington, DC, United States
May 16, 2000

In several days, Congress will make a decision on one of the most important foreign policy issues of recent years: whether or not to grant Beijing permanent normal trade relations status (PNTR).

Some politicians, business leaders, and scholars in America have so framed the public debate over US relations with China that the choice is either "engagement" or "isolation." According to this dichotomy, to advocate the granting of PNTR is to support engagement with China, and to oppose it is tantamount to wanting to isolate the country. The debate over PNTR has been, for me, something much larger than economics and far more complicated and delicate than this simplistic dichotomy can ever describe.

No doubt, a more open China is better for the Chinese people and the rest of the world. Looking at the last hundred years of Chinese history, one can readily find that the darkest times in China were when it locked itself in; people were hopeful when the doors were open. I do not think China can or should be isolated. Quite to the contrary, I can hardly wait to see China brought into the global free economic system. But the question, of course, is how.

It is certainly unwise to retreat all together from using trade as a leverage to proactively push China to change for the better. The Beijing regime, by its very nature, has not and is not expected to automatically behave according to accepted international norms, much less to the universal human rights standards. This, even if it is granted WTO membership and/or PNTR status. The free world, as it endeavors to bring China into the global trade system, should carefully husband any leverage, not surrender its ability to influence Beijing's behavior. Both the multilateral trade organization WTO and the unilateral trade regime PNTR are meant to promote a free global economy. For an economy to be called free, it must permit, sometimes even advance, the free exchange of capital, goods, information, and labor. For the foreseeable future, however, the globally free exchange of labor is impossible. The workers in China, for example, cannot come to the United States simply for a higher labor return, or better working conditions, or an improved human rights situation. Therefore, both WTO and PNTR must address the issue of human rights in the countries like China. International trade that does not use its leverage to push for the freedom of the individual does not deserve the name of "free trade."

Until alternative ways are found to keep meaningful pressure on the Chinese authorities to reform their egregious practices, I suggest that China's access to normal trading privileges in the American market be subject to annual Congressional review. Granting China PNTR would send two wrong messages. One is that rogue states can be rewarded because they have economic resources. The other is that Americans are hypocritical in protecting the universal values of human rights; when it comes to their economic interests, however, these values can be sacrificed. These two messages will undermine US world leadership and will surely be used by the Beijing regime to advance its political purposes both at home and abroad.

The experiences of the past ten years have shown that it is very unlikely for the normal US-China trade tie to be severed. It was so even in the aftermath of the Tiananmen Square Massacre. Thus, those who worry about American economic and security interests, those who worry about hurting ordinary Chinese people and entrepreneurs, those who worry about keeping China out of the global free economic system, those who worry about isolating China would all have little reason for concern. Trade between the US and China will not be diminished because of Congress's failure to grant the permanent trade status.

Next, the annual review of Chinese human rights abuses is not about threatening, as some of the advocates of PNTR accuse; it is more about providing a most important forum to scrutinize the Chinese authorities' practices and to get out the message of human freedom and liberty to the Chinese people. Some of the advocates of PNTR argue that the US government has been playing the annual threatening game since the aftermath of the Tiananmen Square Massacre and that it has proved a failure because the threat holds no credit at all. To say the least, they simply overlook the effects of the annual debate on the spreading of the idea of human rights among the Chinese people. Each year, the Congress draws its largest Chinese audience in addressing this issue. Through the annual review, if continued, the idea of individual liberty, the most valuable commodity produced in America, would keep being exported to China.

Lastly, the annual-scrutiny approach sits right at the fulcrum. And balanced on the scale is what forms the foundation of US foreign policy, namely, American national economic interests vs. the core value that defines America as a nation. The annual threat has been less than credible simply because Chinese leaders have understood that Washington lacks the will to endure the costs of the former for the sake of the latter.

They have called Washington's bluff. I believe it is time to move toward a more balanced position.

Nobody expects the democratization of China will be effected overnight, no matter what decision Congress makes on May 24, 2000. But some day in the future, when we look back, if we discover that trade did help bring about democracy in China, it would be because we made it so.

CHAPTER 2

There Must Be a Better Way

Opening Speech at the First Interethnic/Interfaith Leadership Conference
Campion Renewal Center, Weston, MA, United States
October 2, 2000

Tom, Mr. Yao, Dr. Liu, Mr. Flum, Ambassador McDonald, distinguished guests, my dear friends, ladies and gentlemen:

It is heartening and encouraging to see so many younger-generation leaders from Mainland China, Taiwan, Hong Kong, Macau and ethnic Mongolians, Muslims, Tibetans and Uyghurs, gathered together at the beginning of the new century. It is unprecedented. It is the first time in history that leaders from these ethnic and religious groups and regions have come together without coercion to stand up together for justice and love without fear and hesitation.

We are here for the future of all, a future that should be better than our past and our present. Nobody would agree that our past or present is beautiful; it is actually even nowhere close to being satisfactory. Dominance of one by another, ethnic divisions, killings, atrocities, war, the threat of force, ethnic culture destruction… all these have prevailed in the history of our relations, especially in the past half-century of communist rule in China. We are lying if we say there is no hatred, resentment, distrust among us, whether they are planted by autocratic rulers or grow out of the Satan dwelling in our own hearts.

It is my deep belief, and I hope it is also yours, that there must be a better way, a better way to live together, a better way to cherish one another, a better way to honor our sacred potential, a better way to serve the life force, a better way to build justice and peace into the fabric of our lives. We are, most of us, beginning to see that the way we have been going about things has not been working. We may still not be clear about, or disagree on, which way will work, but we are becoming very clear about, and more agreed on, which way will not. More and more of us, after experience with the Chinese communist one-party dominance, are shaking our heads, saying "That system doesn't work."

Yesterday marked the fifty-first anniversary of the founding of the People's Republic of China. Business as usual, the communists celebrated with boasting about their achievements in the fifty-one years of their ruling, including inevitably that of their policies toward ethnic minorities and Taiwan and that of their practices of "one country, two systems" in Hong Kong and Macau. Our assembly here is the most obvious and vivid demonstration of the failure of these policies and practices. Fifty-one years of communist rule has widened the existing rifts and planted new seeds of hatred. Ethnic and nationalistic tensions are mounting as Chinese communists continue to crack down on ethnic minorities, especially Tibetans and Uyghurs, to threaten democratic Taiwan with military build-up in the Taiwan Strait, and to project a restructuring of the democratic systems in Hong Kong and Macau against the wishes of Hong Kong and Macau citizens. We must have learned the lesson, from our own experiences as well as from world history, and we must know instinctively that nationalism cannot always be justified and that what submission brings about is often not peace but the reinforcement of that logic: Might is right. Real lasting justice and peace among us can never be assured as long as someone is not free, whether that someone is a Han Chinese or Tibetan. In order to find the better way, we must tear down the mountain of the communist tyranny and erect democracy in China. This is our shared cause.

We must also tear down the mountain of the old ways of thinking. Somebody has said, "Many people want to change the world, but few want to change themselves." Yes, we are deeply embedded in the thoughts of dominance. Relationships based on dominance create conflicts. They ultimately lead to recurring cycles of violence, war, revenge, and breakdown of order. Now we have to reap the inevitable bitter fruits of such thoughts and to learn hard lessons from the backlash. Now it is time for all of us to reprogram our thoughts, words, and deeds from dominance to partnership. A partnership is not about sameness but about being equal and sharing. We have multiple differences. But whoever we are and whatever we bring, we can bring fully to the relationship. We can honor one another as equals and treat all parties with respect within the bounty of our diversity. Relationships based on partnership create peace and justice. They ultimately lead to cooperation, sharing, goodwill, and building.

In order to find the better way, we must tear down the mountain of lies that stands between us. We cannot make right relationships if we cannot know each other truly.

It is especially important that the Mainland Han Chinese develop a deeper understanding of the history, culture, current situations, concerns, and aspirations of the Tibetans, Mongolians, Uyghurs, and other Muslims, as well as the needs of the people of Hong Kong, Taiwan, and Macau. The first step for us to find the better way is to make authentic human contact, heart to heart and mind to mind, and discover how we make sense to each other, build up mutual trust among us. Only then can we cross through the mountain of lies to find the way leading to the place where we all say that we want to be. We are gathering here to take the very first step. This is encouraging news.

We have had difficult times in the past; we will have difficult times down the road ahead. It is going to take determined and widespread leadership to find a better way to live together in love, harmony, peace, and justice. My dear friends, you are leaders of your people. You are needed. You have committed to the values of human rights and human dignity; you have the power of human kindness; you also have the skills and knowledge to make a difference; you can build bridges across the deepening chasm among us; you must lead in the great crusade to build peace, restore justice, and establish a democratic governance on the great land we all call home.

Early this year, when I went to many individuals and organizations asking for help for this assembly, I remember one day after I enthusiastically talked to an executive of a big peace-promoting organization about the idea of organizing an event like this, and of course about my vision for the future, he said disdainfully, "You like to think big." "Yes, I do!" I stood and answered and left, with as much determination as I could muster. Yes, we like to think big and we are prepared to do big. A new system based on the values of freedom and premises of partnership is only one possible outcome of the breaking down of the old system that was built on domination. We must not act small when history entrusts us with a big mission.

My dear friends, we are meeting in the spirit of Mahatma Gandhi, whose birthday we celebrate today—that we may transcend the differences among us and live in harmony together. At last, let me ask you to lift your eyes beyond the dangers of today to the hopes of tomorrow, beyond the freedom some of us are enjoying outside Mainland China to the advancement of freedom of the people there. When all of us are free, then we look forward to that day when we will be joined as one.

Thank you all.

CHAPTER 3

Please Remember This Warm and Friendly Night

Toast at the Banquet of the First Interethnic/ Interfaith Leadership Conference
Weston, MA, United States
October 4, 2000

Dear friends,

Good evening.

It is now three days into our conference. We have had three days of heated discussion, and what has been achieved is already exceeding our expectation. Nevertheless, tonight I would like to repeat once more the two important reasons why we are gathered here. First, there are still serious issues between us, many of which are very difficult to resolve. That's why we need to get together to identify these issues and search for resolutions. Second, but more importantly, our futures are closely tied together, and we together make a common entity of fate. That's why we need to get together to plan our common future.

Some people may ask, at this age of advanced media and communication, why do we need to get together to communicate face to face? There is an old Chinese saying that says "meeting brings affection." In a sense, we are gathered here for such affection. I believe that this affection will be a positive factor in our common cause of dissolving hostility and creating a common future.

The atmosphere tonight is very warm and harmonious, and people from different groups are taking pictures together. Please do safely keep these pictures. In the unfortunate event when we might have to go into conflict, especially when we might have to resort to arms, please get out these pictures and take a look. That might well help us turn hostility into friendship. Dear friends, please remember this warm and friendly night.

Finally, please allow me to propose a toast to the achievement of freedom by all the nationalities under the rule of the Chinese Communist Party, to the health of everybody here and your families, and to our bright common future!

Thank you all.

CHAPTER 4

Supporting Each Other in Our Common Cause of Fighting Dictatorship

Closing Statement at the First Interethnic/ Interfaith Leadership Conference
Weston, MA, United States
October 5, 2000

Dear Friends,

The first Interethnic/Interfaith Leadership Conference is about to adjourn.

These four days of meeting is a good process of educating each other. During these four historical days, delegates from various ethnic groups and regions made extensive exchanges, including some intensive debates. But debates are better than no debates. It is possible to have no debates only in CCP meetings. The four days of meeting have seen both friendly occasions and emotional conflicts. Such conflicts are not only allowed at a meeting like this but also expected. Just think about the animosity that has been there for hundreds or even thousands of years among different nationalities and geographic regions, think about the separation, anger, hatred, misunderstanding, and distrust that were created among us during a half-century of communist rule; isn't it just natural that our feelings are expressed emotionally when we get together?

The whole course of the meeting was videotaped. Mr. Zhang Weiguo suggested that not only we videotape the meeting but also we watch the videotapes of previous meetings and compare them during later meetings. This way we can monitor our own progress to see if we are making advances or not. I think this is a very good suggestion.

Mr. Sonam Dagpo from Tibet said just now that the goal of this meeting has been achieved. I agree with him. We listened wholeheartedly to each other, started to understand each other's problems, and increased understanding of each other's positions. This has at least raised the mutual respect for all the participating young leaders. We developed our personal friendship, and we opened up a new prospect for the dialogue between the nationalities and regions that are in conflict with each other, establishing a new model for further exchanges. More importantly, through such get-together and exchange, we boosted our support for each other in our common cause against the dictatorship of the Chinese Communist Party. In case when the CCP uses military threat against Taiwan again, we will not only provide greater support for the democratic Taiwan, but also know better than before how to support them. We will not only have more sympathy for the ordeals suffered by our brothers and sisters in other nationalities but also know better than before how to express our support for them. When the CCP continues to restrict freedom of press and interfere with the rule of law in Hong Kong, we will not only support the democrats with greater effort, but also know how to support them. We have not only gained a better understanding of the situation for the democratic forces in Mainland China but also understood better how to promote democratization in the Mainland. In the last ten years, under very difficult and dangerous conditions, scholars like Mr. Wang Lixiong have been tirelessly studying and introducing the religion, culture, and history and current situation of the minority nationalities in China, and trying to reduce the hatred, misunderstanding, and conflict among different nationalities. His heart is sincere. Suppose one day Mr. Wang Lixiong were to be persecuted by the CCP, would any of us here remain indifferent?

A phenomenon at the meeting that is thought-provoking is that people who live in different areas or who are of different nationalities hold rather different views about unification and independence. Mr. Chen Jingci, who is from Hong Kong, just said that if he were living in Taiwan, he probably would be a Taiwan independence pursuer; if he were a Tibetan, he would probably be a Tibetan self-determinist. We have also seen that representatives from the Mainland are all for China's unification. This phenomenon itself indicates that none of us here holds the absolute truth. We are all young leaders of our own nationalities or geographic regions. History often demands leaders make painful choices and difficult decisions. Chances are that all of us may have to make concessions at future historical moments. Nevertheless, we should all have this conviction: We will never concede to the inhuman and anti-civilization forces represented by the CCP.

Thank you all and have a nice trip home.

CHAPTER 5

Globalization, Global Democratization, and China

Opening Remarks at the International Conference on Globalization, China, and the Cross-Strait Relations
American University, Washington, DC, United States
July 1, 2001

Globalization, as an expanding process of some sort of internationally interdependent relations, is no novelty. Without going too far back, at the beginning of the last century, a capital internationalization had been widely spread. Sometime between the two World Wars, "Capital Needs No Boundary" became a familiar slogan in the western capitalist countries. Going in an opposite direction, on the other hand, the Communist movement with the "Working Class Needs No Motherland" slogan was also widely spreading. These two types of opposing globalization were both trying to establish a just, lasting, and more convincing order that would tie the world capital, states, and even individuals together, one way or another. Much to the same, a new tide of the globalization movement at the end of the last century, especially after 1989, was also powered up by the desire for a more human and sustainable relations between capital, states, and individuals. Although internationally we saw protests in Seattle, Washington, and Quebec against free trade and domestically we witnessed an anti-globalization trend from China's new leftists, the resistance to globalization this time is almost unspeakably weak in comparison with those in the earlier times. We can't help asking why. I think it is because this time we have a more fundamental component in addition to the internationalization of capital and free trade. This new component is the global democratization based on the universally accepted human rights value. This is reflected not only in the foreign policies of many democratic countries, but also in the democratic pursuant of the people in non-democratic nations and their expectation of support from the world's democracies. The entire human society has never had as much faith in democracy as today.

However, in practical courses of promoting a global democratization, we face a difficult problem. Behind the globalization of capital are the international capitalists who have the money. It's a natural trend for capital to move to the places that will generate the greatest return. In other words, the capital globalization is realized by individual actions of many investors. But a global democratization needs collective actions, just as what's needed for the democratization in a single country. For example, from the most selfish angle, every democratic country would hope it is the other countries that take the responsibilities of human rights diplomacy when facing China but itself in good terms with the Chinese government and thus positioned better to get a big bite of the Chinese market. Also, every democratic country may assume everyone else is thinking the same, resulting in worries in everyone's mind of being left behind in business deals and becoming so foolishly the only "devil" for being tough on human rights issues. Of course, many foreign businessmen in China acted exactly like this. Therefore, although a global democratization meets the interests of every democratic country, all these countries together will likely take no action because of this "collective action" dilemma. Let's take the World Trade Organization (WTO) as an example. The WTO's mission is to promote a free economy in a global scale. A free economy has to have free flows of capitals, products, labor, and information in combination with fair competitions based on these free flows. However, in a foreseeable future, a free labor flow won't be possible. Therefore, if the WTO is to promote a really free economy, it can't ignore the universality of the human rights standard. But human rights issues are not on WTO's agenda. In addition, free information flow in countries like China is severely impaired. Not only did the WTO not let people in those countries know more about, and thus monitor, their government's trade policies, but the WTO's own operations are carried out pretty much in a black box. I think this is exactly the "democracy deficit of the global economy" said by Lori Wallace, one of the key leaders of the Seattle protest. In other words, the economic globalization owes a great deal to the global democratization! We can compare this with China's current situation. We can use "democracy deficit of the Chinese economy" to describe what the Chinese modernization owed to China's democratization. Just as what we often ask, "Where can the driving force for democratization in China translate to effective collective action?" we can't help asking, "Where can the driving force for *global* democratization translate to a collective action?"

Besides this, there are still many unanswered questions about globalization.

What types of government responsibilities can be overtaken by multi-nation companies? What can be left alone? Does globalization demand a single world government or a few? If so, what responsibilities should the world government take over from the governments of individual countries or companies? Should these world governments be democratic? Who are the voters then? Should non-democratic countries be allowed to take part in the affairs of the world government? If so, how can the people's will in those countries be represented? State sovereignty is no longer absolute and human rights must be above state sovereignty. This has been a consensus of all but some governments and scholars in a few non-democratic countries. But how do we implement this in practice?

Some people think that globalization will make the rich countries richer and the poor poorer. This is not always true. Many countries have become advanced because of their trade with advanced countries. The question is, under what domestic and international circumstances can an undeveloped country close up its gaps with advanced countries by involving itself in a global economy and vice versa? Market economy does not always make the rich richer and the poor poorer; but why is it so and more and more so in China?

The worst times in China were when it closed its doors. In the past century, no single country in the entire world was able to realize its economic modernization and political democratization with closed doors. To open up should be a consensus among the Chinese. But we all know that China's state enterprises are incapable of competing with foreign companies. Joining the global economy will hit hard on China's industries as well as finance sector. Should China only join the global economy after completing its economic privatization and political democratization, and after a true market is matured with many really competitive business executives who have the real power to run China's economy? But if we wait, are we going to miss the opportunities and lag behind even more?

We all know that the interests of the Chinese government and the capitalists are converging in today's China. Market economy in China is deepening the conflicts between the government and the workers and peasants. Therefore, the working people's demands for democracy out of their own interests may well appear to be anti-capitalist. What is its implication to China's modernization? Is the fundamental value of democracy really always in line with a capitalist economy? Where is the balance if not? Along with the continuing inflow of international capital and capitalists, how will the government-people relationship in China change and to what extent? What does all this mean to China's democratization?

In the globalization process, the capitalist countries that are geographically and culturally close tend to integrate their economies. For example, there have been the European Union (EU) and the North American Free Trade Agreement (NAFTA). However, few have faith in a unified market between China and Taiwan in a foreseeable future, even though the two parties have the same people and culture. Why is it so? After entering the

WTO, how are the relations across the Taiwan Strait going to change? What kind of democratization in China can benefit the public interests in Taiwan? Is Taiwan obligated to support China's democratization? Is Taiwan's effort to gain international recognition going to hurt the public interests in China?

All these globalization-related questions have a lot to do with the future of China and Taiwan, and they worth our study. These questions have bothered me for many years. What's exciting today is that we are lucky to have some thirty outstanding scholars here to study and debate these issues. Of course, we don't expect answers to all these questions out of a conference. We may, in fact, never find satisfactory answers. But I believe our two-day conference will uplift our discussions to a new level. I am looking forward to everyone's opinions while I expect free and even heated discussions from all of you.

Thank you all.

CHAPTER 6

Our Proposed Constitutional Democracy of (Con)Federation and Constitutional Democracy Movement

Speech at Conference "Planning for a Democratic China"
San Francisco, CA, United States
August 1, 2001

In the early 1990s, as the executive director of Foundation for China in the 21st Century, I organized a series of academic seminars on planning for a democratic China. Based on these discussions, the foundation's task force wrote up a draft constitution that outlines a constitutional democracy of (con)federation in a future China. The task force, under the direction of Professor Yan Jiaqi, consisted of several dozen scholars of different nationalities from Mainland China, Taiwan, Hong Kong, and overseas.

Since its publication, this draft constitution has attracted attention in various circles. In 1996, this foundation hosted a dialogue between the Dalai Lama and scholars of Han nationality. During the dialogue, the Dalai Lama relayed that the spirit of the constitution was acceptable, informing his opinion to my team, which included myself, Dr. Liu Kaishen, Mr. Yan Jiaqi, and Mr. Zhang Weiguo. Three years later during my first visit to Dharamsala, India, I met with the Dalai Lama and he once again commended the foundation's effort on the constitutional design. Scholars affiliated with KMT participated in the research from the very beginning. Taiwan's Democratic Progressive Party has been attending the seminars hosted by the foundation since 1999 and has started to study this draft constitution. Many scholars from Hong Kong, Taiwan, and overseas have mentioned the constitutional outline proposed in their publications. During the first Interethnic/Interfaith Leadership Conference, organized by our foundation, this topic was also extensively discussed. So far, the foundation has been fielding suggestions from all circles, including those by well-known scholars such as Wu Jiaxiang, Liu Junning, Wang Lixiong, and the late Gong Xiangrui. At this time of launching our online publication *Yibao*, we once again introduce this draft constitution to the general public, hoping that there will be wider participation and more in-depth discussion.

Some may say that it is premature to talk about which kind of national structure and political systems China should adopt in the future when it is still under the totalitarian rule. That is not true. History tells us that brainstorming possible future choices will lead to better outcomes. Therefore, discussion over future China's constitutional democracy is highly necessary. In fact, even discussion is not enough. What China needs is a constitutional democracy movement.

In broad terms, a constitutional democracy movement consists of two parts. First, a clear constitutional goal needs to be established. Then promotion is needed to push various political forces and interest groups to participate in jointly building and implementing these broad constitutional goals. The broad constitutional goals refer to some general principles, such as the (con)federation system. They do not include fine details such as the term of office of parliament members. Virtually all the details of the future constitutional system, including general principles, will be realized in a process involving various political forces and factions, interest groups, nationalities, and geographic regions. The finally realized constitutional arrangements are basically the results of compromises among different interests. From the point of view of a scholar, such results may not be the best arrangements. However, this process cannot be bypassed. For instance, any well-trained constitutional scholar can write a very good constitution after working in seclusion for a period of time. However, a constitution that has not gone through the due process will not be collectively cherished. And it will not inspire public trust. Such a constitution therefore is not implementable. As an analogy, a constitutional democracy is like a child. If it is raised by many people collectively, everyone will treat it like their own child and will cherish it, love it, protect it, and trust it. A constitutional movement is thus a process of promoting the realization of constitutional democracy. Only through such broad participation will we Chinese foster the kind of constitutional habit and legal mentality that have never been established before.

As Mr. Zhang Weiguo said in his editorial in the first issue of *Yibao*, the political system under the rule of the Chinese Communist Party is a system with a constitution but without constitutional governing. To a certain extent, this is the source of all of China's conundrums. Due to a conflict of interests, the Chinese Communist Party still has not proposed any clear goals for a constitutional democracy. In such a political situation, pro-democracy forces are obliged to bear the responsibility of initiating the process toward a constitutional democracy. Also, as an important part of the constitutional movement, we should propose certain constitutional goals to be discussed by the people and certain constitutional blueprints to be selected by the people. The constitutional democracy of (con)federation outlined by this draft has led to a discussion broadly participated in by various nationalities from both sides of the Taiwan Strait (including Mainland, Taiwan, Hong Kong, and Macau). This is a good start. Many ordinary Chinese people are not clear about the goals of the constitutional democracy movement and are afraid that democratization may lead to the disintegration of their country. The constitutional democracy movement is a forward-looking movement. We believe that the goal of a democracy without disintegration, and a unification without totalitarianism, would reflect the wishes of the people of Mainland China. Such a goal can only increase people's confidence in democracy.

Currently, Mainland China faces two kinds of danger. First, the breakdown of the existing order in the political system may lead to the collapse of the country. Second, due to the authorities' continual blocking of the democratization process, China is slipping into Nazism. The only way out for China is for all the nationalities, all the geographical regions, and all political forces to work together to initiate a democratization process and to build a constitutional democracy of (con)federation for China. This will meet not only the interests of the Mainland Han people, but also the interests of other nationalities in the Mainland as well as the people of Taiwan, Hong Kong, and Macau. I hope our friends here will spread this important idea, build a common base, and form a force so as to complete the development of a constitutional democracy of (con)federation.

I look forward to your valuable suggestions as well as actions.

Appendix
Draft Constitution of Federal China
The Constitution of the Federal Republic of China
(Drafted in 1993 by the Foundation for China in the 21st Century, led by Dr. Yang Jianli)

This Constitution is made so as to end the politics of dictatorship in the history of China, to change the system of centralization of power, to establish the rule of law, to safeguard the freedoms and rights of citizens, to improve the well-being of all, and to maintain peace and tranquility for all nationalities and all areas.

Chapter One: General Principles

Article 1: The Federal Republic of China is a free and democratic federal republic with the rule of law.

Article 2: The sovereignty of the Federal Republic of China belongs to all people.

Article 3: People with the nationality of the Federal Republic of China are citizens of the Federal Republic of China.

Article 4: The Federal Republic of China is composed of Autonomous States, Autonomous Provinces, Autonomous Cities, and Special Regions (hereinunder, states, provinces, cities, and regions for short).

Article 5: All nationalities of the Federal Republic of China have the right to keep and develop their cultures, religions, and practices.

Chapter Two: Citizens' Rights and Obligations

Article 6: The citizens of the Federal Republic of China are equal before the law. They are not unequal because of difference in sex, in origin, in language, in nationality, in religion, in wealth, in party affiliation or in political persuasion.

Article 7: Citizens' personal freedom is inviolable. See below for the handling of the arrest of offenders against existing law. Nor may anybody be arrested and detained by the judiciary or the public security authority except in due process of the law, nor may be tried or sentenced by the count except in due process of law. Arrest, detention, trial, and sentencing may be resisted and actionable if they do not comply with the provisions of law. Where a citizen is arrested and detained as a crime suspect, the arresting and detaining authority should tell him the reason for his arrest and detention, and hand him over to the appropriate court for action within the time limit prescribed by law. He or any other person may apply to the appropriate court for a writ requiring that he be removed from his place of detention and brought before the court within the time limit prescribed by law. The court may not refuse such an application. The detaining authority may not refuse to comply, or delay in complying, with the writ. The suspect's personal dignity is inviolable. He has a right to be tried independently and openly by a court of justice and to defend himself therein. He may not be treated or punished in a cruel, inhuman, or humiliating manner. He may not be forced to testify against himself.

Article 8: The home of a citizen is inviolable. Nobody may force his way into it or search it except in due process of law.

Article 9: A citizen who is not a military person on active duty may not be tried by a military court.

Article 10: Citizens are free to choose their places of residence and to change them. Each autonomous State or Special Region may make its own entry and exit regulations as warranted by local circumstances.

Article 11: Citizens have the freedom of speech, lecture, writing, publication, and operating news media.

Article 12: Citizens have the freedom of confidential communication.

Article 13: Citizens have the freedom of assembly, association, procession, and demonstration.

Article 14: Citizens have the freedom of organizing political parties and conduction of political activities. Political parties must be lawfully registered. Fundings and expenditures of such parties must be declared in accordance with law.

Article 15: Citizens have the freedom of religion and belief.

Article 16: Citizens are free to choose their occupations.

Article 17: Citizens have the freedom of organizing and joining trade unions and going on strike.

Article 18: Citizens have the right of lawful access to information.

Article 19: Citizens have the right to present petitions, air grievances, and to take legal proceedings.

Article 20: Citizens upon reaching the age of 18 have the right to vote in elections. Citizens upon reaching the age of 20 have the right to stand for elections.

Article 21: Citizens' property rights should be protected. Nobody may be expropriated of his property except for a public cause, except in due process of law, and except upon payment of reasonable compensation.

Article 22: Citizens have the right and obligation to receive national education.

Article 23: Citizens have the obligation to perform military service as required by law.

Article 24: Citizens have the obligation to pay tax as required by law.

Article 25: All other rights and freedoms of a citizen, except where they are detrimental to peace and order or to public interests, are safeguarded by the Constitution.

Article 26: No law should be made to curtail the above listed freedoms and rights. Exceptions are where they hinder the rights of others, when there is an emergency, and where they must be curtailed in order to maintain peace and order or to promote public interests.

Article 27: Any public servant who unlawfully violates a freedom or right of a citizen should not only be punished under law but also incur a criminal or civil liability. The victimized citizen may ask the state to compensate him for the damage that he has suffered.

Chapter Three: Federal Structure

Article 28: The Federal Republic of China is made up of:

The Autonomous State of Inner Mongolia, the Autonomous State of Taiwan, the Autonomous State of Tibet, the Autonomous State of Xinjiang, the Autonomous State of Ningxia, and the Autonomous State of Guangxi.

The Autonomous Province of Shanxi, the Autonomous Province of Shandong, the Autonomous Province of Sichuan, the Autonomous Province of Gansu, the Autonomous Province of Jiangxi, the Autonomous Province of Jiangsu, the Autonomous Province of Jilin, the Autonomous Province of Anhui, the Autonomous Province of Hubei, the Autonomous Province of Hunan, the Autonomous Province of Qinghai, the Autonomous Province of Hainan, the Autonomous Province of Zhejiang, the Autonomous Province of Guizhou, the Autonomous Province of Yunnan, the Autonomous Province of Heilongjiang, the Autonomous Province of Fujian, the Autonomous Province of Guangdong, and the Autonomous Province of Liaoning.

The Autonomous Municipality of Shanghai, the Autonomous Municipality of Tianjin and the Autonomous Municipality of Beijing, and the Special Region of Hong Kong and the Special Region of Macau.

Article 29: Any power that is not constitutionally vested in the Federal government is exercised by the individual Autonomous States, Autonomous Provinces, Autonomous Municipalities, Special Regions, and the entire citizenry.

Article 30: Each Autonomous State makes its own constitution. Each Autonomous Province, Autonomous Municipality, or Special Region makes its own Basic Law. A State Constitution or Basic Law may not conflict with the Constitution of the Federal Republic of China or violate the lawful rights of another State, Province, Municipality, or Special Region.

Article 31: The Federal government makes and enforces laws in the following areas:

- Foreign policy, the declaration of war, and the making of peace
- Nationality
- National defense and military affairs
- Federal budgets and taxes
- The Federal legal and judicial system
- The election of the National House
- The Federal civil service system
- The Federal public security and police system
- Federal customs and excises and entry/exit controls
- The regulation of space flights, aviation, ocean shipping, inland waterways, national roads, and national railways
- The establishment of the Federal Central Bank and the issue of the national currency
- The regulation of postal service and telecommunications
- Standard weights and measures and national statistics
- The protection of copyrights, patents, trademarks, and intellectual property
- The regulation of relationships among the States, Provinces, Municipalities, and Regions

Article 32: The individual States, Provinces, Municipalities, and Regions make and enforce laws in the following areas:

- The legal and judicial system
- The education system
- The selection of members to the Federal House
- The regulation of agriculture, forestry, animal husbandry, mining, industry, and commerce services
- Budgets and taxes
- The land system and nature conservation
- The regulation of labor, social welfare, and social services
- The provision and supervision of medical and health services, sports facilities, and recreation facilities

- The promotion and protection of science, technology, culture, and the arts
- The regulation of banks and financial services
- The regulation of public utilities and joint operations
- The supervision of charities and community services
- The registration of religious organizations and social groups
- The public security and policy system
- The civil service system
- The system of local autonomy
- Other areas that are constitutionally not under the jurisdiction of the Federal government

Article 33: Each Autonomous State has the right, in the name of an Autonomous State of China, to sign non-military agreements with foreign countries and the right to make its own decisions about joining international organizations and setting up representative offices in foreign countries.

Article 34: The Federal government may send representatives to, and set up representative offices, in the individual States, Provinces, Municipalities, and Regions.

Article 35: No military alliances shall be formed, or military agreement signed, among the States, Provinces, Municipalities, and the Regions.

Article 36: The Federal House must approve by a three-fourths majority vote before any new State, Province, Municipality, or Region can be created. Before any change is made to any State, Province, Municipality, or Region, the legislature of the particular State, Province, Municipality, or Region must give its approval and the Federal House must approve by a two-thirds majority vote.

Article 37: Before the year 2050, the Special Region of Hong Kong and the Special Region of Macau will have the authority to issue regional currencies and regional passports, travel documents and visas; set up regional court of final appeal; regulate regional postal service and telecommunications; protect copyrights, patents, and other kinds of intellectual property;

and in the name of the Special Region of the Federal Republic of China, sign non-political and non-military agreements with foreign countries, take part in non-political and non-military international organizations, and set up economic and trade offices in foreign countries. The Special Region of Hong Kong and the Special Region of Macau are financially independent and not required to pay federal tax. The Special Region of Hong Kong and the Special Region of Macau are authorized by the Federal House to regular aviation and ocean shipping. In the year 2050, the Federal House will review the position of the Special Region of Hong Kong and the Special Region of Macau under the terms of the second clause of Article 36.

Article 38: The Autonomous State of Taiwan has the authority to issue its state currency, passports, travel documents and visas; set up its state court of final appeal; regulate space flights, aviation, ocean shipping, postal service and telecommunication; and protect copyright, patents, trademarks, and intellectual property. The Autonomous State of Taiwan is financially independent and not required to pay federal tax. The Autonomous State of Taiwan has the right to maintain armed forces and the right to refuse a federal military presence.

Article 39: The Autonomous State of Tibet is a national nature conservation area where the testing of nuclear, chemical, and biological weapons and the storage of nuclear wastes are prohibited. The Autonomous State of Tibet is financially independent and not required to pay federal tax. The Autonomous State of Tibet has the right to set up its state court of final appeals. The position of the Autonomous State of Tibet will be reviewed twenty-five years after this Constitution is promulgated. The review will be in the form of a referendum by the citizens in the state and not subject to Article 36 of this Constitution.

Chapter Four: The Parliament

Article 40: The Parliament of the Federal Republic of China is the supreme federal legislative body. The Parliament of the Federal Republic of China is composed of two houses: the National House and the Federal House, which jointly exercise the legislative powers.

Article 41: The National House has a total of 501 members, returned from the individual State, Provinces, Municipalities, and Regions, each in a number proportional to its population, provided that each return at least one Member. The term of office of a Member of National House is four years. He can be reelected. The assignment of house seats, the demarcation of electoral district boundaries, and the methods of election are stipulated by law.

Article 42: The Federal House is composed of Members returned from the individual States, Provinces, Municipalities, and Regions: Four each from the Autonomous States, three each from the Autonomous Provinces and Municipalities, and two each from the Special Regions. Each of the States, Provinces, Municipalities, and Regions decides for itself how its Representatives to the Federal House are elected. The term of office of Member of the Federal House is six years. An election is held every three years to return on half of the Federal House Members. A citizen of the Federal Republic of China must have reached the age of 30 before he or she can serve as a Federal House Member.

Article 43: Each house has a Speaker and Deputy Speaker, who are elected by its Members from among themselves.

CHAPTER 7

We Must Break the Cycle of Violence

Opening Remark at the Second Interethnic/
Interfaith Leadership Conference
Boston, MA, United States
September 25, 2001

Ladies and gentlemen, my dear friends:

Last October, we successfully organized the first Interethnic/Interfaith Leadership Conference. That assembly was unprecedented; it was the first time in history that leaders from Mainland China, Taiwan, Hong Kong, Macau and ethnic Mongolians, Muslims, Tibetans and Uyghurs, came together without coercion, to stand up together for justice and love without fear and hesitation. Just by gathering together, we had accomplished a significant first step toward the goal of eternal peace and harmony.

At that conference, we all admitted that dominance of one by another, ethnic divisions, killings, atrocities, wars, the threat of force, ethnic culture destruction… have prevailed in the history of our relations, especially in the past half a century of the communist rule in China. We all realized that it is time for all of us to reprogram our thoughts, words, and deeds from dominance to partnership, and to tear down the mountain of lies that stands between us. More importantly, we all agreed that there must be a better way for us to live together.

At the same time, no one can ignore the fact that nothing is more difficult and formidable than the resolution of ethnic, religious, or regional conflicts. The history of humankind has repeatedly shown us that a civilization built for many years can be destroyed overnight by barbarian forces. The terrorist attacks that took place exactly two weeks ago, once again, heavily punctured our confidence in our lives and in the coexistence of human beings. As we sorrowfully prayed for those lives buried in the rubble, we could not help but cry out: Do human beings still have hope? President Bush declared: "We will direct every resource at our command—every means of diplomacy, every tool of intelligence, every instrument of law enforcement, every financial influence, and every necessary weapon of war—to the destruction and to the defeat of the global terror network." I believe, as the majority of the world's people do, that this is the right thing to do. Nevertheless, if we search in the deepest recesses of our hearts where we cannot reach in ordinary times, we cannot refrain from asking ourselves: Is this really what we want? If we say yes, the violence goes on and on; if we say no, the terror spreads. This is the dilemma we must wrestle today.

We who dream for a just and peaceful China face the same dilemma. We deeply understand that the process of democratization in China is fraught with dangers of violence and terror. It is so simply because the communist tyranny has planted too many seeds of cruelty and hatred. From Beijing to Tibet, from Shanghai to Xinjiang, from Inner Mongolia to the Taiwan Strait, in prisons and schools, in plants and markets, in churches and temples, everywhere we can see an evil process at work. Tyranny is violence of violence, is the hotbed of barbarian thoughts and acts. Democracy is necessary for peace, therefore, bringing the communist tyranny to an end and erecting democracy in China is our shared cause.

The first thing we must do to that end is to entirely abandon the logic of power and violence harbored by world dictators and terrorists. We must resolve our differences by nonviolent means, we must take a civilized road to look for freedom, and we must build our future through democratic ways so that all people and individuals are free, not exploited, living so they can grow to their full potential.

Some people may wonder why we have not dropped all these ideals because they seem so absurd after so many evil things have happened. We keep them because, in spite of everything, we still believe that people are really good at heart, and thus the power of love will eventually prevail over the love of power.

My dear friends, you are leaders from different ethnic, religious, and regional groups that are in age-old conflicts and can so easily be pulled into bloody war. Always bear in mind: It is easier to lead your men to combat, stirring up their passions, than to restrain them and direct them toward the patient labors of peace. What our future calls for is not the coward leadership that makes war but the brave leadership that makes peace.

To conclude, let me quote Eleanor Roosevelt: "If we want a free and peaceful world, if we want to make the deserts bloom and man grow to greater dignity as a human being, we can do it."

Thanks be to you all.

SECTION II

RETURN FROM PRISON: THE STRENGTH TO PERSEVERE

August 2007—April 2008

"I have lived a lifetime since I left home in April 2002 to support the labor movement in northeastern China. While I never would have wished for the pain for my family, we all now truly understand that through adversity comes strength... I am here today stronger than I have ever been. More determined than I ever thought possible. More convinced that the one-party system in China is fatally flawed. And deeply heartened by the knowledge that the democratization process in China is irreversible."

CHAPTER 8

My Heart Is Filled with Thanksgiving

Remarks at Press Conference "Dr. Yang Jianli Has Returned to America"
Capitol Hill, Washington, DC, United States
August 21, 2007

Ladies and gentlemen, my dear friends:

It is heartening to be able again to stand on this great land as a free man freely expressing my thoughts and ideas before you. Five years and four months. This moment has not come easily. There is no way to know how many good-hearted people have put their efforts to secure my release and safe return to the United States, how many prayers have been said, how many wishes have been made, how many tears have been shed. At this emotional moment, my heart is filled with thanksgiving.

While it is impossible to thank everyone by name now—and I look forward to giving proper thanks to people individually, in person, and in good time—there are a few people that I would be remiss if I did not thank publicly now.

It is most appropriate for me to begin with the US Congress as I stand today in this great democratic institution. I thank its members for their genuine concern, compassion, and perseverance to secure my freedom and family reunion.

My family could not have been luckier to have chosen to live in Brookline, Massachusetts, and to happen to have been represented by Congressman Barney Frank. His support to my family and his relentless support has been the backbone of the effort to secure my release.

In addition, Chairman Chris Cox, prior to leaving the Congress, spent many years, and Chairman Tom Lantos, all from the very beginning working to secure my release.

I feel deeply indebted to the Bush Administration—President Bush, Secretary Powell, Secretary Rice, Secretary Paulson, Ambassador Randt, and so many others for their tireless work on the front line, which has brought this day to fruition.

Standing with me today also is my dear friend Jared Genser, President of Freedom Now, who has supported my family since the very beginning. He brought my case before the United Nations, which prepared the vital and necessary groundwork for this entire endeavor. And he pressed the Bush Administration and US Congress to care about my imprisonment. He fought for five long years without one minute of wavering. Just like I knew from within my cell that this day would come, he, too, on the outside, was just as resolute in his determination. My special thanks to him—and to Jerry Cohen as well—who could not be here today but who was a tremendous support to my family.

My gratitude to all of you in the media for publicizing my case, which in turn created enormous support around world. And to human right groups worldwide and my colleagues from the Chinese community, I thank them for their constant and unflagging support.

I also cannot express enough my profound affection and appreciation to my entire family. Without their love, devotion, support, and understanding, I would have not been able to survive these difficult years.

But my rock, my source of strength, and the person who helped me get through these many years is my devoted wife, Christina. No one, when they get married, quite knows what will be required when they take their wedding vows. I know that was certainly the case with us, and especially for her. I have only begun to understand, mostly since my release, what a vital leadership role she played in this entire effort. Her grace and dignity—and her unflagging dedication to get me home—inspired countless people to put in an extra effort on my behalf.

Without her summoning the inner strength required to persevere, I would not be home today. I love you, and I am blessed and so proud that you are my wife.

Five years and four months.

I have lived a lifetime since I left home in April 2002 to support the labor movement in northeastern China. While I never would have wished for the pain for my family, we all now truly understand that through adversity comes strength.

I am here today stronger than I have ever been. More determined than I ever thought possible. More convinced that the one-party system in China is fatally flawed. And deeply heartened by the knowledge, especially after the four months I spent in Beijing since my release, that the democratization process in China is irreversible. While the Chinese Communist Party may choose to fight this process every step of the way, it shouldn't.

The Chinese people are increasingly demanding accountability from their government. They want to know that the resources being invested and spent are being used wisely, efficiently, and without corruption, fraud, waste, or abuse. They want transparency and good governance. They want to know that their government has their best interests in mind. And, most important, they are educated enough that they want a say in directing how those resources are invested and spent.

One only needs to understand that there are, literally, tens of thousands of protests in China every year, to see that the Chinese government is sitting on a powder keg as frustration with the one-party system mounts. The Chinese government claims that what is required is stability to deliver on its promises to the people and that it needs to control people's lives. But the tighter they grip on to power, the more difficulty they will have in holding on.

If a thirsty man plunges his fist into a bucket of water to get a drink and then pulls it out, he will have nothing. It is only by extending an open hand into the bucket that he can get the drink he requires.

So too it is with the Chinese government. While counterintuitive for those who are too convinced of the righteousness of their cause, it is only by opening up their hands and trusting the wisdom of its own people that China can reach its full potential.

The answer to China's major challenges is not suppressing the countless protests across the country for fear they will spiral out of control. But rather it is to acknowledge that they are a symptom of a broader, deeper, and more fundamental problem—that the people do not believe that their government has their best interests in mind. It is only by embracing public debate and placing more power to make the decisions that affect people's lives into the hands of the Chinese people that the Chinese government has the opportunity to relieve the tremendous pressure it is under. And by making these decisions, inevitably, China will also play a more responsible and less self-centered role on the world stage.

Information is power. And with the internet, mobile phones, text messaging, education, trade, and greater travel abroad, the Chinese people have had a taste of freedom—and they like what they see. The Chinese government has a fundamental decision to make. It can swim against the tidal wave or it can surf it onto shore.

I believe that, inevitably, we will see vibrant democracy take root in China. And my time in prison only reaffirmed and strengthened my resolve to continue this struggle.

First, as I hope you will understand, I need to take the time to rest and be with my family.

There is so much more that I have to say, but with the freedom to express my views, I will have the time to do that in the right way.

Again, my profound thanks for your years of support. Knowing from inside my cell how much was being done on the outside gave me the strength to persevere.

Rather than getting into any further specifics, I would be pleased to let the discussion be guided by what you are interested in hearing about.

God bless America. God bless China.

CHAPTER 9

Brief Report at Board Meeting of National Endowment for Democracy

Washington, DC, United States
September 7, 2007

Based on my reflections during the five years of imprisonment plus the nearly four months of my experiences as "a free man" in China after my release (the importance of the networks I made during that time to our future work cannot be overestimated), I am in the process of writing up an "Assessment on China's Public Political Space and My Strategic Plan." Given the amount of information I need to acquire and digest the complexity of the questions we are facing, it will take some time for me to straighten out my thoughts and finish it. Today I can but give you a brief, incomplete report.

My emphasis on the public political space does not imply that I don't attach any importance to the CCP inner power struggle and its impact on China's political development. Rather, I have no capacity whatsoever to have a direct intervention in the top inner party politics, and more important, that we, the Chinese Democracy Movement, are naturally and historically best placed to work from grassroots level up. In addition, it is my personal belief that a democracy is most real and solid if it grows from bottom up within the society.

I want to talk about a few things. 1) Institutional Inertia: Political rights are lagging much behind personal liberties; 2) The Main Conflict in the Chinese Society; 3) China: 100% Police State; 4) The Overall

Conditions of the Chinese Democracy Movement (CDM) inside China (unless otherwise clarified, by the Chinese Democracy Movement I mean the Movement inside China); 5) The CCP's treatment of CDM; and 6) Prescription of Our Future Work.

1. **Institutional Inertia: Political rights are lagging far behind personal liberties**

   In general, the Chinese people are enjoying more personal freedom: information, assets, more choices among goods, and greater ability to decide where to work, live, and travel. Expression is tolerated to the degree that is not made at organized gatherings or in black and white. Small-scale demonstrations airing grievances or protesting local officials are also more acceptable if they are not directed to challenging higher-level government, absolutely not challenging CCP's rule. Yet the degree of repression on the protesters varies from locality to locality and from case to case. But the level of political rights enjoyed by the Chinese people is much lower than that of personal liberties; the rights of free press, free expression association, free ballots, gatherings and demonstrations, are, as they were, tightly controlled. There are as yet no real institutional channels through which societal interests, political groups, and ordinary citizens can influence the selection of rulers or the making of public policy, nor regular ways of supervising the government conducts of any level. Personal liberties have not yet been institutionalized. The current situation leaves little doubt that the space of personal liberties will continue to expand, which in turn leads to increasingly stronger demand for political rights. The pressures on the government are mounting. The CCP leadership does not like the ever-widening gap, which may portend coming political instability. It might seek to close this gap by relaxing the control over political rights or by taking away people's recently acquired personal liberties, bringing them to the level of political rights. I see both mentalities existing in the mindset of the CCP system; therefore, both tendencies of opposite directions drive their practices at the same time. That is why we see many contradictory phenomenon (mixed signals and trends) coexist in present China. It is safe to say that the latter is dominant and will continue to be so in the near future. Based on this analysis, I wrote articles while in prison on China's taxpayers' revolution, which are intended to promote the awareness of taxpayers' rights and to initiate meaningful Chinese constitutional democracy movement by combining the concrete interests of the people with our ideal of democratic governance.

2. **The Main Conflict in Chinese Society**

   The main conflict in Chinese society is the tension between the existing institutions, mindset, and ways of governance at all levels and the ever-growing demands of the people for free expression, protection of their rights and interests, and social justice. Over 80,000 mass protests were reported in the year 2006. The figure is continuing to climb. If the government continues to try to manage the economic with its monopoly on political power, unstable factors will continue to accumulate, and China's transition to democracy will more likely be crisis-induced than peaceful evolution.

3. **China Is a 100% Police State**

   After the Tiananmen Massacre, China has been enlarging its police forces, updating their weaponry, and increasing their pay and benefits. China now has all together 4.6 million police troops: 1.7 million regular police, 2 million armed police, and 900,000 para-police personnel. China's police forces will continue to expand. The Chinese authorities are able, if they are so determined, to crack down on any mass protest at any time at any place unless protests occur at the same time and in all places.

4. Overall Conditions of CDM

CDM is active but scattered. It consists of different parts (there are of course overlaps, yet the partition will assist my analysis).

Independent Intellectuals (public intellectuals): The group has grown rapidly in recent years and quite a few inside the CCP system have become involved, and as an encouraging result, the division between the inside and the outside has become increasingly blurred. They are enjoying greater freedom of speech than ever and firmly and actively defending the hard-won space, especially the space on the internet.

Independent-minded journalists: Enlarge freedom of press by their courageous truthful reports.

Human rights lawyers and defenders in other professions: Grows fast, active, often with concerted efforts.

Grassroots activists: Locally elected representatives, representatives and spokespersons of local interest groups, organizers of mass protests, potential independent candidates, trainers, and educators.

NGO activists: Some have association with the government system, some with dissidents, some neither. They are well networked and enjoy a relatively good space to function.

Internet activists: Active on the internet writing articles, conveying, exchanging and spreading information which is forbidden, helping defend dissident websites, and overcome the government firewall with computer skills. (Censorship remains a fact of life. Indeed, the Chinese government has led the world in taming the Web.)

Traditional dissidents: Members of banned political parties, maintaining their organizations is the main task, challenging the government ban on associations.

New Organization Fan Lan: Believers of Sun Yat-sen's theory San Min Zhu Yi, mainly consisting of young people with relatively low education, unstable thoughts, and ideas.

CDM is lacking widely recognized organizations and leaders, concerted efforts, mutual support and protection, and shared, clearly defined, long-term goals. It is lacking resources for their activities.

5. The Government Treatment of CDM

Tolerant toward intellectuals without organizations, without engagement with grassroots mobilizations, NGO activists, high-profile dissidents (largely due to Olympic). Harsh on human rights defenders, journalists, newly emerging activists.

The central government sets broad rules and policies on dissidents and activists leaving much authority to local governments. The degree of control varies from place to place and from case to case.

6. Prescription of Our Future Work

A. Establishing mediating organizations between CDM and the outside world—toward a support system for CDM

- Making their voices heard, their real situations and activities known
- Helping them with information, thoughts, and ideas

(websites like *Yibao* serve as an effective platform for above two)

- Providing 911 help for closed down websites
- Setting up a help and mutual help system for persecuted and imprisoned dissidents and their families
- Helping newly emerging weak NGOs by making associations with international NGOs in their respective fields
- Collecting, reviewing, and screening their proposals and doing fundraising for them, and monitoring their operation and doing audit work

B. Organize democratization research (bring intellectuals in and outside China together)

- Annual, semi-annual, quarterly reports (depending on funds) on China's Public Political Space, present to various supporters and interested organizations and individuals
- ProduceSchemes and Strategies for Democratization, crisis management strategies and plans
- Handbooks on taxpayers' rights, for free and fair elections, strategies for independent candidates
- Introduce experiences of other countries
- Training programs, virtual or real world (toward enlarging political activist groups)

C. Deepening and enlarging dialogue and exchange between ethnic groups. The question of ethnic relations has not entered the field of vision of the intellectuals and dissidents and activists, let alone its importance in the democratizing process. The ethnic crisis is most likely to outbreak in which most Chinese, given their ever-robust nationalism sentiment, would not accept the prospects and turn to blame democratization for this, and they might choose to abandon democratization all together. We must plan ahead and bring this critical issue to the attention of those who would make the constituency of China's transition to democracy.

D. Begin to establish China's first Web University

- Recruit democracy-oriented intellectuals for teaching and research, provide them resources and the stage to act. (This is especially important for those still working inside the CCP system. Most of them have no alternative resource for their living and work and no alternative stage for them to act to realize themselves.)
- Training programs
- Actual unified organization for CDM but safe because major administration work is done in the US (dilemma of CDM), organize concerted efforts

- Produce shared program, plan for future constitutional democracy

E. Exchange program between Chinese and American younger-generation leaders

My experience of staying in China as "a free man" proves equally, if not more, important to our future work. In nearly four months' time, I traveled four provinces, two municipalities, and one autonomous region and met up with nearly 200 people from various political backgrounds and professions -- including radicals, Fan Lan members, and democratic party members, for example, human rights defenders mainly consisting of lawyers, grassroots political activists, independent intellectuals, reporters and editors, professors within the system, white collar professionals, NGO activists, businesspeople, big and small, workers and farmers, taxi drivers, people in the entertainment business, former high-ranking party officials, and even incumbent party officials. The importance of the network I built up cannot be overestimated. Based on this experience of mine and on my reflection while in prison and my readings after I got back to the States, I have made the following observations.

1. People agree that democracy is inevitable in China but disagree on how and when.

I did not come across a single person who disagreed that democracy in China is necessary and inevitable. I believe that China's leadership also shares the view. But people are divided on how long the democratic transition will take, how much price the Chinese people as a whole is going to pay for the transition, and who is going to pay and how much.

Please don't mistake me. Agreeing on the inevitability does not necessarily mean supporting the democratic transition, let alone beginning the process now. To the ruling elite who benefit disproportionally from the existing political system and their monopoly on political power, democratization obviously means a heavy loss of privileges, and for the most corrupt and brutal ones, even a severe punishment through legal process or mass retaliations. They are jealous of power and oppose initiatives for change. Government officials of all levels readily use police force to put down all kinds of protests, especially when it is directed toward challenging their authority, privilege, abuse of power, and corrupt practice. They agree to change only when facing pressure or social crisis that may threaten to lose their grip on power. I call this institutional inertia. We will surely see a lot of crisis-induced changes in China ahead.

Some people don't think it will happen any time soon, not even in their lifetime, so democracy is too distant for them to care, although they believe in its inevitability. Their natural choice is coming along with the existing society and capitalizing on it when and where it is possible. A majority of the Chinese people desire changes because they are powerless under dictatorship and constantly subject to repression and exploitation.

Yet, they run into collective action dilemma: Everybody wants others to take action against the regime pushing for changes but not themselves, so as to avoid paying higher prices and running higher risks while waiting to take a free ride. This is understandable. Autocratic regimes are brutal by nature anyway.

Some people engage in various protests not because they have a long-term goal of democracy in mind to accomplish but simply because they are braver to air their grievances or more conscious of their rights or even their situations are more unbearable. They take action on specific issues directly concerning their interests. I believe there lies real motivation to change, and they may become solid forces to push for democratic transition if well organized and well guided.

Thank God. Given all the difficulties, there are very active democratic forces existing in China. I will come back to talk about their work and predicaments later.

2. **Political rights are lagging much behind personal liberties.** I have talked about this topic earlier rather thoroughly. I won't repeat it.
3. **Collective action legitimacy is rationed by the authorities.** Exercises of political rights more often than not involve collective actions. But the resources of collective action legitimacy in China are controlled by the authorities.

   In a democratic country with rule of law, the resources of collective action lie in the laws and public opinions. But in China, provisions in laws are contradictory, let alone ambiguous, allowing the authorities to interpret laws at will and to follow the laws they prefer. The public opinions are tightly controlled and censored.

In conclusion, I want to say a few more words about the Taxpayers Revolution, which I thought so much about while imprisoned.

1. True relationship of the people and the government
2. Raise awareness of taxpayers' rights
3. Most government problems can be made clear through these ideas:
   - Government intrusion on rights, private fields
   - No government budget or not made public
   - Lack of public service
   - Corruption
4. Taxpayers are entitled to have political rights to ensure their servants serve their interests
5. Initiate meaningful Chinese constitutional democracy transition by combining the concrete tangible interests of the people with our ideals of democratic governance
6. All-inclusive Chinese democracy movement

The left-wing and right-wing debate has been going on for years in China. Both wings are missing a target because the normal relationship of the people and the government has yet to be established. The CMD should not solely represent the poor nor the rich only. They are taxpayers and everyone has the right to hold the government accountable.

CHAPTER 10

Let Us Launch a "Speak the Truth" Movement

Speech at Annual Meeting of Chinese Democracy Education Foundation
San Francisco, CA, United States
November 30, 2007

Recently, Chinese officials, democratic activists, scholars, and businessmen who are traditionally considered members of the Chinese communist system have stood up one after another to write open letters to top leaders of the Chinese regime to present their analysis and voice their deep concerns about the political, economic, cultural, religious, and environmental situation in China. With great courage, they have pointed out the calamities brought about by one-party totalitarianism and have earnestly called for a political reform toward democracy, social justice, and harmony.

We are glad to see that the "insiders" of the communist system are starting to join the "outside" democratic forces. What's even more inspiring is, despite the fact that outspoken Chinese often risk the danger of being persecuted by the repressive communist regime, more and more people have spoken their consciences with remarkable wisdom and courage.

The CCP's kaiserdom, just like any totalitarian regime, is built on a three-legged table. One is the loyalty of its followers, which is entirely based on the huge material interests and gains obtained through monopolization of power. The second is violence, and the third is lies. The CCP regime will come to a swift end even if only one leg is cut off.

In China, the time is now ripe for taxpayers to unite themselves to combat the dictatorship with their lawful rights, resist violence with peacefulness and rationality, and overthrow lies by speaking out the truth. Let's start from the simplest steps. I call upon all Chinese to start a Grand Movement of Speaking the Truth.

Why Launch Such a Movement?

In a normal society, there is no need to launch a movement to encourage people to speak out the truth. In a civilized society, to tell the truth should be as natural as breathing the air. However, in China, people have long been submerged in violence and lies imposed on them by the dictators—falsified history, fabrication, forged greatness, counterfeit virtue, fabricated happiness, and so on. All the regime's crimes that are committed in broad daylight are protected by these lies. How many people have been imprisoned, tortured to death, or have had their families torn apart because they have told the truth?

Even today, in the twenty-first century, Chinese people still have to suffer financial punishment, political persecution, incarceration, and physical and mental torture. They even have to lose their lives for telling the truth! China's society has become unaccustomed to speaking the truth. Instead, we have become accustomed to tolerating and complying with lies. Moreover, we have developed the ability to tell and live on lies. The entire society is lying and has taken it for granted. Even kindergarten kids would speak about the "Three Represents" in front of a TV camera. Even those in the esteemed "pure land"—the institutions for higher education—are trading their diploma for official positions and money. As a result, we are indifferent toward those who are being ruthlessly persecuted for telling the truth; some of us even consider them abnormal people who have sabotaged social "harmony."

As time goes by, our spiritual lives have withered. We manage to survive, or strive to survive in an inauthentic way, at the cost of our inner dignity. Those who do not belong to the privileged class are being exploited and abused until they have nowhere to turn to seek redress for the injustices they have suffered. It's precisely because we completely accept the rule of lies that the dictators act so sanctimoniously. It's precisely because we completely succumb to lies that the totalitarian regime appears to be strong. Our spiritual realm has fallen into deep ruin, because by lacking courage to speak the truth, we have failed to defend it.

Under such circumstances, without launching a movement, that is, having a group of people take the initiative to speak the truth with their noble loftiness and courage, we will be unable to save this lie-drenched society. In today's China, it is a phenomenal feat for any individual to openly speak the truth, a feat that will in turn greatly encourage more people to stand up to speak the truth. A movement disobeying communist rule will surely be on the horizon. As a result, a campaign for all Chinese people to speak the truth is necessary and inevitable.

What Truths Should be Told?

The Speak the Truth movement is targeted at the field of public life. We do not advocate violating personal privacy, which is irrelevant to public life. Public life refers to all public people and activities that are supported by taxes paid by citizens, with the purpose of enhancing citizens' welfare. Any citizen is entitled to and has the right and responsibility to speak freely in public life in order to prevent corruption and damage to civic rights.

However, any dictator starts from controlling the right to speak in public through monopolizing civic rights. They use violence and lies to weaken people's ability to speak and think freely, thus destroying people's dignity and independent personalities. Hence, having an honest civic life will definitely be the most fundamental disintegration of an autocratic society.

To speak the truth, one must first speak one's mind and avoid saying things against one's conscience. Voice your own heartfelt evaluation of history, your opinion about the current situation of China and the world, your genuine wishes for your country, your criticism of your local government, and your genuine demands for what you think your government should or should not do.

When you speak from your heart, you refuse to go along with the language and language patterns that have been created by the lying machine of the dictatorial regime for controlling people's minds. The words that first come to mind may not necessarily be correct. Yet the essence of freedom of speech is not about being allowed to speak correct opinions but about being able to speak freely. Nobody can guarantee that one's words will be 100 percent correct, but everyone knows if someone is speaking one's true mind. Let us start by speaking our mind and not against our heart, gradually smooth out this mental state that has been distorted for so long, throw off the shackles that the dictatorial regime has placed on free thoughts, and fearlessly speak our mind in the field of public life.

To speak honestly, one must use the real facts. Autocratic societies are sustained through covering up and distorting history and reality. Once its true history and nature is known, the CCP's revolution and ruling of China would have no chance to exist on the right side of history. It will lose the shadows it relies on for survival. We will use the light of truth to drive away the lies that have been created by the CCP and are crawling all over China. We will restore the health and beauty of China's society.

We will no longer be a political cosmetician, nor will we accept his work or collaborate with him. We will no longer write "red" classics, take "red" tours, or use words that have been created to cover up history and distort people's minds, such as the "liberation" of China (which in reality is a cruel form of slavery), three years of "natural disaster" (which were actually manmade calamities), the "June 4th incident" (which was actually a massacre), and so on. We will evermore loudly proclaim the true facts of history, no matter how big or small, and explain the true situation in the world, in China and its localities, and of those around us.

We will tell all emperors, large or small, "The emperor is naked!" Let the saying of "whoever controls history controls reality and whoever controls reality controls history" end with our generation speaking the truth.

To speak the truth, we need to let out our complaints. One of the characteristics of a totalitarian regime is to continuously create dissatisfaction yet not allow people to express it. When the CCP regime had full political control, it demanded that people sincerely believe in it and praise it from their heart. Now that the CCP has already been put on the defensive by the forces of political democratization, it can only hope that people do not oppose it or recognize what it really is, and instead continue to praise it against their wills. From today onward, the Chinese people should begin to discard the cynicism that comes from accepting, recognizing, praising, and being indifferent to the CCP regime against our wills. We must voice our dissatisfaction with both history and reality, speak of the inequity that has been forced upon us and others, speak out against bureaucratic corruption, expose the CCP regime's crimes against humanity and crimes in destroying human nature, let people know how disharmonious the society is under the rule of an autocratic regime, and fully expose corruption and lies.

We must let people understand that an authoritarian regime has no ability to reduce official corruption or to establish a harmonious society. The taxpayers, as masters of the government, naturally have the right to oppose corruption and the abuse of civic rights. To allow citizens to fully voice their concerns is the first step toward a harmonious society.

How to Speak the Truth

In today's China, citizens have no reliable channels to be heard through the mass media and to influence regime decisions. What this Speak the Truth movement wants to achieve is to build such channels.

This movement must first inculcate in us the habit of telling the truth, as it requires us not to lie, not to attend mendacious celebrations, not to support face-saving projects that waste people's money and manpower, not to watch China Central TV's news programs or any other fake media reports, not to read party newspapers and magazines, nor to cooperate with the propaganda department's deceitful policies. We should use honest language in our daily, public lives. If we do so, our mouths will break away from the chain of lies.

To participate in this movement, we should write either private or open letters to local government leaders or central leaders. If you agree with the content of an open letter published by someone else, you could also cosign the letter and send it to the leaders. We should continuously publish open letters and send them to those leaders, leaving them no way to ignore citizens' voices.

We should also publish internet articles, write on our blogs, comment on others' articles, or even send cell phone text messages. The idea is to saturate the wavelengths surrounding China with the honest words and complaints of the Chinese people.

We should openly accept interviews from free media outlets and bring their stories back to China. Just as the free flow of capital can bring people material wealth, the free flow of information can bring people spiritual fulfillment.

The Speak the Truth movement is a campaign to establish a system of public opinion. We need to speak the truth, speak from our heart, express our dissatisfaction to the representatives of the people, let them get used to listening to the people, and bring these messages to the People's Congress.

Conclusion

Under the long rule of the communist dictatorship, we Chinese have lost too much. Most importantly, we have lost our right to speak and have forgotten how to do so. To take back this right, we need to constantly and determinedly speak the truth and relearn how to do so. For any individual, being able to speak the truth in China is the self-salvation of one's own soul. Physically, it is difficult, but spiritually, it is the only choice. For our nation to establish a democratic system, we, as a unified entity, need to clean up our political culture, which has been marked by lies and dictatorship.

The history of human civilization is the history of truth overcoming lies. Let us overcome our fear of dictatorship through speaking consciously and publicly. Let us unify people with courage through the Speak the Truth movement, regain our dignity and confidence as citizens, recover our spiritual realm, which has long been occupied by the enemy, and build the foundation of civic culture—all necessities for establishing a democratic society in the future.

My compatriots, let us act at once!

CHAPTER 11

Overcome Fear

Speech at Harvard Kennedy School of Government Forum
Cambridge, MA, United States
December 5, 2007

In each Sunday service that I have attended since returning to the United States from my five-year ordeal in China, our priest Leslie Sterling says, "Dear Brothers and Sisters: Live without fear!" This simple but powerful blessing strikes a resounding chord in my heart each time I hear it.

My five-year imprisonment was a fear-overcoming experience, which deepened my understanding of how fear works to subdue prisoners, and further, how an autocracy, which can be considered a prison at large, employs fear to make people's minds captive minds. I have come to realize that, to end a dictatorship, we must begin with efforts to end deep-rooted fear in ourselves and in the people whose freedom we are fighting for.

Look at these methods that the prison authorities applied against me or my inmates: stark-naked violence and intimidation of the use of violence, demonstration of omnipotence of arbitrary persecution, degradation and humiliation, isolation, monopolization of perception and brainwashing, harassment and psychological torture, induced debility and exhaustion, occasional indulgence, enforcing trivial demands, arbitrary intrusion of privacy, and so on and so forth. In a broader sense, the Chinese regime uses the same tactics to create fear and then compliance among the Chinese people. As a result, fear permeates. Everybody under the regime is filled with fear. Fear of persecution, imprisonment, and death for voicing dissents or just for telling the truth, fear of losing a job or other means of living, fear of being banned from publishing, fear of bringing troubles to family and affecting the future of our children… Fear becomes habit and habit becomes second nature. Fear is internalized to the degree that people sometimes do not even feel fear but always know how to behave and not cross the lines.

A number of recent surveys conducted by foreign scholars wrongly revealed 60, 70, or even up to 80% of support for the Chinese government among the Chinese citizens. The surveys misrepresented the real situation just because the scholars overlooked this very fundamental psychological state of the Chinese populace.

The Chinese regime is able to continue its rule not because the Chinese people love autocracy but because, as in any dictatorship, they are trapped in a collective action dilemma: Everybody, fearing that the cost of resistance is far more damaging to his situation than capitulation, wants others, and not themselves, to take action to bring an end to the unpopular regime, although he wants to see its fall.

Collective action dilemma may not be the worst part of reality in China. Pervasive fear with selective repression and selective indulgence induces cooperation, and then voluntary cooperation and, finally, willing accomplices. It is common in Chinese prisons that prisoners offer help to the guards to repress other inmates in exchange for favors. Almost every device of torture in prison is invented and made by prisoners and almost all prison regulations are drafted by prisoners. We can see that the Chinese elites have been caught in a situation similar to the prisoners' dilemma and, because of this, the Chinese regime has been able to co-opt them and shore up its powerbase.

We hope for, but cannot rely on, the Chinese autocratic rulers' initiative to open up the field of political rights. A democratic transition in China is more likely to come as a logical result of the growth of people's democratic forces. But the collective action dilemma and the prisoners' dilemma I described above constitute major hindrance on the road and the deep-rooted fear is their underlying spell. To break the dilemmas, we must break the spell of fear.

I think every fear consists of three components, which I call spiritual fear, material fear, and self-imposed fear.

Spiritual fear is fear that can be overcome spiritually by ideas, beliefs, and heroic actions. The Chinese leading democrats, one generation after another, have stood up for their ideas and beliefs. Their heroic actions and the ordeals they endured have revealed again and again the truth: "The biggest fear is fear itself." They have not only morally encouraged many to follow their cause but also paved the way for their followers to more easily apply the domestic and international pressures that have pushed the Chinese regime to make concessions. So, we must encourage more heroic actions, promote publicities for them, and propagate their impact on the Chinese society as a whole.

I experienced spiritual fear myself. When the Chinese authorities first brought groundless charges against me, I had a fear. I feared that the espionage charge might tarnish my name and that I might end up in prison for a long time with that serious charge. But during an interrogation, a police officer, knowing that I was a Christian, asked me to pray for her family and expressed her sympathy to my situation by saying, "A good person like you shouldn't have such a bad future." Her words opened my heart and vision. I might not be as good as she thought I would be but, to be sure, I was innocent, and the Chinese authorities had more fear than I did. They feared my return to China, and they brought a bad name on me because they feared my good name. I was a formidable force to the Chinese autocratic regime. Why should I fear?! So, I said this in the court, "No matter how long I will be sentenced, I will stay in prison until the last day to enjoy the right to move freely in China, my beloved homeland. During my imprisonment, I will reject any arrangement to expatriate me even if it is based on good will. I made my words good by rejecting an early release on the condition to leave China right after. I had gradually overcome the fear spiritually and reaffirmed my old belief that "Courage is not without fear, but to choose to do the right thing even with fear."

Material fear, the second component of fear, is concrete and can be overcome but by external reduction of actual costs: the severity of persecution. Everybody has a reason to fear because everybody might have something to lose, real or perceived.

Again, my experience. When the police blindfolded me upon my escorted arrival in Beijing from Kunming where I had been first detained, fear sent a chill to my bones: What are they going to do to me? Are they going to kill me? I began praying to God. I was sent to nearly fifteen months of solitary confinement where I was totally cut off from any meaningful human contact and reduced to animal-level physical life with tremendous human worries and anxieties. I was forced to sit up and look straight without moving four hours a day and was not allowed to go out for fresh air or sunshine for several stretches, the longest lasting nearly eight months. Also, I was constantly subjected to psychological torture inflicted by the interrogators. In the beginning I was only able to muster courage enough not to cooperate but no more. Yet when I was informed of the outpouring of support for me from outside, I was greatly encouraged to protest because I knew I was not alone, I was not forgotten and, with so many people around the world standing behind me, I could bear the pain. I began to stage the first of a series of protests and successfully ended the forced sitting up practice in the detention center.

My experience shows that support from the outside world can help reduce the cost and risk the democracy activists may have to face. In fact, the Chinese regime has become increasingly worried about its international image; your voice can be heard even in Chinese prison cells and, when it is heard, change may be quietly made.

The third component of fear, self-imposed fear, is self-evident and it can be reduced or overcome through education. The climate of tension created by autocratic rulers readily produces and reproduces fear to the extent that fear itself is a major source of fear. In many cases risk is much lower than perceived and fear can be seen as imaginary. For any autocratic ruler, generating self-imposed fear is the most cost-effective way to maintain its rule and, unfortunately, oftentimes people unwittingly contribute to the consolidation of an autocracy by simply exaggerating its strength and acting accordingly.

Much self-imposed fear will be dispersed if the ordinary Chinese people understand that the Chinese regime is actually on the defense in the battlefield of human rights. The rulers, with so many human rights violations, have more reasons to fear than we do. The best strategy is to move little by little to touch the boundary of freedom and little by little push it outward.

I believe that we, who enjoy freedom of speech and who stand to incur the least cost, if any, for criticizing an autocratic regime, have the responsibility to help educate the Chinese people by speaking out the truth. But some American scholars have exercised self-imposed censorship when conducting their China studies and abstained from voicing their views on China. Their messages have been misleading to both the Chinese people and the international community. They act in this manner out of fear, self-imposed fear. They are fearful of being banned from study in China, of losing the access, or the competition to others for the access, to the top Chinese leaders, of losing the prestige, or the competition to others for the prestige, the Chinese regime confers on them. They, too, run into a collective action dilemma and a prisoners' dilemma. I would have an uneasy feeling if I heard a Harvard professor saying, "I cannot be critical because I want to maintain a good relationship with the Chinese government." During the period of the South African people's struggle against apartheid, a great American citizen, Leon Sullivan, authored the Sullivan Principles to help the US business community exercise their collective strength to defend fundamental values of human dignity. I respectfully suggest that the community of China scholars in the United States should do the same. When a member of this community is banned from entering China for his outspokenness, for example, what should other members do? I think we all know the answer.

In prison, I respected everybody, inmates and guards, as human beings and offered them my knowledge and shared with them my democratic ideas. When my situation improved, I taught my inmates English, Mathematics, Economics, Logic, and Chinese calligraphy, and I also coached a basketball team for three years until my last day there. The inmates gradually overcame their fear and joined in my work to bring about positive changes in prison, and sane guards gradually overcame their fear and became my friends and, thanks to their sympathy and protection, I was able to organize a bible study group. The inmates overcame their fear because they saw me as their protector, they saw some hope, and my guards overcame their fear because they saw me as an alternative; they saw an alternative future. They all began to see that our cause is right and just and the democracy activists represent a brighter future.

I am here tonight not to tell you why democracy is good and why China needs a democratic order; I believe most of you are democracy lovers and are interested to see democracy take root in China. Instead, I want to share with you my views, based on my own experience, on how to help the Chinese people and even ourselves reduce or eradicate the deep-rooted fear in our hearts, which is the major obstacle on the road to collective wisdom and collective strength needed for a democratic transition in China. We should openly engage with the Chinese democratic forces both in and outside China, give them moral and material support, provide them with ideas and resources, bring their situation to the attention of the international community, speak the truth about China and the world, and provide protection to those in danger. All of these ideas and actions will contribute to the reduction of the cost and risk the democracy activists have to face. As fear lessens, more and more people will join the democratic forces. The collective action dilemma will consequently be broken. The growth of the democratic forces will go on to help break the prisoners' dilemma because it will provide an alternative future to the Chinese ruling elite who will one after another split from the autocratic regime to join the democratic forces. Who, after all, wants to be on the losing side?

CHAPTER 12

China: From Prison to Freedom

Speech at National Endowment for Democracy
Washington, DC, United States
January 15, 2008

During my five-year imprisonment, I experienced firsthand the games played between repressive prison authorities and repressed prisoners. With seemingly unlimited power, prison guards constantly use the following methods against prisoners: violence and intimidation, arbitrary persecution, degradation and humiliation, isolation, brainwashing, harassment and psychological torture, induced debility and exhaustion, occasional indulgence, enforcement of trivial demands, and the like. At the same time, capitalizing on prisoners' fear and their desire for the reduction of their prison terms and other benefits, the guards constantly exploit prisoners and their families economically. Until I was put in prison, I had no idea that being a jailer is such a profitable occupation!

How do prisoners react to all this? On the one hand, they harbor such bitter hatred toward the prison authorities that they would, if they could, torture the guards even more than the guards have tortured them. On the other hand, due to longtime persecution and fear, they have unknowingly been transformed into fawning slaves who do everything possible to win favor with the guards, even competing with other prisoners for pitiful benefits and for a domineering position over their fellow inmates. Both in behavior and in psychology, a Chinese prison is a mix of tyrants, mobs, and slaves.

I became intent on creating and cultivating a new and different environment—a civil and healthy environment. Otherwise, things would inevitably keep going around in a vicious circle. Despite extremely unfavorable circumstances, my efforts achieved limited success, and I learned the following lessons: First, somebody needs to show moral courage and to protest, awakening and inspiring the consciences of inmates and guards alike. Second, issues must be carefully selected and strategies wisely chosen to achieve small victories, especially at the outset, thereby strengthening the confidence that positive results can be achieved. And last but not least, outside support is vital.

Although it is not a perfect analogy, Chinese autocracy is like a prison writ large, with its authorities relentlessly persecuting and even seeking to annihilate its civil and healthy elements. As a result, Chinese society is, to a large extent, also a mix of tyrants, mobs, and slaves. Our challenge is how to nurture new and different elements—civil and healthy ones—in present-day China. Until we find a solution to this problem, the prospects for democracy in China will remain hopeless, because neither tyrants, nor mobs, nor slaves can create a truly civil society.

Ignorance Is Not the Problem

Many people assume that there has been no democratic transition in China because the Chinese people, especially the ruling elite, do not understand democracy, let alone its essential importance to the country's future. This assumption is false. During the nearly four months I spent in China following my release from prison on April 27, 2007, I met and had meaningful conversations with about 200 friends, both old and new. They ranged from dissidents to government officials, from peasants and taxi drivers to renowned professors and successful entrepreneurs, from freelance Web writers to official journalists, and from show-business people to retired senior officials of the Chinese Communist Party (CCP). These personal interactions actually began more than five years earlier, when I entered China in April 2002. I interviewed nearly a hundred migrant and unemployed workers during the short period of freedom before my arrest. These interactions continued during my imprisonment.

I seized upon every possible opportunity to exchange views on various questions concerning democratization in China with my fellow inmates and guards. Almost none of the people whom I met denied the intrinsic importance of democracy to China's future. Almost everyone agreed that democracy is inevitable, although they might disagree about how long it would take to achieve it and who should pay the price and take the risks of the potential disorders that might accompany a transition. I also discovered that most of the ruling elites have been exposed to Western democratic theories and practices. It is fair to say that they understand what democracy is almost as well as Westerners do.

Now, if these people have a good understanding of democracy, realize its vital importance to the future of China, and accept its inevitability, then why has a democratic transition not yet begun? The standard answer is that the ruling elites do not want to loosen their grip on political power because they do not want to give up their privileges. Who does? This answer is absolutely right—but the story does not end there. The real question has to do with what distinguishes China from other autocracies. Many autocratic societies began the process of democratization in an even less favorable international environment when the universal standards of human rights were much less acknowledged worldwide than they are today. Why not China? The answer lies in the unique history of the CCP rule.

Over the course of its nearly sixty years in power, the CCP has conducted two diametrically opposed pieces of the devil's business. At first, the CCP forced the Chinese people to surrender their private property to the state in order to establish a comprehensive planned economy. Later, the CCP began to steal public property and to put it into the private pockets of party officials and their associates. As a result, the CCP has turned China into a system that combines a monopoly of political power and crony capitalism with Chinese characteristics. Almost every member of the ruling elite has committed the double sin of being both a political persecutor and an economic embezzler.

So political change might lead not only to the surrender of the elites' vested privileges but also to serious lawsuits or even violent mob revenge against them. If the CCP had committed only political repression, things would be much easier: Upon the arrival of political change, the ruling elites could explain their past behavior by saying, "We conducted governmental business that way because we believed in communism," or "We just carried out orders from above," or "We were deceived by Chairman Mao and did everything he told us to do." But I cannot imagine how they could rationalize both evils. How could they explain embezzlement? They cannot easily say: "I am corrupt because of my political ideals," or "President Jiang Zemin told me to use political power to make money," or "President Hu Jintao told me to steal."

Because of their evil deeds, the ruling elite have concluded that the political status quo is the only safe haven for them. So, their first political priority is to stall the democratization process as long as they can. This mentality and policy were clearly embodied in the political report made by Hu Jintao at the CCP's recent Seventeenth National Congress. The CCP's political paralysis has trapped itself and China in a vicious circle: Initial resistance to political reform only aggravates existing problems and gives rise to new ones. This sharpens tensions, which then increase the risks that any reform will get out of control. This, in turn, deters the CCP from undertaking any reform, further fueling state-society tensions as individual and collective grievances continue to mount, compounding the risks of future reform.

When political change took place in the former Soviet Union in the 1980s, the resistance from the ruling elite was not as stubborn, since the Bolsheviks had largely conducted only the relatively "easy to get away with" evil business of imposing political autocracy. The 1997 transition in Suharto's Indonesia was not so difficult because corruption was pretty much limited to one family and its associates—unlike in China, where the hands of almost every member of the ruling elite are stained by either blood or dirty money. In Taiwan, the long-ruling Kuomintang (KMT) party's opposition to democratization was even less bitter. The KMT government had respected private property rights and managed to contain government corruption and income disparities within an acceptable range. Thus, KMT officials had little to fear in facing political change.

It is an impossible task for the CCP to convince people that the two opposite pieces of evil business are both right. In fact, the CCP has been unable to close its legitimacy gap despite all the theoretical bridges that it has tried to build—from Marxism to Mao Zedong Thought, from Mao Zedong Thought to Deng Xiaoping Theory, from Deng Xiaoping Theory to the Three Represents, and from the Three Represents to Harmonious Society and Scientific Development Concept.

In all of China's long history, the CCP one-party dictatorship has conducted the cruelest theft of private property. In times of peace, the CCP government has been responsible for the bloodiest turmoil, the most horrific starvation, and the greatest number of non-natural deaths. It has created the most numerous cases of injustice and perpetrated the most barbarous destruction of China's historic heritage, natural environment, and religious beliefs. The CCP has carried out the most notorious crackdown on a student movement, and it continues to produce the most widespread human rights violations and government corruption.

CCP policies have produced the most unjust income disparity, and, in the name of socialism, they have left the country without a social safety net. Both in theory and in practice, the CCP's rule has no basis of legitimacy. The only straw at which the CCP can grasp is rapid economic growth. The slogan strongly promoted by the CCP in recent years—"Growth is the hard truth"—stems from this hard fact.

Yet the fruits of this growth are not justly distributed. The ruling elites have been systematically pilfering the spoils. Permitting graft in exchange for loyalty, the CCP has tolerated predatory practices on all levels, so long as the mass grievances and protests that they cause can be kept under control. But the grievances are mounting. The number of incidents of collective protest has risen to about a hundred thousand per year. This total is even more telling given that protesters face the threat of a severe crackdown.

In order to ensure a "Harmonious Society" without having to reform its political system, the CCP continues to expand and upgrade its police forces. About 4.6 million well-paid and well-equipped police stand ready at any time to crack down on and persecute so-called unstable elements around the country. Make no mistake about it: In some ways China is still a police state.

Nevertheless, the CCP is on the defensive with regard to political rights, facing resistance not only from abroad but, more importantly, from within. Political rights in China lag far behind personal liberties, and more and more people are coming to realize that, so long as they lack political rights, their social and economic rights can be arbitrarily violated. Two typical examples are land-grab cases in the countryside and instances of forced demolition and eviction in the cities. Protests against such violations of rights, as well as voices demanding political reform, are besieging the communist regime on all sides. Although the CCP understands that it is on the wrong side of history, it lacks the confidence to welcome a democratic transition. Instead, it tightly defends the system that it considers necessary to its survival.

What Is to Be Done?

Given all that I have said, where do our hopes lie? What can and should we do to advance democracy in China? Scholars often talk about prerequisites for democratization. For me, the most important prerequisite of all is that there must be democratic forces in Chinese society. One should not count on tyrants or slaves, and certainly not on mobs, who would only scare the ruling elite into a more determined defense of their positions. But how can we nurture the civil and healthy elements that we need in China?

Based on my experience in prison, I believe that for democratic forces to thrive, the first step is for someone to stand up with moral courage and vision and openly challenge the undemocratic features of our society, thereby inspiring the civil and healthy elements in our country. Second, we must continually improve our organizational work and our strategies for assembling civil and healthy elements into democratic forces; it is imperative to secure some initial advances, for this can convince people that success is possible and inspire them to join. Third, support from the international community is essential.

The good news is that more and more civil and healthy elements are surfacing in virtually every geographic area, profession, and social class. But the bad news is that these elements remain scattered. They lack a unified organization, broadly accepted leadership, and commonly shared long-term goals and strategies. These three factors are indispensable to facilitate communication, to coordinate efforts, and to transform all grievances, protests, and independent voices into a movement toward a constitutional democracy. Without them, democratic forces can operate only on a very low level, with little impact on the overall situation.

To know what we need is to know what we should do. All my work here in the United States is aimed at assisting our colleagues back in China so that they can successfully bring together moral leadership, improved internal organization of democratic forces, and support from the international community.

We will not be able to get very far without a strong commitment from the international community, and particularly the United States, to support Chinese democratic forces both within and outside China. Today China is open to the world, and its leadership can no longer afford to ignore the pressures, voices, and norms emanating from the international community. Western governments should bring up human rights issues with China on every possible occasion, even in the context of economic talks or cultural exchanges. Even a single request for the release of an individual prisoner of conscience can have a significant impact. All these efforts can help to enlarge the political space in China. Over the past twenty years, international attention and pressure have helped to raise Chinese public awareness of human rights to a significant degree. It is very important to keep China's door open, and I have never opposed a policy of engagement with China. But I believe that a crucial part of such a policy is to engage openly and systematically with Chinese democratic forces and to nurture their growth, as they offer the most promising means to limit the arbitrary and predatory power of the CCP regime and to foster positive changes in China.

Let me add a word addressed to the international business community. I would like you to realize that the legitimacy of CCP rule now hangs by but a single thread—the gossamer strand of continued stratospheric economic growth. In every region of China, economic growth is the single most important measuring rod for evaluating the performance of local leaders. They want you to do business in their regions regardless of your stand on human rights issues. Why be silent like a cold cicada? Much of your fear of speaking out is actually self-imposed. During the period of the South African people's struggle against apartheid, a great American citizen, Leon Sullivan, authored the Sullivan Principles (1977) to help the US business community exercise its collective strength to defend fundamental values of human dignity. I respectfully suggest that you do the same when dealing with China.

We can hope that China's autocratic rulers will take the initiative to grant their people political rights, but we cannot rely on them to do so. A democratic transition in China is most likely to occur through the growth of popular democratic forces. Our real hope lies with them. Our sacred duty is to nurture their growth.

CHAPTER 13

A Different Approach for the Beijing Olympics: Conditional Participation

Speech at Action Group Organized by US Senator Sam Brownback
Capitol, Washington, DC, United States
March 11, 2008

When I returned to the United States last year after serving five years in prison in China, many people asked me about my views about the 2008 Beijing Olympics and what can be done to bring about positive changes in China's human rights situation before the Olympics. The Olympics are indeed a major event. There are many in the international community that are disappointed or even angry about China's human rights record after its prior commitments to clean up its act. And there are regrets about why the IOC (International Olympic Committee) remains unwilling to make public, as in past cases, the agreement it signed with the Chinese government in 2001. It is believed this is because China has failed to abide by numerous commitments contained in that document.

When Burma's military junta ruthlessly suppressed peaceful protests last September, I heard many people expressing regrets that if the international community had insisted on its principles back in 1988 and 1989, when the governments in both Rangoon and Beijing carried out large-scale killings of peaceful protesters and had pressured the Chinese government to compromise on political reform and human rights, both Burma and China would be different places today. Why do we allow ourselves to live with so many regrets?

The Chinese government places great value on the opportunity to host the Olympics to showcase its achievements as the ruler in a one-party system. The Chinese leaders are extremely nervous about any potential mistake or embarrassments in relation to how the Olympics are run. As a result, it cannot afford to ignore pressure from the international community. There is, therefore, a real window of opportunity for us to press the Chinese government to improve human rights conditions.

I have been asked, "Should the international community boycott the Olympics?" In my view, the Olympics are going to happen in Beijing, so our effort should be spent on how to use it as an opportunity to bring about a positive change. I believe that rather than trying a futile boycott that will be viewed as a failure, it would be much more effective to initiate a conditional participation campaign.

Imagine if we could find world-renowned athletes or sport teams who would indicate their intent to participate in the games but only provided certain conditions are met. Similarly, imagine if well-known politicians, scholars, and entrepreneurs specify to the Chinese government the conditions under which they attend the Olympics. When President Bush accepted President Hu Jintao's invitation, his press secretary said he was going to the games as "a sports fan, not to make any political statement." This was disappointing as surely President Bush must understand that no president can attend any event without there being a political element to it. And his mere attendance will make a political statement and will be explained by the Chinese government in the state-controlled media as such. So, I urge President Bush to explain to the Chinese government the conditions that will need to be met for him to participate in the Beijing Olympics.

Then, what conditions should we raise to the Chinese government? And what are the things that we could achieve and that would have a long-term impact? I think we can focus on the following issues:

1. Ratify in the Chinese People's Congress next March the International Covenant on Civil and Political Rights, which the Chinese government signed in October of 1998.

2. Extend the rights of travel and reporting granted to foreign journalists in January of last year to China's domestic journalists, and let both domestic and foreign journalists retain these rights after the Olympics.
3. Release all those who remained imprisoned for their involvement in Tiananmen Square almost twenty years ago.
4. Stop the ongoing arrests of human rights activists and defenders.
5. Abolish the border-crossing blacklists so that all Chinese citizens, including pro-democracy activists, can leave and return to China. Give all people the freedom of movement.

Since I am overseas, I want to say a little more about the fifth condition, which is very personal for me. We cannot overlook this one. Just as the free flow of domestic and international capitals has propelled the development of market economy in China, allowing all Chinese citizens to enter and leave China in accordance with the Chinese law will propel the development of democratic politics in China.

As the Olympics approach, the international community needs to remain vigilant. Increasing resistance, harassment, or suppression must be brought to the attention of the international community, and we need support for the dissidents inside China. Most importantly, anyone with a connection to the Olympics should take the liberty that those inside China do not have—to articulate the conditions to the Chinese government required for their attendance at the games.

CHAPTER 14

Darkness Cannot Drive Out Darkness

Speech at Commonwealth High School
Boston, MA, United States
April 2, 2008

Good afternoon. I wish to thank you for inviting me to speak with you today. I will talk to you about an event that happened to me when I was not much older than you. This event changed my life and the lives of many other people and, I believe, will ultimately change the future of China. The event took place on June 4, 1989. It is called in the United States the Tiananmen Square Massacre. In China, it is not called anything because the Chinese government does not want anyone to know what really happened.

In the middle of May 1989, I was elected by my fellow Chinese students at the University of California at Berkeley to go back to China to support the students who were protesting for democracy. The protest was peaceful but was very large. On June 4th, the Chinese government sent in the army to crush the protest. They had orders to kill anyone who resisted. By the end of June, thousands of protesters were killed. No one knows the exact number.

About 6:30 on the morning of June 4th, I was among the students who last retreated from Tiananmen Square. I was a few yards away when Chinese army tanks ran over students, and among them was Fang Zheng, who was a little luckier than the other eleven students who lost their lives on the spot. He only lost both his legs. Fang Zheng went on to become a very good athlete despite his disability, but the

Chinese government to this day will not allow him to compete in any international sports activities. Those who will participate in the 2008 Beijing Olympics as competing athletes or sports fans will surely not be able to see Fang Zheng because he belongs to the part of China that China doesn't want the world to see.

I managed to avoid arrest and return to the United States to finish my studies in Mathematics at UC Berkeley. Tiananmen Square taught me that freedom is not free. We must work for it and work to protect it. If not, we will surely lose it. So, I committed my life to exposing the lack of human rights in China and to promoting the peaceful transition to democracy.

In 2002, I returned to China to support the labor movement and to better understand the growing number of the protest. I went because I believed, as I still do today, that more people must stand by them with moral courage and vision to form civil democratic forces because there is no democratization without democratic forces to fight for it. The visit was longer than I intended. Two weeks after I entered China I was arrested by the Chinese police and put in jail. I remained in jail for over a year before I was finally charged with treason and sentenced to five years in prison. I was tortured and placed in solitary confinement for nearly fifteen months.

This was very difficult for me. Imagine having no contact with anyone having no materials, nor a pen to write for over a year. I kept busy by writing poems and books in my head. I was determined not to become angry or hateful. However I was treated by others, I responded with respect and love. In this way, I was able to turn many of my guards into friends who made my life there bearable. It also taught me that the best way to achieve change is through peaceful resistance and love. This is what Martin Luther King Jr. taught us when he said "Darkness cannot drive out darkness; only light can do that. Hate cannot drive out hate; only love can do that." This is still true today.

In prison, I also experienced firsthand the games played between prison authorities and prisoners. With seemingly unlimited power, prison guards constantly use various physical and psychological torture methods against prisoners. How do prisoners react to all this? On the one hand, they harbor such bitter hatred toward the prison authorities that they would, if they could, torture the guards even more than the guards tortured them. On the other hand, due to longtime persecution and fear, they have unknowingly been transformed into fawning slaves who do everything possible to win favor with the guards, even competing with other prisoners for pitiful benefits and for a domineering position over their fellow inmates. Both in behavior and in psychology, a Chinese prison is a mix of tyrants, mobs, and slaves.

I became intent on creating and cultivating a new and different environment—a civil and healthy environment. Otherwise, things would inevitably keep going around in a vicious circle. Despite extremely unfavorable circumstances, my efforts achieved limited success, and I learned the following lessons: First, somebody, in this specific case myself, needs to show moral courage and to protest, awakening and inspiring the consciences of inmates and guards alike. Second, issues must be carefully selected and strategies wisely chosen to achieve small victories, especially at the outset, thereby strengthening the confidence that positive results can be achieved. And last but not least, outside support is vital; to tell you the truth, without it, I might not be able to muster enough courage to protest.

Although it is not a perfect analogy, China is like a prison at large, with its authorities relentlessly persecuting and even seeking to annihilate its civil and healthy elements. As a result, Chinese society is, to a large extent, also a mix of tyrants, mobs, and slaves. One should not count on tyrants or slaves or mobs to advance democracy. But how can we nurture the civil and healthy elements that we need in China?

Based on my experience in prison, I believe that in order for democratic forces to thrive, the first step is for someone to stand up with moral courage and vision and openly challenge the undemocratic features of our society, inspiring the civil and healthy elements in our country. Second, we must continually improve our organizational work and our strategies for assembling civil and healthy elements into democratic forces; it is imperative to secure some initial advances, for this can convince people that success is possible and inspire them to join. Third, support from the international community is essential. You are a very important part of the international community.

It is quite possible that I would still be in jail today except for the fact that many, many people in the United States spoke up about my imprisonment. They wrote many letters to the Chinese government asking for my release. The leaders in the US government also spoke on my behalf. The Congress of the United States, both the House of Representatives and the Senate, passed a resolution calling for my release. Again, I learned how powerful and necessary it is to speak for the rights of people. That is the best way to ensure that our rights will not be taken away.

As a result of the tremendous support I received, I was finally released from prison in April of 2007 and returned home to my family and friends in Brookline.

There is no way I can personally thank all the wonderful people in the United States who worked for my freedom. But I feel I must do something to thank them for standing up for my human rights in the face of totalitarian repression.

So, I will make an announcement today to you. You are the first to know. On May 4 of this year I will walk 500 miles from Boston to Washington, DC, over a period of thirty days. Each step will be an expression of thanks to all the great people of America for their courage in asking for my freedom. Each step will also be a call to remember the thousands of Chinese people who remain in prison and the many millions of others who are repressed and abused for no other reason than they spoke freely, protested an injustice, or tried to worship as they please.

Each day of the walk, I will call on you and all the wonderful people of America to remember the struggle for human rights and democracy is not over. As President Lincoln said: "Our nation cannot survive half free…" I say to you who will be the future leaders of America, freedom cannot survive in a world that is only half free. With this idea in mind, I ask you to walk with me in spirit to Washington and be with me in spirit when I arrive in Washington on June 4th, the anniversary of the brave students who stood up and spoke for democracy in Tiananmen Square.

To conclude my speech, I would like to read to you one of the over 100 poems I wrote while in prison.

The first anniversary of 9/11 happened during my solitary confinement, and I wrote a poem commemorating that awful event.

A Lamentation

Two huge new waves of glory crashed down,
Cast so cruelly into history, the towering twins.
Five thousand ships, with sails full-blown,
Now scattered and thrown.
To the Four Winds.
Civilization wept and groaned.
Greatness fell down on her knees to pray.
The red setting Sun, all arrayed in light,
On the back of a Swan,
Turns into Dark Night.
A crystal tear falls, seed upon a pillow.
The Moon grows, rising up from the sea,
Cradles her face within both her hands
Looking down at the world,
From her abode of peace.
An Old Man smiles, face riddled with ripples,
Undulating, propagating, ripples on ripples…
Another year's tears, dreams and emotions
Sink into the deep,
The deep, vast ocean.

Above the foam,
A white feather flies low,
Drifts to and fro,
Then floats…
A sail,
…without
…a boat.

SECTION III

FREEDOM WALK: AWAKENING CITIZEN POWER

April 2008-July 2008

"This May 4, I will begin walking 500 miles to Washington, DC, to thank America for all you have done for me, and to remember those still imprisoned in China. We are calling this walk 'GongMin,' which means 'citizen and citizen power.' My presence here today is testimony to the power of free citizens speaking freely in a free country. It is this citizen power that will keep the hopes of the Chinese people alive and ultimately bring about a peaceful transition to a democratic China."

CHAPTER 15

I Will Walk 1,408,000 Steps as a Free Man from Boston to Washington

State House of Massachusetts
Boston, MA, United States
April 15, 2008

Good afternoon. First, I want to thank Joshua Rubenstein for his very kind introduction and, more than this, for his persistent efforts to get me released when I was a political prisoner in China.

I also want to thank State Representative Frank Smizik and State Senator Cindy Creem for holding this wonderful celebration of freedom at the State House for me and my family and, in a symbolic sense, for all the Chinese people who do not yet enjoy freedom that is their right, just as it is the right of every citizen of the world.

Many American people and organizations came to my aid while I was imprisoned: from my neighbors in Brookline to the national leaders in Washington, DC, from my son's and daughter's elementary schools to Harvard University, from grassroots rights groups to the US Congress, from personal friends to compassionate strangers, from lawyers to journalists, from my Christian brothers and sisters in Massachusetts to American diplomats in Beijing…

It is impossible to thank them one by one, and I cannot thank any of them enough.

If it weren't for these dedicated Americans, I would not be standing here today. And for that, I offer you my deepest and most humble gratitude for all the support you have given me and my family during the very dark days of my five years in prison.

With my heart so full of gratitude for my adopted country, the United States of America, I've often reflected on what would have happened had I gone to another country to further my studies instead. When I went back to China in 2002 and was detained without due process and then sentenced to five years as a political prisoner, where would I be now?

I'm certain that after hearing from my wife, Christina, my second country would have taken an interest in my plight and would have done everything it could to get me safely released. Yet, would everything it could have done have been enough? Or might I still be languishing in prison, along with countless others, my health failing, as one's health tends to fail in Chinese prisons? Would I be on my way to dying there?

The truth is that this great country, the United States of America might well be the only country in the world with both the moral conscience and the political strength to have been able to get me safely home.

It is said that with power comes responsibility; with great power comes great responsibility. This great country, the United States of America, must continue to demand that the Chinese government stop repressing its citizens. And what better opportunity could there be than in the time leading up to the Olympics in Beijing?

You might be aware that this is China's second attempt to win the coveted role of Olympic host. Its first attempt in 1991, in the aftermath of the Tiananmen Square Massacre, was denied. Ten years later, with the harrowing cries of the victims of Tiananmen faded and almost forgotten, its second attempt was successful. But I stand here today knowing that there are still thousands of smaller Tiananmen Squares all over China. And I stand here today knowing that the Chinese Olympic slogan, "One World, One Dream," is the furthest thing from the truth in China.

For I dare say that the Chinese government's dream is not the same as the dream of Mr. Hu Jia's activist wife, Zeng Jinyan, and their three-month-old daughter, who have now been under house arrest for more than 200 days. If convicted, Hu Jia will join Olympic dissidents, including Yang Chunlin, who was last week sentenced to five years in prison for his involvement in a petition, "We Want Human Rights, Not the Olympics," signed by farmers protesting land seizures; nor is it the same dream as the dream of Ye Guozhou, who is serving a four-year prison sentence for organizing protests against Olympics-related forced evictions; and Wang Ling, sentenced to fifteen months of "re-education" in November of 2007 for opposing demolition of her property for an Olympics-related project—does she and the Chinese government share the same dream?

The list goes on. Think of Chen Guangcheng, the blind rural activist from my hometown, who was sentenced to four years and three months in prison for exposing forced abortions and sterilizations in eastern China. Or Dr. Wang Bingzhang, who was abducted in Vietnam by Chinese secret agents, and held secretly for six months before his arrest was even announced, and later sentenced to life in prison. Think of the Tibetan monks, with unknown numbers of them slaughtered just last month. What is their dream? Think of Falun Gong practitioners. Think of underground house church members. What is their dream? Is it the "one dream" of the Chinese government?

No. That is not their dream. It is their nightmare. "One World, One Nightmare," might be the more appropriate slogan for the Chinese people whose thirst for basic human rights and dignity is akin to a barren parched desert where it never rains. I lived in this nightmare for five years in prison. And when I called out to my God in prayer, I was beaten down by the guards.

But now I stand before you, fully awakened from my nightmare—a free man in a free country—with a heart so full of gratitude that I fear it might burst. How can I ever express this thanksgiving for all the support and hard work that you and so many other Americans gave so generously to help me be released? How can one say thank you for one's life and liberty using only words, when words, no matter how lovely or sincere, no matter how often repeated, could never be enough? I must say thank you in such a way that you will know it comes right from my heart.

In February of this year, I founded "Initiatives for China." GongMin LiLiang in Chinese means "citizen power." We are dedicated to empowering the citizens of China by sowing the seeds of hope and giving voice to their struggles for initiating a peaceful transition to a democratic China. We are now busy at work on a daily basis, with an electric energy surging through our staff and volunteers. Some may say we are engaging in dreams that will never come to fruition, but I like to think that every day we are throwing a little more tea in the harbor.

You may have noticed this small blue and yellow ribbon that I am wearing on my lapel. We are introducing this ribbon today as a symbol for the great need for human rights in China. Yellow is the color of my homeland and the yellow part is shaped in the Chinese character "Ren," which means "human." Blue is for the open sky. The ribbon is in the shape of an English "R," standing for "rights." This ribbon says, "The Chinese people, under the blue sky of Creation, are entitled to human rights." I ask that you join with us in wearing this ribbon to make clear to the Chinese government that they must stop repressing their citizens.

I am so pleased to be here in Boston today as I announce Initiatives for China's upcoming action.

This May 4, I will begin walking 500 miles to Washington, DC, to thank America for all you have done for me, and to remember those still imprisoned in China. We are calling this walk "GongMin" which means "Citizen and citizen power." My presence here today is testimony to the power of free citizens speaking freely in a free country. It is this citizen power that will keep the hopes of the Chinese people alive and ultimately bring about a peaceful transition to a democratic China. My journey will commence here in Boston, and I will walk through Wellesley, Providence, New Haven, Bridgeport, New York, Philadelphia, Wilmington, and Baltimore. On June 4th, the nineteenth anniversary of the Tiananmen Square Massacre, I will conclude my journey in Washington, DC.

Along the way, I will speak out on the human rights situation in China, and I will make the critical call for continued moral leadership from the United States. I will speak out on land grabbing, on Tibet, Darfur, on political prisoners, and I will speak about the need for conditional participation in the upcoming Olympics.

Once again, I find myself humbly asking for your generous support with this vast endeavor. I will be posting my route and whereabouts online and welcome you to join with me in my journey. The address is printed in today's program leaflet. We will broadcast the walk LIVE every day, and I encourage you to talk about my walk, to blog about it, to message me, to spread the word, to share some miles with me. Yes, it will take much help and support and the power of the free citizens in America for me to complete this GongMin Citizen Walk.

This event today is also being broadcast live all over the world on HelloWorld. I am told it will even be broadcast in China, if it can make it through the great fire wall of the Chinese internet police, so I'd like to take a minute to say something to all of my Chinese compatriots right now.

亲爱的同胞们：我将于五月四日开始从波士顿徒步行走，六月四日抵达华盛顿，这个徒步行走活动叫做“公民行一从五四到六四”。我坚信，中国的希望在于公民精神的觉醒和公民力量的成长。亲爱的同胞们，让我们一起宣誓：不做恶官，不做暴政的帮凶，不做奴隶，也不做暴民。我们要做公民。中国将由于公民精神的觉醒而文明，中国将由于公民力量的成长而民主，中国将由于成为公民社会而成为真正伟大的国度。

(In addition to introducing GongMin Walk, I said: My dear fellow compatriots, I believe that our country's hope lies in the awakening of Citizen Spirit and the growth of Citizen Power. Let us not be accomplices to tyranny, let us not be slaves nor mobs, let us be citizens. China will be civilized with the awakening of Citizen Spirit; China will be democratized with the growth of Citizen Power, and China will be a truly great nation when our society becomes a civil society.)

Now, knowing a little about mathematics has helped me figure out how many steps my 500-mile journey will add up to and, averaging my stride at 22.5 inches, I calculate that I will walk 1,408,000 steps.

Yes, I will walk 1,408,000 steps as a free man, with a heart full of gratitude for my wonderful adopted country, the United States of America, and a soul full of hope for a better future in China, my homeland. I thank you all so very much.

CHAPTER 16

Help Form a Coalition of Human Rights Patriots

Speech at the Hearing on the Political Situation in China on the Eve of the Olympics Held by the Political Affairs Committee of the Parliamentary Assembly of the Council of Europe
Strasbourg, France
April 17, 2008

Good morning, everyone. Thank you for giving me this opportunity to speak to you about the current political situation in China, less than four months before the Beijing Olympics. I want to look at the situation through the prism of Chinese nationalist fervor, the effects of which have again captured worldwide attention last month.

In almost every Olympics-related discussion I have engaged in during the past few months, I was asked whether it was the right thing to use the opportunity of the Beijing Olympics to push China to improve its human rights records. The international pressure seems to have played right into the hands of the CCP regime by triggering nationalist emotions and rallying indignant Chinese people behind the Chinese Communist Party (CCP). This is a common worry, which is quite understandable.

In order to answer this question, we need first to distinguish and understand the different types of nationalism existing in China today.

One is what I call CCP pragmatic nationalism. The CCP is struggling for its survival as the single legitimate ruling party because communism in China, for all practical purposes, is dead. Yet, the CCP has never retreated from seeking new ways to manipulate, if not control, the mindset of the Chinese people. Nationalism has, over time, become one of the two life-saving strings it clutches. Another lifesaver, actually a stronger one, is fast economic growth. China's pragmatic leaders understand well that continued prosperity is the key to its continued rule and that China's economic growth relies very much on its integration with the outside world, especially with major powers. Therefore, it has engaged in a sophisticated balancing act of fanning nationalist emotion to promote loyalty among the populace, while at the same time tightly controlling this emotion so as not to bring damage to the international environment needed for its development. So CCP pragmatic nationalism is an interest-driven, not ideological, doctrine.

The second is what I call vassal pragmatic nationalism. The pragmatism of vassal pragmatic nationalists, a majority of them being elites in Chinese society, is embodied in their keeping in line with the CCP pragmatic nationalism. In a sense, showing their nationalist sentiment is probably the only way they choose to showcase their morality in public life, but quite ironically, their sentiment can be instantly weathered with that of the party's. They become angry and indignant in the right time and place, when and where the party thinks they should. Sometimes I am amazed by their ability to get over their emotion almost instantly when the party hints, not even orders, them to. As the world watched in the past several weeks, many Chinese who don't normally feel uneasy toward China's state-controlled media for its everyday propaganda or the regime's never-tired online policing, protested very indignantly against some western media's unsatisfactory reports on Tibet. The inconsistency in their mindset shown so poignantly in this case is the essential character of vassal pragmatic nationalism.

CCP pragmatic nationalism and vassal pragmatic nationalism can together be called Chinese pragmatic nationalism. Since pragmatism has been such a dominant doctrine in the mindset of the Chinese people during the past twenty years, we can know for sure that Chinese pragmatic nationalism constitutes a major part of the Chinese nationalism we are experiencing. It is no wonder that many observers are often puzzled by Chinese nationalism's superficiality, phoniness, affectedness, theatrics, and flexibility.

The third kind of Chinese nationalism is what I call popular nationalism. Chinese popular nationalism traces the roots of weakness to the impact of imperialism on China's self-esteem. It pursues China's unity, strength, prosperity, and dignity. With that dominant in the mindset, it may or may not take human rights and democracy as its core value, and it may occasionally call for democracy as a way for China to become strong and rich. Chinese popular nationalists can be quite reasonable, accurate, righteous, and democracy-oriented when it comes to local politics because their judgment is based on their own experiences. But they can be very illogical, inconsistent, and emotional when it comes to remote issues concerning international relations, Taiwan, or minorities, which they cannot directly experience and must rely on the state-monopolized source for information. Being idealists, Chinese popular nationalists can be manipulated by the Chinese government but cannot be fully controlled by it. They may well turn against the government if they deem it as having failed to fulfill its nationalistic promises. They sometimes call for public participation in the foreign policymaking process, which poses a threat to the CCP's monopoly on power because this idea has great potential to extend to all public policy fields.

So, nationalism in China is a double-edged sword: being both a means to legitimize the CCP's rule and, if not adequately upheld, a means for the Chinese people to judge the performance of the communist state.

Thank God, there is still another kind of nationalism existing in China, which may be more properly called patriotism than nationalism: that is human rights patriotism represented by people like Chen Guangcheng and Hu Jia. Human rights patriotism, with human rights as its core value and democracy as its goal, loves the country through loving the people, pursues the glory of the country through gaining dignity for each compatriot, promotes the strength and prosperity of the country through the liberation of the people's minds, ideas and potential for creation, and seeks to safeguard the integrity of the country through the recognition of the integrity of each individual and ethnic group. It harmoniously integrates nationalism and democracy. The human rights patriotism is the best candidate to fill the vacuum left by communism because it will bring about positive change in Chinese society without causing chaos or the collapse of the country, which would serve nobody's interest. It is fair to say that the Dalai Lama, having long taken the middle road approach through nonviolent means, is a human rights patriot even from the perspectives of the greater China. So is Taiwan's elected president Ma Ying-jeou.

Now with so much being said, what should we do before the Olympics, and how will these different kinds of Chinese nationalists react to it? With less than four months left, our challenge is this: how to help Chinese human rights patriots grow in strength, win over popular nationalists, form a coalition of human rights patriots from China, Tibet, Taiwan, and overseas, and how to work in solidarity with them to press the Chinese government into more desirable behavior.

The worst scenario is that we are silent and stop protest activities out of fear of the counteraction from Chinese fanatical nationalists. If this were to become the reality, the CCP's hands would be strengthened with the emboldened confidence that they can get away with whatever they have done and want to do: with the Tiananmen Square Massacre nineteen years ago; with the ongoing violent suppression in Tibet; with imprisonment of human rights defenders, journalists, land petitioners, Falun Gong practitioners, and house church members, with continued forced evictions for Olympic beautification, and the list goes on. That would be a human rights disaster in China. And more than this, Chinese popular nationalists, with national strength and prosperity dominant in their minds and hearts, might well align closer with CCP because they, excited by the Olympic spectacular gala, would tend to believe it is the

CCP that brings them the closest proximity to the national glory that they desire. With strengthened dictatorship, with fast economic growth and ever-expanding military forces, with fervent idealistic nationalists rallying behind the regime, what road do you think China would take? It is not impossible that China would be Nazified. A Nazified China would pose a grim threat to world security. I think the thirty Chinese secret police officers' presumptuous presence in Paris and London has sent a warning sign to us all. The much loved Reverend Martin Luther King Jr. told us long ago that "Injustice anywhere is a threat to justice everywhere." So, we must continue our protest activities and raise up our voices. The best strategy is still conditional and partial participation, which I have been advocating since I left prison nearly one year ago. Everyone's participation in the Olympics must be conditional on some minimum standard of human rights. Raise your condition to the Chinese government or set a minimum standard in your own heart: This, then, will inform you as to whether or not you should participate, or which part you will attend.

Our pressure will help enlarge the public space of discourse for the human rights patriots in China and encourage their brave action inside. Our pressure may irritate Chinese popular nationalists at first, but our continued action will engage them in extensive debate for which they will become increasingly inquisitive for information other than provided by the Chinese government. I believe they will soon ponder the question—"What is the true source of 'humiliation'?"—which will turn more and more of them to the side of human rights patriotism.

We, the international community, should help form a broad-based coalition of human rights patriots from across the world and encourage and support their concerted peaceful protest activities both in and outside China and, at the same time, continue to induce the Chinese government to renounce its strategy of violent repression and to enter into a dialogue with the coalition of human rights patriots. If this were to happen, in the end we would all support wholeheartedly the Beijing

Olympics and the games would be a great celebration for the beginning of a real democratic transition in China. "We want human rights as well as Olympics" is the slogan of Chinese human rights patriots.

In conclusion, a life-saving straw can turn into a hanging string. The Chinese government has surely lost the battle to keep human rights issues from the games. With the rapid emergence and growth of the force of human rights patriots and the ever-increasing pressure from the international community, the Chinese government, who values so highly the Olympics, may cede some ground before the games because pragmatic nationalists are intrinsically pragmatic. Being able to understand the language of pressure pragmatically well, they can change and can change in a very short time. So, the goal I have just envisioned is not impossible. It largely depends on our persistent efforts.

Thank you.

CHAPTER 17

The Lord's Grace is Sufficient in Good Times and in Bad

Speech at St. John's Lutheran Church
Sudbury, MA, United States
April 27, 2008

My dear brothers and sisters,

I'd like to talk to you today about the strength that I have received from Christianity. You see, I was not born a Christian. I was not raised in a Christian family. I was raised in Communist China, where religion was forbidden. I came to Christianity from a place of confusion and pain in the aftermath of the infamous massacre at Tiananmen Square.

You all know the awful details of this massacre, about how lives and spirits were literally crushed under the force of the Chinese military. For those of us lucky enough to survive, there was tremendous loss and emptiness. Painful as it was to mourn for our brothers and sisters whose lives had been snuffed out prematurely, we were also forced to mourn for a lost truth. You see, before the massacre, we had all been very hopeful. We had talked about equality and liberty and how the truth would overcome all obstacles. But after the unspeakable events that ended our call for change, many of us, including me, lost faith in that idea of truth. But if I no longer had that, what did I have? I began to search and seek and question. Looking at the history of mankind, I discovered that man's stupidity, weakness, and evilness have been repeated one generation after another and man does not seem to have a way out.

Thus, if the very ideas of equality and liberty are ever to be realized, even to a moderate degree, there must be something greater than the power of every human being combined. Is that something the truth or the source from which the truth flows? I was not sure.

Not long after the massacre, I remembered back to the day when I decided to go back to Beijing to support the students who were protesting. A Christian friend of mine at U.C. Berkeley had asked me about the dangers I might face going back to China. What were the risks? Might I end up in prison? I told her that prison was a possibility. She opened up her bible and read from it. I must confess, I don't remember what the verse was. It had something to do with prisoners. It might have been this verse from Psalm 146:

–5 Blessed is he whose help is the God of Jacob, whose hope is in the LORD his God,

–6 the Maker of heaven and earth, the sea, and everything in them—the LORD, who remains faithful forever.

–7 He upholds the cause of the oppressed and gives food to the hungry. The LORD sets prisoners free,

–8 the LORD gives sight to the blind, the LORD lifts up those who are bowed down, the LORD loves the righteous.

–9 The LORD watches over the alien and sustains the fatherless and the widow, but he frustrates the ways of the wicked.

–10 The LORD reigns forever, your God, O Zion, for all generations. Praise the LORD.

Now, this Christian friend of mine was the wife of a fellow graduate student. She didn't have a strong educational background or any further educational aspirations. But her words spoke to me powerfully, and I felt something I had really never felt before, even in all of my years of schooling.

As I say, after I had experienced the horrors of the Tiananmen Massacre, I remembered the feeling upon hearing these words, and I longed to hear such words again. I wanted more meaning for my life. After I returned from China, I met with Christians on the Berkeley campus, and shortly thereafter, in 1991, eighteen months after the massacre, Praise the Lord, I was baptized and became a born-again Christian.

In 2002, I made my first trip to China since I was helped to escape in 1989. I went back to help the labor movement with nonviolent struggles. I stayed for two weeks and while seeking to leave China, I was detained at the airport in Kunming, and twelve days later I was transferred to Beijing, where I was blindfolded, handcuffed, and put into the back of a car. I had no idea where they were planning on taking me or what they were planning on doing to me. I began to feel real fear. I feared they might secretly kill me. Every cell of my body was terrified. I began to pray:

"Lord, you know what is happening here," I said. "There must be a purpose. I may not understand what the purpose is, but I know I will be able to understand it whatever the outcome is. I ask you now to be with me, to help me overcome my fear. Wherever they take me, wherever I go, I know you will be with me and will open the road for me."

I prayed like this for about three hours in the car, and that day my fear was gradually overcome, even as I was imprisoned at the end of the car ride.

They kept me in solitary confinement for nearly fifteen months without books, with no one to talk to, with no news from outside, and with no pen or paper. They subjected me to both physical and psychological torture. This left me with a constant and unprecedented deep connection with God. I prayed and prayed to our Lord to sustain the movement of my living Christian spirit, for faith, for courage, and for peace. Once they even beat me for praying. They saw my lips moving and asked me what I was doing. "I am praying," I said. They ordered me to stop and I refused. "I have a right," I replied. Then four police officers took me into a cell, pushed me down, put their feet on me so I couldn't get up, and beat me and tortured me.

At times, I became very weak and at one point almost collapsed, but the Lord's strength was made perfect in my weakness. I never stopped praying, and with the support of the Spirit, I survived, endured, even overcame all the torments the authorities inflicted on me.

Thanks to international pressure and the help of many, many friends in the United States, my situation gradually improved. I was transferred to another prison in Beijing where I got more freedom. In that prison I organized a bible study group; between twenty and thirty prisoners came at different times. I myself baptized three of them and they became born-again Christians. Praise to the Lord! Finally, just one year ago, I was released from prison.

The ordeal I went through was an experience that solidified my relationship with God. My thanks and praise be to God, our heavenly father. He and I trudged through these difficult years together with me leaning upon him at every moment. I have emerged a stronger person and, more than that, a better Christian. Standing here after what I have been through, I am wholly confident in these words: The Lord's grace is sufficient in good times and in bad. And in very bad. The Lord will provide.

Let me conclude by sharing with you from Romans 8:35, 38 and 39:

–35 Who shall separate us from the love of Christ? Shall tribulation, or distress, or persecution, or famine, or nakedness, or peril, or sword?

–38 For I am persuaded, that neither death, nor life, nor angels, nor principalities, nor things present, nor things to come, nor powers

–39 Nor height, nor depth, nor any other creature will be able to separate us from the love of God which is in Christ Jesus our Lord.

Thank you. God bless you all.

CHAPTER 18

GongMin Walk: Freedom Trail to Beijing

Speech at the Kick-off of GongMin Walk
Government Center Plaza, Boston, MA, United States
May 4, 2008

Good afternoon. Today, we people of different faith and different ethnicities came together for a peaceful assembly to make a profound statement that under God we are equal and we can live together without fear and we can speak out without facing persecution.

Today, May 4, is a very significant date in the history of China. Eighty-nine years ago, Beijing students took to the street to call for democracy in China for the first time. And today, this cause is not yet accomplished.

That is why we start our "GongMin Walk" today. GongMin in Chinese means citizen. It is my firm belief that China's hope for the future lies in the awakening of citizen spirit and the growth of citizen power—GongMin LiLiang. Being a citizen means that you have a voice and a right to vote on important issues that matter in our lives. Being a citizen has many responsibilities for the country you love.

Our walk will conclude in Washington, DC, on June 4th, another significant date in China for the past nineteen years. On that day I will join a large group of human rights advocates and political and spiritual leaders to remember untold numbers of Chinese compatriots who were killed on that date nineteen years ago in Tiananmen Square.

After five years as a political prisoner in China, I am once again free thanks to the efforts of countless friends in the United States, but I am not walking simply for my personal freedom, as blessed as I am to have it. I am walking on behalf of the millions of others who cannot walk with freedom, who cannot speak for freedom without fear of persecution. At a time when the eyes of the world are on China as it prepares to host the Olympic games, I am walking to draw attention to the people the Chinese regime tries to make invisible: the powerless whose land has been grabbed by government officials and their associates, the powerless who have been forced to be evicted because their homes were demolished for Olympic beatification or making way for government-supported developers; the powerless who are constantly subjected to exploitation by predatory officials and deprived of all means to make their grievance be heard. I am walking for the Tibetan monks, for the Falun Gong practitioners, the underground house church members, the petitioners, the political prisoners who fill China's prisons. I am walking for all citizens of China who wish for freedom and democracy.

Earlier today I walked the Freedom Trail. My heart was filled with hope. This great monument to the funding principles of this country—the Freedom Trail—will resonate more broadly in the twenty-first century—it must extend beyond Boston, it must extend to Tiananmen Square, it must extend to the Chinese countryside as well as to the people of Tibet. Chinese farmers, workers, thinkers, holy men, students, and ordinary citizens: Men and women are entitled to a government that respects their rights as human beings. Rural Chinese deserve land; urban Chinese deserve housing. Both deserve shelters in which they are protected not just from wind and rain, but also from the king's unwanted entrance.

Today, this 500-mile GongMin walk is only our first step to continue the same walk that Beijing students started eighty-nine years ago. My friends, freedom is to live without fear. Freedom will come only as a result of the brave efforts inside China and our supportive efforts outside China.

Our cause is true and just because freedom is our birthright. It is, in the words of Jefferson, "inalienable" because "the God who gave us life gave us liberty." As American people work hard to secure the blessings of liberty for this generation and our posterity, she has also been the brightest beacon of liberty and hope for the world over the past few centuries, and her flame burns more brightly, more steady, more sure because of the wisdom and unflinching courage of this great country and its people. I believe the onward March of Freedom is irreversible, and with the grace of God, freedom will prevail.

Thank you and God bless you all.

CHAPTER 19

GongMin LiLiang—Citizen Power

Providence, RI, United States
May 7, 2008

Good evening. Some of you may think it odd that I call my walk GongMin Walk. GongMin in Chinese means citizen. I believe China's hope for the future lies in the awakening of its citizen spirit and the growth of its citizen power, GongMin LiLiang, the democratic forces.

Here, in the home of Roger Williams, I am very much humbled to say that we all know the power one great citizen can have and what one citizen can accomplish by his walk.

In China, the most populous country on earth, we are not short of people but citizens.

In prison, I experienced firsthand the games played between prison authorities and prisoners. With seemingly unlimited power, prison guards constantly use various physical and psychological torture methods against prisoners. How do prisoners react to all this? On the one hand, they harbor such bitter hatred toward the prison authorities that they would, if they could, torture the guards even more than the guards tortured them. On the other hand, due to longtime persecution and fear, they have unknowingly been transformed into fawning slaves who do everything possible to win favor with the guards, even competing with other prisoners for pitiful benefits and for a domineering position over their fellow inmates. Both in behavior and in psychology, a Chinese prison is a mix of tyrants, mobs, and slaves.

I became intent on creating and cultivating a new and different environment—a civil and healthy environment. Otherwise, things would inevitably keep going around in a vicious circle. Despite extremely unfavorable circumstances, my efforts achieved limited success, and I learned the following lessons: First, somebody, in this specific case myself, needs to show moral courage and to protest, awakening and inspiring the consciences of inmates and guards alike. Second, issues must be carefully selected and strategies wisely chosen to achieve small victories, especially at the outset, thereby strengthening the confidence that positive results can be achieved. And last but not least, outside support is vital; to tell you the truth, without it, I might not be able to muster enough courage to protest.

Although it is not a perfect analogy, China is like a prison at large, with its authorities relentlessly persecuting and even seeking to annihilate its civil and healthy elements. As a result, Chinese society is, to a large extent, also a mix of tyrants, mobs, and slaves. One should not count on tyrants or slaves or mobs to advance democracy. But how can we nurture the civil and healthy elements, the citizen spirit and power, that we need in China?

Based on my experience in prison, I believe that in order for democratic forces to thrive, the first step is for someone to stand up with moral courage and vision and openly challenge the undemocratic features of our society, inspiring the civil and healthy elements in our country. Second, we must continually improve our organizational work and our strategies for assembling civil and healthy elements into democratic forces; it is imperative to secure some initial advances, for this can convince people that success is possible and inspire them to join. Third, support from the international community, particularly the United States, is essential.

I am walking this GongMin walk to encourage the continued leadership from the United States for the global cause of human rights and democracy.

One may wonder why the support of American people is so important and why it can work.

The Chinese Communist Party is struggling for its survival as the single legitimate ruling party because communism in China, for all practical purposes, is dead. Yet it is clutching lifesaving economic growth. China's pragmatic leaders understand well that continued prosperity is the key to its continued rule and that China's economic growth relies very much on its integration with the outside world, especially with major powers.

So, they care about its international image, and quite contrary to many people's understanding, whatever stance you take on human rights issues, they want to do business with you.

Our pressure will help enlarge the public space of discourse for the human rights patriots in China and encourage their brave action inside. We should openly engage with the Chinese democratic forces both in and outside China, give them moral and material support, provide them with ideas and resources, bring their situation to the attention of the international community, speak the truth about China and the world, and provide protection to those in danger. All of these ideas and actions will contribute to the reduction of the cost and risk the democracy activists have to face. As fear lessens, more and more people will join the democratic forces. The collective action dilemma will consequently be solved.

Thank you.

CHAPTER 20

Calling for a Democratic System of Checks and Balances to Monitor Earthquake Aid

Speech in New Haven City Hall Press Conference during the GongMin Walk
New Haven, CT, United States
May 14, 2008

Dear friends,

I cannot begin to tell you the many wonderful people who have given me shelter, food, and spiritual encouragement on this GongMin Walk from Boston to Washington, DC. This truly has been a spiritual journey as well as a physical one.

I am walking with deep love for my homeland and my compatriots. The events of the past forty-eight hours regarding the earthquake centered in Sichuan, China, leaves me shocked and worried. Over 12,000 of my countrymen are now dead. Tens of thousands are homeless and the news, I fear, will only get worse in the coming days. My heart is with them.

Please join me in a moment of profound silence as we convey our pain to our Creator and ask for his mercy upon the victims of this great misfortune.

I was going to begin my talk today by reading a letter I received from His Holiness, the Dalai Lama of Tibet. Instead, I will read just a paragraph:

"China today is an emerging world power. The international community has acted wisely by making efforts to bring her into the mainstream of the

world economy. But economic integration alone is not sufficient. China needs human rights, democracy, and the rule of law. These values are the foundation of a free, dynamic, stable, and peaceful society. Such a society would also offer far greater economic freedom, security, and other advantages to all citizens of the People's Republic of China."

These wise words from His Holiness are the basis of what I want to share with you today.

First of all, I call on President Bush as leader of the most powerful democracy on earth and on the United States Congress, as the duly elected representatives of the American people, to call on the generosity of the American citizen to donate to the Red Cross Disaster Relief Fund. I also humbly ask all of you who might be inclined to donate to Initiatives for China to go to our website and click on the link to the Red Cross and make a donation to the Red Cross instead. In my short life I have seen no greater example of democracy in action than the response of American citizens to victims of misfortunes and disasters. Please exercise that great generosity on behalf of my fallen countrymen.

Secondly, I call on the US government to encourage the Chinese government to cancel the Olympic Torch Relay that is scheduled to pass through Sichuan in June and to mobilize all available resources toward relieving the great suffering of its citizens.

Thirdly, based on common sense and past experience, disaster relief funds without a system of checks and balances can and will be misused and misdirected to benefit the corrupt and only add to the misery of the unfortunate. A democracy that freely and generously gives cannot allow its generosity to be subverted by the corruption inherent in a one-party system with no checks and balances. I therefore plead with President Bush and the US Congress to work with the Chinese government to set up a system of citizen run controls that ensure the generosity of the American government, the American taxpayer, as well as donations from Chinese taxpayers and people from all over, are used for its intended purposes and reach the hapless people for whom it is intended.

Fourthly, again based upon common sense and past experience, no system of controls will be effective without the oversight of a free and unhindered press and the free speech of citizens. I therefore call on President Bush and the US Congress to urge the Chinese government to engage in a grand gesture in the name of the victims of this terrible tragedy to lift all restraint on the press. To tear down the Great Firewall that controls the flow of information over the internet. Let the people, the citizens of China, be the eyes and ears that ensure the great generosity of people from all the world goes to those with the greatest need and not the greatest greed.

These are common sense actions that will ensure that the suffering caused by this great tragedy will not be compounded by the built-in flaws of unregulated power accountable only to itself.

These actions will also demonstrate to the Chinese government and to my fellow Chinese citizens that there is a better way of governance. These actions will not only bring the greatest amount of relief to the earthquake victims but will demonstrate for all to see that free citizens, exercising free speech and enjoying a free press, living without fear, are the basic ingredients for a truly just society. This is the opportunity to show democracy in action. To demonstrate the power of individual citizens to produce a greater good. This is the opportunity for the Chinese government to truly demonstrate its commitment to human rights and learn that democracy is not to be feared but to be embraced.

I pray that the wisdom of citizen power be visited upon the leaders of China so the misery of the earthquake victims is relieved quickly and with love and not greed.

Please pray with me for a moment for the victims and their families, for my fellow citizens, and for the leaders of China that their great power be used for the common good of all its citizens. For this let's pray to God.

Thank you.

CHAPTER 21

Continued Calling for a Democratic System of Checks and Balances to Monitor Earthquake Aid

Speech in Front of Columbia University in the GongMin Walk
New York, NY, United States
May 20, 2008

Dear friends,

Good afternoon and God bless you all. As some of you know, I have a doctorate degree in Mathematics. So, I can tell you very truthfully that both from theory and experience that New York is 70,4000 steps from Boston! I cannot begin to tell you the many wonderful people, such as yourselves, who have given me shelter, food, and spiritual encouragement on this GongMin Walk to Washington, DC. This truly has been a spiritual journey as well as a physical one.

So, this afternoon my spirits should be high. However, the events of the past week regarding the earthquake centered in Sichuan, China, leaves me shocked and worried. Over 8,000 of my countrymen are now dead. Tens of thousands are homeless, and the news, I fear, will only get worse in the coming days.

Please join me in a moment of profound silence as we convey our pain to our Creator and ask for his mercy upon the innocent victims of this great misfortune.

(SILENT PRAYER)

In light of this unfolding tragedy, I will begin my remarks by emphasizing a paragraph from the letter sent to me by His Holiness, the Dalai Lama of Tibet. I quote from this letter:

"China today is an emerging world power. The international community has acted wisely by making efforts to bring her into the mainstream of the world economy. But economic integration alone is not sufficient. China needs human rights, democracy, and the rule of law. These values are the foundation of a free, dynamic, stable, and peaceful society. Such a society would also offer far greater economic freedom, security, and other advantages to all citizens of the People's Republic of China."

Human rights and democracy are indeed the foundation of a free, dynamic, stable, and peaceful society. The issue of human rights is not political. It is not situational. It is not fashionable… something that can be given and taken away by whim. It is the very bond between humans and their Creator. Human rights give us dignity and purpose. The protection of these rights, for all its citizens, is the first responsibility of any government. Any government that does not protect the God-given rights of its citizens is irresponsible. Any government that actively denies human and political rights for its citizens cannot have any claim to legitimacy, regardless of its wealth or power.

So, my dear friends, human rights are indeed the foundation of life and a civil society.

However, when tragedy strikes, such as the devastating earthquake of this past week, the exercise of human, political, and civil rights is no longer a matter of life. It is the difference between life and death.

The answer is GongMin LiLiang. I therefore call on the Chinese government and the donor governments and humanitarian relief agencies to work together in the spirit of openness and cooperation to get as much aid to those with the greatest need in the quickest amount of time. Specifically, the following must occur:

Firstly, I call on the US government to encourage the Chinese government to cancel the Olympic Torch Relay that is scheduled to pass through Sichuan in early June and to focus on mobilizing all available resources toward relieving the great suffering of its citizens. GongMin LiLiang. Citizen Power!

Secondly, based on common sense and past experience, disaster relief funds without a system of checks and balances can and will be misused and misdirected to benefit the corrupt and only add to the misery of the unfortunate. A democracy that freely and generously gives cannot allow its generosity to be hijacked by corrupt government officials and their agents. I therefore plead with President Bush and the US Congress to work with the Chinese government to set up a system of citizen run controls that ensure the generosity of the world community and the Chinese taxpayers will be used for its intended purposes and reaches the hapless people for whom it is intended. GongMin LiLiang. Citizen Power.

Thirdly, again based upon common sense and past experience, no system of controls will be effective without the oversight of a free and unhindered press and the free speech of citizens. I therefore call on President Bush and US Congress and the Chinese government to engage in a grand gesture in the name of the victims of this terrible tragedy to lift all restraints on the press. To tear down the Great Firewall that controls the flow of information over the internet. Let the people, the citizens of China, be the eyes and ears that ensure the great generosity of people from all over the world goes to those with the greatest need and not the greatest greed. GongMin LiLiang.

These are common sense actions that will ensure that the suffering caused by this great tragedy will not be compounded by the built-in flaws of unregulated power accountable only to itself.

These actions will also demonstrate to the Chinese government and to my fellow Chinese citizens that there is a better way of governance. These actions will not only bring the greatest amount of relief to the earthquake victims but will demonstrate for all to see that free citizens, exercising free speech and enjoying a free press, living without fear, are the basic ingredients for a truly just society. This is the opportunity to show democracy in action. To demonstrate the power of individual citizens to produce a greater good. This is the opportunity for the Chinese government to truly demonstrate its commitment to human rights and learn that democracy is not to be feared but to be embraced.

In my short life I have seen no greater example of civil and human rights in action than the response of American citizens to victims of misfortunes and disasters around the world. The American generosity powered by free speech and the ability to freely organize is democracy in action. In Chinese, it is called GongMin LiLiang. "Citizen Power." Just two days ago, as part of the GongMin walk, I was welcomed to Bridgeport, Connecticut, by Mayor Bill Finch and his staff. I mentioned to him how saddened I was by the earthquake and how in need of assistance my countrymen were. I asked for any help he could provide. Without hesitation, Mayor Finch said he would use all appropriate channels to encourage all municipal employees, urging them to donate to the Red Cross Disaster Relief Fund. Mayor Finch's office has confirmed this morning that such communications have gone out to all municipal departments.

What a beautiful example of Citizen Power!

So, with great humility, I thank Mayor Finch and with a heart filled with hope, I call on this great city of New York and to all American citizens from all the great cities of America to please emulate the great citizens of Bridgeport in helping my countrymen at this time of great misfortune. GongMin LiLiang!

While my heart is full of hope because of the Citizen Power of America, it is also burdened with sadness because I know, and you are all gathered here today because you know, there are no human rights for Chinese citizens. There are no civil rights for Tibetans. There are no religious rights for Falun Gong practitioners. In the face of this great tragedy confronting my countrymen, this lack of rights not only deprives Chinese citizens of a life of dignity but also deprives them of life itself.

Common sense and experience tell us that the Chinese government—an autocratic, one-party system with virtually unbridled power, with no system of checks and balances, with no independent judiciary, with no free speech, with no free press—is incapable of ensuring that life-giving aid, so freely given, will be equitably distributed to those in need. So, I fear that my countrymen will become double victims. Victims of a great natural disaster and victims of a corrupt government. How can we rely on a government that denies human and civil rights to its citizens in the best of times to extend human relief in the worst of times?

Since the earthquake struck, I have walked over 100 miles with this question on my mind. How can we help the Chinese government do the right thing? What must the Chinese government do to ensure that humanitarian aid from both the world and Chinese taxpayers gets to those in need? I pray that the wisdom of Citizen Power be visited upon the leaders of China. So, the misery of my countrymen will be relieved quickly and with love and not greed. GongMin LiLiang.

I pray that my brothers and sisters suffering under this great misfortune will be relieved quickly and with compassion by the awakening of Citizen Power. GongMin LiLiang.

My brothers and sisters, I pray that Citizen Power will come to all of us. I pray that it will bind us together as friends, as brothers and sisters, living under the blue sky of a free China, speaking freely, worshipping freely, respecting our mutual dignity, and seeking our own chosen path to happiness. For this I pray. For this I walk. For this I will not rest until I will embrace you all in a Tiananmen Square that is free. For this I pray. GongMin LiLiang.

Thank you!

CHAPTER 22

The Freedoms Given by the Bill of Rights Are What Gives Dignity to Life and Purpose to Our Existence

Speech in Philadelphia in the GongMin Walk
Philadelphia, PA, United States
May 25, 2008

Dear friends:

Good afternoon and God bless you all. As many of you know, I am walking the 500-mile GongMin walk from Boston to Washington, DC. GongMin in Chinese means citizen. As I pass the 300-mile mark on my 500-mile journey, I am happy to stop here in Philadelphia, the birthplace of American liberty, of the Bill of Rights, on this Memorial Day weekend to pause, remember, and reflect with you.

We pause and remember the great sacrifices that generation after generation of Americans have made and continue to make to preserve and protect freedom around the world.

I think the best way to remember and appreciate the value of these hard-won freedoms is to consider what the world would be like without these freedoms. Consider what this country would be like without the Bill of Rights to protect people from the excesses of government.

It could be a country where journalists are thrown in jail for reporting on government activities. A country where students, your sons and daughters, and scholars are routinely jailed for sharing ideas over the internet. It could be a country where lawyers are grabbed off the street and intimidated for defending the civil rights of their clients. It could be a country where health care workers are put under house arrest for reporting on health issues. It could be a world where you are persecuted for your religion or your culture or your ethnicity. It is a country where your land, your home, might be taken away without recourse. This could be the country without the Bill of Rights. This country is not hypothetical.

This is the China that the Chinese government does not want us to see. The China that the Chinese government wants us to ignore as it choreographs the Olympic pageantry it does want us to see. I am taking this walk to raise awareness of this China.

The China today is a world where citizens have no rights, no system of government with checks and balances to protect them. No freedom of press to alert them. No freedom of religion to nurture them. The China today is a world where entire cultures, such as the Tibetans and Uyghurs, are repressed, their houses of worship destroyed, and their language forbidden. This is a world without the Bill of Rights. Without the rights of citizens to defend themselves against the arbitrary excess of the government. I am taking this walk to encourage the awakening of its Citizen Power.

The freedoms given by the Bill of Rights are what gives dignity to life and purpose to our existence. This is what Americans have fought so bravely for. This is why I walk, to ask you to continue your great leadership in the cause of human rights across the world.

When tragedy strikes, such as the devastating Sichuan earthquake of this past week, the exercise of human, political, and civil rights is no longer a matter of life. It is the difference between life and death.

Common sense and experience tell us that the Chinese government—an autocratic one-party system, with no system of checks and balances, no independent judiciary, no free speech, no free press—is incapable of ensuring that life-giving aid, so generously given by the world, will be equitably distributed to those in need. So, I fear that my countrymen will become double victims: victims of a great natural disaster and victims of a corrupt government.

How can we rely on a government that denies human and civil rights to its citizens in the best of times to extend human relief in the worst of times? A case in point: It is well known that government buildings and the homes of party officials are built to withstand severe earthquakes, while the homes of ordinary citizens and schoolhouses are not built to code. How many parents have lost their children because of such negligence?

Since the earthquake struck, I have walked over 200 miles with this question on my mind. How can we help the Chinese government do the right thing? What must the Chinese government do to ensure that humanitarian aid from both the world and Chinese taxpayers gets to those in need?

The answer is GongMin LiLiang. I am greatly encouraged by the outpouring of Citizen Power among Chinese citizens in response to this terrible disaster. I have received reports from inside China that thousands and thousands of citizens are donating their time and their resources directly to aid the victims. They are setting up citizen-run systems of checks and balances so aid money and resources do not wind up in the hands of corrupt officials. This is very encouraging news.

This must be encouraged, continued, and protected. I therefore plead with President Bush and Congress to work with the Chinese government to set up a system of citizen-run controls to ensure that the generosity of the world community and the Chinese taxpayers will be used for its intended purposes. A committee should be set up in each devastated Chinese county through election.

In addition, no system of controls will be effective without the oversight of a free and unhindered press and the free speech of citizens. I therefore call on President Bush and Congress to urge the Chinese government to engage in a grand gesture in the name of the victims of this terrible tragedy to lift all restrictions on the press. To tear down the Great Firewall that controls the flow of information over the internet.

Let the citizens of China be the eyes and ears that ensure that the great generosity of people from all over the world goes to those with the greatest need and not the greatest greed.

Lastly, I ask all of you to go to the Initiatives for China website to give a donation, however small, toward our goal of $300,000 to build a GongMin "Citizen Elementary School" as a living tribute to the innocents who were crushed when their school collapsed on them. This school will educate a new generation of citizens with the empowerment to live, speak, and worship freely.

I pray that the wisdom of citizen power be visited upon the leaders of China so the misery of my countrymen will be relieved quickly.

I pray that my brothers and sisters suffering under this great misfortune will be relieved quickly and with compassion by the awakening of Citizen Power.

My brothers and sisters, I pray that Citizen Power will come to all of us. I pray that it will bind us together as friends, as brothers and sisters, living under the blue sky of a free China, speaking freely, worshipping freely, respecting our mutual dignity, and seeking our own chosen path to happiness. For this I pray. For this I walk. For this I will not rest until I can speak to you all freely under the protection of our own Bill of Rights in China.

Thank you all.

CHAPTER 23

Freedom Is Not Free. It's Earned.

Speech at the Nineteenth Anniversary Memorial Concert and Lecture
Chicago, IL, United States
June 1, 2008

Today we gather, once again, to remember those who, on this date, nineteen years ago in Tiananmen Square, gave up their young lives for freedom. In remembering so many young lives crushed and lost, we must recall that freedom is not free. Freedom must be earned. It was not free for those who paid with their lives. It is certainly not free for those of us who, while still blessed with our lives, have yet to complete the mission for which these brave students gave their lives and their freedom.

In the movie *Saving Private Ryan*, Captain Miller led a platoon of soldiers to find a soldier called Private Ryan to get him out of harm's way. Most of the platoon, including Captain Miller, were killed trying to save Private Ryan. As he was drawing his last breath, Captain Miller leaned forward and what would be his last command as a captain, whispered in Private Ryan's ear: "Earn this."

Many years later, Private Ryan returned to Miller's burial site in Normandy, France. As a now elderly man, this would probably be his last visit to the grave site. He spoke to the white cross above the grave in a soft, emotion-filled voice. "Every day I think about what you said to me that day on the bridge. I tried to live my life the best that I could. I hope that was enough. I hope that, at least in your eyes, I've earned what all of you have done for me."

In my own life, I have never stopped asking myself if we, as survivors, have earned what our Tiananmen heroes sacrificed for us. As survivors, have we earned what these heroes died for?

I believe none of us can answer with any certainty. But what we can say is that many people have forgotten or have chosen to ignore that which I mentioned in my opening poem.

What is more, the communist regime has tried in every way to wipe the slate clean of all historical memory. As a result, younger generations following the Beijing massacre of June 4th have little or no knowledge of the pro-democracy movement and why that movement ended up in blood.

Three weeks ago, not long after I started the GongMin Walk, the Sichuan earthquake struck. We have lost almost 100,000 lives in this catastrophe, including almost 20,000 young students. Our hearts are bleeding. On this particular day of June 4th, I have been thinking about the connection between the lives lost in the earthquake and the student lives lost nineteen years ago in Tiananmen Square. If the students who were killed in Tiananmen were living today, their own children would the same school age as the earthquake victims. But that is not the connection of which I want to speak.

The pro-democracy movement of 1989 carried a second important theme that is not as widely known—the theme of stopping corruption in government. But the communist regime responded with machine guns and rolling tanks. As a result, political reform ceased in China, and the government has become even more blatant in its corruption. Now, nineteen years later, it is known to almost everyone in China that the schools in the earthquake area would not have become concrete coffins if they had met the same quality construction standards as government buildings and the homes of party officials. In other words, if the communist party had not slaughtered the students with tanks in Tiananmen, but had accepted their requests for political reform, many of our children's lives would have been spared. That is the connection of which I speak. The corruption that spawned the 1989 protests, the cancerous corruption that took the lives of students in Tiananmen Square, has metastasized, crushing 20,000 innocents in Sichuan. This connection should not be covered up by the dust of the earthquake. The corruption continues, and the sacrifices continue to grow. June 4 and May 12 are dates that challenge the conscience of every Chinese.

Today we are here to remember these young people and children who died in the earthquake—many of whom may well have lived through the earthquake had it not been for government corruption. We must confront the fact that the difference made by democracy is not only whether we have a life of dignity but very often is the difference between life and death itself.

Therefore, our memory today is not just a sad recall. Our memory concerns life and death. It concerns the ultimate value of life. Whenever we think of those lives lost so young, we need to challenge ourselves and ask ourselves how we can live so we truly earn what their sacrifices have given us. We truly cannot say we have earned them at this point. For me, I will not be able to kneel at their graves and whisper, "I have done my best to earn what you have died for." For me, I will not be able to say these words until I stand in Tiananmen Square, breathing the air of a free China, a China blessed with the dignity of human rights for all its citizens, and a China secure with the freedoms to speak, to worship, to publish, and to seek redress. Only then can I kneel before the fallen. Only then can we look each other in the eye and say: We have earned this. We have earned this. Rest in peace my dear brothers and sisters of Tiananmen. Rest in peace my sons and daughters of Sichuan.

Let me conclude with a stanza from the poem I read at the beginning of my speech:

No poem can stop a tank
But some poems can stop the forgetting
Stop the forgetting
The skeleton of my soul is as slender as the lines of my poem

The skeleton of my soul, like my poem, is emotional
Oh, the skeleton of my soul is naked and has nowhere to hide
Over this emotional body of my poem tanks are rolling over
Rolling over, over…

CHAPTER 24

The Weapons We Fight with Are Not the Weapons of the World

Speech at the Nineteenth Anniversary Commemoration of the Tiananmen Square Massacre
Washington, DC, United States
June 4, 2008

Today, I have arrived in the great city of Washington, DC, the final destination of the GongMin Walk. I can tell you, both from mathematical calculation and experience, Washington, DC, is 1,408,000 steps from Boston.

When I started this walk in Boston, Washington, DC, was my goal. But I knew I could only reach Washington by taking one step, followed by another step, followed by another step. So is it with our pro-democracy movement. No matter how great and noble our goal is, no matter how clear it is in our heart and vision, we can only achieve our goal by moving step by step. Tenacity and audacity are the spirit we seek for this larger GongMin Walk toward democracy in China.

More than one hundred years ago, the Chinese people started a GongMin Walk toward democracy. And nineteen years ago, the whole world turned its attention to Tiananmen Square, where hundreds of thousands of Chinese citizens took more steps in this GongMin Walk. But nineteen years ago, on this very day, those footsteps were brutally crushed by the tanks of the communist government. Today, we have gathered here to remember those who lost their lives in that brutal massacre.

To remember means to look back, but oftentimes remembering is also a way of looking forward. To remember Tiananmen Square is once again to make ourselves, as well as people all over the world, aware of this simple truth: If a country is to have hope, human rights must be respected and life must be valued. China cannot be an exception.

The steps of the GongMin Walk have never stopped. Tiananmen Mothers bravely opened a website in China only a week ago. I have seen great promise for the future of China based upon the power demonstrated by the Chinese people in their solidarity with earthquake victims. The earthquake and the atrocities of nineteen years ago both prove that the free exercise of human rights is not simply the legal basis of citizen's life; it can be the difference between life and death. We saw this demonstrated by the crushing tanks of Tiananmen and we saw this in the hundreds of schools that collapsed onto their young students because they weren't built to earthquake code. The protection of these rights for all citizens, therefore, is the first responsibility of any government, and any government that actively denies these rights is not only irresponsible, it is also illegitimate, and illegitimate governments must be fought against and ultimately transformed.

Throughout the ages, many have pondered the question: Can good prevail over evil? It may appear that when good and evil compete on a level battlefield, evil will triumph. But when we rise up to the higher level, the level to the ultimate source of justice, good can be victorious. We must reach higher ground. Consider these words from Second Corinthians:

"For though we live in the world, we do not wage war as the world does. The weapons we fight with are not the weapons of the world. On the contrary, they have divine power to demolish strongholds."

Therefore, I would like to make this coming year, from today until the twentieth anniversary of the June 4th Massacre, a year of prayer for the Chinese leaders. For this period of one year, I will not stop traveling in order to make it known to people of faith all over the world that they need to pray for the Chinese leaders, to pray that the Chinese leaders will exercise their power in order to do common good to their citizens, to pray that the Chinese leaders will introduce a system that places limits on their power. I particularly want to ask all people of faith to pray in your local sanctuaries, homes, offices or parks, from 11:00 a.m. to 12:00 p.m. on May 31, 2009, which is the Sunday before June 4th. Globally, we will engage in twenty-four hours of continuous praying for the leaders of China. The power of these prayers will be felt by China's leaders. This power needs to be felt by China's leaders, for the present governing strategy of the Chinese Communist Party is to appeal to the worst instincts in human beings in order to control the Chinese populace and thus strengthen its grip on power.

The process to realize democracy relies on a different set of principles; it is a process which succeeds by appealing to the abundant good in people's hearts.

Democratization in China is the biggest and a most important challenge of our century. What we are engaged in is a great experiment; our hypothesis is that it is possible that a Chinese political system can be compatible with the good, the fair, and the just. Proving this will take persistent, creative, and tireless efforts on the part of good, fair, and just people all over the world. When I consider the countless who fill our ranks, I am confident we will succeed.

We the Chinese people all want our country to be glorious. To this we say: What is truly glorious is justice, fairness, and the protection of the fundamental rights of every citizen. What is glorious in life is the opportunity to peacefully enjoy all of its facets. What is glorious is the spirit we glorify when we live lives in which we recognize and honor the essential dignity, decency, and humanity of every member of the world's community.

God bless America. God bless China.

Thank you.

CHAPTER 25

"One World, One Nightmare"

Opening Remarks at US House of Representatives' Hearing "China on the Eve of the Olympics"
Rayburn House Office Building, Washington, DC, United States
July 23, 2008

Thank you, Chairman Berman, Ranking Member Ileana Ros-Lehtinen, and distinguished members of the House Foreign Affairs Committee. I am grateful for the opportunity to address you today.

As you know, between May 4 and June 4 of this year, I walked 500 miles from Boston to Washington, DC, to express my gratitude to the US government and to the American people for their courageous support during my imprisonment in China. Because of this support, I am here today a free man in this great hall of democracy, speaking freely. I will speak not for myself, but for the thousands, yes tens of thousands, of my countrymen who cannot speak because they are either full of fear, in jail, or dead for what I will be doing today. Speaking freely. I will never forget the great compassion of America. And I ask you never to forget, or underestimate, the powerful voice for freedom that is America. It is because of you that I am free. And it will be with your continued support that someday soon all the people of China will be free. Thank you.

You have asked me to address two issues today:

1. To give my perspective on China's foreign and domestic relations in the context of the upcoming Olympic Games.
2. To provide a perspective on what China's behavior tells the world about the nature of China's political development and how China will conduct its foreign relations going forward.

First, my perspective on China's foreign and domestic relations in the context of the upcoming Olympic Games. It is moot to discuss whether or not the Olympic Games should have been awarded to China. The vast scope of the Chinese government's systematic abuse of its citizens has been well documented and is well known to the committee members. The Chinese government's promises back in 2001 to improve its human rights record are also well known. The fact that the Chinese government has actually intensified its disregard for the civil and human rights of its citizens in the lead-up to the Olympics is also well known.

This desperate crackdown on its citizens and its blatant disregard for its commitments to the international community speak loudly about how the CCP views the Olympic Games and its role as the governing body in China. The Chinese government wants to host the Olympics so it can use the pageantry and the equity of the Olympic rings to project an image of China under its rule as a great, stable, and harmonious society. For the Chinese government, the Olympic games are nothing more than a tool for orchestrating a thin veneer of harmony over a society that, underneath, is a cauldron of frustration, disillusionment, discontent, and fear. It is sweet irony that the numerous recent protests, crackdowns, and natural disasters made even worse by government corruption have repeatedly punched through this veneer to reveal images of a Chinese society that is more like "One World, One Nightmare" rather than its official line of "One World, One Dream." In this regard, the lead-up to the Olympics has been somewhat of a media disaster for the CCP. The Chinese government needs the Olympics to project an image of legitimacy to the world and to its people. However, its actions clearly reveal how corrupt and illegitimate the Chinese government really is. It knows it has no ideology to offer its people. It knows it rules by fear. And its actions tell us it will do anything to any of its people and tell anything to the outside world to maintain its hold on power.

The Chinese government's position as an Olympic host gives us the right, if not the duty, to hold China accountable. Even at this hour, the United States and the world democracies can leverage the Chinese government's desperate need to have a successful Olympics to engage in a constructive and assertive dialogue regarding its human rights record and its persecution of minorities. At the very least, President Bush should demand the release of political prisoners as a condition for his attending the opening ceremonies. President Bush should also work in concert with other world leaders to develop a coordinated strategy of conditional participation in the Olympics tied to specific and measurable actions by the Chinese government. We should have no fear in doing this because the Chinese government needs President Bush at the Olympics much, much more than President Bush needs to be there. Such a coordinated strategy will also send a powerful message of support for the many courageous Chinese citizens inside and outside of Chinese jails who are putting their lives, their families, and their fortunes at risk every day to advance the cause of liberty.

Finally, I urge all of you and all the national and international press to remember the climate of fear and repression we have seen in the events that have preceded the Olympic Games. We have seen the repression of the Tibetan protests. We have heard of the arrest and intimidation of numerous journalists and human rights activists. We have witnessed the agony of parents in Sichuan province who know that their school-aged children would be alive today if it were not for the government corruption that allowed schools in a known earthquake zone to be built to substandard codes. Do not forget this as the carefully orchestrated Olympic festivities unfold. Journalists may be free to move around Beijing and ask anything of the people they meet. *But the true test of a society is whether people are free to respond.* This is clearly not the case in China today.

I will conclude by giving my perspective on the most important issue: *What China's behavior tells the world about China's political development and how China will conduct its foreign relations going forward.*

In his brilliant book, *The Case for Democracy*, noted Soviet dissident Natan Sharansky states that governments, which rule by fear, are inherently unstable. The world community cannot rely on leaders who do not rely or trust their own people. The government of China remains a one-party totalitarian system, driven by the fear of losing power and committed to the use of fear to incapacitate any person or organization, which it deems a threat to its illegitimate hold on power.

The hope of many people that political openness in China will follow economic progress is an illusion. Structurally, the Chinese government is organized to maintain its absolute power at the expense of its citizens. For example, the Chinese constitution admits the CCP as the only legitimate ruling power in China. Therefore, anyone who speaks against the government is subject to charges of treason. The Chinese constitution establishes that the judiciary reports directly to the Chinese Communist Party. The CCP tells the judges who is guilty and what sentences to give. Trials are no more than preordained showpieces. People have no means of redress. This is why, according to the Human Rights Watch Report of 2007, there are more than 100,000 protests against the government each year in China. This is remarkable, given the great risk people assume for participating in these protests.

The Chinese government will continue to rule by fear. It knows no other way. The CCP will continue to invest inordinate amounts of resources into controlling the population through fear, hatred, and division. It will make demons of the Tibetans. It will make terrorists of the Uyghurs. It will make subversives of Christians and Falun Gong practitioners. This control will stifle political, social, and ultimately economic development and increase social unrest. As unrest grows, it will export its fear abroad to create enemies or situations that rally the people at home under the banner of nationalism. It will use its economic clout to intimidate and induce foreign governments and organizations to capitulate to its rule by fear. We need not look further than the case of Yahoo, whose executives capitulated to the Chinese government by turning over private emails, which the government used to send a young man to prison. We need not look any further than Flushing, New York, where peaceable demonstrators were attacked by mobs incited by the Chinese government. Sowing fear, discord, and instability wherever it sees threats will be the underlying modus operandi of the Chinese government's foreign policy.

Strong and sustained American support for human rights in China is not only the morally correct position, it is strategically the right approach for advancing American interests. America cannot allow its great way of life to be subverted by fear. It is important to realize that China needs the approval of the world community to legitimize its power. It is important to realize that China needs its economic engine to mollify its citizens. We need not be afraid to challenge the Chinese government on its human rights record. Indeed, it is in our strategic interest to do so. China will respond. It will continue to do business with us regardless of our challenges because it needs the approval of the world community and integration with the world economy to maintain a veneer of legitimacy.

At Initiatives for China, we are working very hard as catalysts for peaceful and incremental change by helping Chinese citizens exercise their citizen power or GongMin LiLiang in Chinese. It is this display of Citizen Power that will ultimately overcome the corruption and the fear induced by the CCP. It is GongMin LiLiang that ultimately will drive China toward a more open, just, and democratic society. America's strong, vocal, and consistent support will send a powerful and enabling message to this struggle for peaceful change. And when the time comes, the tipping point if you will for decisive action, the American government must be prepared to give the right signals in defense of freedom so the forces for freedom and democracy will prevail for the good of China—for the good of the Chinese government and for the good of America and the international community.

If the committee will be so kind, I will conclude by telling you a story that was told to me by a fellow inmate while I was in prison. This story speaks to the depth of the frustration of my countrymen and the hope that America holds for them. A young man was sentenced to death for a minor crime. He spent many years on death row in China. The night before he was executed, he said to a fellow inmate, "If I am to be reborn, I shall look outside first. If I see the Chinese flag over the land, I will refuse to be born. However, if I see an American flag waving in the blue sky, I will gladly leap into the world.

Thank you.

SECTION IV

INTERETHNIC/INTERFAITH CONFERENCES: UNIFIED IN A COMMON BELIEF

November 2008–October 2009

"A unified struggle against the Chinese regime must first eliminate the obstacles of suspicion, distrust, antagonism, and even outright hostility between different ethnic groups. Those who have lived under the communist Chinese dictatorship are well aware that the enmity between ethnic groups as it exists today was stoked by the regime, whose monopoly on media control allows it to stir up the fears and hatred that form one of the primary pillars of its power....But our better nature is quite capable of seeing the similarities, rather than differences, that exist between and among all members of the human race. Is the desire for freedom a Han desire, a Tibetan desire, a Uyghur desire, or a Mongolian desire? Or is it a human desire? In order for us to coexist peacefully, we must simply remember to be loyal to those fundamental human traits we all share. This both honors us as people and makes us better citizens of our nations and our world."

CHAPTER 26

Our Strive for Freedom Is an Integrated One and Cannot Be Separately Carried Out

Opening Speech at the Fourth Interethnic/ Interfaith Leadership Conference
Harvard University, Cambridge, MA, United States
November 6, 2008

Dearest friends,

First, allow me to thank you all for coming to the fourth Interethnic/ Interfaith Leadership Conference. It is inspiring and moving to see so many faces from all over the world. When I think of the distances that many of you have traveled to be here, I am blessedly reminded that, even with all of the work we have ahead of us, so much has already been done to establish the foundational spirit of community that is essential to our labors in, and on behalf of, the future.

Indeed we, the participants in this conference, are as diverse in history, culture, religion, language, and race and ethnicity as we are unified in a common belief in the possibility of a future of equality, love, freedom, and a real democracy for all.

We, and the people we come from, have been fighting for this future for a very long time. Some of us, such as our Taiwanese brothers and sisters, have achieved remarkable successes, which have energized us with proof that progress is possible. Even so, great numbers of the people we represent are living either in the partial light of half-freedom and semi-democracy—like those in Hong Kong and Macau—or are still struggling in the deep darkness of outright dictatorship and tyranny. Today, even the people of Taiwan, who have boldly brought about a transformation from dictatorship to a democracy, still live in the shadow of the intimidation by the Chinese communist regime.

While this illegitimate power is often formidable and fearsome, it is also always insecure because it is always defending itself against its potential dismantling. Knowing that the basis of its authority lies in nothing more moral or legal than its power to brazenly bend people to its will, the tactics it uses are as limited in variety as they are effective in results. One of autocracy's tried and true methods of maintaining its hold on power is to divide and conquer those it subjugates. This is an especially effective method because its victims are also its practitioners. We who have been working for change in China must recognize that in the past we too have fallen into this time-tested trap set for us by illegitimate power. Each group, be it racial, cultural, regional, or religious, has tended to believe that it could achieve its own goals, through its own means, on its own terms. Some of us have tried to negotiate with the Chinese communist regime; others have used more radical tactics; we have all, however, mistakenly attempted to go it alone. Today we must realize that this strategy has failed. Today we must recognize what the Honorable Dalai Lama and myself agreed upon in a meeting this past July:

"It's only wishful thinking that the Chinese government gives freedom to the Tibetans and not to the Han Chinese majority or the Uyghurs at the same time. It is also impossible that the Chinese government would give freedom only to Falun Gong practitioners and not to the underground church members. And the dictatorial threat hanging over Taiwan, Hong Kong, and Macau can be alleviated only through the continued fighting and successful effort for freedom by the people in Mainland China. Therefore, our strive for freedom is an integrated one and cannot be separately carried out."

But a unified struggle against the Chinese regime must first eliminate the obstacles of suspicion, distrust, antagonism, and even outright hostility between different ethnic groups. We, and those who have lived under the communist Chinese dictatorship, are well aware that the enmity between ethnic groups as it exists today was stoked by the regime, whose monopoly on media control allows it to stir up the fears and hatreds that form one of the primary pillars of its power. As Ms. Kadeer has wisely noted in a meeting with me not long ago, "The Chinese Communist Party rallied the Han Chinese to prejudicial treatment of the Uyghurs by means of Han Chauvinism; on the other hand, the CCP deceived the Uyghurs into hatred of the Han Chinese by claiming that the oppression of the Uyghurs came from the Han Chinese people. Our hope lies in the termination of racial hatred."

We also have to recognize that it is because of our intrinsic weakness as human beings that we have been susceptible to the deceptive tactics of the communist Chinese dictatorship. This, in fact, is one of the vulnerabilities of humankind—we place too much value on differences. This unfortunate emphasis on differences and resulting allegiance only to those whom we perceive to be "our own" has very often, throughout history, led to racial, religious, or regional hostility, hatred, and bloodshed. But this need not be so. Our better nature is quite capable of seeing the similarities, rather than differences, that exist between and among all members of the human race. Are there great differences between our physical, material, and spiritual needs? Is the desire for freedom a Han desire, a Tibetan desire, a Uyghur desire, or a Mongolian desire? Or is it a human desire? In order for us to coexist peacefully, we must simply remember to be loyal to those fundamental human traits we all share. This both honors us as people and makes us better citizens of our nations and our world. Indeed, the fundamental dignity and value of every human being, the ethos that must be the basis of all of our work going forward, is the same philosophy that the universal Declaration of Human Rights promulgates. The Universal Declaration of Human

Rights, whose sixtieth anniversary we will soon celebrate, does not seek to eliminate differences among people and cultures, but simply recognizes a series of fundamental human rights to which every individual is entitled by virtue of humanity in which we all share. These rights are guaranteed irrespective of race, culture, religion, language, and geography precisely because, while these things are aspects of being human, in no instance do they supersede the fundamental rights that exist to protect this humanity. This idea must be the ideological foundation of our common cause.

And based on this ideological foundation, we must work out a plan for a constitutional democracy in China; we must foster a commitment to a democratic constitutional system that all of us can agree upon and trust.

Especially in those lands under the actual jurisdiction of the People's Republic of China, history—no matter how you look at it—has intertwined our fates. It is therefore essential for us to work from a common starting point. The dedication to the creation of the rule of constitutional law in China is such a starting point and, as a starting point, it will nurture a relationship of co-existence based on mutual respect. Without an agreement of this kind, our pursuit of equality, love, freedom, and democracy is only a utopian dream; the dictatorship will manipulate us, divide us, and destroy us by preying on the fundamental weakness of our lack of a common ideal.

We must also pledge to each other that, in addition to working from a common starting point toward a common goal, we will repudiate violence as a political tool. Indeed, in addition to our commitment to constitutional democracy, we must also commit to nonviolent means to effectuate our goals. We must not allow blood to stain the ink that will mark our new constitution; a new China must be birthed peacefully so that peace and stability are as much a part of its creation and future existence as dictatorship and disrespect for its citizens are a thing of its communist past.

Without question, the Chinese communist dictatorial system is the primary obstacle standing between us and constitutional democratic order.

If it remains in place, there will be no meaningful future for any of us who are fighting for a new beginning in China. This obstacle must be removed. But none of the group we represent can single-handedly carry out this task by ourselves. We are therefore faced with necessity—and it is a necessity—of building a unified democratic front in order to further our common cause. This is no longer an academic dispute; it is now a practical question of implementation. We all understand that it is much more difficult to practice than to theorize, but we must also understand that it is only through the work of the far-sighted, open-minded leaders of the different ethnic groups present here today that, with perseverance and political skill, we will be able to push forward and finally realize our shared goal of a constitutional democracy that recognizes the rights of all of our people and of all the world's people.

I hope this conference will serve as a start.

CHAPTER 27

Reciprocity Should Be US China Policy Platform

Eastern Kentucky University, Richmond, KY, United States
January 22, 2009

Just two days ago, I was among the millions of men and women who witnessed Barack Obama take the oath of office and become America's forty-fourth President. This was a moment that none but few would have even dared to dream about when Rosa Parks refused to give up her seat on a Montgomery, Alabama, bus more than a half-century ago. And yet, it was precisely the labors and struggles of the many people who, like Ms. Parks, worked over the years in the service of the ideals of democracy that made this once-unimaginable moment possible. The saying that Rosa sat so Martin Luther King Jr. could walk so Obama could run is a very good picture of the situation.

When President Obama spoke of "the God-given promise that all are equal, all are free, and all deserve a chance to pursue their full measure of happiness," I was moved to tears thinking both of the strength and resilience of America's democracy and the future of my home country, China.

* * *

Everywhere on the globe, if ordinary people are given the chance to choose, the choice will eventually be the same: freedom, not tyranny; justice, not discrimination; equality, not slavery. But there exists a persistent, at times self-serving, always short-sighted, myth among many

American sinologists, business elite, and policymakers. This myth says that while Americans love freedom and fundamental rights, some other people do not. A recently published Pew Research survey purports to find that a large majority of Chinese approve of the communist autocratic regime that is their government. On July 23 of last year, during the lead-up to the Beijing Olympics, I was one of the three people who testified before the Congressional Foreign Affairs Committee on the state of Human Rights in China. Professor Kenneth Lieberthal of the University of Michigan also came before the Committee, and in his testimony, he referenced the Pew Research survey in order to bolster his claim that the Chinese government is on the right track "searching for a Chinese path of political reform."

A Chinese path of political reform? In the context of the regime's behavior, Professor Lieberthal's testimony amounted to an endorsement of the idea that democracy and human rights are not essential components of political reform in China. What, then, are people like Professor Lieberthal looking to reform if they jettison democracy and human rights—the fundamentals, that is, of a just society? Does Professor Lieberthal, and those of like mind, really believe that the people of China do not want democracy or the basic human rights that democracy is intended to safeguard?

My mind cannot help but go back to May 30, 1989. In the midst of a national movement of millions—millions—demanding democratic reforms in China, the statue of the Goddess of Democracy was unveiled in Tiananmen Square by students who declared:

"The statue of the Goddess of Democracy is made of plaster, and of course cannot stand here forever. But as the symbol of the people's hearts, she is divine and inviolate. Chinese people, arise! Erect the statue of the Goddess of Democracy in your millions of hearts! Long live the people! Long live freedom! Long live democracy!"

The statue, together with thousands of young lives, was crushed four days later by government tanks. I was a witness to these events, and I saw protesters die before my eyes.

But the desire for democracy was not crushed by these tanks. Indeed, the desire for democracy cannot be crushed in the hearts of any people. On December 10, 2008, the sixtieth anniversary of the Universal Declaration of Human Rights, 303 Chinese intellectuals published Charter 08. Its opening statement asserts:

"A hundred years have passed since the writing of China's first constitution. 2008 also marks the sixtieth anniversary of the promulgation of the Universal Declaration of Human Rights, the thirtieth anniversary of the appearance of [the] Democracy Wall in Beijing, and the tenth of China's signing of the International Covenant on Civil and Political Rights. We are approaching the twentieth anniversary of the 1989 Tiananmen Massacre of pro-democracy student protesters. The Chinese people, who have endured human rights disasters and uncountable struggles across these same years, now include many who see clearly that freedom, equality, and human rights are universal values of humankind and that democracy and constitutional government are the fundamental framework for protecting these values. By departing from these values, the Chinese government's approach to 'modernization' has proven disastrous. It has stripped people of their rights, destroyed their dignity, and corrupted normal human intercourse."

Despite the Chinese government's heavy-handed measures against the organizers of the Charter 08 petition, the number of signers continues to rise and today it stands at more than 10,000.

The meaning of numbers is important to understand. Some academics in China and in the United States cite the scales of popular participation in activities encouraged or even orchestrated by the authorities as evidence of the people's approval of the government. But statistics based on the coercion of the tyrant's baton obviously misrepresent the true state of the minds of people living under dictatorship. More telling indicators are the numbers of people who engage in activities the government aims to prevent—or actually cracks down upon once they have begun.

"Mass incidents" is the term the Chinese government uses to describe protests in which 100 or more people participate. The number of these "incidents" has risen to 10,000 per year—which means that on average a new, large protest against the policies of the Chinese government takes place every five minutes.

Do you, or anyone you know on this earth, not want to have dignity? Who don't want to be respected as human beings, who don't want to have freedom to pursue their full measure of happiness? You may go to China, or indeed any of the existing autocracies in the world, and ask any person you meet, using the language they can comprehend, whether or not they want to enjoy the rights specified in the Universal Declaration of Human Rights. In almost every case, you will hear the answer "yes." Certainly, the values of democracy and human rights are not only American values nor only Western values but universal values that should and can be treasured by all people in this world.

On my walk last year from Boston to Washington for human rights in China—the GongMin Walk, I met an American man who said to me, "What you say is all well and good, and I am myself convinced about the universality of democracy and freedom, but other than that, why should we care about whether, and how fast, China becomes democratic?" I am asked similar questions on an almost daily basis.

My answer is simple. If China continues its path of economic development under a one-party dictatorship, it will pose a serious threat to our democratic way of life in the United States. China will serve as a model for dictators and juntas. In fact, it is already a model and leading supporter of these regimes. Pick a dictator anywhere on the globe—from North Korea to Sudan, from Burma to Zimbabwe, from Cuba to Iran—and you'll almost certainly find that the Chinese regime is supporting it today. This idea that tyrannies inevitably export their repression and discord was superbly presented by the great Soviet-era dissident Andrei Sakharov when he said, "The world community cannot rely on governments that do not rely on their own people."

Some of you may say these dictators are far away and what they do has little bearing on our lives here.

Reverend Martin Luther King Jr.'s admonition that "injustice anywhere is a threat to justice everywhere" is not an abstract call to action based on a vague sentiment. It is a demand for practical vigilance. The Chinese regime is a corrosive, antidemocratic force that promotes a pernicious model for other dictators. For the long-term stability of China, the world, and for the protection of our own hard-won freedoms, we must challenge this tyranny of the CCP and the corruption, fear, and violence it propagates. Its power must be countered, diminished, turned back—its legitimacy must be challenged on every front until its authority is subjected to the rule of law and international norms and the light of justice is allowed to shine in on all of China's people.

In the United States today, the Chinese government takes advantage of our freedom and democracy to solidify its position at home. It, or its surrogates, have wide access to our universities, think tanks, and media through which they can advance their opinions and rationalize their actions. Most recently, a well-regarded think tank in Washington, DC, hosted a forum on the challenges facing the practice of religion in China. The forum consisted only of Chinese government officials and government-sanctioned religious groups. None of the groups who are widely recognized as persecuted by the Chinese government were represented. Chinese state media were in the back of the room recording every minute of the forum's "discussion," from which China miraculously emerged as a model of religious tolerance.

The Chinese government has co-opted numerous American businessmen and academics by providing them with favorable business opportunities and all manner of privileges; in turn, they serve the purposes and interests of the Chinese government back in America as lobbyists for favorable policies toward China. Professor Lieberthal's troubling view of China and the Chinese people, for example, perhaps was compromised by his involvement with a consulting firm that gave advice to people seeking business opportunities in China, a fact that Congressman Dana Rohrabacher raised during the congressional hearing I mentioned earlier. Indeed, are not many of our opinions on China clouded by what has been the "business-first" priorities of our China policy, which has benefited neither working-class Americans nor ordinary Chinese?

In the spring of 2008, the Chinese Consulate in New York pushed the envelope on the freedoms provided by American democracy by directly instigating and supporting violence against peaceful Falun Gong practitioners who were handing out literature. These people were physically assaulted and denied access to restaurants and other facilities by Flushing residents and business owners who were incited by Chinese officials based in the New York consulate. Recordings of phone conversations between Chinese officials and Flushing residents and leaders have been widely distributed to support this contention. The Chinese government uses our freedoms here to threaten freedom in their own country and even intimidate residents in this country.

* * *

Make no mistake, the expansion of China's military power is also a significant and alarming development. Throughout the past decade, China's defense budget has increased at an annual rate double that of its GDP growth. The Chinese People's Liberation Army is acquiring more than enough power to intimidate surrounding East Asian countries, some of them America's allies. It seems clear that at present, China wants to avoid any military confrontation with the United States and seeks instead to concentrate on developing its economy. Yet this could well be a temporary strategy, aimed at delaying conflict with the United States while giving China the time it needs to develop a more powerful military. Who can say what grandiose dreams and ambitions Chinese leaders may harbor twenty or thirty years hence if their regime is richer and stronger?

History and a well-developed body of political theory show that established democracies rarely go to war with one another. If this is true, then the United States has a clear national security stake in whether China becomes an established democracy.

* * *

But what leverage do we have with the Chinese government to push for positive change in China in the field of political rights? Some—even those who want to restore human rights as a centerpiece of foreign policy—will say that we have little leverage to effect meaningful change.

Exactly the opposite is true. But a detailed list of effective policies can emerge only after we rid ourselves of the delusions and false assumptions upon which our China policy has long been based. Above all, we must understand democracy in China is homegrown and not imposed by the outside world as many have suggested and many others would worry it would be. But this does not mean that we must sit back and wait for democracy to bloom. Instead, it means engaging with and nurturing democratic forces already at work in China. People often talk about prerequisites for democratization; for me, the most important of all is that there must be democratic forces in Chinese society, and I believe today more than ever that a visionary part of the US engagement policy with China is to openly and systematically engage with the Chinese democratic forces and to nurture their growth.

The ostensible legitimacy of the Chinese communists' rule hangs by one tenuous thread: economic growth. GDP in a particular region is the single most important criterion by which local leaders' performances are evaluated. The United States should take advantage of this fever for ever more business by bringing human rights issues to the fore in all exchanges with China, be they economic or cultural. Even a single request for the release of an individual prisoner of conscience can have significant impact. In fact, in the past twenty years, the human rights talks in which the Chinese government has engaged as a result of pressure exerted by the Chinese Democracy movement, international rights groups, and the US government have helped to significantly raise the Chinese public's awareness of human rights issues.

More than this, we need political leaders who will call attention to the fact that trade has not yet brought, and will never alone bring, an end to political repression or the Chinese Communist Party's monopoly on power. America has been carrying out a policy that benefits business interests in both the United States and China far more than it helps ordinary people in either country. It is time for change.

To that end, I want to offer the idea of Reciprocity as a foreign policy platform.

In 1997, Harvard University invited Jiang Zemin, then-president of China, to speak at the campus. In response to this invitation, I organized a student demonstration, which became the largest campus protest at Harvard since the Vietnam War. Those in favor of Jiang's visit argued for it on the basis of freedom of speech. Our protest argued against it on the grounds of Reciprocity.

The lack of reciprocity gives the Chinese government a huge advantage in the field of world opinion and in tamping down internal dissent. By insisting on reciprocity, the United States and the rest of the world's democracies can showcase their own freedoms while forcing the Chinese government into an untenable position with respect to its denial of basic rights to its own citizenry.

As I said earlier tonight, in the United States today, the Chinese government and its surrogates have wide access to our universities, think tanks, and media outlets through which they can advance their opinions and rationalize their actions. When a Chinese government official speaks at a university such as Harvard or Yale, the government-controlled media in China uses the association with these prestigious institutions to enhance its credibility to its own people at home.

When US government officials travel to China, their movements, their contacts, and their communications are tightly controlled. If officials give a speech, it is not typically broadcast to the Chinese people.

Congressman Chris Smith of New Jersey reported that on his last trip to China, his meetings with reform-minded Chinese citizens were suddenly canceled and that he could not access his own website on the internet. Even Presidents Bush and Clinton had their speeches to Chinese citizens blocked when they visited China. Virtually all the American media are blocked in China. Here in the United States, China can freely broadcast. In fact, it is estimated that over 90% of the Chinese-language media in the US are Chinese-government controlled. The Chinese government exploits our freedoms to extend its influence with Chinese communities in the United States.

In short, there exists no reciprocity between China and the democratic world.

Now, some people may argue that pushing for Reciprocity with respect to human rights will unduly antagonize the Chinese government. This is nothing more than self-imposed fear—an attitude that the Chinese government would desire most from American foreign policymakers. In response to this fear, I adduce the European Parliament's recent awarding of the Sakharov Prize for Freedom of Thought. The Chinese government mounted a furious lobbying effort that included many threats of dire consequences for European relations with China if the Parliament followed through on its decision to give the award to Hu Jia, the now imprisoned Chinese AIDS activist. To the chagrin of the Chinese government, and to the credit of the European Parliament, Hu Jia received the award. The Chinese government's reaction amounted to nothing more than ritualistic fulminating. For one must understand that more than anything else, the Chinese government knows that it must maintain and advance its integration with the global community. Without this continuing integration and the economic benefits that follow, the regime's hold on power will lose whatever apparent legitimacy it claims. The US must realize this and mount a consistent, frequently repeated call for Reciprocity in the exercise of freedom and human rights.

It is fair and appropriate to ask the Chinese government for the same freedoms for its people that we ourselves enjoy; the same access to the Chinese people for our officials and delegations; the same open discussion and exchange of ideas that we extend to the Chinese government here in the United States. This idea of Reciprocity will allow us to directly and indirectly infuse the issue of human rights into all sectors of our dialogue with China in a way that would make it very difficult for the Chinese government to refuse. It would give the United States, and the other democracies of the world, further leverage in their discussions with China and help to restore the moral compass of the United States as it navigates the choppy seas of world diplomacy.

The United States was founded on the principles of freedom, democracy, and certain inalienable rights. But the desire to meet short-term interests tends to compromise faithfulness to these principles. That inconsistency weakens American credibility. But the United States remains a great country and its people a great people. I have an incurable confidence in American democracy, knowing as I do that its structure always makes it possible for its citizens to correct past mistakes. At present, isolationism is not the solution to the problem of a tarnished international image. Promoting democracy and freedom around the world will panic dictators and gain the interest of even those who have been hoodwinked by their rulers.

The time has come to have a consistent, cogent, concrete policy aimed at democratic change in China. I have great hope in the new president. More than that, I have a great hope in you, the great citizens of the United States of America.

CHAPTER 28

Charter 08: A Wake-Up Call for America and China

Address to Congressional Defense and Foreign Policy Forum
Washington, DC, United States
February 27, 2009

Good afternoon.

Thank you Ambassador Middendorf and Ms. Suzanne Scholte for inviting me to address the Defense Forum Foundation. And thank you, Ed, for sharing Dr. Edwards' letter with us. I applaud Dr. Edwards and everyone associated with the Victims of Communism Memorial for their vision and their fortitude in making this monument a reality.

I also thank everyone here, particularly the hard-working staff from Congress and the executive departments, for taking the time to come to this luncheon. I will do my best to give some good food for thought that will assist you with the difficult work you have in turning information into effective legislation and policy.

I will talk of three things this afternoon. Then I will answer any questions you may have:

1. The importance of the struggle for democracy in China to the long-term strategic interest of the United States and the world
2. The three conditions that must be present at the same time to effect a political change in a country like China
3. The specific foreign policy options Charter 08 presents for achieving an open, stable, democratic China

Regretfully, I was not here for last month's luncheon; I understand that Bill Gertz gave a very cogent summary of the security challenges facing the Obama Administration. Bill observed that China's military buildup, coupled to a dictatorship that is not in any way accountable to its people, can only be perceived as a growing challenge to American security. I would add to Bill's observations that China's emergence as an economic as well as a military power poses the very real question of whether the Chinese government model of a one-party dictatorship without the rule of law and the protection of individual rights will become the model for the world in this new millennium. The very real question for us is will China be integrated into the world community or will China integrate the world community within its system. I urge everyone in this room to reflect on where the Chinese dictatorship was twenty years ago in 1989. It was on the brink of collapse. It was unthinkable for everyone, including the then-leaders of China, that its brand of communism would be considered by so many people in the world today as a challenge to the American model for the rest of the world. What has the US done wrong in the past twenty years?

Most recently, on December 8, 2008, 303 brave Chinese citizens published Charter 08, a well-reasoned call for peaceful constitutional reform. Rather than engage in dialogue with these citizens, the Chinese government arrested Liu Xiaobo, a lead signatory, and harassed and intimidated the others. Nonetheless, almost 9,000 other Chinese citizens have signed Charter 08. Like H.W. Bush's sending a private envoy shortly after the Tiananmen Square Massacre to reaffirm his recognition of Deng Xiaoping as the legitimate leader of China, Secretary Clinton's recent remarks regarding the low priority of Human Rights in her discussions with the Chinese leaders sends the wrong message at a particularly critical moment. Her remarks demoralized Chinese activists and protesters, many of whom had gathered at the US Embassy for her visit to seek her support. The Chinese government can only read Secretary Clinton's remarks as giving it a free hand to exercise their arbitrary rule. The freedom fighters can only see this as a slap in the face. The world can only see this as the rise of the Chinese political system over the weak US model. As a result, I can only see greater repression of Chinese citizens in the future and bolder actions by the Chinese government on the world arena.

What will our inconsistency and compromise bring us? Again, I ask you to think where the Chinese government was nearly twenty years ago. Look at where China is today. I hold up Charter 08 as a virtual roadmap for a peaceful transition to democracy in China, which Secretary Clinton has chosen to ignore. What course are we chartering with this mindset? If this continues, think about where the Chinese model will be twenty years from now. Will our silence on human rights eventually come back to silence us here in America? Can we hear a future Secretary of State say, "We can't let the First Amendment stand in the way of a harmonious society and economic progress"?

So, Bill's conclusion that the best solution for the challenge China presents to our security and our democratic way of life is that China has a peaceful transition to democracy. I will add to this by saying that a peaceful transition to democracy in China is not only the best outcome for America, but also the best one for China and world peace as well.

If a peaceful transition to a democratic form of governance in China is the optimum solution for removing this challenge to American security, it then follows that advancing human rights and supporting democratic forces within China must be a vital, integral, and fundamental basis of our bilateral relations with the Chinese government. It is counterproductive to compartmentalize human rights and democratic reform in our discussions with China. We cannot make progress on this issue so vital to our security by raising it only every so often when the wind blows just right. Human rights and democratic reform must be the platform upon which all other issues are based.

This brings us to the topic at hand. What are the options for American foreign policy in constructively assisting this peaceful transition to democracy in China? And what role does Charter 08 play in this transition?

In China or any other country, three conditions must be present at the same time for a peaceful transition to democracy to occur:

1. A viable opposition
2. A crisis
3. International support

A hundred years ago, China experienced a serious political crisis and also enjoyed a viable democratic opposition led by Dr. Sun Yat-sen. Unfortunately, there was no international support. This caused Dr. Sun to turn to Lenin in 1917—a fateful and disastrous turn of events for China and the world.

Many of us in this room vividly recall the Pro-Democracy Movement of 1989. A viable opposition had formed and a crisis was clear and present. One million students and sympathizers gathered around the Goddess of Democracy statue erected in the middle of Tiananmen Square; the likeness of this statue adorns the Victims of Communism Memorial here on Massachusetts Avenue. In addition, numerous smaller demonstrations were erupting in cities across China.

Again, the third component. The international support needed failed to materialize.

We can easily draw from these two examples an understanding of how the three conditions of a viable opposition, a crisis, and international support must interplay for our desired outcome of a peaceful transition to democracy.

International pressure in and of itself cannot and should not bring about democracy. The desire for democracy must come from the hearts of Chinese citizens. This desire must be distilled into a viable opposition that is distinctly and undeniably home grown. But as we have seen from the above two examples, international support provides the critical counterweight that tilts the outcome in the right direction. The lack of international support proved disastrous for my countrymen in 1989. On the positive side, the wonderfully orchestrated support of the Western world and in particular of Pope John Paul provided the final nudge that brought the swift collapse of the communist regime and the birth of democracy in Poland.

Then what significance is Charter 08 bringing to make up the three conditions I just elaborated?

Charter 08 has three significant attributes: First is its authorship. It is 100% homegrown with an impeccable pedigree. The original 303 signatories are all widely known and respected citizens of China. In addition to the original signatories, almost 10,000 Chinese citizens have affixed their real names to Charter 08. This number should not be underestimated. How many of us in this room would sign such a petition with the full knowledge that in so doing we are putting our jobs and even our freedom at risk? This fact renders moot any contention by the CCP that Charter 08 is the rambling of subversives or the work of outside agitators. It also renders as absurd the conventional wisdom of many academics and so called "sinologists" that the desire for freedom and democracy really does not exist in China.

The second important fact about Charter 08 is that it is a clear and detailed roadmap for achieving the goal of a peaceful transition to democracy. It is a cogent and factual description of the problem as well as the solution:

I quote from the opening remarks of Charter 08:

The Chinese people, who have endured human rights disasters and uncountable struggles, now see clearly that freedom, equality, and human rights are universal values of humankind and that democracy and constitutional government are the fundamental framework for protecting these values.

By departing from these values, the Chinese government's approach to "modernization" has proven disastrous. It has stripped people of their rights, destroyed their dignity, and corrupted normal human intercourse.

Charter 08 goes beyond describing the situation. It details nineteen specific recommendations for peaceful constitutional reform. So, Charter

08 is not only a homegrown, unequivocal call for democratic reform, it is also a roadmap for achieving that reform. It is the basis for discussion and dialogue with the CCP.

And lastly, because it is homegrown and because it has attracted such widespread endorsement, Charter 08 is now a catalyst for the formation of a viable opposition. Remember that a viable opposition is the first condition for democracy to take hold. There now exists a body politic of almost 9,000 people who have gathered around a common principle for forming a democratic alternative to the current one-party dictatorship. And I assure you that the number is growing every day, and this is just the tip of the iceberg. Not since 1989 have the forces for democracy so visibly formed inside China.

It is therefore not surprising that the communist government has reacted so swiftly by arresting Liu Xiaobo, putting numerous others under city arrest, intimidating almost everyone involved, and desperately attempting to remove any trace of Charter 08 from the internet. The CCP knows all too well that this is the most fearful of viable organized opposition—one of the conditions for the peaceful transition to democracy.

A crisis, the second condition for democratic reform, is also taking shape. Virtually, the only support propping up the Chinese government is its claim of creating economic prosperity. This support is rapidly eroding. The economic downturn is producing an army of unemployed workers and disaffected peasants all across China. As the economic situation worsens, the Chinese government's credibility will rapidly dissipate. The swamp will be drained, if you will, laying bare the underlying frustrations, grievances, and contempt for the CCP. Recognizing that they have nothing to lose, people will become bolder and bolder in publicly expressing their dissatisfaction. Charter 08 will become the focal point for the people's demands for reform.

The viable opposition and the crisis will come together to challenge the sixty years of corruption, repression, and disregard for humanity which the CCP has delivered to the Chinese people.

So, two of the three conditions for a peaceful transition to democracy are now forming as we speak.

The stage is now set for America and the Western democracies to provide the third condition, international support. The timing is right because the situation is still manageable. Assertive engagement with China can push the government to engage in a constructive dialogue with the opposition. A dialogue that will create the climate for peaceful and orderly democratic reform. Assertive American engagement with the Chinese government at this time can induce the Chinese government to realize that the tide of history is going against them and now is the time to strike a bargain.

Without a forceful and consistent message from America now for the Chinese government to enter a dialogue with the opposition, the Chinese government will be lulled into a false sense of security. That it can delay the inevitable, just as it did in 1989. That just as in 1989, it can intimidate and crush the opposition into submission. This could and probably will set in motion cataclysmic confrontations of unpredictable proportions. At the very least, America will have lost another opportunity to tip the scales toward democracy in China. America will lose a vital opportunity to eliminate the biggest challenge to its own security and for freedom for fully one-quarter of the world's population.

I must add at this time that America has little to lose and much to gain by assertively and consistent engaging China on the subject of democratic reform. Many argue that China will react by pulling the plug on their considerable holdings of US debt. This is self-imposed fear. The Chinese government knows this would be suicide for them.

China indeed will raise the volume and issue all sorts of threats privately and even publicly. But I urge everyone to consider what happened earlier this year when the European Parliament was about to award the Sakharov Prize for Freedom of Thought to the Chinese activist, Hu Jia. The Chinese government made forceful and even belligerent threats to the EP. Much to their credit, the European Parliament went ahead and awarded the prize to Hu Jia. China did nothing more than issue a pro forma protest.

At this critical moment America cannot be driven by self-imposed fears. The conditions for a peaceful transition to democracy are coming into play. The signers of Charter 08 are giving America and the world a wake-up call. We cannot afford to miss that call.

But a detailed list of effective policies can emerge only after we rid ourselves of the delusions and false assumptions upon which our China policy has long been based. Above all, we must understand democracy in China is homegrown and not imposed by the outside world as many have suggested and many others would worry it would be. But this does not mean that we must sit back and wait for democracy to bloom. Instead, it means engaging with and nurturing democratic forces already at work in China. I believe today more than ever that a visionary part of the US engagement policy with China is to openly and systematically engage with the Chinese democratic forces and to nurture their growth.

We must send a clear and consistent message to the Chinese government that the time for constitutional reform has come. We must engage our democratic partners around the world to give China the same message.

Specifically, I strongly urge all of you involved in legislation to exercise this great tool of freedom to introduce resolutions that give voice to our commitment to freedom. I applaud the Senate resolution, introduced by Senators Casey and Brownback, supporting Charter 08, calling for the release of Liu Xiaobo and urging democratic reforms in China. I congratulate Congressman McCotter for drafting a similar resolution for the House.

Furthermore, we must become proactive in our support of democracy. By proactive, I mean we should take actions that put the Chinese government on the defensive in a way that forces them to confront the fact that they are on the wrong side of history. And at the same time gives hope to the democratic forces inside of China. I will give you this example of proactive policy: I call it the Doctrine of Reciprocity. When

US government officials travel to China, their movements, their contacts, and their communications are tightly controlled. If officials give a speech, it is not typically broadcast to the Chinese people. Congressman Chris Smith of New Jersey reported that on his last trip to China, he could not access his own website on the internet. Even President Obama's inauguration speech was edited before it was published in China.

Virtually all the American media are blocked in China. Here in the United States, China can freely broadcast. In fact, it is estimated that over 90% of the Chinese language broadcasts in the US are Chinese-government controlled. The Chinese government uses such freedom to extend its influence with Chinese communities in the United States. In the United States today, the Chinese government and its surrogates have wide access to our universities, think tanks, and broadcast studios through which they can advance their opinions and rationalize their actions. When a Chinese government official speaks at a university such as Harvard or Yale, the government-controlled media in China uses the association with these prestigious institutions to enhance its credibility and validity to its own people at home. Chinese people can protest here. Chinese people cannot protest in China. US citizens cannot protest in China. Under the Doctrine of Reciprocity, the United States would demand the same rights and freedoms be extended to American citizens and officials, an American media in China that we extend to Chinese citizens and officials, and Chinese media here in the United States. In the exchange of ideas with China we must demand a level playing field.

I firmly believe that it is not too late to summon our better angels and to stand on the right side of history. We must apply a much more strategic yardstick to determine the right policies toward the Chinese government. We must realize that at the most fundamental level, we are engaging in a struggle between two completely different views of humanity. One says man is just a serf of the state with no rights. The other states that human beings have rights and it is the purpose of the state to protect them. In this regard, we must strive to restore Human Rights to its rightful place as the very fabric that binds our foreign policy together. This will not earn the retribution of the Chinese government but respect and the realization that it is dealing with people of strength and character. This is what the Chinese government fears the most. This more than anything else will put America on equal footing in its negotiations on other bilateral issues and restore America's standing in the world.

To do so will not only make a historic leap toward world peace, but it will also reaffirm America's moral standing in the world. It will reaffirm that the lifeblood of America is not in what it consumes but in what it believes. It will tell the world once again that America's commitment to freedom and democracy is not a costume that it wears only on special occasions but the very foundation of its existence. Through this we will ensure that the American model of the freedom and justice of a government of the people, by the people, and for the people will be the model we pass on to our children.

CHAPTER 29

China's Economic Miracle: A Model Built on Massacre

Speech at Gustavus Adolphus College
St Peter, MN, United States
April 30, 2009

My talk today will address the following questions:

How did China's economic miracle come about? What role did the Tiananmen Square Massacre play in that miracle? What is the nature of the so-called China model? Is it sustainable? Why should we here in the US care? What can we do to promote democracy in China and the world?

I hope as I speak, these questions will be answered.

China started its market-oriented reforms in the late 1970s. In addition to fast economic growth, two others soon became apparent.

One was the negation of the ideology on which the Chinese Communist Party (the CCP) had waged its revolution, which in turn negated the legitimacy of the CCP's rule itself. The original purpose of the revolution and the new communist regime was to destroy private ownership, markets, and capitalist elements altogether and establish socialism and even communism. The CCP's market-oriented reforms obviously undermined socialism, which in effect said the revolution was a mistake.

The other was corruption. As economic reform continued, official business dealings and manipulations thrived, and corruption became rampant. Widespread corruption caused widespread discontent and became a major reason for the 1989 democracy movement, which culminated in Tiananmen Square.

The democracy movement, which caused an unprecedented split within the CCP leadership, had two demands. One was "freedom and democracy," the other was "no official business dealings, no corruption." Many moderates in leadership as well as among the rank and file led by the Party's then-General Secretary Zhao Ziyang were sympathetic to the movement and opposed to crackdowns, but the Chinese paramount leader Deng Xiaoping insisted on ending the movement in bloodshed.

Deng Xiaoping acted mainly out of fear. He feared the CCP regime would be toppled, so he massacred the movement, creating terror in order to preserve power.

The massacre did create a strong sense of fear and dismay among ordinary people in China. Any room for a public system of checks and balances against governmental abuse of power was gone.

It also created a sense of fear and crisis within the communist regime because it brought unprecedented public awareness to human rights and democracy. Although the Chinese communist regime cracked down on that movement, life was no longer the same for the rulers. The regime had to face a completely different domestic and international environment and had to resort to new tactics to meet its "overwhelming" need for stability.

The subsequent disintegration of the Soviet Union and the Eastern European Bloc cast an even darker cloud over the heads of Chinese communist officials. "How long can the red flag continue to fly?" they started to worry. Their concern was two-fold: First, for how long can the communists stay in power and what would happen after they were gone? Second, what does the ongoing, market-oriented economic reform have to do with communist doctrine?

Shortly after Deng Xiaoping's famous 1992 Southern Inspection, where he proposed accelerating economic reforms without asking whether they were socialist or capitalist, communist bureaucrats at all levels realized three facts: First, the Chinese Communist Party's stay in power has nothing whatsoever to do with communist ideals. Second, "economic growth means everything;" that is, continued economic growth is the last, best hope to keep the CCP ship afloat. Third, an unjust regime can only be upheld through the work of unjust officials. In order to uphold the one-party dictatorship, it had to rely on capitalizing on the dark and evil side of human nature: spoiling the elite in exchange for their loyalty. Therefore, the corruption of the powerful elite became accepted, endorsed, and necessary.

With the understanding of these three realities, the communist officials developed an undocumented but almost unanimously accepted code of conduct—or rather, code of corruption. Every piece of governmental power was now on sale in the market and every corner of the market was invaded by political power.

Officials in nearly all government agencies spend most of their energy beefing up GDP, engaging in power arbitrage, bribing their superiors, and seeking luxurious personal perks. They are doing this because it is a natural choice for them, probably the only choice. They gain enormous financial and material benefits without taking any political risk. As a result, the Communist Party elite, who used to label themselves "the vanguards of the proletariat class," have either turned themselves into get-rich-overnight capitalists, or become brokers, patrons, and backers of (domestic and foreign) capitalists. All this was made possible thanks to the Tiananmen Massacre and the political terror that was imposed on the entire country in the years following. There may have been some officials in the regime with some vision and ideals before the massacre, but afterwards almost nothing of the kind existed.

In such a political environment, political power was dancing a full-swing tango with capital operation. Low human rights standards, low wages, lack of environmental protection, regulations and enforcement, and the illegality of collective bargaining all contributed to creating a golden opportunity for domestic and international speculative capitalists.

As a result, money quickly courted political power. Business venture takers go to any length to seek out someone in power to serve as backers so they can obtain market opportunities without fair competition. They also use political connections to shed all legal and social responsibility. In a sense, the Chinese Communist Party, which used to be China, Inc.'s sole shareholder, has now offered its shares for capitalists to purchase.

The CCP's sixteenth National Congress published a new Party Charter that welcomed capitalists as Party members. As a result, capital has become the greatest advocate of the current system. For the past two decades, the marriage of power and capital in China has been an ongoing soap opera that shows no signs of being canceled. This marriage has also extended to Hong Kong, Macau, Taiwan, and the international community writ large.

While the shares of China, Inc. are open for domestic and foreign capitalists to purchase, they were offered to China's intellectuals for free as performance-related stock options. The regime knows that in addition to economic growth, there is something else critical to its survival; that is so-called "political stability." In order to sustain such stability, the CCP regime offers all kinds of bribery incentives to buy off anyone and everyone of importance and influence in society. The bribery list includes bureaucrats at every level of governmental, military officers, and business leaders who the regime deems direct relatives. The list also includes college professors, research institutions, journalists, publishers, authors, art performers, high-profile athletes, etc. The government pays all these people off in the form of salaries, bonuses, state-covered expenses, free medical insurance, subsidized housing, free pension plans, and so on. Laws and policies increasingly favor this group of people in exchange for their recognition and acceptance of the political status quo. Their income and perks add up to wealth that is disproportionately higher than that of ordinary workers, farm workers, clerks, and small business owners. The gap is much larger than in any other country in the world.

Such a policy of co-opting and buying off potential opposition is quite effective in conjunction with the high-pressure purges and persecution after the Tiananmen Massacre. The crackdowns created terror in the minds of intellectuals as a psychological deterrent. As time went on, fear turned into cynicism, becoming increasingly indifferent to what was right and what was wrong. Indifference and hypocrisy rapidly became the new fashion that all modern Chinese intellectuals tried to follow. Coupled with a piece of the action in China, Inc., many intellectuals—who had once been independent and considered the conscience of the society—softened up their position against the post-1992 status quo.

In today's China, power (political elite), capital (economic elite) and "intellect" (social and cultural elite), are bonded together with corruption as the adhesive to form an alliance that maintains the existing political order. This alliance owns and runs China, Inc., dazzling the entire world with its wealth, might, and glory. With China's vast geographic size and population, the shareholders of China, Inc. have impressed many observers with their prodigious wealth accumulation and astonishing growth rates, making those same observers believe that one-party dictatorship is good for economic growth. By the same token, these shareholders also control all the channels of the information flow and dominate the public discourse. They can make their voices loud enough so outside observers believe that they represent China, that they are China—the whole of China. This is the China model based on massacre.

Is the Chinese model sustainable? My answer is "No." First and foremost, the model is built upon an unfair, illegitimate foundation that goes against humanity, against human rights, and against democracy. People in China, as elsewhere in the world, demand fairness, human rights, and democracy.

My mind cannot help going back to May 30, 1989. In the midst of a national movement of millions—millions—demanding democratic reforms in China, the statue of the Goddess of Democracy was unveiled in Tiananmen Square by students who declared:

"The statue of the Goddess of Democracy is made of plaster, and of course cannot stand here forever. But as the symbol of the people's hearts, she is divine and inviolate. Chinese people, arise! Erect the statue of the Goddess of Democracy in your millions of hearts! Long live the people! Long live freedom! Long live democracy!"

The statue, together with thousands of young lives, was crushed four days later by government tanks. But the desire for democracy was not crushed. Indeed, the desire for democracy cannot be crushed in the hearts of any people. On December 10, 2008, the sixtieth anniversary of the Universal Declaration of Human Rights, 303 Chinese intellectuals published Charter 08. Its opening statement asserts:

"The Chinese people, who have endured human rights disasters and uncountable struggles across these same years, now include many who see clearly that freedom, equality, and human rights are universal values of humankind and that democracy and constitutional government are the fundamental framework for protecting these values. By departing from these values, the Chinese government's approach to 'modernization' has proven disastrous. It has stripped people of their rights, destroyed their dignity, and corrupted normal human intercourse."

Despite the Chinese government's heavy-handed measures against the organizers of the Charter 08 petition, the number of signers continues to rise, and today it stands at more than 10,000.

The significance of these numbers is important to understand. There are academics in China and in the United States who point to statistics about Chinese citizens participating in activities encouraged or even orchestrated by the authorities as evidence of the people's approval of the government. But statistics based on the coercion of the tyrant's baton obviously misrepresent the true state of people's minds. More telling indicators are the number of people who engage in activities the government aims to prevent—or actually cracks down upon once they have begun.

"Mass incidents" is the term the Chinese government uses to describe protests in which 100 or more people participate. The number of these "incidents" has risen to 10,000 per year—which means that on average a new, large protest against the policies of the Chinese government takes place every five minutes.

I am often asked by American friends, "What you say is all well and good, and I myself am convinced about the universality of democracy and freedom, but other than that, why should we care about whether, and how fast, China becomes democratic?"

My answer is simple. If China continues its path of economic development under a one-party dictatorship, it will pose a serious threat to our democratic way of life in the United States. China will serve as a model for dictators and juntas. In fact, it is already a model and leading supporter of these regimes. Pick a dictator anywhere on the globe—from North Korea to Sudan, from Burma to Zimbabwe, from Cuba to Iran—and you'll almost certainly find that the Chinese regime is supporting him today.

In the United States, the Chinese government takes advantage of our freedom and democracy to "solidify its position at home." It, or its surrogates, have wide access to our universities, think tanks, and media through which they can advance their opinions and rationalize their actions.

The Chinese government has co-opted numerous American businessmen and academics by providing them with favorable business opportunities and all manner of privileges; in turn, they serve the purposes and interests of the Chinese government as lobbyists in America for favorable policies toward China. Indeed, are not many of our opinions on China clouded by what has been the "business-first" priorities of our China policy, a policy which has benefited neither working-class Americans nor ordinary Chinese?

Make no mistake, the expansion of China's military power is also a significant and alarming development. Throughout the past decade, China's defense budget has increased at an annual rate double that of its GDP growth. The Chinese People's Liberation Army is acquiring more than enough power to intimidate surrounding East Asian countries, some of them America's allies. It seems clear that at present, China wants to avoid military confrontation with the United States and seeks instead to concentrate on developing its economy. Yet this could well be a temporary strategy, giving China the time it needs to develop a more powerful military. Who can say what grandiose dreams and ambitions Chinese leaders may harbor twenty or thirty years hence, once their regime is richer and stronger?

History and a well-developed body of political theory show that established democracies rarely go to war with one another. If this is true, then the United States has a clear national security stake in whether China becomes an established democracy.

But what leverage do we have with the Chinese government to push for positive change in China in the field of political rights? Some—even those who want to restore human rights as a centerpiece of foreign policy—say that we have little power to effect meaningful change.

Exactly the opposite is true. However, a detailed list of effective policies can emerge only after we rid ourselves of the delusions and false assumptions upon which our China policy has long been based. Above all, we must understand democracy in China is homegrown and not imposed by the outside world. This does not mean we should sit back and wait for democracy to bloom. Instead, it means engaging with and nurturing democratic forces already at work in China.

More than this, we need political leaders who will call attention to the fact that trade has not yet brought, and by itself will never bring, an end to political repression or the Chinese Communist Party's monopoly on power. America has been carrying out a policy that benefits business interests in both the United States and China far more than it helps ordinary people in either country. It is time for change.

To that end, I want to offer the idea of Reciprocity as a foreign policy platform.

In 1997, Harvard University invited Jiang Zemin, then-president of China, to speak at the campus. In response to this invitation, I organized a student demonstration, which became the largest campus protest at Harvard since the Vietnam War. Those in favor of Jiang's visit argued for it on the basis of freedom of speech. Our protest argued against it on the grounds of Reciprocity.

The lack of reciprocity gives the Chinese government a huge advantage in the field of world opinion and in tamping down internal dissent. By insisting on reciprocity, the United States and the rest of the world's democracies can showcase their own freedoms while forcing the Chinese government into an untenable position with respect to its denial of basic rights to its own citizenry.

As I said earlier tonight, the Chinese government exploits our freedoms to extend its influence with Chinese communities in the United States. The Chinese government and its surrogates have wide access to our universities, think tanks, and media outlets through which they can advance their opinions and rationalize their actions. Here in the United States, China can freely broadcast. In fact, it is estimated that over 90% of the Chinese-language media in the US are Chinese-government controlled.

But when US government officials travel to China, their movements, their contacts, and their communications are tightly controlled. If officials give a speech, it is not typically broadcast to the Chinese people. Congressman Chris Smith of New Jersey reported that on his last trip to China, his meetings with reform-minded Chinese citizens were suddenly canceled and he could not access his own website on the internet. Even Presidents Bush and Clinton had their speeches to Chinese citizens blocked when they visited China. Virtually all the American media are blocked in China.

In short, there exists no reciprocity between China and the democratic world.

It is fair and appropriate to ask the Chinese government for the same freedoms for its people that we ourselves enjoy; the same access to the Chinese people for our officials and delegations; the same open discussion and exchange of ideas that we extend to the Chinese government here in the United States. This idea of Reciprocity will allow us to directly and indirectly infuse the issue of human rights into all sectors of our dialogue with China in a way that would make it very difficult for the Chinese government to refuse. It would give the United States and the other democracies of the world further leverage in their discussions with China and help to restore the moral compass of the United States as it navigates the choppy seas of world diplomacy.

The United States was founded on the principles of freedom, democracy, and certain inalienable rights. But the desire to meet short-term interests tends to compromise faithfulness to these principles. That weakens American credibility. The United States remains a great country and its people a great people. I have an incurable confidence in American democracy, knowing as I do that its structure always makes it possible for its citizens to correct past mistakes. At present, isolationism is not the solution to the problem of a tarnished international image. Promoting democracy and freedom around the world will panic dictators and gain the attention of even those who have been hoodwinked by their rulers. We must always remember Reverend Martin Luther King Jr.'s admonition: "Injustice anywhere is a threat to justice everywhere."

CHAPTER 30

The Pain of Victims and Their Families of Tiananmen Massacre Will Endure until This Justice Is Served

Speech Kicking Off the Second GongMin Walk
Boston Commons, Boston, MA, United States
May 19, 2009

Twenty years ago, Tiananmen Square swelled with millions of Chinese students and citizens. They called for the Chinese leaders to address government corruption, protect individual rights, and allow transparency and public participation in policy-making. These reasonable requests conform with China's constitution and law. However, on June 4, 1989, the petitioners were rewarded with machine guns and tanks.

Despite twenty years of repression, the struggle for freedom endures: from the tears of the Tiananmen Mothers to the persuasive logic of Charter 08; from the prayers of the underground Christians to the meditations of the Falun Gong; from the cries of the Uyghurs and the chants of the Tibetan monks; from the mourning of the peasants to the agony of urban citizens who had their lands and homes confiscated, the calls for justice, human dignity, and the rule of law in China are stronger than ever.

GongMin Walk, the peaceful way of promoting civil and political rights, is taking place all over the world including China. We are most encouraged to learn that Mr. Li Guohong, a courageous rights defender, has begun GongMin Walk inside China two weeks ago on May 4. Despite the tremendous risks and difficulties that he is facing, he is determined to continue. Today we begin our GongMin Walk in the United States to show our solidarity with the human rights fighters in China and to urge the American general public to be concerned about and support the Chinese democratic cause. I am encouraged by Speaker Nancy Pelosi's upcoming visit to China on the eve of the twentieth anniversary of the Tiananmen Massacre. Speaker Pelosi has been one of the most consistent and outspoken supporters of the Chinese democracy movement and I anticipate she will deliver a clear, strong message to the Chinese leaders. I urge her to meet with the Tiananmen mothers and the GongMin Walker, Li Guohong.

Now, on this twentieth year following the Tiananmen democracy movement, we come together with one voice to call on the Chinese authorities to initiate the following actions, which are consistent with China's constitution and international laws:

1. Acknowledge the Tiananmen Massacre and begin a dialogue with the victims and their families of the June 4th protests.
2. Release all the political prisoners, repeal all arrest warrants, and renounce the blacklist for all those involved in the June 4th protests.
3. Establish an impartial "truth and reconciliation" committee of citizens to document a full and truthful account of the events surrounding June 4, 1989.

We believe the above are actions expected of a reasonable and responsible government. They are nonpolitical and nonpartisan and reflect fundamental human values to which the world community subscribes. The pain of victims and their families from the Tiananmen incident and the suffering of Chinese citizens will endure until this justice is served.

CHAPTER 31

Key to Reconciliation Is the Growth of the Democratic Forces

Statement at Congressional-Executive Commission on China Hearing "The 20th Anniversary of the Tiananmen Square Protests: Examining the Significance of the 1989 Demonstrations in China and Implications for US Policy"
Dirksen Senate Office Building, Washington, DC, United States
June 4, 2009

Thank you, Mr. Chairman. It is a great honor for me to testify here today, to provide the point of view of a Chinese human rights and democracy advocate. I'm not going to repeat what the other panelists have said. Twenty years ago, Tiananmen Square swelled with tens of thousands of Chinese students and citizens. They called for the Chinese leaders to address government corruption, protect individual rights, and allow transparency and public participation in policymaking. These reasonable requests conform with China's constitution and law. However, on June 4, 1989, the petitioners were rewarded with machine guns and tanks.

The massacre left thousands dead and injured, and thousands more imprisoned. Tiananmen Mothers have identified and documented 195 fatalities and, according to their assessment, "these are definitely not all, nor even a majority." Hundreds of activists fled China into exile and most of them, joining the existing overseas dissidents of China, have been blacklisted from returning home ever since.

The massacre also set China's reforms down on the wrong path. If the recently published memoirs of Zhao Ziyang tell us anything, it is that we were so close to embarking on the road of peaceful transition to democracy, but now as then, very few people believe that China stood a real chance. The truth is the tragedy took place only because of four or five hardliners. The massacre created universal fear and universal cynicism in China that, in turn, has resulted in a moral disaster, a human rights disaster, and an environmental disaster. These three disasters have in the past twenty years minimized the short-term cost of capitalists and that of government embezzlement. That is how China's economic miracle has become possible.

The Chinese regime is a four-legged table. The regime will collapse should any one of the four legs be cut. One leg is fear, behind which is violence. One leg is untruth; the Chinese government, for example, has kept the truth about the 1989 movement and the magnitude of this tragedy from the ordinary people. One leg is economic growth; this is the only source of the legitimacy of its rule. The fourth leg is corruption; the Chinese government exchanges the loyalty of the elite with opportunities for corruption. It has not only co-opted the Chinese elite but also the foreign elite who are the sinologists, the businesspeople, and the policymakers. The Chinese government appeals to the universal tendency for corruption, which conflicts with the universal value of human rights.

This is the so-called "China's model," and this model is now challenging the democratic way of life worldwide. The model is not sustainable for many reasons but primarily because the Chinese people will abandon it. One evidence being that every year there are hundreds of protests against corruption, such as the incident when Chinese people were outraged by tainted milk or by the tragic deaths of children in the earthquake. We also have seen a growing willingness to make public statements through publication, as is the case with the internet posting of Charter 08 last December.

People are eager to find a breakthrough point. A reversal of the verdict on the Tiananmen incident is widely considered one such breakthrough point. I agree. With this good intention, some democracy-oriented intellectuals have recently called for reconciliation with regard to the tragedy. I think the notion of reconciliation is very important; we sooner or later will have to come to terms with our troubled past. But putting forth the proposal of reconciliation now is premature; primarily because the Chinese government has not even acknowledged any mistake in all this. One cannot reconcile to a non-event. The admission of the events of June 4th must precede any reconciliation. Rather than acknowledge the past events, the CCP continues on the path of untruth. It continues to persecute the victims and their families, tens of those known as "June 4 prisoners" are still being imprisoned, no compensation has been made to victims or their families. The government remains a one-party repressive regime continuing to lie about the tragic events, to ignore the pleas from its own people, and to demonstrate an unwillingness to listen. They repeatedly show us that they have no intention to change.

The truth is not out. When it is, perhaps it will be through an impartial truth-seeking committee, one of the major demands from Tiananmen Mothers. It should be the regime, the more powerful party, and not the victims who first raise the issue of reconciliation. First, an honest admission of the incident. Truth must come before reconciliation.

The democratic forces in China are not strong enough to get the regime to sit at a negotiation table and begin a process toward the truth and toward reconciliation. And the regime has no willingness to engage in any such program because it has accumulated too many grievances of incredible magnitude. Tiananmen is just one of the many tragedies. So, to reach the end point of reconciliation, we must first develop the critical mass of democratic forces. This is necessary for any breakthrough. The key to reconciliation is the growth of the democratic forces in China.

What the international community, particularly the United States, can and should do:

First, we should put the Chinese regime on the defensive by raising the human rights issues on any occasion possible. It is the Chinese that should worry more about economic relationships with other countries. This is one of the four legs on which the Chinese government stands.

Second, we should nurture the growth of Chinese democratic forces.

Third, we should help tear down the firewall that has been erected by the Chinese Communist Party [CCP]. If the United States is not in a position to face down the regime's violent forces—one of its four legs—it is most certainly in a position to expose its lies—another leg. Truth liberates.

Fourth, when a movement similar to the one in 1989 arises, national leaders in the United States should openly recognize and support the democratic forces and any democracy-oriented factions within the party. Had US leaders had access to Zhao Ziyang's memoirs beforehand, I believe they would have openly supported his faction during the Tiananmen uprising. The least the United States should do would be to press the CCP to enter into dialogue with the opposition leaders.

Thank you.

Addendum to Statement

Regarding the question of reassessment/reconciliation, the basis of any relationship, whether between people or nations, is truth. Without truth there can be no trust. Without trust there can be no security. The failure of the Chinese government to fully acknowledge the events of June 4, 1989, is a failure of truth and a black cloud over this regime to this day.

It is in the interests of both the Chinese government and the US government to work aggressively toward the following actions in order to build the foundation for a lasting bilateral relationship.

1. A full accounting of the events of Tiananmen Square in 1989. This can be in the form of a truth commission or a dialogue with the Mothers of Tiananmen or some combination thereof.

2. A release of all citizens imprisoned for their activities related to the Pro-Democracy Movement of 1989.
3. The removal of the firewalls imposed by the Chinese government to censor information over the internet that prevents the free exchange of ideas and information.
4. The support of the US government for the scaling up of firewall-busting technology that will make a free and secure access to the internet available to a minimum of 50- to 100-million people in China and related totalitarian regimes such as Vietnam and Iran. This action more than any other will bring truth and freedom to the people struggling under these regimes.
5. The immediate release of Liu Xiaobo and Wang Bingzhang, whose only crime was to speak their consciences.

CHAPTER 32

You Shall Know the Truth and the Truth Will Make You Free

Speech at the Rally Commemorating the 20th Anniversary of Tiananmen
West Lawn of Capitol Hill, Washington, DC, United States
June 4, 2009

"You shall know the truth and the truth will make you free."

After the passage of twenty years, there are those who wish to cloud the legacy of Tiananmen by saying that democracy has many faces and Western-style democracy is not for China. Some even say that the Chinese people do not want democracy. Some say that for the sake of stability, China needs a strong single-party government. Any logical analysis of this reasoning quickly reveals it as self-serving rhetoric designed to rationalize the illegitimacy of absolute power. If one accepts this logic, then one must also accept the concept of slavery. That some people actually desire to be slaves. That one human being actually has the right to tell another human being how to think, how to pray, and how to associate. The absurdity of this logic is quite evident.

Freedom and democracy may indeed have many faces. But freedom and democracy in whatever form have a common foundation. That foundation is truth. We are here today to call for truth. Without truth there is no basis for any relationship between people or between nations. We are here today to ask why the Chinese government is so afraid of truth. We are here today to call on the government of China to confront the truth. To acknowledge what happened on the morning of June 4,

1989. We call on the Chinese government to end the blacklist of people who participated in Tiananmen. We call on the Chinese government to end its persecution of its best and brightest citizens who dare to speak the truth. In particular, we call on the Chinese government to release Liu Xiaobo, signer of Charter 08, and democracy patriot Wang Bingzhang who, as we speak, is in solitary confinement for life for his lifelong advocacy for democracy.

But most of all we call on the US government and likeminded defenders of freedom to support truth by supporting an open and free internet for all people. The technology exists to bypass the firewalls constructed by tyrannies to block the truth from their people and enslave their minds. With a modest investment, the democracies of the world can open the internet to millions of people in China, Vietnam, Iran, Cuba, Burma, and North Korea. Such a large-scale access to the truth will destroy these firewalls and strike a blow to tyranny much in the same way the collapse of the Berlin Wall brought an end to communism in Europe.

We are here today to remember, but we are also here to call for truth. It is truth that tyrannies fear most. It is truth that builds stable societies and creates international stability. We must demand truth from the government of China. We must take up the call of our fallen brothers as they brought the goddess of democracy into Tiananmen Square, "Chinese people, arise! Erect the statue of the Goddess of Democracy in your millions of hearts! Long Live Freedom! Long Live Democracy!"

CHAPTER 33

The Nonviolent Tiananmen Democracy Movement

Lecture at the ICNC Summer Institute for the Advanced Study of Nonviolent Conflict
Tufts University, Medford, MA, United States
June 25, 2009

From mid-April to early June of 1989, hundreds of thousands of students gathered in Beijing's Tiananmen Square to protest government corruption and to call for more public participation in government. It was a phenomenon unprecedented in history: a long-lasting, large-scale, nonviolent demonstration. The campaign drew broad involvement from all walks of life throughout China. The protest lasted six and a half weeks and ended in bloodshed on the morning of June 4th when a government military crackdown took place, killing hundreds, if not thousands, of innocent Chinese people longing for freedom.

For the past twenty years, people have reflected on the movement and its bloody ending. Debates continue over what the students should or shouldn't have done to avoid the bloodshed. How did an essentially nonviolent struggle end so miserably? What did the students do right? What did they do wrong?

To understand what "could have been," we need to examine the movement in the context of the power struggle within the CCP. This examination is now possible with the publication of the memoirs of Zhao Ziyang, the liberal-minded general secretary of CCP who was purged following the massacre.

Let's begin by considering a few important features of the movement:

The student movement was totally unpremeditated. It was triggered by the death of Hu Yaobang, the previous open-minded Party general secretary who had been ousted by Deng Xiaoping two years earlier. His death generated a deep, spontaneous outpouring of protests against rampant government corruption and repression of liberal ideas and acts. These protests had no organization and no recognized leaders to plan and lead the demonstrations in the beginning.

The movement lacked clearly defined goals other than to express discontent. Later, students put forth different demands, which were mainly responses to the authorities' rhetoric. But they did not seek to overthrow the government; they didn't envision regime change but rather its reform.

One of the remarkable features of the movement was its use of strictly nonviolent forms of protest. The students had limited knowledge about nonviolent struggle strategies and past cases of nonviolent resistance in other parts of the world. Their motivations were neither moral nor religious. They chose to avoid violent actions for very practical reasons; they wanted to prove that they were good patriotic kids and to give the government no excuse to use violent means. One well-known incident involved student guards turning into the police three workers from Hunan province who threw eggs filled with red, blue, and yellow paint at the large portrait of Mao Zedong near Tiananmen Square. The students explained they turned them in because of the purity of their demonstrations.

Unlike most of the protests taking place in China today, the 1989 democracy movement was purely idealistic, motivated by noble ideas beyond self-interests. The backbone of the movement was young, idealistic students. Most had no experience in politics of any kind, no clear understanding of the nature of the CCP, and little knowledge of the power struggles within the party.

The students had virtually no insight into the split within the CPP leadership regarding the movement. They did not know that two major factions within the Party—moderate Zhao Ziyang and hardliner Li Peng, then-premier—were competing for the ear of the paramount leader Deng Xiaoping regarding the protests.

When Zhao Ziyang left on a trip to North Korea on April 23, hardliners led by Premier Li Peng took advantage of Zhao's absence and maneuvered Deng Xiaoping to their side. On April 25, Deng angrily and openly denounced the demonstrations. On April 26, an editorial in the *People's Daily* echoed Deng in describing the student demonstrations as "premeditated and organized turmoil with anti-party and anti-socialist motives." The students had no idea that their destiny and that of the movement had been largely determined the moment that editorial was published.

In a totalitarian world, a dictator cannot be wrong. Once Deng had issued his verdict, it had almost no chance of being reversed. Deng had to be vindicated. Li Peng and his faction would make sure that they were right. The protests had to be counter-revolutionary turmoil or even worse. This was the major theme as the events in the spring of 1989 unfolded.

By the time Zhao left for North Korea in April, most of the students had already left Tiananmen and Xinhua Gate, the main entrance to the CCP Central Committee's Compound. The few who remained were cleared away by police and taken back to school. However, students drew new fervor from the April 26 editorial. They were particularly incensed that their own patriotic inclinations had been called into doubt. The editorial's warning weighed heavily on the hearts of the students; anybody in China, then as now, knew a verdict like that would eventually lead to severe punishment.

To the students, the way to remove that weight was to demand that the government reverse the verdict. The next morning, the students took to the streets, joined by the largest crowd yet, estimated to be somewhere between a quarter of a million to half a million people. Walking in rows with their arms linked, the students remained peaceful throughout and pierced each of the police blockades easily.

The march of April 27 was a great success. It galvanized popular attention and brought the first phase of student protest to its climax. The students thought they had been proved innocent of the charge of counter-revolutionary turmoil. They also believed they had established a power base to demand government reform. Instead, they were moving one step closer to the trap set by Li Peng and Deng Xiaoping.

Upon his return from North Korea, Zhao Ziyang continued his moderate approach toward the students, downplaying the judgment of the April 26 editorial and hoping to gradually turn the situation around. In his May 4 speech, whose tone was distinctly different from the editorial, he conveyed the need to resolve the matter in a cool, reasonable, restrained, and orderly manner based on the principles of democracy and law. He pointed out the student demonstrators were absolutely not against the basic foundation of the political system; instead they were merely asking the government to correct its flaws. He also promised dialogue and to take measures on the key topics raised by students—such as corruption, government transparency, democracy, rule of law, and public scrutiny of government.

There were positive responses to Zhao Ziyang's speech from a wide range of sources, both domestic and overseas. In the days to follow, many universities in Beijing resumed classes.

But Li Peng and his allies did everything possible to prevent carrying out Zhao's proposals. They spread the notion at a meeting held by State Council with several university Party chiefs that Zhao's speech represented only his personal opinion and did not represent the Central Committee's. This message quickly spread among the students, who now worried that the government would indeed uphold the April 26 editorial. Li Peng and his people blocked any student organizations that had emerged during the demonstrations from participating in dialogue; they also prohibited the students from selecting their own representatives. They insisted on letting only students from official student organizations participate, organizations that were not at all representative of the student demonstrators. This suggested that the independent student organizations would be outlawed.

The students began to feel deceived by the government and felt they had no choice but to resume their protests. Even if they could not achieve reforms, at least they had to press the government to reverse the judgment of the April 26 editorial and acknowledge that the students' actions were based on patriotic motives and that their organizations were legal. Without such a reversal and legalization, the students knew they would be threatened with retaliation even if they refrained from further protest activities. The students decided to use the occasion of Gorbachev's visit to stage large-scale street demonstrations and a hunger strike. Then they occupied Tiananmen Square, one of most important symbols of government power. A more intense confrontation was inevitable.

In retrospect, Zhao's May 4 speech might have been the ideal opportunity for students to withdraw and for the government to take credible measures to address the questions raised by students. But the hardliners sabotaged this prospect, setting up the students and defeating their moderate rivals in the power struggle. In Zhao's own words, Li Peng "revealed his evil intentions. He used resistance and sabotage to ensure that efforts to resolve the student demonstrations on the basis of democracy and law would fail, with the intention of looking for an excuse to crush the student demonstrations using violent means."

History knows what happened next. Deng Xiaoping, Li Peng, and others sabotaged Zhao's constructive measures and lured the students to become "counter-revolution rioters," all to provide justification for the bloody crackdown that came on June 4th.

Despite the tragic ending, the students could claim some remarkable achievements. They resisted provocations to violence. They conducted what was probably the largest hunger strike in history, which aroused mass participation and brought the split within party leadership to one step short of a real democratic revolution. They successfully used international media, especially on the occasion of Gorbachev's visit.

But there were too many problems strategically. Given the genesis and nature of the movement, it is probably unfair to criticize the students on a strategic level. But it is always worth examining what one did wrong, or what one should have done differently, in order to draw lessons for the future. The movement had:

- No universally recognized organization.
- No credible viable leadership.
- No strategic planning; demands varied with the situation.
- No understanding, let alone strategy, for taking advantage of the split within the party leadership.

And yet, despite all these shortcomings, the movement remains the greatest in history. It contributed to peaceful democratic change in Eastern Europe, while in China, it voiced an open challenge to the system, set a pattern of nonviolent struggle, and most importantly sowed the seeds of democracy. Over the past twenty years, the Chinese government has made various efforts to ensure young people do not know about the movement and the massacre. This fact itself proves that the spirit of the 1989 democracy movement frightens the regime.

The regime should be frightened. The hunger for democracy has not disappeared but has reincarnated in the society as various resistances. Human Rights Watch estimates that there are over 100,000 protests against government policies and actions each year. Last December, on the sixtieth anniversary of the UN's Universal Declaration of Human Rights, Charter 08 was published on the internet. This document clearly outlines the failures of the CCP and proposes nineteen specific reforms. Originally signed by 303 well-known and respected citizens, Charter 08 has now gathered nearly 10,000 real names and signatures, despite the best efforts of the government to suppress it.

Protesters today have one important advantage that my colleagues did not have in 1989: the internet. The power of the internet to communicate ideas, promote truth, organize actions, and inspire hope is a great threat to the Chinese government or any other dictatorship. Truth is the greatest weapon against tyranny. That is why regimes, particularly in times of crisis, restrict and block the media. Perfidy always prefers to operate in darkness. The power of the internet to spread truth to break down the walls of lies and deceit of tyrannical regimes like China and Iran will prove pivotal in the ultimate success of freedom. You can play a part in this. Please write your congressmen urging their support for internet freedom initiatives. The technology now exists to bypass internet firewalls. Modest funding can put this capability in the hands of 50- to 100-million citizens of China, Iran, Vietnam, and North Korea. This will provide a critical mass of citizens with unrestricted access to information, truth, history, and each other. This can be done and, with your help, will be done. It would be a worthy tribute to the heroes of Tiananmen Square. Thank you.

CHAPTER 34

Statement Regarding the Continued Violence in Xinjiang Region of China

Speech at Rally Supporting Uyghurs' Peaceful Resistance
Washington, DC, United States
July 7, 2009

The endless carousel of repression and recrimination in Xinjiang Region of China must be replaced with more responsible actions that address the underlying tensions between the Uyghurs and the Han Chinese. The Chinese government's accusations that Ms. Rebiya Kadeer, the Uyghur leader in exile, is responsible for the rioting is blatantly absurd and only adds to this cycle of violence. Likewise, Uyghur leaders must confront reports that many of the victims of the recent rioting are Han Chinese as well as Uyghurs. Ethnic violence cannot be condoned and only serves to perpetuate the violence that claims victims on all sides.

I call on the Chinese government, my fellow Chinese citizens, and my Uyghur brothers and sisters to take the following constructive actions: 1) Establish an impartial commission to gather the facts and establish the truth. The purpose of this commission will be to determine how and why did a peaceful protest turn into violent rioting that caused so many innocent deaths and injuries. 2) Based on the commission's findings, bring the offending parties to justice through a fair and open trial. 3) For all responsible parties to take actions that build bridges of trust and understanding rather than dig divides through inflammatory rhetoric and stereotyping.

In this regard, the Chinese government bears a great responsibility. As the ruler of China, the CCP is responsible for promoting stability and harmony throughout society. Such a goal can only be achieved by recognizing and respecting the just and peaceful grievances of its citizens. The CCP's tradition of intimidating, demonizing, and incarcerating people whose opinions or beliefs or way of life is different from the Han Chinese model is counterproductive and promotes the very instability it claims to prevent. As a minimal first step, the CCP must cease its divisive and troubling behavior of stereotyping the Uyghurs as "terrorists," the Falun Gong practitioners as "subversive," and the Tibetan people as "ingrates." At the same time, the Uyghurs must realize that violence is neither a strategy nor a solution for their unjust conditions. Violence serves only to strengthen the stereotypes promoted by the CCP. I call on all the Uyghur people to publicly and unequivocally eschew violence in any shape or form.

In conclusion, I call on all friends of freedom and justice, in particular the United States, to work with all concerned to break this violent cycle of ethnic hatred and to restore the rule of law and respect for the dignity of all people living in China.

CHAPTER 35

Leverage the Power That American Values Hold for Billions of People Around the World

Address to US Senator Brownback's Values Action Team
Washington, DC, United States
July 28, 2009

I thank Senator Brownback for inviting me to address you today. I often hear the comment that naturalized Americans make the best citizens because they have a greater appreciation for the values that many native-born Americans take for granted.

I do not know if this is true, but I can tell you with great certainty that many Americans do not fully appreciate, nor does American government today fully leverage, the power that American values hold for billions of people around the world.

So, I will use the few minutes I have with you today to share two stories.

The first story is widely circulated in the prison where I was imprisoned. The story tells of a young man on death row for a crime that should have put him in prison for just a few years. The evening before his execution, he said to his cellmates that next time, before he agrees to be born, he will first look out to see what flag is flying. If he sees the red flag of China, he will refuse to be reborn; he will jump into the world again only if he sees the Stars and Stripes of the United States. Now, no self-respecting Chinese citizen has the desire for China to be the fifty-first state, but the story tells of the Chinese people's deepest respect and yearning for freedom, democracy, and basic rights—values they associate with the United States more than any other place on earth.

When Charter 08, the document signed by leading intellectuals calling for democratic reform, appeared on the internet on December 8, 2008, there was great excitement in China. In the ensuing months, more than 10,000 ordinary Chinese citizens signed the document. Chinese citizens looked to Secretary Clinton's visit last February with great expectations. Thousands gathered around the new Embassy to hear some word of endorsement for Charter 08. I can't tell you how pleased the Chinese Communist Party was, and how devastated millions of Chinese people were, when Secretary Clinton announced that human rights would take a back seat to other issues such as trade and security. We cannot undo what is already done. But I urge all of you to vigorously support the bipartisan Senate Resolution 24 sponsored by Senators Brownback and Casey in support of Charter 08. This is particularly critical as we all know that Dr. Liu Xiaobo, the lead signatory for Charter 08, has now been arrested and charged with inciting subversion of the State. Passage of this resolution before his trial will send a powerful message to the Chinese government.

The second is my personal story.

When I first entered prison, life was hard. I had no reading or writing materials. I spent long days in solitary confinement. I composed poems in my head and committed them to memory as a way of keeping my sanity. I also made a conscious decision to return the hatred and cruelty of my guards with expressions of love. Over time I was able to touch the humanity in some of them. Gradually, I won respect and consideration. One guard obtained a bible for me, clearly in violation of prison rules. One guard in particular took a special interest in my work and provided me with writing materials and magazines. He was instrumental in sending my writings back to the United States. Just before I left prison, he came to me and asked a special favor. He said that he had a very bright and beautiful daughter. He did not want her to be educated without being exposed to the values and the humanities to which I had exposed him. He requested my help in situating his daughter so she might finish high school in the US and go on to an American university.

The humility and the reverence this man showed me brought me to tears. This man is the same one who treated me so cruelly during my early days in prison. Today I am most pleased to share with you that this man's daughter is now living with my family and attending the Commonwealth High School in Boston on a full scholarship.

I shared this story with you so your belief in the universality of justice, truth, and the dignity of the individual will be strengthened. To say that some nationalities do not care about human rights, that they need an authoritarian government, is absurd and self-serving. Regimes that repress their citizens ferment instability, not stability. Just look at the recent events in Iran, Tibet, and Xinjiang Region. The Soviet-era dissident Andrei Sakharov, one of the few people to predict the fall of the Soviet empire, said it correctly when he observed that the world community cannot rely on governments that do not rely on their own people.

You might ask: What options are open to us to promote these universal values? Well, you need look no further than Iran and Xinjiang Region of China. These protests not only show the universal desire for justice and truth, but they also clearly show how we can support those desires. Tyrannies know they cannot survive in the light of truth. That's why regimes like Iran and China spend so much effort in controlling information. That's why the first thing Iran did when their citizens began to protest was to limit media access and disrupt the internet. The free flow of information is the soft underbelly of tyranny and the most powerful sword of freedom. The technology exists to bypass the firewalls erected by governments like China, Vietnam, and Iran. We just need to put this technology in the hands of a critical mass of citizens. This will overwhelm firewall protocols and open the floodgates of freedom. American support for this is vital. I urge your ongoing support for internet freedom initiatives. I especially commend Senator Brownback and Senator

Specter for their bipartisan leadership of the current appropriations bill that earmarks monies for putting firewall-busting technology into the hands of millions of Iranian, Chinese, and Vietnamese citizens. This is putting money behind American values. This is the kind of investments that will secure a peaceful and free world for all Americans and for all of God's children.

Thank you.

CHAPTER 36

Tiananmen's Legacy in Today's Demand for Democracy

Speech at Southern Utah University
Cedar City, UT, United States
September 22, 2009

Good morning. I want to thank you for inviting me to be with you here today. I'd like to begin by talking about an event that I experienced when I was not much older than you are now. It was an event that changed my life and the lives of many others; and it is an event that I believe will ultimately change the future of China.

In the spring of 1989, college students in China led a pro-democracy movement that called for freedom, democracy, more transparency, and less corruption from China's communist leaders. Their protest was peaceful and nonviolent; the protesters were unarmed.

The students gathered in Beijing's Tiananmen Square and erected a statue that resembled the Statue of Liberty. Their version was dubbed the Goddess of Democracy.

Their protest soon gained widespread support, attracting intellectuals, journalists, and labor leaders. Millions of people in Beijing joined them, and almost all classes of Chinese society—including many high-ranking officials—were on their side. These supporters were not just in Beijing; people from all over China sympathized with the protests.

In the middle of May 1989, fellow Chinese students at the University of California at Berkeley selected me to go back to China to join with the students of Tiananmen. I went back as a representative of the overseas Chinese students and fought side by side with the student leaders there.

On the night of June 3, 1989, the communist leaders decided to crack down on the student movement. Chinese tanks and troops swept into the square and opened fire on students and civilians. I was among those who last left the square.

Thousands of people were killed throughout China, and many more were wounded.

But after the massacre, the Chinese government claimed that no students or civilians had been killed by the army, no massacre had happened in Tiananmen Square. It was the "mob" that had blood on its hands; they had killed Chinese soldiers.

Even today, the peaceful pro-democracy movement is still officially described as a "riot" by the communist government.

I was lucky. I managed to avoid arrest and return to the United States where I finished my studies in Mathematics at Berkeley. Tiananmen taught me that freedom is not free. We must work for it and continuously protect it. If not, we will surely lose it. So, I have committed my life to the promotion of a peaceful transition to democracy in China, a China that will not ride roughshod over the fundamental human rights of its people.

After the massacre, the hope that the demonstrations had engendered appeared retrospectively naive to some around the world. Their apparent failure was seen merely as a tragic inevitability—as doomed as the Hungarian Revolution of 1956 or the Prague Spring of 1968.

But the demonstrations of 1989 were not a discrete anomaly in the otherwise tyrannical history of China. Instead, they were a manifestation of a spirit that has always been present in the Chinese people—indeed, a spirit that has always been present in all of humanity. The desire for individual and collective freedoms, and the protection of those freedoms (most successfully embodied in our own times by constitutional democracy), is a fundamental human want—as basic as the need for dignity, respect, and love.

So, while we mourn the fallen of June 4th, let us also honor them by remembering that theirs was not a hopeless, romantic errand. Indeed, the iconic image we have all seen so many times of one nameless man standing down a column of tanks is too often viewed only as a symbol of individual bravery, and ultimate defeat, in the face of overwhelming odds; instead, it should remind us of the dogged practicality of ordinary people in the face of illegitimate authority's hopeless goals.

The democracy movement of 1989 was not confined to students in Beijing. It included millions—millions—of supporters from across China. And even in Beijing, one must remember that at least one quarter, and maybe as many as one third, of officials joined the protestors. And many of those who did not join were sympathetic to some of the demands of the student demonstrators.

Numbers are important to keep in mind when talking about the desire for democracy in China. We have often heard the lie from Chinese dictators that the Chinese people don't much care about enjoying fundamental human rights, and over the years this lie has frequently been explicitly or tacitly accepted by many Western governments, businesses, and ordinary citizens. And yet, consider that not too long after the excesses and bloodletting of the Cultural Revolution, a democracy movement appeared that included millions of Chinese among its supporters and only ended after the merciless and bloody Tiananmen crackdown that momentarily quelled dissent and chilled debate.

Not long after the massacre of the Prague Spring of 1968, Czech writer Milan Kundera gave voice to the hope of those who would remember history: "Before long the nation will forget what it is and what it was. The world around it will forget even faster. The struggle of man against power is the struggle of memory against forgetting."

By that measure, the struggle that began in Tiananmen Square over twenty years ago continues today. It lives in memory and in legacy. It gave birth to an era of protest and the rise of a human rights consciousness among the Chinese people. For the first time in history, the Chinese government faced massive international criticism for its human rights record. Pressure from abroad and rising dissent at home have together helped bring about significant developments in the area of human rights, though much work remains to be done.

Today, with the Tiananmen Massacre still serving as a reminder of the lengths to which China's autocratic, illegitimate, and violent regime will go to suppress dissent, 303 Chinese intellectuals recently published Charter 08, whose signatories now number nearly 10,000.

Charter 08 is a remarkable document that begins, "A hundred years have passed since the writing of China's first constitution. 2008 also mark[ed] the sixtieth anniversary of the promulgation of the Universal Declaration of Human Rights, the thirtieth anniversary of the appearance of [the] Democracy Wall in Beijing, and the tenth of China's signing the International Covenant on Civil and Political Rights. [...] The Chinese people, who have endured human rights disasters and uncountable struggles across these same years, now include many who clearly see that freedom, equality, and human rights are universal values of humankind and that democracy and constitutional government are the fundamental framework for protecting these values."

Charter 08's signatories remind us that the Chinese people's desire for freedom cannot be eliminated by even the most violent and repressive measures. In spite of the ruthless control that is exerted by the Communist Party over Chinese society, the people's longing for democracy regularly manifests itself—even though it is so often answered with violence. And the Chinese government recognizes this—which is why they are now communists in name only.

I said earlier that the nameless hero who bravely stood in front of a column of tanks was acting in the service of practical ends, and not hopelessness, and I want to talk a little bit more about that. You see, today we are in a situation that is both more dire and more hopeful than that faced by the brave demonstrators of 1989. On the one hand, the Chinese government has adjusted to new realities in order to maintain their hold on power. They have responded to pressure because they know that, in the long-term, their rule will be impossible to sustain. Thus, they have willingly jettisoned their ideology and allowed a distinctly undemocratic capitalism to supplant undemocratic communism in hopes that individual wealth will end demands for individual freedoms. But it will not. It cannot, because the desire for freedom is too great; it is too deeply rooted in all of the people who make up our common humanity. Violence, repression, coercion, and propaganda are tyrant's tools utilized in a desperate—and ultimately hopeless—quest to maintain autocracy.

Consider the number of people who engage in activities the Chinese government, with all of the resources at its disposal, aims to prevent—or actually crack down on once they have begun. "Mass incidents" is the term the Chinese government uses to describe protests in which 100 or more people participate. Even underneath the ever-ready tyrant's baton, the number of these "incidents" has risen to 100,000 per year—which means that on average a new, large protest against the government's policies takes place every four or five minutes. Is it not logical to infer from this fact that no amount of violence or propaganda can ever suppress the desire for freedom? One may as well attempt to outlaw love, friendship, or rain.

I am often asked by American friends: "What you say is all well and good, and I am myself convinced about the universality of democracy and freedom, but other than that, why should we care about whether, and how fast, China becomes democratic?"

My answer is simple. If China continues its path of economic development under a one-party dictatorship, it will pose a serious threat to our democratic way of life in the United States. China will serve as a model for dictators and juntas. In fact, it is already a model and a leading supporter of these regimes. Pick a dictator anywhere on the globe—from North Korea to Sudan, from Burma to Zimbabwe, from Cuba to Iran—and you'll almost certainly find that the Chinese regime is supporting it today.

In the United States today, the Chinese government takes advantage of our freedom and democracy to solidify its position at home. It, or its surrogates, has wide access to our universities, think tanks, and media through which they can advance their opinions and rationalize their actions.

The Chinese government has co-opted numerous American businessmen and academics by providing them with favorable business opportunities and all manner of privileges; in turn, they serve the purposes and interests of the Chinese government back in America as lobbyists for favorable policies toward China. Indeed, are not many of our opinions on China clouded by what has been the "business-first" priorities of our China policy which has benefited neither working-class Americans nor ordinary Chinese?

Make no mistake, the expansion of China's military power is also a significant and alarming development. Throughout the past decade, China's defense budget has increased at an annual rate double that of its GDP growth. The Chinese People's Liberation Army is acquiring more than enough power to intimidate surrounding East Asian countries, some of them America's allies. It seems clear that at present, China wants to minimize military confrontation with the United States and seeks instead to concentrate on developing its economy. Yet this could well be a temporary strategy, aimed at delaying conflict with the United States while giving China the time it needs to develop a more powerful military. Who can say what grandiose dreams and ambitions Chinese leaders may harbor twenty or thirty years hence if their regime is richer and stronger?

History and a well-developed body of political theory show that established democracies rarely go to war with one another. If this is true, then the United States has a clear national security stake in whether China becomes an established democracy.

But what leverage do we have with the Chinese government to push for positive change in China in the field of political rights? Some—even those who want to restore human rights as a centerpiece of foreign policy—will say that we have little leverage to effect meaningful change.

Exactly the opposite is true. But a detailed list of effective policies can emerge only after we rid ourselves of the delusions and false assumptions upon which our China policy has long been based. Above all, we must understand democracy in China is homegrown and not imposed by the outside world as many have suggested and many others would worry it would be. But this does not mean that we must sit back and wait for democracy to bloom. Instead, it means engaging with and nurturing democratic forces already at work in China. People often talk about prerequisites for democratization; for me, the most important of all is that there must be democratic forces in Chinese society, and I believe today more than ever that a visionary part of the US engagement policy with China is to openly and systematically engage with the Chinese democratic forces and to nurture their growth.

More than this, we need political leaders who will call attention to the fact that trade has not yet brought, and will never alone bring, an end to political repression or the Chinese Communist Party's monopoly on power. America has been carrying out a policy that benefits business interests in both the United States and China far more than it helps ordinary people in either country. It is time for change.

To that end, I want to offer the idea of Reciprocity as a foreign policy platform.

In 1997, Harvard University invited Jiang Zemin, then-president of China, to speak at the campus. In response to this invitation, I organized a student demonstration, which became the largest campus protest at Harvard since the Vietnam War. Those in favor of Jiang's visit argued for it on the basis of freedom of speech. Our protest argued against it on the grounds of Reciprocity.

The lack of reciprocity gives the Chinese government a huge advantage in the field of world opinion and in tamping down internal dissent. By insisting on reciprocity, the United States and the rest of the world's democracies can showcase their own freedoms while forcing the Chinese government into an untenable position with respect to its denial of basic rights to its citizenry.

As I said earlier tonight, in the United States today, the Chinese government and its surrogates have wide access to our universities, think tanks, and media outlets through which they can advance their opinions and rationalize their actions.

When US government officials travel to China, their movements, their contacts, and their communications are tightly controlled. If officials give a speech, it is not typically broadcast to the Chinese people. Congressman Chris Smith of New Jersey reported that on his last trip to China, his meetings with reform-minded Chinese citizens were suddenly canceled and that he could not access his own website on the internet. Even Presidents Bush and Clinton had their speeches to Chinese citizens blocked when they visited China. Virtually all the American media are blocked or jammed in China. Here in the United States, China can freely broadcast. In fact, it is estimated that over 90% of the Chinese-language media in the US are Chinese-government controlled. The Chinese government exploits our freedoms to extend its influence with Chinese communities in the United States.

In short, there exists no reciprocity between China and the democratic world.

It is fair and appropriate to ask the Chinese government for the same freedoms for its people that we ourselves enjoy, the same access to the Chinese people for our officials and delegations, and the same open discussion and exchange of ideas that we extend to the Chinese government here in the United States. This idea of Reciprocity will allow us to directly and indirectly infuse the issue of human rights into all sectors of our dialogue with China in a way that would make it very difficult for the Chinese government to refuse. It would give the United States, and the other democracies of the world, further leverage in their discussions with China and help to restore the moral compass of the United States as it navigates the choppy seas of world diplomacy.

The United States was founded on the principles of freedom, democracy, and certain inalienable rights. But the desire to meet short-term interests tends to compromise faithfulness to these principles. That inconsistency weakens American credibility. But the United States remains a great country and its people a great people. I have an incurable confidence in American democracy, knowing as I do that its structure always makes it possible for its citizens to correct past mistakes. At present, isolationism is not the solution to the problem of a tarnished international image. Promoting democracy and freedom around the world will panic dictators and gain the interest of even those who have been hoodwinked by their rulers. We should always remember Reverend Martin Luther King Jr.'s admonition that "injustice anywhere is a threat to justice everywhere."

The most practical, and moral, course to follow, in other words, is one which supports and stands together with those many, many nameless individuals in China who bravely put themselves forward as obstacles against the forces of autocracy. Their fight is our fight, and we need only repay their courage with our love, support, and unified and consistent engagement to see their victory through to its rightful end: a just and democratic China.

CHAPTER 37

Only in Friendship Will We Find Freedom, Truth, Equality, and Peace

Opening Remarks at the Fifth Interethnic/ Interfaith Leadership Conference
Washington, DC, United States
October 8, 2009

Dear Brothers and Sisters, Dear Friends,

Many of us have traveled great distances to be here today, but all of us have traveled even further mentally to make this conference possible. The tensions and hostilities that have divided us are like so many open wounds on the body of our common cause. Only by healing these wounds will we march strongly toward the horizon where the dawn of freedom, truth, equality, and peace for us all will one day break.

No matter whom you sit here representing, you have been victimized by the Chinese Communist Party. Tibetans, Uyghurs, Mongolians, and Han; Christians, Falun Gong, and Muslims; all have suffered, and all now suffer, at the hands of this cruel regime. The people of Taiwan, Hong Kong, and Macau: Their freedoms are being compromised by its political and economic intimidation.

The Chinese Communist Party's rule is entirely based on a calculated combination of fear, violence, truth-suppression, ethnic tension and, most recently, a capitalism that trades wealth for silence, money for obedience. The Communist Party's sixty years in power testify to the effectiveness of these tools. But even with efficiency and ruthlessness at its disposal, it has no real future. Its ideals run so counter to the most fundamental human drives for freedom, truth, equality, and peace that it will always be beating back the tide in order to maintain its existence.

We ourselves are part of the crest of this tide, and we are gradually eroding the fortifications of China's ruling regime. Perhaps this is happening more slowly than we would like it to, but we must not allow our occasional impatience to blind us to the fact that this very gathering is one more example of just how much of a failure the last sixty years of communist rule in China have been.

My friends—and let us resolve upon brotherhood as a guiding and uniting principle for our work together—we are each other's keepers, we are each other's freedom, we are each other's peace, we are each other's hope. Over two thousand years ago, the Roman poet Horace wrote, "When your neighbor's house is on fire, your own property is at risk." Today, in China, each one of the houses of freedom is on fire. Mine, yours, and everyone else's. Han, Tibetan, Uyghur, and Mongolian; Christian, Falun Gong, and Muslim; those of the people of Taiwan, Hong Kong, and Macau—we all see and smell the flames that only the strong tide of freedom will quench.

My friends—and let us also resolve that only in friendship will we find freedom, truth, equality, and peace—under the circumstances I have just described, we have no choice but to work together and avoid the divisiveness, apathy, fear, and hatred that will only play into the hands of the Chinese government and feed the status quo.

Make no mistake, the regime is doomed, but inaction or fragmented action will only forestall its eventual crumbling. The world cannot afford another sixty years of Chinese Communist Party rule.

Our plight as people of conscience dedicated to freedom and truth is like that of Ngawang Sangdrol, a 29-year-old woman who was born in Lhasa, Tibet. Before her birth, much of her homeland and its culture had been destroyed by the Chinese government. Ngawang's parents sent her to a nunnery so she could study Buddhist traditions, and when she was thirteen, she joined some people who were demonstrating for freedom of religion.

Her reward was a rope around her neck and a beating by the police. But this did not silence her. Soon after she was released, she joined another demonstration. This time she was sentenced to three years in prison, where she was beaten to unconsciousness and forbidden from practicing Buddhism. Still, she was not silenced. She and some of her fellow prisoners secretly recorded songs praising the Dalai Lama. The recording was smuggled out and it traveled the world. China was pressured to release Ngawang and her fellow prisoners, but it added six years to her sentence instead.

After eleven years in prison, she was sent home. In 2003, she was offered asylum here in the United States. "Freedom is wonderful," she said. She now lives in New Jersey with two other nuns from the prison. Each morning they begin with a prayer, and each day she studies English because, in her words, "It is my duty to speak well enough to explain how my country is suffering, to tell the world that Tibetans deserve freedom, too."

Like Ngawang, it is our duty to learn a new language—it is our duty to speak well enough so that we can put aside our differences and talk to each other anew. Our language must be a unifying language of friendship and common cause. We must use this language to speak to each other, and to the rest of the world, about our joint struggle for freedom, truth, and peace.

Let us start putting these words together today. For not only do our various people deserve freedom for the sake of one another, but so too does the world deserve our freedom for its own sake. Your freedom is my freedom and mine yours.

In the name of brotherhood and friendship, I thank you.

SECTION V

TWO CHINAS AND CHINA, INC: A SOCIETY OF TYRANTS AND SLAVES

March 2010—November 2010

"China, Inc. uses its vast wealth and power to compromise and neutralize the intellectual elite. China, Inc. impresses many observers with its enormous wealth and astonishing growth rate. These observers begin to believe that one-party dictatorship is a good model for economic growth and the progress of society. China, Inc. promotes this idea by controlling all the channels of communication. China, Inc. makes its voice loud enough and suppresses other voices so outside observers believe that they represent China, the whole China.... But there is another China. A China increasingly separated economically and socially from China, Inc. Seventy percent of China's national wealth is divided between just 0.4 percent of Chinese households. That means that a billion Chinese citizens have benefited very little from the economic growth.... Increasingly the picture of two Chinas on the Mainland comes into focus: China, Inc., the tyrants; and the citizens of China, the powerless and exploited."

CHAPTER 38

A Society Divided into Tyrants and Slaves Cannot Last for Long

Speech at the Third Geneva Summit for Human Rights and Democracy
Geneva, Switzerland
March 8, 2010

Good morning, friends, delegates.

Mr. Chairman, thank you for giving me the opportunity to speak today.

I have been asked to share my personal story with you. My story is important not because it is different or exceptional, but because it is very similar to the stories of my 1.4 billion fellow citizens.

I was born three years before the Cultural Revolution, which lasted an entire decade. At an early age, the unspeakable sufferings that most families had at the hands of the communist dictatorship, including mine, made me disenchanted with the Communist Party. After the Cultural Revolution came to an end, however, I was enticed into joining the party with the idea of reforming it from within. This all changed when I returned from my PhD studies in the United States to join tens of thousands of my fellow students as army tanks, at the direction of the Communist Party hardliners, rolled across Tiananmen Square on the morning of June 4, 1989.

After the Tiananmen Massacre, I narrowly escaped back to the United States. While I went on to finish my PhD degree in Mathematics at U.C. Berkeley and then another PhD degree in Political Economy at Harvard, I immersed myself in advancing a peaceful transition to democracy in China. Forgive me, but time and respect for my audience does not allow me to elaborate except that I decided to return to China in 2002 to help the democracy movement with nonviolent struggle strategies. During my attempt to leave China, I was arrested by Chinese authorities and sentenced to five years in prison. Much of those years I spent in solitary confinement. I resorted to composing poems in my head and committing them to memory as a means of maintaining my sanity. Thanks to the overwhelming international support generated by the persistence of my wife, Christina, and with the incredible help from Jared Genser, who represented my case in the United States, my treatment in prison gradually improved.

My prison experience gave me the perfect analogy to describe the course of China under the communist dictatorship. The events of Tiananmen caused a seismic rupture in Chinese society. It was as if China separated into two landmasses: one containing the ruling elite; the other containing the vast majority of powerless Chinese citizens.

The "Two China" society is not so different from the society I experienced in jail: a society of tyrants and slaves. In jail, the tyrants make up all the rules, arbitrarily administer justice, and control what the slaves eat, read, and do.

After Tiananmen, the communist rulers discarded any pretense of communist ideology. They threw open the doors to rapid economic development at any cost. The political elite quickly bonded with the economic elite to become the ruling tyrants of China, Inc. China, Inc. uses its vast wealth and power to compromise and neutralize the intellectual elite. China, Inc. impresses many observers with its enormous wealth and astonishing growth rate. These observers begin to believe that one-party dictatorship is a good model for economic growth and the progress of society. China, Inc. promotes this idea by controlling all the channels of communication. Over 300,000 "cyber cops" monitor and censor information over the internet. The recent disclosures regarding

Google reveal that government cyber espionage is a fact of life for everyone inside and outside of China. China, Inc. makes its voice loud enough and suppresses other voices so outside observers believe that they represent China, the whole China.

But there is another China. A China increasingly separated economically and socially from China, Inc. Data shows that 70% of China's national wealth is divided between just 0.4% of Chinese households. That means that a billion Chinese citizens have benefitted very little from the economic growth. China's minimum wage is only 15% of the world's average, ranking number 159 globally. The minimum wage's contribution to GDP also ranked number 159 globally, behind thirty-two African countries. What ranked on the opposite end of the spectrum is its Tax Misery Index. It ranked two or three for several years in a row. These data do not take into account any undocumented but heavy and widespread fees and uncompensated property takeovers. Up to today, the powerless China has been refused to any form of basic universal social security. However, a member of China, Inc. enjoys all kinds of privileges till death. A billion Chinese citizens have no political protection or means for redressing grievances. The judicial system of China reports to the Communist Party. Freedom of expression and ideas are systematically repressed. Increasingly, the picture of two Chinas on the Mainland comes into focus: China, Inc., the tyrants, and the citizens of China, the powerless and exploited.

History tells us that a society divided into tyrants and slaves cannot last for long. So too, China, Inc. and the powerless, exploited China will not endure for long. The question is how these two Chinas can be made whole again in a way that is peaceful and enduring.

The vehicle for a peaceful unification of these two Chinas is already designed. Charter 08 has defined the terms and set the language for building a new bond between rulers and the ruled. It defines a new covenant of governance through the rule of law and the respect for cultural diversity. Despite every possible attempt by the Chinese government to eradicate it, over 11,000 Chinese citizens have given their real names and signatures to this document.

Like Charter 77, the designers of Charter 08 can be jailed and vilified, but the ideas they drew live on. Charter 08 provides the vehicle to carry a billion Chinese citizens to the threshold of freedom. This is why the communist rulers reacted so harshly in its handling of many Chinese civic leaders represented by Liu Xiaobo, a leading signatory of Charter 08, who was sentenced to eleven years in prison on Christmas Eve of last year. These civic leaders believe in and work for integration of the two diverged societies based on justice. But the Chinese government is afraid of such an integration and, therefore, has always tried to contain and persecute Chinese civic leaders. Some of them have been sent into exile overseas, others were put in jail. Still others were followed, monitored, or put under house arrest.

Chinese civic leaders have no public space before China can make any real progress toward democracy. So, we must work relentlessly on their freedom.

If Charter 08 is the vehicle to carry the citizens of China to freedom, then the internet is the highway along which they will travel. The internet is the product of the Information Age and represents a new ladder for human civilization. Wherever the internet reaches, it enhances commercial productivity, increases government transparency and stimulates social vitality to the benefit of all mankind. Only the regimes like the CCP view the internet as a scourge and exhausts its mental, financial, and manpower resources to infiltrate, intercept, block, and close it off, creating a succession of internet "Berlin Walls" such as "Golden Shield" and "Green Dam," and training and employing myriad internet police, informers and "50 Cent Party" members. In a recent meeting of the Party leadership, President Hu Jintao emphasized that the survival of the Communist Party's leadership was dependent on its ability to control the internet.

But the economics of internet control does not bode well for the tyrants of China. As the internet base expands in China, the costs of censorship outpace the cost of bypassing that censorship by a factor of 10:1. Soon there will be so many holes in the great firewalls that like the proverbial dike, it will be impossible to maintain. Without the ability to control the internet, the CCP will not be able to control the will of one billion Chinese citizens.

As that day approaches, a crisis of confidence will emerge during which the power elite will be thrown off balance, and the one billion citizens of China will realize they are no longer slaves. It will not be a green or a velvet revolution, but perhaps it will be called the cyber revolution. But nonetheless, a crisis will occur, just as the crisis occurred in 1989. A key to ensuring that this crisis ends peacefully and concludes with the transition to a democratic form of governance will be the response of the international community.

China must determine its own future. But just as America looked to France during its struggle for independence and Europe looked to America for its liberation from National Socialism, the citizens of China will be looking to the world to weigh in on the side of the people. It cannot, for the sake of China and the future of stability of the world, stay on the sidelines as it did in 1989.

CHAPTER 39

Our Diverse Cultures and Histories No Longer Separate Us from an Unprecedented Unity of Purpose

Vietnam Freedom Day Speech
Washington, DC, United States
May 11, 2010

Good afternoon, Senator Brownback, Dr. Binh Nguyen, and friends. I am pleased to be here today to observe with you the Sixteenth Commemoration of Vietnam Human Rights Day and to celebrate our common belief that freedom and human dignity will come to our respective homelands.

I have just returned from an extensive trip to Europe and Asia, where I had the honor to co-chair with Atebi of Iran, the committee on Internet Freedom at the Geneva Summit for Human Rights and Democracy, and also lead a Han Chinese delegation to Dharamsala, India, to visit with his Holiness the Dalai Lama during the fifty-first anniversary of the exile of his Holiness. I also was invited to address a Uyghur convention in Istanbul, Turkey. I returned here to the United States invigorated by the experience of a new sense of unity. A realization that our diverse cultures and histories no longer separate us from an unprecedented unity of purpose. A realization that mutual respect, understanding, and common action are necessary ingredients for the achievement of our common goals of freedom, justice, and dignity. As I spoke with his holiness the Dalai Lama, his freedom is my freedom, so I tell you today that your struggle for justice in Vietnam is also my struggle.

I would like to talk with you today about two aspects of internet freedom. We are all united in belief that control of the internet is vital for the rulers in Vietnam, Iran, and China to maintain their authoritarian power. Over the past year, we have worked together through letters to Secretary Clinton, with Senator Brownback, and concerned patriots like Michael Horowitz, to push funding for the quick expansion of proven protocols that will give uncensored and unmonitored internet access to tens of millions of citizens in these closed societies. We must continue to work together on this initiative as there is no doubt that the electronic superhighway is the fast track to freedom in our respective countries. The delegates to the Geneva Summit for Human Rights and Democracy were unanimous in this belief and in their support for the Geneva Declaration of Internet Freedom, which was drafted at the Summit. I call for a concerted effort among the world's concerned citizens, from closed societies and free ones alike, to push this document to the UN so that the UN will pass its version of a World Declaration of Internet Freedom.

I look forward to our collaboration on this important initiative.

The other aspect of internet freedom I want to share with you is equally important. On January 21, Secretary of State Hillary Clinton gave a great speech on internet freedom. In that speech, she remarked that internet censorship contributes to an imbalance of information that "increases both the likelihood of conflict and the probability that small disagreements could escalate." This is a profound statement. Censorship causes conflict because it generates misinformation, incomplete information, and lies. We must consider that the internet firewalls constructed by China, Iran, and Vietnam control what people see and think on both sides of the wall. We in the West and, in particular, here in the United States are victims of the Great Firewall almost as much as the Chinese and Vietnamese people living behind these walls. We know what is going on in China and Vietnam. But most people see the China and Vietnam that these authoritarian governments want us to see. Their media control and censorship allow them to project a carefully fabricated picture that does not reflect the reality of life for citizens in Vietnam and China.

Time does not permit me to elaborate, except to give you a very specific example of how we are victimized by internet censorship and how this censorship affects our opinions and, ultimately, our policies.

On May 1, the world's largest international trade exhibition opened in Shanghai. The Western media was full of articles praising what the *New York Times* called "a monumental" achievement. The *New York Times* article went on to detail the effort expended by the Chinese government to make the expo a reality. According to the *Times*, this effort included "moving 18,000 families and 270 factories employing 10,000 workers." This effort was presented as a positive and significant achievement. The entire article reinforced the impression of China as a progressive, harmonious, and advanced society. Thousands of similar articles appeared in the Western media.

What these articles overlooked in their praise of Chinese progress was the fact that "moving" 18,000 families involved forced eviction, destruction of homes, and disruption of lives for tens of thousands of people. These people had no recourse for compensation or redress of their grievances. This is not an isolated instance, but a common practice in China, and I am sure in Vietnam as well. These are countries that are not progressive or stable or harmonious. They are countries without the rule of law, without any system of checks and balances, without any process for citizens to redress their grievances. These homes are now entombed beneath three square miles of exhibits from international corporations and organizations, including the United Nations.

One of the victims of forced eviction in Shanghai was Hu Yan, a young mother whose home was destroyed. She has waged a five-year battle for justice. Earlier this year, she came to the United States and has been camping out across the street from the UN in a tent called the "Hidden Shanghai Expo." Last week she had a press conference across the street from UN headquarters in New York. Not one US media showed up at the conference.

The information that people received on both sides of the wall was one of a China that is progressive and advanced. The other China, the sad reality of Hu Yan and hundreds of millions of other citizens, was a China without respect or care for its citizens.

This type of misinformation and incomplete information is repeated every day thousands of times. It becomes a source for decision-making and policymaking. Bad information makes bad policy, and bad policy leads to misunderstanding and, ultimately, conflict.

As we fight for internet freedom, we must fight for freedom and truth on both sides of the wall of censorship. We must reach out to journalists and newspapers to push for balanced reporting and take them to task when they do not. We must make sure congressman and senators get complete information and facts in a timely manner. We must make sure that we do not give the governments of China and Vietnam free passes to spread sugar-coated information about life inside these regimes. If each of us works together to do this, we can put these governments on the defensive. We may not have might on our side, but we have right. And as the famous proverb goes: You shall know the truth and the truth shall make you free.

Thank you.

CHAPTER 40

Jared Genser Is One of Those People

Speech at the Charles Bronfman Prize Presentation Ceremony
New York, NY, United States
October 28, 2010

Thank you, Stephen, for that kind introduction and my sincere thanks to Charles, members of the Bronfman family, and the judges for honoring my good friend and former lawyer, Jared Genser, along with Sasha Chanoff with the 2010 Charles Bronfman Prize. In my brief remarks today, I'd like to speak about my own experience with Jared and the power of Freedom Now's efforts to support prisoners of conscience around the world.

Through Freedom Now, Jared served for more than five years as my family's attorney—entirely pro bono—after I was detained in China in April 2002. By way of some background, I was in Tiananmen Square in the early morning hours of June 4, 1989. I had returned to China several weeks previously to support the students from a PhD program I was pursuing at the University of California at Berkeley. I witnessed dozens of people gunned down in the streets. I returned to the United States several days later and testified to the US Congress about what I had seen. For this and for my continued activism, I was blacklisted by the Chinese government and no longer able to return to my country.

I helped found a few major pro-democracy organizations overseas, including the Foundation for China in the 21st Century, of which I was president for more than ten years until April 2002.

In April 2002, despite the informal prohibition on my return to China, I entered the country to help the emerging labor movement with nonviolent struggle strategies. I was detained on April 26, 2002, and was initially held *incommunicado* for more than fourteen months, denied access to reading material and exercise, and interrogated over 120 times.

I later learned that within a few days of my arrest, a budding human rights lawyer got in touch with my wife, Christina, to offer to help. Those early days were especially tough for Christina and our two children, and he made clear that it was going to be a tough fight but that with persistence, they would persevere. That young man was, of course, Jared Genser, whom I had met while pursuing a second PhD in Political Economy at Harvard Kennedy School of Government. We worked together as part of a core group that organized the protests against then-Chinese President Jiang Zemin during his trip to Harvard in November 1997. Back then, Jared may have been younger, but his sense of purpose was just as strong.

Working with NYU Law Professor Jerome Cohen, Jared initially filed a petition to the UN Working Group on Enforced and Involuntary Disappearances because the Chinese government, in violation of its own law, refused to tell my family where I was being detained. He subsequently filed a petition to the UN Working Group on Arbitrary Detention, which ultimately found I was being detained in violation of international law. In announcing the Working Group judgment, Jared organized a press conference on Capitol Hill with a bipartisan group of members of Congress and my wife. With the widespread media coverage this attracted, the Chinese government was on the defensive. I felt the results immediately within my cell. With a week of the decision being released, I was provided access to my domestic lawyer.

Through regular updates from him, I was to learn of Jared's remarkable and unyielding support from the outside. After the UN judgment, he guided my wife and family to persuade more than fifty members of Congress to support a congressional resolution calling for my release. After being unanimously adopted on the floor of the House of Representatives in June 2003 on a vote of 412–0, a subsequent Senate resolution was introduced and also unanimously adopted.

Meanwhile, Jared led a relentless campaign of political and public relations pressure against the Chinese government, using every key moment to attract attention to my ongoing detention. He secured 119 members of Congress and forty US Senators to write to President Bush and Chinese President Hu Jintao calling for my release. He held countless press conferences at key moments in my detention. And he published op-eds in such newspapers as the *Washington Post*, *International Herald Tribune*, *South China Morning Post*, and others. His campaign raised the profile of my case to a top priority of the Bush Administration. Perhaps the best illustration of this is that by the time I was released, my case had been raised personally by President Bush twice to the Chinese president and by former Secretaries of State Rice and Powell. And former US Ambassador to China Clark Randt had raised my case more than sixty times.

With all of the pressure on the Chinese government, it ultimately put me on trial for espionage and illegal entry but gave me only a five-year prison sentence. While I served my full prison term, the impact of Jared's work was nevertheless profound. First, from within my cell, I knew I had a special measure of protection. I was treated far better than most inmates. Second, while at first glance a five-year sentence might seem like a lot of time in prison, the context makes a big difference. For the espionage charge alone, I could have been executed or even given life in prison without parole. In a judicial system where the conviction rate for political offenses is virtually 100 percent, I was given the lowest sentence possible under the circumstances. And third, on three occasions, I was actually offered early release, but I declined because the Chinese government insisted that I accept a number of conditions, including my agreeing never to return to my homeland again.

At the end of it all, I finally returned to Boston's Logan Airport more than five years after I left, on August 18, 2007. Along with my wife, daughter, son, and other family members, Jared was there to greet me. As he promised my wife, he was there every step of the way to the very end. I have no doubt that without Jared's relentless efforts, instead of being here today, I would still be languishing in a Chinese prison.

Beyond his success on my case, the results he has achieved through Freedom Now are extraordinary. Since 2001, with his colleagues, he has built from scratch an organization that has achieved the release of an ever-growing number of prisoners of conscience. Each former prisoner has a personal story like mine to tell, such as Nyi Nyi Aung, a Burmese American imprisoned wrongly in Burma who is with us here tonight—and each of us are profoundly grateful for Jared and Freedom Now's help.

Since returning to the United States in August 2007, I founded a new organization called Initiatives for China, which is working to advance a peaceful transition to democracy for China. One of our first big projects was a 500-mile walk that I completed from Boston to Washington from May 4th to June 4th, stopping in ten communities along the way to speak to government officials, community groups, and the media to raise awareness of why Americans should care about the challenges facing the Chinese people.

I've helped organize a series of Interethnic/Interfaith Leadership Conferences to facilitate dialogue and foster understanding among Uyghur, Tibetan, Mongolian, native Taiwanese, people from Hong Kong, people from Macau, Han Chinese, and other nationalities; Falun Gong; and the Christian House Church Movement. In that context, we discussed the way to promote a democratic China that embraces all of its ethnic and religious people, something that is adverse to the approach of the Chinese Communist Party, which has sought centralized control and to divide Chinese people from each other.

None of these broader impacts from my work would have occurred but for Freedom Now's approach of selecting high-impact cases where freeing a single person could have this kind of ripple effect. And it's not just me. Without Freedom Now having successfully helped free the journalist Lewis Medjo in Cameroon, his newspaper would no longer exist. And Cameroonians would have one less outlet for independent media—an ever-endangered category. I could go on. It's clear that Freedom Now's targeting of clients who will make a deep impact in their country once freed is vital.

And Freedom Now's efforts to choose those cases that are representative of a broader set of abuses in a country have an equally important impact. This means that Freedom Now can draw the world's attention to the increasing practice of the Uzbek government in targeting human rights defenders with extortion charges, such as with their client Akzam Turgunov. Or as with my own country, Freedom Now can draw attention to the Chinese government's growing targeting of human rights lawyers, such as with the disappearance of Gao Zhisheng.

As you can see, it's a truly remarkable organization. And since my return, I am especially pleased to have played a small part in supporting Freedom Now's transition from an all-volunteer to fully staffed organization by providing it free office space in Washington during its first year of staffed operations. Now Freedom Now is rapidly expanding and has in the last few months been able to take on ten new cases of prisoners of conscience, each of whom will have their own ripple effects.

One of those new cases is that of a friend and colleague of mine. I am so very proud to have introduced Liu Xia to Freedom Now so we could work collaboratively to secure her husband's release from prison. While many of you may not know her name, earlier this month her husband Liu Xiaobo won the 2010 Nobel Peace Prize.

But back to Jared. While he is Jewish and I am Christian, we share a common and strong faith in God. I know that his faith and his values, instilled in him by his parents, and shared by his wife, Lisa, both provide the foundation for his work and will be passed on to their son, Zachary.

Very few people in the world have the combination of intelligence, charisma, determination, and humility to have the power to save human lives. But Jared is one of those people. And the ripple effect of his efforts will be felt for generations to come. In my own case, instead of languishing in a Chinese prison, I am now able to dedicate the balance of my life pursuing freedom and democracy for the Chinese people. My family and I are eternally grateful.

CHAPTER 41

China's Repression of Its People Calls into Question China's Contention That Benevolent Authoritarianism Can Coexist with a Genuine Rule of Law

Testimony at Canadian Parliament International Subcommittee
Ottawa, Ontario, Canada
October 28, 2010

Thank you for inviting me to speak to you today. I will use this valuable time at this historic moment of the award of the Nobel Peace Prize to our great countryman, Liu Xiaobo, to put into context what this award means to the people of China and what an opportunity it is for democracies around the world to finally bring freedom to our homeland and true peace and stability to the world.

In the opening paragraph of its announcement of selection of Liu Xiaobo to receive the 2010 Nobel Peace Prize, the Nobel Committee made a simple but profound statement. I quote: *"The Norwegian Nobel Committee has long believed that there is a close connection between human rights and peace. Such rights are a prerequisite for the 'fraternity between nations' of which Alfred Nobel wrote in his will."*

I am here today to plead with you, representatives of a great democracy, to consider this statement very carefully. For too long, the democracies of the world have too often ignored this unbreakable bond between democracy and world peace. For too long the democracies of the world have lulled themselves into thinking that human and political rights for the Chinese people will automatically follow in the wake of China's embrace of a market economy. All we need to do is to be patient and let nature take its course.

The people of the world have welcomed the Chinese government into the community of nations. We have welcomed it without strings attached. We have awarded it the privilege of hosting the Olympics. We have given it membership in the World Trade Organization. It is a member of the UN Security Council and the inner circle of the G20. We have done all this and more driven by the misguided, unfounded, and blind belief that the Chinese government will unilaterally embrace democratic reform.

We must now recognize that just the opposite has occurred. The *Washington Post* raised the warning flag in an editorial of July 11 of this year. The title of the op-ed piece was "China's Thin Skin." In it the *Post* clearly stated that Western democracies' toleration of China's disregard for human rights and the rule of law has only emboldened the government to increase its repression. I quote: *"China's human rights record is dismal enough that the latest crackdown on political opposition should not surprise, but there is a disturbing new element, human rights activists say: the government's total lack of reticence in going after even high-profile targets... The brazenness is a reflection of Beijing's increasing assertiveness in the international sphere—and its calculation that there is little or no price to be paid in its relations with the United States or other nations for abusing its own citizens."*

The article went on to say that the Chinese government's repression of its people *"calls into question China's contention that benevolent authoritarianism can coexist with a genuine rule of law. And the regime's fear of criticism from its own people calls into question the self-confidence that supposedly undergirds its increased assertiveness abroad."*

The vociferous reaction of the Chinese government to the award of the Nobel Peace Prize to Liu Xiaobo shows how out of touch the government in Beijing is with the world community and how fearful it is that the world will see that its claim that authoritarian rule has created a stable and harmonious society is nothing more than a myth right out of the fairy tale *The Emperor's New Clothes.*

The fact is that the Chinese government's repression of its people is accelerating with its fear of losing its illegitimate and unilateral hold on power. From the Uyghurs of East Turkestan to the Tibetan people, to the burgeoning Christian community, to the intellectuals such as Liu Xiaobo and Gao Zhisheng, the Chinese government has alienated virtually every segment of Chinese society. Instead of harmony and stability, its philosophy of destroy dissent at any cost has created a cauldron of discontent. This discontent is beautifully explained in the opening words of Charter 08, the document whose authorship resulted in Liu Xiaobo's imprisonment. The *"Chinese government's approach to 'modernization' has proven disastrous. It has stripped people of their rights, destroyed their dignity, and corrupted normal human intercourse. So, we ask: Where is China headed in the twenty-first century? Will it continue with "modernization" under authoritarian rule, or will it embrace universal human values, join the mainstream of civilized nations, and build a democratic system? There can be no avoiding these questions."*

Increasingly the Chinese's government's answer is NO!

Its persecution of its citizens is more widespread than ever before. Imprisonment, intimidation, and torture take place everywhere, against all strata of society and all areas of human endeavor.

Forced evictions of citizens to make way for grandiose schemes of the government and for enriching the pockets of local officials is rampant: 300,000 people were forced from their homes in Beijing to make way for the 2008 Olympics; 18,000 families were displaced with little or no compensation and without recourse to make way for the Shanghai Expo, an act that the UN-Habitat called a "monumental achievement."

Forced abortions under the most inhumane circumstances are a fact of life for women in China and accounts for the fact that of all the industrialized nations, only China has more females who commit suicide than their male counterparts.

Workers slave in factories making goods for Western consumers for below subsistence wages.

The cases of Liu Xiaobo and Gao Zhisheng highlight the brutal repression of free expression and the emasculation of the independent scholars, human rights lawyers, and professionals.

The discontent and alienation are so deep and widespread that more than 120,000 large scale demonstrations occur each year in China that go largely unreported in the West.

To keep a lid on this cauldron of discontent, the Chinese government has constructed an unprecedented police state, or as the Chinese government calls it, "a stability preserving system." This huge security apparatus costs the Chinese people over five trillion yuans of RMB each year. This security system is out of control and clearly shows the paranoia of this regime and its attitude that its citizens are enemies to be mentally and socially controlled at all costs. For instance, Chen Guangcheng, the recently released blind human rights lawyer, is closely watched by about thirty security agents at any given time. It has become common practice for the government to hire thugs and gangsters to beat and kidnap dissidents and family members to intimidate them into silence.

I could go on all day, but the record is clear. The Chinese government is increasingly backed into a corner. It cannot hold a gun to its people forever, and now with the award of the Peace Prize to Liu Xiaobo, its myth of benevolent dictatorship is exposed. Its empty threats to the government of Norway and to the West show how precarious the Chinese government sees its situation.

The question is, "Will we continue to ignore reality and allow the Chinese government to continue its self-destructive ways with serious consequences to the Chinese people and to world stability? Or will we help the Chinese government to truly join the world community by embracing the universal values of democracy and the rule of law?"

In this regard I offer the following suggestions:

- We replace the policy of patience and acquiesce with a policy of Reciprocity. That is, in our relations with China we connect its ability to enjoy the fruits of an open society through trade relations, academic exchanges, media, etc. to its demonstrated advances in opening freedom of speech and internet access in their own society.
- Canada and China had a human rights dialogue between 1996 and 2006. I urge that it be reopened with the caveat that human rights groups be involved.
- The Canadian Parliament establishes a foundation that actively supports the Chinese democracy movement based in North America.

Time does not permit me to elaborate on these points. But I will leave you with this counsel. Proceed with strength. Engage with confidence. Democratic reform must come to China for the sake of world peace. We must help the Chinese government make this transition peacefully. Do not fear negative reaction by the Chinese government. It knows that it is in a precarious position. All its rhetoric is the bluffing of a desperate regime that knows its time is running out. It does not know what to do. We must help them with our firmness and guidance. Above all we must back our words with actions.

Addendum for the General Situation

1. The persecution is more widespread than before, although the punishment may be milder in many cases.

   Persecution, imprisonment, harassment, and physical torture take place everywhere, in any field, against all kinds of people: dissidents, independent scholars, rights lawyers, and petitioners.

   The number of protests with participation of 100 or more people has climbed to 120,000 each; this alone produces numerous targeted people.

2. In the past twenty years, the Chinese government has built up a so-called "Stability Preserving" system, which costs taxpayers five trillion yuans of RMB each year. We all know what "preserving stability" means. It takes the general public as enemies, the Olympics, the Shanghai World Expo, the National Day Saga... The Chinese government is resolved to keep "stability" at all costs.

   Chen Guangcheng, the newly released blind lawyer, for example, and his family have been closely watched by about thirty people at any given time, literally placing the entire family under house arrest.
3. It has become a common governmental practice to hire thugs, members of gangsters, in keeping "stability," force evictions, land grabbing, and so on and so forth. Sun Wenguang, Li Heping, Liu Dejun, Liu Shasha, and numerous other rights defenders have had experiences of being kidnapped and beaten up by "unidentified" people.
4. The authorities have revived the old strategy in many cases of implicating family members. It has become increasingly common, especially when it comes to the persecution against the victims of family-planning policy and forced evictions.
5. Attack on "online crimes" has intensified. Last week, for example, a girl who posted on Twitter a sentence suggesting having a slogan, "Hello, Uncle Xiaobo," in an anti-Japanese demonstration was soon taken away by the police, and released only under pressure generated by Twitter.
6. Whenever the government-deemed sensitive dates come around, numerous people in municipalities like Beijing would be placed under house arrest or taken to police station or a restaurant for "a cup of tea." Beijing alone involves more than 200 people.

CHAPTER 42

This Will Happen If We Walk Together in the Path of Truth, Peace, and Freedom

Speech at the Sixth International Conference of Tibet Support Groups
New Delhi, India
November 5, 2010

Your Holiness, ladies and gentlemen, distinguished guests, and my dear Tibetan brothers and sisters:

I am honored and humbled to speak with you today. I am honored because I am with YOU, whose extraordinary struggle for freedom has won worldwide respect. I am humbled because your suffering has been at the hands of a government that is largely Han Chinese, of which I am a member. Yet, you reach out your hands in friendship. You hold your suffering close to your heart while keeping a smile on your face. The wisdom and guidance of His Holiness the Dalai Lama have shown a path to justice paved with peace and nonviolence for all to follow. I am indeed honored and humbled to follow the path of His Holiness and to walk with you and call each of you my brother.

The Middle Way Approach recognizes that the policies of the Chinese government against the Tibetan people are not the intention of the Chinese people. It is these policies that are the obstacles to peace and justice and not the Chinese people who suffer with you and alongside you. In recognition of this distinction, His Holiness has consistently reached out to Han Chinese in the spirit of peace and justice for all. His embrace communicates that the struggle of the Tibetan people is really a struggle for the heart and soul of all people living under the rule of the Chinese communist regime.

I am here today to share with you some great events that are proving the wisdom of His Holiness' vision.

The first event is the Nobel Peace Prize awarded to Liu Xiaobo. In announcing this prize, the Nobel Committee stated, "The Norwegian Nobel Committee has long believed that there is a close connection between human rights and peace. Such rights are a prerequisite for the 'fraternity between nations' of which Alfred Nobel wrote in his will."

This statement clearly puts the spotlight on the policies of the Chinese government as a challenge to world peace as well as to the dignity of man. The hateful reaction of the Chinese government to this award clearly shows the fear of a cornered beast. The fear of a beast that is confronted with the truth that its lies and hatreds have run their course and it has nowhere to hide. Let's hear what Charter 08 has to say: "The Chinese government's rule has been a disaster for all people of China. It has stripped people of their rights, destroyed their dignity, and corrupted normal human intercourse. So, we ask: Where is China headed in the twenty-first century? Will it continue with 'modernization' under authoritarian rule, or will it embrace universal human values, join the mainstream of civilized nations, and build a democratic system? There can be no avoiding these questions."

These words of truth have put Liu Xiaobo in jail. But now the Nobel Peace Prize has turned the light of justice on the jailer. We must all seize this opportunity to stand shoulder to shoulder to show the world that his suffering is our suffering. We must seize this opportunity to show the world that the policies of the Chinese government are not bringing harmony and stability but rather despair and discontent.

The second event, I am happy to say, is that the patience of His Holiness is bearing fruit among the Han Chinese. We are now seeing the threat to the people of Tibet as a threat to us all. More and more leading Han Chinese intellectuals have come to condemn the policies of the Chinese government that seek to eradicate the Tibetan language from the face of the earth. Without the Tibetan language, the Tibetan culture will cease to exist. The Tibetan language, which is the soul and blood of the Tibetan culture, must be the first official language spoken in Tibet. Prejudice against a language is always discrimination against its speakers. Cultural genocide begins with linguistic genocide. By the same token, a genuine autonomy is foremost a cultural autonomy, which begins with a linguistic autonomy. The people of Tibet have every right to preserve their culture and determine their future. The Chinese people must embrace this and see to it that our Tibetan brothers and sisters can freely express their own minds in their own mother tongue on their own land, free of fear and full of hope.

I look forward to the Nobel Peace Prize award ceremony when the delegation to receive the prize will be not just Han Chinese but a rainbow of people who share a common democratic destiny, a rainbow of languages, cultures, and religions standing together to tell the world and the Chinese government that if Liu Xiaobo is subversive, then we are all subversives; if the Dalai Lama is a terrorist, then we are all terrorists.

I also look forward to hosting another Interethnic/Interfaith Leadership Conference that will continue to embrace diversity and make the promotion of the right to speak and preserve one's language its cornerstone theme.

We will follow the conference with cooperative actions that keep the light on the jailer and keep the pressure on the world to get this government to recognize, respect, and preserve the dignity of its people.

This can be done, and it will be done. For I now live in a country, the United States, where one man had a dream that the black children of the US would sit side by side with the white children. It is because of the dream of this one man that black people now share in the American dream in ways that were unthinkable a generation ago.

I too have that dream that Tibetans, Uyghurs, Christians, and Buddhists can live their lives, raise their children in a rainbow of diversity that will spread across the sky over our homelands, that is, diversity under universality of human rights.

This will happen if we walk together in the path of truth, peace, and justice. Let me close with a little story. Earlier this year in Dharamsala, I was in the audience with His Holiness with a group of Chinese freedom fighters. At the end of the meeting we all stood up together. I noticed that he had a pair of shoes of very good quality. I whispered to His Holiness that he had a pair of very fine shoes, much nicer than mine. "Yes," His Holiness replied. "I will walk home in them." I replied, "Yes, your Holiness, I will walk with you." We suddenly found ourselves embracing each other.

Now is the time for us to embrace one another as we walk together united in our diversity and toward our common goal of peace, justice, and freedom. The time has come. Thank you.

SECTION VI

THE LIU XIAOBO STORY: THE UNIVERSAL HUMAN DESIRE FOR FREEDOM

December 2010—February 2012

"Around the world, buried in prison cells, in sunless living graves, there are rights activists whose sole ray of hope is a beacon of freedom they only know about from the dedicated people at these human rights organizations....The prisoners of conscience have not always been in chains. Let me remind you. Liu Xiaobo worked as a visiting scholar here at Columbia University. At Columbia University, he could freely voice his opinions....But today, as I stand here talking so calmly and openly with you, Liu Xiaobo sits in a jail in Liaoning in northeastern China, far from his wife and family. His crime...? Merely proposing that those very same freedoms, which we enjoy here and have enjoyed for centuries, apply in his home country as well....Liu Xiaobo represents a new kind of politics in China; a politics not based on hatred of an enemy but on love for human dignity and the fundamental human desire to be free."

CHAPTER 43

If Liu Xiaobo Is Guilty, Then We Are All Guilty

Speech at Event Supporting Liu Xiaobo Hosted by the Visual Artists Guild, PEN America, and Reporters Without Borders
Columbia University, New York, NY, United States
December 5, 2010

Thank you, Ann and Anna, for organizing this conference and for giving me this chance to address you. I feel honored and humbled standing here.

For the past several years, my friends at the Visual Artists Guild, PEN, and Reporters Without Borders have supported Liu Xiaobo and his work and his cause and Charter 08, unfailingly. Your valuable work represents the profound international community support for human rights in my country, China. It keeps us sane in a situation which could easily be characterized as its opposite.

Around the world, buried in prison cells, in sunless living graves, there are rights activists whose sole ray of hope is a beacon of freedom they only know about from the dedicated people at these human rights organizations.

The prisoners of conscience have not always been in chains. Let me remind you. Liu Xiaobo worked as a visiting scholar here at Columbia University. At Columbia University, he could freely voice his opinions.

But today, as I stand here talking so calmly and openly with you, Liu Xiaobo sits in a jail in Liaoning in northeastern China, far from his wife and family. His crime…? Merely proposing that those very same freedoms which we enjoy here and have enjoyed for centuries apply in his home country as well.

Why…? Why are these proposals a crime in China…?

After his sentencing last year, Liu Xiaobo said in a statement: "I have long been aware that when an independent intellectual stands up to an autocratic state, step one toward freedom is often a step into prison. Now I am taking that step; and true freedom is that much nearer."

Now Liu Xiaobo is taking that first step. Now we are standing together to send a message to the world and more directly to the Chinese government: If Liu Xiaobo is guilty, then we are all guilty; if Liu Xiaobo is subversive, then we are all subversives.

In a few days, I will be in Oslo, bearing witness to another important moment in the history of China's democracy movement: the Nobel Prize Committee will hold the ceremony to award the 2010 Nobel Peace Prize to Liu Xiaobo for "his long and nonviolent struggle for fundamental human rights in China."

This is a moment millions of Chinese have been waiting for.

I also have waited for this moment. But as I plan my Oslo journey, my joy is tinged with sorrow. My mind is weighted with the solemn memories of friends who cannot travel with me.

Liu Xiaobo and Liu Xia are not allowed to see the day themselves in Norway. There will be an empty seat when the spotlight moves to where the Nobel laureate should be. Speeches, like this, will be made by everyone except the most deserving one.

The Prize brings people joy, but it also brings more pressure for results. At this moment, Liu Xiaobo is still incarcerated and has lost all contact with the outside world, and Liu Xia has been "made missing" as well. A few days ago, one internet commenter I saw joked about dreaming he had won the Nobel Peace Prize himself and that this scared him awake. Under such circumstances, the only thing I could say is that there is much left to be done and our mission is far from finished. Yet we have enough knowledge to make a judgment, namely, that we are on the correct road. As long as we commit ourselves to our goal, we can achieve it.

I am proud to tell you that despite CCP's repression, the civil movement in China is making solid progress. The best example is that, by now, 12,000 people inside China have signed off on Charter 08. And they've signed using their real names despite the possible consequences. Those signatures stand for themselves. They tell the CCP 12,000 times over that we do not intend to be silent about our predicament.

And every day we see still more people stand up against the government to defend their own rights. More and more people are making their true voice heard. All these changes are incremental, but they are solid, they are sincere, they are powerful and they are leading to a paradigm shift in the future.

Yes, Liu Xiaobo is taking these steps; so are many other prisoners of conscience.

Each prisoner of conscience has a sad but still inspiring story to tell. Each of these stories is a China story. Each incorporates China's past, present, and future. The long-term dedication and sacrifice made by Liu Xiaobo, as well as by all the prisoners of conscience, have lowered the risk for others to participate in the pro-democratic movement in China. Their courageous efforts are gradually turning the cause that was originally done by heroes into work that can be done by ordinary people. With our united efforts, I assure you this process will continue, and it will continue until the day when the people of China will live free of fear and full of hope. Thanks to generations of struggle of the Chinese people represented by Liu Xiaobo, thanks to your unwavering support from the international community, that day is much nearer.

Thank you!

CHAPTER 44

To You, Xiaobo and Liu Xia, to the People of China, to Freedom!

Toast at the Banquet for Liu Xiaobo on the Eve of the 2010 Nobel Peace Prize Award Ceremony
Oslo, Norway
December 9, 2010

Ladies and gentlemen, distinguished guests:

Thank you all for coming.

Many of you have traveled great distances to be here in Oslo. We came here in a common cause, and I hope we will meet with each other well enough tonight so that by the time we leave from this place, we will call each other brothers and sisters in that cause.

I want to take this opportunity to thank the Norwegian Nobel Committee for its brave and visionary decision to award the 2010 Nobel Peace Prize to Liu Xiaobo. The future will prove this is one of the most important awards in the history of the Prize.

You and I came here to honor a man who is a part of our thinking and cherished in your hearts and in mine. We crossed the skies and traveled miles of roads to tell the world that we believe in the values that this man fervently believes in. We came here because the desire for peace, justice, and freedom burns strong in our hearts and minds.

The person of honor is himself kept from us. He stays in a place of confinement, a place none of us really wants to ever know. Even those of us who have already been in such places await the day we can tell our children and our children's children that those places don't exist anymore because of the extraordinary work people like this man has done to banish them from this earth.

We came here to celebrate, but our joy is tinged with sorrow. Is this really a celebration when the person to be celebrated is so wrongly held in a prison cell far away from his family and home? And what person would presume to think happy thoughts when this man's wife, for no reason whatsoever, is confined to that home when, at a minimum, she should be free to be here with us now...?

Liu Xia. I can never forget you. You, who serve your husband and his cause so faithfully. You, the artist, the photographer, the painter, the poet, now confined to your home. For no reason at all. A guilt solely by association, not by any action you have taken. Liu Xia, you invited all of us here. You should have been here to share this day with us. You spread the light of this award across the full spectrum of Chinese society.

My mind is weighted with memories of friends inside China who are most deserved to share the honor of this prize but banned from coming here to be with us tonight. Just like Liu Xiaobo, they embarked on their journey to pursue human rights and democracy in their youth. We cannot forget 1989. In that year, the flags waving above Tiananmen Square lit up people's yearning for freedom, but the rolling tanks trampled over so many brave young men and women, crushing a whole generation's dream. From then on, the Tiananmen Mothers have never stopped crying. Amidst the suffering, brave heroes with Liu Xiaobo continued to carry forward that dream as their own destiny. They sacrificed tremendously, fighting for human dignity and for the future of the whole nation. Their stories are not recorded in books. Rather, they are written on the roads of toil and imprinted on the prison walls. All dear friends and colleagues inside China, all prisoners of conscience and their families, we remember you tonight. We honor you here tonight.

We cannot forget those who gave their lives in Tiananmen Square and to whom Liu Xiaobo dedicates this award. Let us take a moment of silence to honor all of our brothers and sisters who have sacrificed their lives for the cause of freedom.

My dear friends, as you see an empty seat tomorrow, do not be sad. Join hands. Wear a smile on your face. Let your thirst for peace and justice and freedom continue to burn brightly in your hearts.

Let's raise our glasses to Liu Xiaobo and Liu Xia.

Xiaobo and Liu Xia, your empty seats will be seen by the world. In that one singular moment of reflection, the world will know all of our struggles as a people through the prism of your silence. Tomorrow, in your unfortunate absence, we will stand tall and proud with the hopes of the Chinese people high on our shoulders for the world to see.

To you, Xiaobo and Liu Xia, to the people of China, to freedom!

Thank you.

CHAPTER 45

I, Too, Have No Enemies

Opening Speech at the Exhibition Honoring Liu Xiaobo
Nobel Center, Oslo, Norway
December 11, 2010

Good evening, ladies and gentlemen.

Today I am humbled to open this exhibition that honors Liu Xiaobo, just as yesterday it was so deeply humbling to recognize the spirit of dignity and humanity that Liu Xiaobo embodies.

"I have no enemies," Liu Xiaobo famously declared in Tiananmen Square. And twenty years later, imprisoned a fourth time for a crime of expression, he said it again: "I have no enemies."

At the root of this declaration is an inspiring challenge. A challenge to all of us to transcend ourselves—our own sacrifices and suffering, our own moment in history—and think in terms of what is necessary. Liu Xiaobo's example demands that we consider our lives in the broader context of the survival and progress of our entire human family.

Liu Xiaobo represents a new kind of politics in China; a politics not based on hatred of an enemy, but on love for human dignity and the fundamental human desire to be free.

Yet in China the vestiges of a simplistic and antagonistic philosophy, cynically deemed "class struggle" by the ruling regime, continue to inform politics. The regime continually prods its population in the direction of resentment and hatred, the steady supply of which is needed in order to maintain its position. The Chinese Communist Party needs the dark side of human nature; it needs a population that either subscribes wholeheartedly to the naked calculus of power politics or one that it is too cynical, fearful, or indifferent to care. What it does not want, indeed, what it cannot survive, is a nation of Liu Xiaobos.

If we base our actions on the principles that Liu Xiaobo has not only espoused but for which the Chinese government has imprisoned him—if we base our actions on the principles that have been honored this year by the Nobel Committee—if we base our actions on the principles on display in this exhibition, then we cannot help but be emboldened in our struggle against injustice.

This struggle is often asymmetrical. As we have seen time and again in China, injustice frequently finds itself favored with far more resources. But we also know, on an even playing field, justice prevails. And what will help even the power calculation will not be a movement based on fear or hatred, but on the transcendent ideals of Liu Xiaobo.

For no deep and sustained manifestation of injustice can long survive a population of people who are willing to take up the challenge, with whatever modest means are at their disposal, and say, "I, too, am Liu Xiaobo. I, too, have no enemies."

Thank you.

CHAPTER 46

It Is the Matter of How Chinese Government Treats Its Own Citizens

Testimony at Hearing Hosted by Chairwoman Ros-Lehtinen of the Committee on Foreign Affairs of the US House of Representatives
Washington, DC, United States
January 19, 2011

Dear Chairwoman:

There are issues of urgent concern for US-China relations: trade, peace on the Korean peninsula, nuclear weapon proliferation, global climate change—just to cite but a few of the outstanding ones. But I want to point you to an even more fundamental complexity in the relationship that must be addressed.

It is the matter of how the Chinese government treats its own citizens.

China is the country with the most prisoners-of-conscience in the world, including a Nobel Peace Prize winner.

In addition, it is practically public knowledge that in China there exist hundreds of black jails established and run by local governments of various levels. These prisons take in numerous innocent petitioners arbitrarily, as long as they are suspected of "affecting society's stability."

Given the time limit, I will not elaborate on all of the human rights violations in China. Instead, I want to give you a brief report on the three new types of measures that the Chinese authorities have been increasingly using in the past three years to control and persecute dissidents, which go beyond the prison system.

1. Direct Violence against Dissidents

Direct violence against dissidents, human rights activists, and petitioners has increased in recent years. The people who have been doing these things are local policemen or thugs hired by the police. Some government officials are also involved.

2. House Arrest

In recent years, house arrest has become more and more widely used as a means for limiting dissidents and petitioners and their family members. Yuan Weijing and Liu Xia are two typical examples. As the wife of the blind human rights lawyer, Chen Guangcheng, Yuan Weijing was placed under house arrest not long after her husband had been arrested. Ever since Chen Guangcheng was released after serving four years and three months in prison last September, the entire family has been put under house arrest. The Chens have been cut off from all contact with the outside world. Those who have tried to visit them were badly beaten.

Liu Xia, Liu Xiaobo's wife, has been put under house arrest ever since October 8, 2010, when her husband won the 2010 Nobel Peace Prize, and her communication with the outside world has been completely cut off since October 20, 2010.

3. "Made Disappearance"

I also urge you to pay attention to the "disappearance" of Chinese citizens as the result of the government's unwarranted actions. The most notorious case is Gao Zhisheng. His case has been well documented by various rights groups.

Another important case is that of Mongolian scholar Hada, who was arrested in December 1995 for peaceful activities demanding more autonomy for the Mongolian region. He was later sentenced to fifteen years in jail. His prison term was set to end on December 10, 2010. But a few days before that, the Chinese authorities detained his wife and their son. Hada was never seen getting out of prison, and to date, the entire family has not been heard from.

Around the time of the Nobel Peace ceremony, more than 100 of Mr. Liu's friends, family members, and supporters, including Tiananmen Mother Ding Zilin and her husband, were either put under house arrest or made missing.

The conventional wisdom that economic growth will help to improve human rights and promote democracy simply does not apply to China as well as people expect. So far, the fruits of economic growth have strengthened rather than weakened the government's confidence in its ability to perpetrate human rights violations. In some special yet widespread cases (such as land expropriation and house demolition, etc.), the need for economic development has become a ready excuse and motivation for human rights violations. As the thirty-two congressional members said in their letter to President Obama last week, "China touts its continued economic progress and integration into the world economy while refusing to acknowledge and uphold universal standards applicable to human rights."

Coming back to the issue I raised at the outset, I guess the question is: Why should China's treatment of its citizens be an important concern for US foreign policy toward China? Pundits and laymen can give a slew of analysis and answers to this question, and some people can even denounce this question as irrelevant. But I just want to echo Phelim Kine's question from his *Wall Street Journal* article last Monday: Will a rising power that fails to honor commitments to its own people act responsibly to fulfill its commitments to other nations and their peoples?

CHAPTER 47

The Time Has Come to Realize That Tolerance for Tyrannies Does Not Promote Security

Speech at Third Annual Geneva Summit for Human Rights and Democracy
Geneva, Switzerland
March 15, 2011

Good afternoon, fellow delegates and distinguished guests. Thank you for the opportunity to address you here today.

I am compelled to begin with a call for a moment of silence for the Japanese people, whose unimaginable suffering continues. Their suffering speaks to our common humanity and to our recognition that their suffering is our suffering.

(Moment of silence)

The nations of the world are providing assistance to the Japanese people, collectively working to help Japan regain its physical well-being. Unfortunately, we are here today because our collective response to willful destruction of the human spirit by the tyrannies of the world is not the same as our collective response to natural disaster.

Please allow me to present this situation and appeal for help; since late February, the Chinese government has launched its biggest clampdown on dissidents and human rights activists in a decade. So far, about thirty have been officially arrested and more than a hundred put under house arrest or made missing. The Chinese government has, once again, outperformed itself in its long-standing history of human rights violations. Although human rights are decreed part of the constitution, the Chinese government has never intended to honor this commitment. As a result, we see all kinds of human rights violations in China. Under the Chinese Communist Party's (CCP) one-party dictatorship, vast numbers of prisoners of conscience are imprisoned, thousands of Falun Gong practitioners perished under persecution, ethnic groups and religious groups are systematically repressed, and there is no free flow of information on the internet. For a long time, the Chinese government has been enforcing forced abortions, large-scale illegal evictions, and farmers were forced to lose their lands without compensation or sell their lands at low prices to government and officials. These are currently taking place in China and is enough to remind us of the severity of Chinese human rights issues.

Last October, the Nobel Peace Prize was announced to be awarded to the jailed Chinese writer Liu Xiaobo. His wife, Liu Xia, designated me to be the liaison to the Nobel Peace Prize ceremony on his behalf. However, not long after her request, Liu Xia was subjected to house arrest by the Chinese government. For five months now, I have not been able to get in contact with her. Since then, none of their family members have seen Liu Xiaobo either. I do not know what Liu Xiaobo is undergoing. I do not know what Liu Xia is undergoing. I do not know when I will be in touch with either of them again. The only thing I can do now is to pray for them, call the world to their attention, and to support them. For those in their situation, every single voice of justice is precious.

The recent uprisings in North Africa and the Middle East remind us that the desire and need for freedom of mind and spirit is as universal and fundamental as the physical need for food, clothing, and shelter.

These uprisings remind us that, today, more than a quarter of the world's population are deprived of basic human dignities of freedom of speech, religion, and assembly. This situation exists even though the United Nations adopted the Universal Declaration of Human Rights more than sixty years ago. This situation exits through the actions of evil human beings and with the acquiescence of the democracies of the world.

Long repressed people are mastering the modern tools of the internet, the social media of Facebook and Twitter, and the locus of power is shifting from the tyrants to the people. These tools are enabling people to organize and to communicate, releasing a tsunami of long-repressed calls for freedom and justice across the globe. If we miss this opportunity to nurture this call for freedom, our indifference will condemn our fellow human beings decades more of darkness and despair.

I know this because in 1989 one million of my countrymen peacefully assembled in Tiananmen Square in a peaceful call for democratic reform. The corrupt remnants of a totalitarian regime stood on the verge of collapse. Then, the unthinkable happened. The world stood by as the tanks and guns of the People's Army were turned on the very people they were sworn to defend.

And this was done with the acquiescence of the Western powers whose shortsighted vision and misguided polices condemned the people of China to decades more of humiliation and degradation. Let us not be blinded by the glitter of economic progress in my country. This same regime that gunned down innocent civilians and students in 1989 is the same regime in power today. Year after year, the United States Congressional-Executive Commission on China reports that the human rights record of this same regime in China is one of the worst in the world. This is the same regime that is now pursuing cultural genocide on our Tibetan, Uyghur, and Mongolian brothers and sisters. This is the same regime whose foreign policies and models of repression enable the morally bankrupt regimes of North Korea, Iran, and Vietnam to suck the freedoms and dignities from their people.

This is the same regime whose paranoid fear of its own allows it to imprison and torture its best and brightest citizens. Why is this tolerated? Are the collective wills of the world's great democracies so impotent that they cannot react? I do not think so. It is because the democracies of the world do not see the repression of basic human rights by tyrannical regimes as a threat to their own security.

The democracies of the world rationalize their acquiescence to tyrannical regimes by citing economic necessities or the need for world stability. In fact, in my own country, the regime plays these false ideas of economic progress and societal stability as reasons for their hardline abuse of human rights.

This rationalization that human rights must be sacrificed for economic progress and societal stability have long justified the world's support for the regimes in Saudi Arabia, China, Vietnam, Egypt, Libya, and others.

Isn't it only through such rationalizations as these that a great country like the United States can witness the empty seat for Liu Xiaobo at the Nobel Peace Prize ceremony in January, and a month later, hold a state dinner for Hu Jintao, the man who put Liu Xiaobo in jail?

We must now recognize that these compromises with tyranny are not only morally wrong but they do, in fact, promote instability and threaten world peace. This is what we are seeing unfold now with the popular uprisings in the Middle East and North Africa.

The time has come to recognize that, in the words of that great champion of human rights, Dr. Martin Luther King Jr., "A threat to justice anywhere, is a threat to justice everywhere." This simple but fundamental idea that support of human rights for others is not optional for us, but is truly necessary for our own security, is clearly stated in the Nobel Peace Prize Committee's announcement of the award to my countryman, Liu Xiaobo. I quote: "The Norwegian Nobel Committee has long believed that there is a close connection between human rights and peace. Such rights are a prerequisite for the 'fraternity between nations' of which Alfred Nobel wrote in his will."

My friends, the time has come to realize that tolerance for tyrannies does not promote security. It just delays the day of reckoning. It intensifies the instability and threat to our security that these regimes present. As such, support for human rights can no longer be an optional component of Western foreign policy. It must be the foundation upon which all other bilateral issues rest.

My friends, the time has come for us to unify our efforts around promoting the connection between human rights and world peace and stability. We must rally our collective constituencies to convince leaders of the world democracies of the undeniable bond between human rights and world peace. We must get them to recognize that regimes that repress their own people are a direct and real threat to the peace and security of all people everywhere.

In conclusion, I propose that we take the first step here today by calling for a new direction in the foreign policies of the world democracies. That we call for foreign policies that make measurable progress on human rights the basis for progress on all other issues from trade to cultural exchanges. At the very least, this new foreign policy must tie progress in bilateral relations with progress in the actual implementation of the Universal Declaration of Human Rights. At a very minimum, these regimes must demonstrate real and measurable progress in the following areas:

- Internet freedom
- Release of prisoners of conscience and the transparent application of the rule of law
- Lifting restrictions and halting state interference in the practice of religion and the free exercise of cultural traditions including: the practice of local languages and customs, the right of assembly, peaceful demonstration, and the ability to petition for redress of grievances without reprisal
- Implementation of this new foreign policy must be consistent, measurable, and tied to defined incentives and consequences for their implementation or lack thereof

To those who say this cannot be done, I say that it has been done. Remember the bold action of the Jackson-Vanik Amendment in the US Congress? This amendment tied trade with the Soviet Union to the implementation of specific and measurable quotas in the emigration of Soviet Jews to Israel. This single piece of "carrot and stick foreign policy" is credited with setting the stage for glasnost and the ultimate demise of Soviet totalitarianism.

To those who say this cannot be done, I remind them of Pope John Paul II, whose quiet but determined diplomacy helped bring freedom to his homeland of Poland.

For those who say that times are different, I say that yes, they are. The universality of human rights has never been more apparent than it is today. If we do not seize the opportunity now, history will judge us harshly.

Thank you.

CHAPTER 48

We Must Prepare Ourselves to Seize That Torch

Speech for Amnesty International Meeting
Seattle, WA, United States
April 25, 2011

Thank you, Larry. Your kind words compel me to remind everyone that it is you and Amnesty International who deserve such praise. For so many people including myself, Amnesty International is the light in the darkness of a prison cell. When political leaders falter and even look the other way, Amnesty International fills the void of conscience that gives tyrants pause and victims hope. I speak from personal experience.

As we all know, the road to change is indeed long. Twenty-two years ago, I was one of a million people in Tiananmen Square, one of a million voices calling for an end to the corruption that, in the words of Charter 08, has "corrupted human intercourse." That corruption revealed itself on June 4, 1989, when the so-called People's Army turned on innocent civilians. In an instant, the legs of my good friend, Fang Zheng, became a tangled mess in the tread of an onrushing tank. Untold thousands of my generation were killed and wounded. The people of China were condemned to twenty-two more years of darkness. Their minds and spirits are slaves to a state that cares for nothing but its hold on power.

Amid the chaos of Tiananmen, I realized that the road to freedom is indeed long. The journey requires not only the desire for freedom but the strategy and the tools for achieving that freedom. It requires leadership and organization that can steer protest in the square to successful negotiation around the table.

So, I returned to the US to begin that long journey. In the past twenty-two years, I have learned, seen, and endured much. I have walked the halls of Harvard as I earned my doctorate in Political Economy. Along the way, I probed the darkness of solitary confinement. I have seen the great leaders of my generation, Liu Xiaobo, Ai Weiwei, Gao Zhisheng, Hu Jia, Wang Bingzhang, Liu Xianbin, and countless others mercilessly beaten, vilified, and incarcerated. I watch as my Tibetan brothers and my Uyghur brothers are systematically decimated to the point of cultural extinction. My own Han Chinese sisters are methodically butchered through forced abortions under the most primitive conditions. Other Han brothers and sisters are routinely beaten and intimidated for no other reason than being Christians or Falun Gong practitioners. We must ask ourselves, "When is enough, enough? Where is the boundary beyond which the behavior of the Chinese government excludes itself from membership in the world community?"

The road to democracy is indeed long and hard. But I stand before you today to give you encouraging news. The end of the road is within sight. We can see the torch of freedom ahead. We must prepare ourselves to seize that torch.

Before us we hear calls for freedom from popular uprisings in Iran, Tunisia, Egypt—all across North Africa and the Mideast. These revolts confirm three extremely important maxims.

Number One. The thirst for freedom is indeed universal. It can be repressed but never extinguished. This repression is the biggest threat to world peace and stability. Tolerating these tyrannies only increases that threat. The Nobel Committee clearly stated this maxim when it announced Liu Xiaobo as the Peace Prize laureate for 2010, saying, "The Nobel Committee long recognizes the connection between democracy and world peace." Active support for the popular call for democratic reforms is not just an internal issue, or a question of human rights, but an imperative for our own survival and world peace and stability.

Number Two. The new technologies of the internet, social media, and mobile communications give repressed people the upper hand in their struggles against tyrannical governments, as witnessed in Egypt and Syria. These powerful tools are enabling what we call in Chinese, "GongMin LiLiang," or Citizen Power, the realization of that power resides with the people and not the tyrant.

Number Three. In almost every case, popular revolts have caught the US foreign policy establishment by surprise. This reveals a great disconnect between our core values and interests and our polices that tolerate tyranny. Unless US foreign policy changes, we will miss opportunities for nurturing democratic reforms around the world and the peace and stability they would bring.

Nowhere is the interplay of these maxims more evident than in China. The repression is unprecedented. Almost twenty-two years after Tiananmen, the Chinese government is compelled to spend more on internal security than it does on national defense to repress the cries for freedom. Its fear of its own people drives it to jail its best and brightest thinkers and to lash out at the slightest affront to its authoritarian rule. My friend Liu Xiaobo is serving an eleven-year prison sentence for his authorship of Charter 08. For the same work, Liu was awarded the Nobel Peace Prize. The Chinese government is so insecure that it not only prevented Liu from going to Oslo, it also put his wife under house arrest. It called anyone who attended the ceremony "clowns" and threatened dire consequences for any country that sent ambassadors to the ceremony. Why did eighteen nations decline invitations to the Peace Prize ceremony? Why did no one from the Obama administration or the US State Department attend? Why did President Obama, himself a Nobel laureate, host a state dinner for Chinese President Hu Jintao less than two months later? Do these actions represent support for freedom or acquiescence to tyranny?

As the third maxim states, such ambivalence—if not outright acquiescence—toward repressive governments only encourages more repression and prefigures the cataclysm of another Tiananmen. Earlier this year, Colonel Gaddafi justified his bloody actions by pointing to what China did to "those people in Tiananmen Square." Does this not show how ignoring crimes in one place only encourages them to spread elsewhere?

Fortunately, the Chinese people are more prepared for democracy today than in 1989. While our thought leaders are in jail, their ideas and ideals are widely circulated. Thanks to firewall-busting technologies, and mobile communications, people are more informed and better organized. Charter 08 is now established as a framework for democratic reform. Through my foundation, Initiatives for China, as well as other democratic movements, citizen power is taking hold. Citizens are becoming more proficient at using the tools of nonviolent resistance. In the past three days, Initiatives for China just sponsored its sixth consecutive Interethnic/Interfaith Leadership Conference, which brings together PRC-ruled ethnic and religious leaders to discuss common goals and actions. The Chinese government is facing a more unified and organized voice for democracy.

The road to change is indeed long. But like our brothers in North Africa and the Middle East, the Chinese people will not be repressed much longer. In the words of the Soviet dissident Andrei Sakharov, a government cannot hold a gun to its people forever.

The Chinese people have the desire and the will in the face of unbelievable repression. We have the technology for organizing and communicating, and thanks to heroic thinkers and practitioners like Liu Xiaobo and others, we have the organizing principles for democracy.

What we need is the clear and compelling diplomacy of the United States to send the unequivocal message that it stands on the side of democracy. It must call for the freedom of Chinese political prisoners, a free and open internet for China, and a transparent rule of law for its citizens. We need the moral voice of Amnesty International to continuously challenge the conscience of America and the world.

In the words of the holocaust survivor and distinguished author Elie Wiesel, the biggest threat to freedom is not hatred or tyranny, but indifference. We can no longer be indifferent.

In closing, I ask for your help on a specific issue. On June 4th, the twenty-second anniversary of the Tiananmen Massacre, Initiatives for China will present a letter to the UN Secretary General regarding the serious and ongoing human rights violations by the Chinese government. Please go to the Initiatives for China website to acquaint yourself with this letter and use your resources to circulate it and endorse it as you see fit.

The road to freedom is long, but the end is in sight. Please walk with us.

Thank you and God bless.

CHAPTER 49

Cultural and Religious Identities Are Allies of Democracy

Opening Remarks at the Sixth Interethnic/
Interfaith Leadership Conference
Los Angeles, CA, United States
April 30, 2011

Distinguished guests, my dear brothers and sisters:

A good day to you. I warmly welcome you to the sixth Interethnic/ Interfaith Leadership Conference.

This Conference was begun in 2000 to facilitate communication between young leaders and members of different ethnicities, religions, and regions. We strive to build friendships, to eliminate biases, and to foster compromise. Our goal is to better understand one another so that together we can form an alliance to promote human rights for us all as individuals and to defend each other's cultural, religious, ethnic, and regional identities.

The young leaders present today bring with them distinct identities. We have leaders of different ethnic, cultural, religious, and political backgrounds, which are links to their regions and their people, and their past, present, and future. Each represents a different way of searching for a more meaningful life. The authoritarian Chinese government perceives these different identities as threats to its political power. It subjects them to systematic persecution and seeks to eradicate them. Authoritarian governments prefer a homogeneous society because it is easier to control. They fear individuality. They fear different cultures. All of you present here know what I speak of because you represent groups trying to extricate themselves from the Chinese Communist Party's authoritarian rule or threat. At the same time, you seek ways of living harmoniously with one another. But how can such a diverse group, with so many different ideas and customs, live together in peace? My answer is, without hesitation, democracy: Identities are allies of democracy, and democracy is the ultimate safeguard of identities.

However, not everyone has confidence in this solution. Some do not believe that people of such distinctive identities can become allies for anything good. When we turn on the television, read a newspaper, or surf the internet, we see stories full of discrimination, mutual suspicion, and deadly conflict, all due to different identities. This causes many to think that different identities are enemies to democracy and peace, that different identities coming in contact with each other will always bring conflict. This also leads some scholars to hasty conclusions like the now famous concept of the "Clash of Civilizations." However, if we carefully analyze ethnic and religious conflicts, we discover that these conflicts are in fact not conflicts between civilizations. Instead, they are conflicts between authoritarianism and democracy or by two autocratic despots either within the border of a country or on an international level. There are never such clashes between democracies. If this is not so, why are there no conflicts between democratic countries based on differing Christian, Judaic, Buddhist, and Islamic faiths? While the authoritarian government of China violently annihilates the cultural identities of the Tibetan, Uyghur, and Mongolian ethnic groups and religious groups such as the Christians and Falun Gong, numerous ethnic and religious groups live in harmony in democratic India.

We all know wealth needs protection, be it material or spiritual.

Almost every person wishes to own private property and hopes that this property will be protected. The best protection for private property humankind has found is the market economy with the rule of law. Those who enjoy private property rights are the most avid supporters of such a system and are those who pursue it where it does not exist. Similarly, almost everyone needs a sense of belonging. Everyone needs a cultural life or even a religious life. This is one's personal spiritual wealth. Just like material property, spiritual wealth must be protected. Thus far, the best protection system for spiritual wealth that humankind has found is democracy. Those with strong identities—more spiritual wealth, so to speak—are like those with large amounts of private property and require the same legal protection a market economy affords property. For this reason, people with a lot of spiritual wealth are firm supporters of democracy. Under an authoritarian regime, these people are the unwavering protesters against tyranny and staunch pursuers of democracy. The Tibetans, Uyghurs, Mongolians, Christians, and Falun Gong practitioners' stories aptly prove this point. The democratic revolution in the Muslim countries of Tunisia, Egypt, Yemen, as well as the rising democratic movement in Iran and Syria, illustrates that mankind's pursuit of the universal values is indeed universal.

Not only does the spiritual wealth require democratic protection, it is also the impetus for the healthy development of democracy. A market economy with its rule of law makes the material free market a possibility. Democracy makes the non-material free market—of spiritual, cultural and thought—a possibility. Ethnicity, culture, and religion are suppliers and shops of such a free market. Different identities greatly add to the richness of society's thoughts and culture. They also enhance humankind's creativity. Even for one immune and desensitized, an encounter with different cultures can sometimes cause awakening, thereby enriching and nourishing life. Distinct identities are essential to the continuation, transmission, and reinvention of human civilization.

Of course, even under democracy, distinct identities can sometimes cause division and conflict. However, democracy is uniquely suited to allow the free exchange of opinions between different groups. Indeed, the risk of conflict is reduced once there is a deliberative democratic body in place.

Even when there is conflict, mankind can learn from it. America offers us an example of this. After the founding of the United States, American Indians, African Americans, women, homosexuals, and other groups were marginalized. However, a democratic society provided the solution to the issues facing these groups. New discussions were introduced. New laws were passed, and now new rights are in place to protect these groups.

People of different identities should be allies. They should form relationships to lift each other up. At this conference, we shall move forward with this in mind. It should give us the confidence to discuss ethnic issues. We will not avoid any issue. Whether the issue is pursuing democracy or urging the protection of different identities, we have a common end: to eliminate the need for mutual suspicion and military conflict. Instead, we will focus on increasing our own autonomy by increasing the rights of different groups. By lifting our fellow man up, we lift ourselves up as well. Just as in previous conferences, we will hear about and be able to learn from experiences beyond our own. Our discussion may not necessarily find us of the same mind—indeed, sometimes there may even be heated debate. But the collision of these differences in opinion will cause us to be more inclusive, more open-minded: in a word, wiser. We will find the impetus for thoughtful creativity from others attending this conference. We will learn through mutual respect, mutual compromise, and mutual support. In the name of democracy, let us unite for the protection of different identities, and work together toward democracy for the bright future of every group. This is my intention, and I believe it is also yours.

Thank you, everyone.

CHAPTER 50

The Myth of Han China

Speech at Oslo Freedom Forum
Oslo, Norway
May 11, 2011

I am very pleased to speak to you today on the topic of "The Myth of Han China."

Time demands that I get directly to my hypothesis that the myth of a Han China as a homogenous and harmonious and stable society is a particularly insidious myth that blinds us from the reality of Chinese society. It is a shroud of deceit carefully woven by the CCP to conceal its true intent. That intent is to reduce Chinese society to a fiefdom of slaves to an all-powerful state.

The myth of a Han China is as racist as the idea of a white America, as repulsive as apartheid in South Africa, and potentially as cataclysmic for China as the myth of Aryan supremacy was to Germany and the world.

The CCP employs the vast resources of China's wealth to perpetuate this myth of a harmonious and stable Han China as a means for rationalizing its otherwise illegitimate claim to power. It craftily weaves the threads of "harmony" and "stability" into a fabric of beguiling lies and half-truths that cover the harsh realities of repression from a world all too eager to look the other way.

A wonderful example of how the Chinese government weaves the myth of Han China is the article written by former Hong Kong chief executive, C.H. Tung, in celebration of the sixtieth anniversary of the PRC (People's Republic of China) and published in the *Washington Post* on October 31, 2009.

In the article, Mr. Tung reflects on the "enormous progress" made by China since the establishment of the PRC in 1949. He states that, "At no other point in history has so much improvement been made for so many people in such a short period." He attributes this progress to the "harmony" and "stability" brought to Chinese society through the "enlightened" policies of the CCP.

This article ran unopposed in the op-ed section of the *Washington Post*. Unfortunately, the view of a harmonious and stable and prosperous China created through the enlightened governance of the CCP hangs over the corridors of power and policymaking in Washington, DC, and other capitals around the world. This view is reinforced by thousands of lobbyists, apologists, and compromised academics—all of whom are seduced, in one way or another, by the power and wealth of the CCP.

My friends, let us remove this shroud of deceit. Let's look at Chinese society today not through the opaque shroud woven by the CCP but rather through hard facts and figures researched and documented by thousands of reports from independent agencies around the world.

Let us ask ourselves: Where is this harmonious and stable society?

Is it with the Tibetans whose culture has been poached to the point of extinction?

Is it with the Uyghurs who are labeled "terrorists" and whose women are systematically enticed to other provinces by the promises of jobs only to find despair and unwelcome marriages to Han Chinese men?

Is it with farmers and peasants whose lands are routinely seized without compensation by unscrupulous developers in collusion with corrupt officials?

Is it with Christian leaders who are routinely arrested and beaten because they want to practice their faith peacefully and privately without the interference of an atheist state?

I ask you again: Where are these enlightened policies of this mythical, harmonious Han China? They are nowhere to be found. The emptiness of this myth was powerfully illustrated by the empty chair reserved for my friend Liu Xiaobo on the stage of the 2010 Nobel Peace Prize award ceremony in Oslo in December 2010. For his writings on democracy. For Charter 08, this eloquent framework for reforming Chinese society, Liu Xiaobo was awarded the Nobel Peace Prize. For this same effort, the enlightened Chinese government awarded him eleven years in prison.

Where are these enlightened policies of the PRC? This unprecedented progress? Is it the land reform of the fifties that caused tens of millions of my countrymen to starve to death? Is it the Cultural Revolution of the seventies that left Chinese society in shreds for decades? Is it in the infamous one-child policy that leaves millions of marriage-age men without women to marry and forces millions of forced abortions a year, causing the highest female suicide rate of any country in the world?

Or perhaps we can find enlightenment in the Tiananmen Square Massacre of 1989 where thousands of my fellow students were killed and maimed by tanks of the People's Army. This massacre is well documented by the world, but its very existence is denied by the enlightened Chinese government.

The answers to any of these questions dictates only one conclusion and proves the hypothesis that the idea of a harmonious and homogenous Han China is an insidious and dangerous myth. China today is a cauldron of repression and discontent. It is a self-serving lie of a government in fear of its own people and in dread of the truth that its rule has been an unmitigated disaster. A disaster eloquently defined in Charter 08. "The Chinese people, who have endured human rights disasters and uncountable struggles across these same years, now include many who see clearly that freedom, equality, and human rights are universal values of humankind and that democracy and constitutional government are the framework for protecting these values. By departing from these values, the Chinese government's approach to modernization has proven disastrous. It has stripped people of their rights, destroyed their dignity, and corrupted normal human intercourse. So, we ask: Where is China headed in the twenty-first century? Will it continue with modernization under authoritarian rule or will it embrace universal human values, join the mainstream of civilized nations, and build a democratic system? There can be no avoiding these questions."

These words from Charter 08, published in December 2008, reverberate today around the globe where we see popular revolts against authoritarian regimes in North Africa and the Middle East.

There can be no avoiding this question: How much longer can we allow ourselves to be seduced by this myth of a harmonious and stable Han China? How much longer will the Chinese people endure this "enlightened" government whose policies have caused the deaths of more people than those caused by Hitler and Stalin combined?

In the words of the Russian dissident Andrei Sakharov, "a government cannot hold a gun to its people forever." When the arm tires and the gun falls to the ground, and a billion people rise against this "enlightened" government, what will that look like?

With that in mind, I ask you how much longer can we afford to support this myth and the government that weaves it?

CHAPTER 51

Why China Should Not Be a Member of the United Nations Human Rights Council

Luncheon Speech at the UN
United Nations Headquarters, New York, NY, United States
May 19, 2011

I am Yang Jianli, a Chinese citizen.

In the course of its affairs as a great nation, China has left large fingerprints on the canvas of human events. With regard to human rights, these fingerprints place China at the scene of so many activities, both domestic and international, that are so outside the norm of civilized nations that its membership in the United Nations Human Rights Council defies logic and reason.

To put it simply, a country's qualification for UNHRC membership is based on how it treats its own people and how it helps promote the human rights of other people around the world. But world history tells us that no country that treats its own people harshly can be relied on to treat another country's people with compassion.

In considering China's record, we need look no further than these individuals, groups, events, and policies:

The Tiananmen Massacre, Tiananmen Mothers, Charter 08... Liu Xiaobo and his wife, Liu Xia, Wang Bingzhang, Gao Zhisheng, Liu Xianbin, Chen Guangcheng, Ai Weiwei, Hada... Tibetans, Uyghurs... House Churches, Falun Gong, Forced Abortions, Forced Evictions, Forced Disappearances, Black Jails...

Next, let's consider internet access among Chinese citizens… I stood in Tiananmen Square on June 4, 1989. I know what happened. That information is readily available to any citizen of the free world, but not to the people of China. While human rights protecting countries actively support internet access as a means of advancing the flow of information and encouraging discourse among their citizens, the Chinese government employs a vast army to monitor and censure such activity. In fact, the Chinese government expends more resources on internal security than it does on national defense.

We all have a copy of the United Nations Universal Declaration of Human Rights.

Surely any member of the UNHRC should, as a minimum, subscribe in practice as well as principle to the rights outlined in these articles.

Conversely, any government that demonstrates its inability or unwillingness to protect and preserve these rights for its citizens is de facto not suitable for membership in the UNHRC. No further examination or debate is necessary.

Therefore, I propose the following thought experiment for you to judge for yourselves whether China, or any country, should be a member of the United Nations Human Rights Council.

The Thought Experiment:

1. Imagine you are a Chinese citizen.
2. You travel to Japan, Czech Republic, or Canada. During your visit, you go to a public place in the capital city of any of these countries.
3. In that place you distribute copies of this Declaration of Human Rights. In doing this you are exercising Articles 18,19, and 20 of the UN Declaration pertaining to freedom of speech and assembly.
4. What is the reaction of the authorities in that city?
5. You then return to your home city of Beijing.

6. You distribute copies of the UN Declaration to people in Tiananmen Square.
7. How will the Chinese authorities react?

No citizens of China would actually conduct this experiment because they know what would happen.

And so do you.

I rest my case.

CHAPTER 52

Justice, Long Overdue

Speech at the Rally Commemorating the Twenty-Second Anniversary of the Tiananmen Massacre
Dag Hammarskjöld Plaza, United Nations Headquarters, New York, NY, United States
June 4, 2011

Dear friends,

For more than two decades, June 4th has been a day of silent mourning in China.

Twenty-two years ago, millions of unarmed Chinese civilians stood in front of tanks and machine guns on Beijing's streets. Hoping to wake the conscience and rouse the slumbering common sense of the dictatorship, their efforts were met with showers of gunfire. Today, these events remain distorted in China's official record.

We do not know the names of all the victims of the Tiananmen Massacre. The noble souls of the Chinese people who died in the crackdown do not rest in peace—not because so many are unknown but because the goals of their sacrifice, courage, and decency are still suppressed by the Chinese regime. For twenty-two years, people of conscience, represented by a group called the Tiananmen Mothers, have persistently sought to replace lies with truth and hatred with understanding. Their appeals have echoed through dimming halls, halls kept dark by ignorance and authoritarianism.

Today, as we have gathered to memorialize the victims of Tiananmen, we also appeal to the United Nations to investigate long-term, systematic violations of human rights in China and hold the perpetrators accountable. When there exists serious injustice in the world, no one can truly enjoy peace.

While we recognize the existence of very real obstacles that may impede a thorough investigation into China's human rights practices, we make our appeal based on fundamental principles of law, justice, and morality.

Let me be clear: The events of June 4, 1989, were not a one-time event. In the twenty-two years since the Tiananmen Massacre, China has never stopped violating the human rights of its citizens. It has never lacked for prisoners of conscience in its jails.

China, with its great territorial expanse and large population, is a very powerful member of the United Nations. But the UN should not apply different human rights standards to different member countries based on considerations of power. The UN should stand for fundamental values and principles. It should say NO to the Chinese government on human rights violations. It should show the victims of human rights violations in China that justice and fairness are valued in our world after all.

United Nations' support for the human rights movement in China will help China and the world. A pro-human rights China will not only be a boon to its citizens but will go a long way toward making the world a more peaceful and prosperous place.

Dearest friends, those who died twenty-two years ago can no longer speak for themselves. It is up to us speak for them, to carry on in their spirit, to try to align our world with their ideals. Let's hope that this gathering refreshes our memory, reminds us of our responsibility, and serves as a source of strength for our struggle.

Let us now stand in silence and strength for one minute in honor of those heroes who died twenty-two years ago.

Thank you all.

CHAPTER 53

Congratulations to the Tibetan People on This Day for Celebration

Speech at the Celebration of the Inauguration of Lobsang Sangay
Dharamsala, India
August 9, 2011

Honorable Prime Minister Lobsang Sangay, distinguished guests, and my dear Tibetan brothers and sisters:

Tashi delek!

I am honored and humbled to lead a delegation of Chinese to attend and speak at today's inauguration of Lobsang Sangay as Prime Minister of the Central Tibetan Administration: honored because I am with YOU, whose extraordinary struggle for freedom and the advancement of democracy has won worldwide respect; humbled because your suffering has been at the hands of a government that is largely made up of Han Chinese, an ethnicity of which I am a member.

Congratulations on this momentous occasion to His Holiness the Dalai Lama, whose leadership has once again proved extraordinary.

Thanks to his wisdom, vision, and determination, Tibetans in exile have, step by step, established full-fledged democracy in their community. His Holiness the Dalai Lama stands as a shining exemplification of the righteous way. The example he sets serves continual notice to the world's power-hungry and greedy dictators—especially those sitting in Zhongnanhai, Beijing.

Congratulations to Mr. Lobsang Sangay, my dear schoolmate and friend, whose commitment, vision, ability, and willingness to serve his people have won him their trust and granted him this important position of leadership.

Lobsang, Mr. Prime Minister, I can feel the heavy responsibility on your shoulders, even on this glorious day. But you are an honest and trustworthy man. I know you are up to the test and wish you all good luck.

Congratulations to the Tibetan people on this day for celebration.

Your achievements in democracy, and your struggle for freedom under the banner of the Middle Way Approach upheld by His Holiness the Dalai Lama, have become twin monuments—not only in the history of Tibet but in the history of mankind. You are a beacon of hope to many people, including the Han Chinese under the rule of the Chinese communist regime. It is your good fortune to have His Holiness the Dalai Lama as your spiritual leader and Prime Minister Lobsang Sangay as your political leader while you continue to travel the difficult road toward home and freedom. My dear brothers and sisters, united under this new leadership structure, continue to fight the good fight. Wish and work for an inauguration that will one day take place in Lhasa.

Congratulations to the world's leaders on this inauguration day.

The Tibetan issue is not an issue limited to Tibet and China; it is a world issue. It is not only a political issue; it is a moral issue facing all of humanity. Leaders of the world, I understand that you often run into awkward situations where you feel that proclaimed principles have to be compromised for the sake of short-term interests. The next time you are in such a situation, think of this principled leader whose moral courage will whisper a powerful message in your ear: Honesty is the best policy.

Last but not least, congratulations to the leaders of China.

I can understand your fear of losing political power, but His Holiness the Dalai Lama's example shows you that being without political power is not that frightening; voluntarily giving away political power can be beneficial. I understand your worry about stability. But please come and see for yourselves the Tibetan community in exile here. It is very stable and harmonious under democracy. The Tibetan community in

Tibet will also be stable and harmonious under democracy and genuine autonomy. So will any community back in China. Now that the Dalai Lama issue has disappeared—for His Holiness is no longer holding any political power in the exiled Tibetan community, nor pursuing any political power or status in China—I think you have no choice but to face the Tibetan issue and open dialogue with Lobsang Sangay. If you say Lobsang Sangay cannot serve in such a capacity because the Tibetans in Tibet did not participate in the election, then we say please let the Tibetans in Tibet freely elect their representative for dialogue with you.

Dear Tibetan brothers and sisters, we have all traveled great physical, mental, and temporal distances to get here. The tensions and hostilities that have divided us are like so many open wounds on the body of our common cause. Only by healing these wounds will we be able to march strongly toward the horizon where the dawn of freedom, truth, justice, equality, and peace for us all will one day break.

This will happen if we walk together.

Let me close with a little story. The last time I was in Dharamsala, I was in the audience with His Holiness. At the end of the meeting we all stood up together. I noticed that His Holiness had a pair of shoes of very good quality, and I whispered to him that his shoes were quite nice. "Yes," His Holiness replied, "I will walk home in them." I replied, "Yes, your Holiness, I will walk with you." We suddenly found ourselves embracing each other.

Now is the time for us to embrace one another and walk together: united in our diversity and toward our common goal of freedom, truth, justice, equality and peace.

The time has come.

Thank you.

CHAPTER 54

Expanding the Reach of the Rights Guaranteed by Both the UN Charter and the Universal Declaration of Human Rights

Speech at We Have a Dream: Global Summit Against Discrimination and Persecution
New York, NY, United States
September 21, 2011

Dear friends, today we live in a land of shadows. Stark shadows cast by what is worst in us on what is best.

In 1945, as one of the worst convulsions of violence in the history of mankind drew to a close, the United Nations was formed and its Charter signed by twenty-six nations. This was a ray of light in a world still shrouded in darkness.

The best of mankind was on display in the UN Charter, which affirmed the "faith in fundamental human rights, in the dignity and worth of the human person, [and] in the equal rights of men and women and of nations large and small."

The Universal Declaration of Human Rights was another milestone in the evolution of man's global consciousness, emerging as it did in 1948 in the aftermath of world war. In 1998, the government of the People's Republic of China publicly proclaimed its commitment to the principles of the Universal Declaration.

But we must ask today how it is that this Charter, which speaks so eloquently to the aspirations of men and women around the world to live peaceful and secure lives, is so readily ignored by some of its signatory states.

And we must ask how this Declaration, which states that "everyone has the right to life, liberty, and security of person," that "no one shall be subjected to torture or to cruel, inhuman, or degrading treatment or punishment," and that "no one shall be subjected to arbitrary arrest, detention, or exile," is so casually traduced by one of the most powerful nations in the world.

Dear friends, what is best in us, what is most hopeful about us, what gives our joint future as a species such promise is beautifully articulated in the Charter and the Declaration. These are the principles of light and hope by which we should organize ourselves as a human family. These are the principles at the core of any meaningful democracy.

And yet, too many of our eyes have adjusted to the shadows that power and greed cast on the existence of our brothers and sisters around the world. Whereas the brave and visionary people who created the United Nations could see a world beyond the catastrophe they had just endured, we live in an age where what has been gained in principle, what has been recognized in fact, has been eroded by an acceptance that it is better to accommodate the evil—and hope it changes on its own—than to seek to change it through pressure, denouncement, and direct confrontation.

What else explains the presence of China on the United Nations Human Rights Council, a body supposedly responsible for strengthening the promotion and protection of human rights around the globe?

Back in March, I had a chance to address the Human Rights Council in the capacity of a Chinese citizen. This was just after Libya was suspended for its outrageous abuses against its own people.

While in front of that body, I recalled the case of Liu Xiaobo, among others. I asked how China's communist regime, whose victims run into the hundreds of millions, could remain a member while Libya was expelled for its abuses.

Where were you, I asked the representatives of the member nations, when there was only an empty chair at the Nobel Peace Prize ceremony in Oslo?

Where were you, I asked, when police and hired thugs brutally beat Mr. Chen Guangcheng, a blind human rights defender whose house has been surrounded all day, every day, since his release from prison in September of 2010?

When, I asked, will you demand accountability from the individuals responsible for the Tiananmen Massacre, and for other gross and systematic violations of human rights in China?

And so on, and so forth.

To be sure, there were many more I did not get enough time to ask.

Unfortunately, I received no answers.

More unfortunate than this, China remains a member of the United Nations Human Rights Council.

Dear friends, it says a lot about the importance of our work that an institution created to represent the best of what we can be retreats from conflict with the worst. It says a lot about the work that must be done that the discussion we are having today must take place outside of the United Nations, instead of inside its halls, and must take place among NGOs instead of governments. Clearly, we have a great deal to do.

And so, we have gathered here, in the shadowy valley of our times, to summon the wisdom and the best heritage of mankind and remind the entire world once again that each one of us has an opportunity to act in a way worthy of the best of our humanity.

The other option is to adjust our eyes to the shadows.

But friends, I have seen firsthand what takes place in these shadows. In 1989, I was in Tiananmen Square. I saw my countrymen crushed beneath tanks and felled by machine gun fire.

Even today, we do not know the names of all the victims of the Tiananmen Massacre. The noble souls of the Chinese people who died in the crackdown do not rest in peace—not because so many are unknown, but because the goals of their sacrifice are still suppressed by the Chinese regime.

The events of June 4, 1989, were not a one-time event. In the twenty-two years since the Tiananmen Massacre, China has never stopped violating the human rights of its citizens. It has never lacked for prisoners of conscience in its jails.

No country that behaves this way toward its own citizens should have a place on the Human Rights Council. No country.

We must demand that the United Nations readjust its eyes to the light and remove China from the Human Rights Council. China's membership will expire next May; it needs ninety-seven votes to remain a member. If each and every democracy says no, China will stand no chance. This is a test of the sincerity and commitment of every democracy to democracy.

Yes, China, with its great territorial expanse, large population, economic power, and military forces is a very powerful member of the United Nations. But the UN should not apply different human rights standards to different member countries based on considerations of power. The UN stands for fundamental values and principles. It must say no to the Chinese government on human rights violations. It must show the victims of human rights violations in China and the rest of the world that justice and fairness are valued in our world after all. It must not capitulate to expedience.

For what does it say to Tiananmen Mothers, to Liu Xiaobo and his wife, Liu Xia, to Wang Bingzhang, Gao Zhisheng, Liu Xianbin, Chen Guangcheng, Chen Wei, Ding Mao, Hada, to Tibetans, Uyghurs, Mongolians, to House Churches members, Falun Gong practitioners, and to the victims of Forced Abortions, Forced Evictions, Forced Disappearances, and Black Jails, if China remains a member of the United Nations Human Rights Council?

What does it say to our brave brothers and sisters in the Arab world, to our friends in Burma and Cuba, to the victims of dictators in Burma, North Korea, and Sub-Saharan Africa if China continues to cynically sit on a council supposedly committed to expanding the reach of the rights guaranteed by both the UN Charter and the Universal Declaration of Human Rights?

No, the behavior of China toward its own people, and internationally, cannot be condoned.

Those people in the middle of the last century who created the UN rose to the challenge of their times in the midst of the worst the world had ever seen. Surely, we, with their work as our foundation, can rise to the challenge of our own times. Surely, we can all see the shadows for what they are and say that it is time to begin living in the light.

Thank you.

CHAPTER 55

Three Chinas and Liu Xiaobo

Speech at Peace, Democracy, and Human Rights in Asia | Forum 2000
Prague, Czech Republic
December 10, 2011

Mr. President Havel, your Holiness the Dalai Lama, distinguished guests, ladies and gentlemen:

It is a great honor for me to share a panel with such a group of world human rights leaders and speak to the audience whose Velvet Revolution I profoundly admire as a Chinese activist.

Exactly one year ago, I attended the Nobel Peace Prize ceremony to honor my friend and colleague, Liu Xiaobo. He was being awarded the Nobel Prize for his pursuit of democratic reform in China. Sadly, he spent the occasion locked alone in a cell. Liu Xiaobo's wife, Liu Xia, was placed under house arrest. Today, a year later, Liu Xiaobo is still imprisoned and his wife is still under house arrest.

This past Thursday also marked the third anniversary of the release of Charter 08, a manifesto in which Chinese citizens demand political reform in their country. Charter 08 was mirrored after Czechoslovakia's Charter 77 of the 1970s, which Charter 08 authors admire greatly. As of today, 12,777 people have signed Charter 08 with their real names. Those who have signed are taking a brave risk; Liu Xiaobo advocated for Charter 08, and that is why he was imprisoned.

Why is China, a seemingly increasingly assertive world power, afraid of a single man like Liu Xiaobo? Why is it afraid of a moderate document like Charter 08? The answer can only be that the rulers of China understand just how unjust, therefore weak, their system is.

Liu Xiaobo and his colleagues recognize there are two Chinas. They have tried to bring together these two severely separated Chinas and construct a society built upon universal values of public political life.

Why do I say two Chinas? I am not trying to distinguish "Mainland China" from "Taiwan." Geographically, there is only one entity of Mainland China, but politically, economically, sociologically, and even sentimentally, it has largely broken into two separate Chinas.

These two Chinas date back to 1989 when the widespread pro-democracy movement, which stood against government corruption, was violently crushed.

The Tiananmen Massacre created a strong sense of fear of political engagement among ordinary people. Any hope for a public system of checks and balances against governmental abuse was swept away by this bloodletting.

But 1989 also created a sense of fear and crisis within the communist regime. The Massacre brought unprecedented public awareness to human rights and democratic causes. Life was no longer the same for rulers, who now faced a changed domestic and international environment. The regime was forced to develop new tactics to meet its "overwhelming" need to preserve the status quo.

Then the Soviet Union disintegrated and the Eastern European Bloc fell. This cast an even heavier cloud over the heads of Chinese communist officials. How long could the communists stay in power?

Shortly after Deng Xiaoping's famous Southern Inspection Tour in 1992, communist bureaucrats at all levels realized three realities:

First, the Chinese Communist Party's stay in power had nothing to do with communist principles.

Second, continued economic growth was the last, best hope to keep the ship afloat.

Third, the elite must be spoiled to retain their loyalty. Corruption was now accepted, endorsed—even demanded.

Understanding these realities over the past twenty years, the CCP regime established a two-China structure and one of the two Chinas, which I call China, Inc. China, Inc. is formed by

1. Red Capitalists
2. Marriage between Power and Capital taking advantage of:
   - Low human rights standards
   - Low environmental protection
   - Low wages
   - Banning collective bargaining power
3. China, Inc. shares open to domestic and foreign capitalists
4. China, Inc. shares free to intellectuals

In today's China, power (political elite), capital (economic elite), and "intellect" (social and cultural elite) are bonded together with corruption as the adhesive, forming an alliance that maintains the existing political order. This alliance owns and runs China, Inc., dazzling the entire world with its wealth, might, and glory. It dominates the public discourse, making its voice loud enough that outside observers believe they represent China, that they are China—the whole of China.

The truth is there is another society named China, a society constituted of over a billion Chinese, who are virtually slave-laborers working for China, Inc. I call this second China the under China.

What is the difference between China, Inc. and the under China?

1. Unprecedented wealth gap between the Chinas.
   For example, 0.4% of the families owns 70% of the nation's wealth.
2. Citizens of the under China are citizens only in name. They are unable to enjoy basic benefits or constitutionally afforded civil rights.
3. The elite's monopoly over power, capital, and information makes mobility from one China to the other nearly impossible.

4. The two Chinas no longer speak a common political language.
5) The two Chinas have almost no common political life.
6. The underclass has grown more and more distrustful of the elite. In recent years, China's official media has adopted a new phrase: "Conflicts caused by non-stakeholders."

Then how does the CCP regime maintain its Market-Leninism System, namely the two China structure?

On top of the traditional lies and violence, which every autocratic ruler uses, the CCP regime has developed new tactics. It is comprised of:

One body: sustaining economic growth at all costs to maintain the regime's ruling legitimacy

Two wings: appeasing the elite with corruption and suppressing the powerless with rogue police

Two claws: purging citizen advocates like Liu Xiao and blocking public opinion.

Nevertheless, it is not enough to just see the severe division of the two societies of China. We must expand our gaze. We must envision the emergence of a new, democratic China: the third China.

Despite the unprecedented division of the two Chinas, there are two often overlooked areas of consensus among Chinese from both societies. The first is that the present China is not "normal." The second, although agreed upon to a lesser degree, is that China will eventually become a normal country through democratic means.

But people disagree over how China can go from an "abnormal" state to a "normal" state.

Where can we find a common ground to lay the foundation for a democratic China? First, we must create a political language that can bridge the gap between the two Chinas. We need to gradually develop a consensus based on universal values. And that is exactly what Charter 08 intends to accomplish.

Change is unlikely to happen from within the CCP. Most of its members come from extraordinarily wealthy families. They value stability above all else and will do everything possible to delay the process of democratization. The persecution of Liu Xiaobo and many others who have exercised their freedom of expression is evidence of this.

Nevertheless, the concept of democracy has prevailed in people's minds. When something does change and people have to make a choice, most people will choose the right direction.

A breakthrough for such a change will surely come from the people.

The Nobel Peace Prize awarded to Liu Xiaobo has a remarkable impact on the hearts of many people inside China, and over the past year, the civil movement has become increasingly mature, skillful, and resilient as evidenced by two cases: Chen Guangcheng and Ai Weiwei. Both took place amid the latest round of heavy-handed crackdowns on the dissent early this year right after the Arab Spring.

Despite the CCP's best effort to impose strict control over the media, the internet has allowed people to connect, to share information.

Following the release of Charter 08, grassroots support for the document was immediate and unprecedented, even though the CCP regime tried to block its spread. Those who signed the Charter with their real names came from diverse segments of society. Because of this, signers could function as a de facto minor-parliament. Their diversity would allow them to effectively represent a wide spectrum of society.

The Charter is a banner. Backed by its real-name signers, the Charter could transform individual protests into a long-lasting movement that demands across the board, systematic change. The Charter could produce a quasi-organization with numerous new leaders. And that is only the beginning.

With a clear direction of the political resistance movement, the people will grow to exert greater and greater pressure on the communist regime. As the non-governmental forces grow and the civil protests escalate, the struggle for power among different factions with the communist regime will become more pronounced. Once the external pressure reaches a critical mass, the rival factions within the CCP will have no choice but to take the voices of the citizens seriously and seek their support to survive.

The release of Liu Xiaobo will help signal the coming of that change.

When a large-scale movement takes place again, as it did in 1989, we will need a group of civil leaders to play the role that the Civic Forum led by Mr. Havel played in the Velvet Revolution twenty-two years ago. We will need a group of leaders who can disrupt the political order and establish itself as the legitimate voice of the people in negotiations with the state. Liu Xiaobo, as a widely accepted leader both at home and abroad, will surely play a unique role in forming such a group, which was most needed but lacking in our 1989 Tiananmen movement.

Therefore, working toward his freedom is vital for a democratic change in China. I am particularly encouraged by the strong support for Liu Xiaobo and Charter 08 from world human rights leaders such as Václav Havel and His Holiness the Dalai Lama. Aung San Suu Kyi was released from house arrest in Burma last November. For the first time, there is hope for reform in Burma. In seeking Liu's release, we hope and struggle for the same in China.

Thank you.

CHAPTER 56

Your Pain Is My Pain and Your Freedom Is My Freedom

Speech at the Tibetan Rally in Front of the Chinese Embassy in Washington
Washington, DC, United States
February 8, 2012

Last Friday, three Tibetans set themselves ablaze within a single day in eastern Tibet. This comes shortly after four Tibetans immolated themselves and others were killed in peaceful demonstrations in Tibet during the month of January. In less than three years, more than twenty Tibetans have self-immolated in protest against Chinese rule. This rule has led to the killing of a million Tibetans, the toppling of thousands of temples, and the more than five-decade-long exile of the Dalai Lama. Each time tensions escalate, instead of showing concern and trying to address root causes, Chinese authorities respond with increasing force and oppression.

I have fallen into deep pain and sorrow. This is more than any heart can and should take. The sufferings of the Tibetans at the hands of the Chinese regime are unparalleled in the history of mankind but so is their brave and peaceful resistance. The question of Tibet is not only a political issue but also a moral one. All of humanity is challenged. Every world leader must take this moral test, and just like any other test, one either passes or fails. To our great dismay, many world leaders have so far either refused to take the test or have failed it. Too many of them looked the other way while our dear Tibetan brothers and sisters were crying in flames. Today, we are standing here carrying this burning message from Tibet: Give me liberty or give me death; we want freedom, and we want our spiritual leader His Holiness the Dalai Lama to return home.

Mr. President Obama, next week, you will meet China's Vice President Xi Jinping who, since last July, has been fully in charge of Tibetan affairs and who should therefore be held responsible for the recent crackdowns. Please summon the moral courage needed to confront him in your upcoming meeting in the White House with this simple and specific question: Why have so many Tibetans set themselves ablaze? Please press China, using every power in your capacity as the president of this greatest and most powerful democracy, to allow an independent international investigation on the self-immolation cases. This is the very least you should do in order to pass the moral test that I think you must take and cannot afford to fail.

Dear friends, we should work together to urge the United Nations state members to remove China, the world's leading human rights violator, from special positions of power in the United Nations human rights system. China's membership in the UN Human Rights Council will expire at the end of this year and it should not be re-elected.

I often find that we live in a land of shadows. Stark shadows cast by what is worst in us on what is best. With burning flames from Tibet, we should see the shadows for what they are and say that it is time to begin living in the light.

As a Chinese, I am proud that I have fought side by side with Tibetans for more two decades, yet this still cannot wash away all my shame. I am ashamed of what the Chinese regime, Chinese officials, and Chinese soldiers have done to my dear Tibetan brothers and sisters.

Dear brothers and sisters, your pain is my pain, and your freedom is my freedom. We, your Chinese brothers and sisters, will continue to join hands with you in your cause of freedom; our numbers in China are growing. As believers in the true principles of human rights, we will resolve to respect you as a people with every right to determine its own future. As believers in the principles of brotherhood, we will resolve to continue to struggle side by side with you for your freedom and ours.

Thank you!

SECTION VII

CHINA'S PLACE ON THE UN HUMAN RIGHTS COUNCIL: A THREAT TO PEACE AND THE DEMOCRATIC WAY OF LIFE EVERYWHERE

February 2012—December 2012

"A country's qualification for UNHRC membership should be based on how it treats its own people and how it helps promote the human rights of other people around the world. But world history tells us that no country that treats its own people harshly can be relied on to treat another country's people with compassion....Why should any dictatorship have a say in world human affairs when it does not allow a voice to its own citizens? Who does a dictatorship represent when it takes its seat at the UN? More importantly, who and what is the UN choosing to recognize when it grants a dictatorship power in a committee or on the Security Council? The time has come to realize that tolerance for tyrannies does not promote security. It just delays the day of reckoning....Regimes that repress their own people are a direct and real threat to the peace and security of all people everywhere."

CHAPTER 57

The Time Has Come to Realize That Tolerance for Tyrannies Does Not Promote Security

Speech at Rally Protesting Chinese Vice President Xi Jinping's Visit
Lafayette Park, Washington, DC, United States
Februrary14, 2012

In the course of its affairs as a great nation, China has left large fingerprints on the canvas of human events. With regard to human rights, these fingerprints place China at the scene of so many activities, both domestic and international, that are so outside the norm of civilized nations that the world's continued acquiescence to this repressive regime defies conscience, logic, and reason of humanity.

Democracies like the US rationalize their acquiescence by citing economic necessities or the need for world stability. In fact, in China, the CCP regime plays these false ideas of economic progress and societal stability as reasons for their hardline abuse of human rights.

Let us not be blinded by the glitter of economic progress in China. This regime that gunned down innocent civilians and students in 1989 is the same regime in power today. This is the same regime that is now pursuing cultural genocide on our Tibetan and Uyghur brothers. This is the same regime whose foreign policies and models of repression enable the morally bankrupt regimes of North Korea, Iran, and Syria to suck the freedoms and dignities from their people.

This is the same regime whose paranoid fear allows it to imprison and torture its best and brightest citizens. Why is this tolerated? Are the collective wills of the world's great democracies so impotent that they cannot react? I do not think so.

My friends, the time has come to realize that tolerance for tyrannies does not promote security. It just delays the day of reckoning. It intensifies the instability and threat to our security that these regimes present. As such, support for human rights can no longer be an optional component of the US foreign policy. It must be the foundation upon which all other bilateral issues rest.

My friends, the time has come for us to unify our efforts around promoting the connection between human rights and world peace and stability. We must rally our collective constituencies to convince leaders of the world democracies of the undeniable bond between human rights and world peace. We must get them to recognize that regimes that repress their own people are a direct and real threat to the peace and security of all people everywhere.

Dear friends, we should work together to urge the United Nations state members to remove China, the world's leading human rights violator, from special positions of power in the United Nations human rights system. China's membership in the UN Human Rights Council will expire at the end of this year and it should not be re-elected.

For what does it say to Tiananmen Mothers, to Liu Xiaobo and his wife, Liu Xia, to Wang Bingzhang, Gao Zhisheng, Liu Xianbin, Chen Guangcheng, Chen Wei, Chen Wei, Chen Xi, Hada, Zhu Yufu, to Tibetans, Uyghurs, Mongolians, to House Churches members, Falun Gong practitioners, and to the victims of Forced Abortions, Forced Evictions, Forced Disappearances, and Black Jails, if China remains a member of the United Nations Human Rights Council?

CHAPTER 58

Saffron Flames: The Voice of the Tibetans

Speech at Launching of the Namesake Book Hosted by International Campaign for Tibet
Washington, DC, United States
March 9, 2012

Dear friends,

It's been nearly two months of intense work editing *Saffron Flames: The Voice of the Tibetans*. The book is done, but I don't feel as if I can now breathe any easier. The subject of this book is just too heavy to bear, and the tragedy is just continuing to spiral down. Just as we put the book in print last weekend, again came the sad news of two more Tibetans who set themselves ablaze, bringing the number to twenty-six in three years. This is more than any human heart can and should take.

What causes a person to self-immolate? Common sense and moral tuition should enable us to realize that the spate of Tibetan self-immolations is revealing four, and only four, grave realities.

First. The increased clampdown on the Tibetans, especially monks and nuns, stepped-up cultural genocide, and ever-growing ethnic oppression have made the situation in Tibet unbearable to the Tibetans.

Second. The self-immolators did not end their lives out of fear or of utter despair as many think because there are a variety of less painful ways of terminating one's life if one acts out of fear or utter despair. Rather their very acts of self-immolation have displayed Tibetans' will power, resolution, and courage. They sacrificed their lives in the most painful way for a message.

Third. They have chosen to take the most desperate step of setting themselves on fire to protest because the message would have not been possible to get across otherwise given the most critical conditions in which they are forced to live.

Fourth. The self-immolators were not hopeless as many would say because hopeless people do nothing. Rather, they had a profound confidence in the conscience of man and set themselves on fire in the hopes that the flames would shine for the world to see the seas of unthinkable suffering and enlighten the hearts of many people around the world including that of the perpetrators. The greatest effect of this struggle is to awaken the world's morality.

Let's listen to the flames. Yes, there are voices in the flames: Free Tibet and Let the Dalai Lama Return Home! When we see the flames, we must hear the voices, and when we hear the voices, our conscience permits us nothing but to act as their transmitters and amplifiers through our words and deeds to awaken more people's moral conscience, letting more people know the truth about these tragedies, and allowing more people to experience these Tibetans' despair and desire to be reborn in the flames.

Here came the idea of editing, publishing, and distributing the book that is now in front of you.

This book includes news coverage of the Tibetan self-immolations, the positions of Western countries, the calls of the Tibetan exiles, as well as the comments of Chinese writers and human rights activists. At the same time, the book also collects some articles published in the official Chinese media for people to reference. This book is not an in-depth analysis of Tibetan self-immolations, but mainly the reactions from difference sources on the subject. We hoped to help the reader to have a broader view and to think more comprehensively and objectively about Tibetan self-immolation and about the nature of the Tibetan issue as a whole.

Lianchao, myself, and many of our colleagues who put efforts into this little book project did so primarily as human beings. Not just any human beings, but people who happen to have been so close to the issue and who are all impatient with injustice anywhere in whatever form. And we are Chinese; we particularly share this moment of sadness and anger and yet we have a unique shame to shake off: The Tibetan sufferings have been inflicted by a government consisting of mainly people of our ethnicity, and we are so ashamed of what the Chinese regime, Chinese officials, and Chinese soldiers have done to our Tibetan brothers and sisters. We are proud that we have fought side by side with Tibetans for more than two decades, yet this still cannot wash away all our shame. We always feel obliged to do more.

We edited the book as very special messengers in the hope of helping the voices in the flames reach out to more Chinese.

In the process of editing this book, we regret that, despite so many self-immolation cases, little is known about each individual incident itself. The information we have obtained is still far from sufficient, and in some cases, we know nothing about their personal background and their suffering—only their names. We don't even know if some of them are still alive. This reflects the high degree of control by the Chinese government in Tibet. Even compared with other parts of China, it is much harder for the outside world to obtain information from Tibet due to the restrictions on Tibetan transportation, communication, and language differences. We believe this is the very reason that the outside world must care more about Tibetan suffering. So far, the reaction to Tibetan self-immolation from the outside world, including Western societies, is far from sufficient. All of us who care about the survival of the Tibetans should make a greater effort to think and explore the question of how to make the outside world wake up from its desensitized state and exert greater pressure on the Chinese government to ease the suffering of the Tibetan people.

I want to take this opportunity to thank all the authors, and my special thanks go to Professor Yan Jiaqi for the preface and Professor Xia Ming for the introduction. During the editing process of this book, Kunga Tashi and other Tibetan friends have provided us with the information on the self-immolated Tibetans; we are grateful to their valuable help. In addition, we also want to express our thanks to those volunteers who have helped in information collection, book layout, and design.

Lastly, let us forever remember and always cherish the memory of each and every one of the Tibetan martyrs:

Tapey, Lobsang Phuntsok, Tsewang Norbu, Lobsang Kunchok, Lobsang Kelsang, Kelsang Wangchuk, Khaying, Choephel, Norbu Damdul, Tenzin Wangmo, Dawa Tsering, Palden Choetso, Tenzin Phuntsok, Tenyi, Tsultrim, Sobha Tulku, Lobsang Jamyang, Kyari, Tsering, Rigzin Dorje,Tsering Kyi, Rinchen…

CHAPTER 59

No Country That Behaves This Way toward Its Own Citizens Has a Place on the UN Human Rights Council

Opening Remarks at the Fourth Geneva Summit for Human Rights and Democracy
Geneva, Switzerland
March 13, 2012

Good morning, my friends. And good day.

I say good day because any time friends join together to openly dedicate themselves to the collaborative work of advancing human rights and democracy, it is a good day. As the United Nations Human Rights Council holds its main annual session, our Geneva Summit for Human Rights and Democracy is assembling hundreds of courageous dissidents and human rights activists, diplomats, and student leaders to shine a spotlight and call for action on urgent human rights situations that require global attention. And so, let me say again, good morning and good day.

Of course, although it is morning in this beautiful city on this very good day, we know too that we are gathered in the shade of shadows—shadows cast by human rights abuses, shadows cast by human rights abusers.

The Syrian autocracy's continuing brutal crackdown on its own people is today the most visible example of the bad and predictable habits of corrupt and unaccountable power.

But while we watch and read in horror as the Assad regime murders Syrian citizens, while we deplore the senseless carnage visited upon our Syrian brothers and sisters, and while we lament that more than sixty years after the promulgation of the Universal Declaration of Human Rights, the world still cannot prevent atrocities like those taking place today in Syria, we should be grateful to the Syrian people for courageously reminding us that human dignity does not compromise when it demands recognition.

We should also be grateful to the Syrian people for reminding us that the work we do here, in Geneva, is concretely connected to their struggle.

You see, I come from China. And just as the people of Syria have friends in people of conscience around the globe, their oppressor has a friend in the Chinese regime.

The Chinese regime that massacred innocent civilians and students in 1989 is the same regime still in power today. This is the same regime that is pursuing cultural genocide on our Tibetan, Uyghur, and Mongolian brothers. This is the same regime whose paranoid fear allows it to imprison and torture its best and brightest citizens.

The list of the Chinese government's crimes against its own citizens goes on and on. The number of the regime's victims runs into the millions, including the twenty-seven Tibetan self-immolators in the recent three years. And this is the same regime whose foreign policies and models of repression enable the morally and philosophically bankrupt regimes of North Korea, Iran, Syria, and so on to suck the lives, freedoms, dignities, and wealth from their people.

Then what is China's punishment for this scandalous behavior?

When it comes to the UN, there is no punishment. Quite the contrary, China is rewarded for its behavior with a seat on the world's highest human rights body, the UN Human Rights Council. It also has a permanent seat on the UN Security Council where it can exercise its veto with impunity.

As a result of this farcical arrangement, the Chinese government—an unaccountable and illegitimate power that does not even represent its own people—is able to influence how other countries, indeed, how other dictatorships treat their people.

No country that behaves this way toward its own citizens has a place on the UN Human Rights Council. No country.

And no country that uses its veto power to prevent UN condemnation of atrocities against the people of another country like those taking place in Syria has any right to the power it has been given by the United Nations. No country.

Indeed, we must ask ourselves serious questions: Why should any dictatorship have a say in world human affairs when it does not allow a voice to its own citizens? Who does a dictatorship represent when it takes its seat at the UN? More importantly, who and what is the UN choosing to recognize when it grants a dictatorship power in a committee or on the Security Council?

In the case of China, the consequences of the dictatorship's power for the people of China is clear enough. So too are the consequences of its power at the UN for the people of Syria. All of these consequences are unacceptable. If China were a pupil in elementary school, its progress reports would never stop reading, "must do better." But because it is not a pupil in elementary school, but a powerful nation at the UN, its progress reports always read, "good enough."

But that's not good enough for the advancement of human rights. "Special friendships" between dictatorships cannot be allowed to continue at the UN.

The continued existence of dictatorships in today's world is an embarrassment to common sense and to our common humanity. Dictatorships today exist as desperate anachronisms, clinging as they do to the nearest and most convenient justifications—be they cultural, historical, or economic—to maintain power.

Human rights heroes from Burma, China, Cuba, Iran, Sudan, Venezuela, Zimbabwe, and other countries will testify today at this summit that their struggles have demonstrated and will continue to demonstrate just how flimsy these justifications are. We are very much looking forward to hearing their inspiring testimony.

We should be grateful to these heroes for reminding us that tyranny's desperate wars against fundamental human dignity are bound to fail. History progresses and older methods of control are swept away as concentrated and illegitimate power faces increased opposition from more and more forces demanding freedom from domination, as has been most recently evidenced by the Arab Spring and the opening up in Burma and will surely be proved again and again by the people's struggle in China, Cuba, Iran, Sudan, Venezuela, Zimbabwe, and other remaining world autocracies. This is the promise of democracy in our own times.

This is truly a good day. But I must remind you, my dear friends, that it says a lot about the work that must be done that the discussion we are having here today must take place outside of the official United Nations meetings. Clearly, we have a great deal to do.

And let us make no mistake as we move forward—the international interconnectedness of our work must always be at the front of our minds. The problems of the people of China are our problems because they are the problems of the people of Syria; the problems of the people of Syria are our problems because they are the problems of the people of Iran, of North Korea, of Russia, and so on. They are the problems that we must confront honestly, energetically, and forthrightly today in order to make good days possible for more and more people tomorrow.

CHAPTER 60

Moving Forward Together

Opening Remarks of the Seventh Interethnic/ Interfaith Leadership Conference
Long Beach, CA, United States
April 19, 2012

Dear friends, dear brothers and sisters,

It is heartening to see all of you coming to the seventh Interethnic/ Interfaith Leadership Conference. When I think of the distances, especially the psychological distances that we have traveled to be here, I am blessedly reminded that even with all the difficulties facing us which, sadly to say, may not have become less daunting than at the beginning of this century when this conference was first started, so much has already been done to establish the foundational spirit of community that is essential to our labors in and on behalf of the future.

When we first undertook this endeavor in 2000, we knew we were taking up one of the most challenging jobs in the world but knew not how long we would be able to persevere. Twelve years and seven major assemblies and hard work in between should justly bestow us some pride. Looking back, my heart is filled with gratitude to the people of conscience and vision like those at the US National Endowment for Democracy and Taiwan Foundation for Democracy. Without their unwavering support, it is truly questionable whether we could have traveled so far as we did. Most importantly, the people and groups that our participants here represent have never, in past decades, spared a single day in their struggle for freedom and dignity. They have been the major source of inspiration to us, and their unflagging spirit has led us every step of the way toward where we are today.

In our past assemblies and our work in between, we have been committed to following the principles of respecting the differences between ethnic groups, embracing human rights as a universal value, uniting as one for the realization of a common democratic future, to nonviolence and overcoming evil with good. We have been committed to maintaining close communication, exercising tolerance and forgiveness toward each other, eliminating hatred, resentment and misunderstanding, pursuing truth, accomplishing reconciliation and loving one another, and we have been committed to mutual concern for each other's human rights, and to offer necessary assistance. I want to refresh every one of us with these principles which, arduously established, should guide us today to move us forward together. "Moving forward together" is the theme of this assembly.

A year ago, we held our sixth assembly in Los Angeles, which is not far from here. This past year experienced the Chinese regime's crackdowns against various ethnic, religious, and political groups with greater frequency and increasing brutality, and people's unprecedented resistances as highlighted by the spate of Tibetan self-immolation protests. During the coming three days, we will discuss these situations as well as strategies for us to take actions as a whole.

In this past year, two major elections took place in regions represented here in this conference, one in Taiwan and the other in Hong Kong. We will hear reports on the elections and the impacts those elections will have on the people in Taiwan and Hong Kong as well as other people represented by our participants sitting here. We will be privileged to hear lectures by prominent professors from both American and Chinese universities that will inform and empower our thinking for our future work. Our most inspiring representative—Ms. Rebiya Kadeer—will share with us her thoughts on how to promote democracy through mutual understanding and cooperation. Very encouraging indeed that this conference will also feature three teenage girls who will present special reports on their quest for freedom as the "second generation" of Tiananmen activists. We will be lucky to have leading voices of nonviolence principles and political changes in the Middle East and Burma, who will share with us their respective valuable experiences. And I am most thankful that His Holiness the Dalai Lama will meet with our participants. I believe every one of you is as eager as myself to hear His teachings.

Now let us begin our program.

Let this meeting lay the groundwork for us to create strategies for us to continue to move forward together.

Thank you.

CHAPTER 61

The Lust of Power and Greed Is No Match for the Thirst for Freedom

CEPOS Freedom Award Acceptance Speech
Copenhagen, Denmark
April 30, 2012

Dear friends,

I am both humbled and invigorated to be honored as the recipient of the 2012 Center for Political Studies Freedom Award. I understand that this prestigious award recognizes individuals who demonstrate a "principled and steadfast commitment to the values and ideas of individual freedom and basic human rights."

Although I stand here before you as your honoree, in my eyes I see in front of me the faces of my brothers in China, my fellow freedom fighters in Burma, Cuba, Egypt, Iran, North Korea, Syria, Vietnam, and other closed societies around the globe whose lifework and whose very willingness to shed their life's blood, each and every day, make each of them so much more deserving of this recognition than I. It is only with this acknowledgement that I can accept this award.

I am invigorated with the knowledge that I inherit this award from last year's recipient, Yoani Sánchez, whose amazing courage, despite huge personal costs, gives daily voice to the reality inside one of the world's most suffocating dictatorships.

And I am truly honored to receive this award from CEPOS who, although young in years, has earned the recognition and respect of much older and bigger sister foundations through its vigorous support of the worldwide struggle for freedom, justice, and human rights.

Your recognition strengthens my commitment to my fallen brothers in Tiananmen Square, to my compatriots including Christians and Falun Gong practitioners, to my Tibetan, Uyghur, and Mongolian brothers and sisters who suffer mightily under the unspeakable repression of a government whose sixty-three years of tyranny have taken more lives than the victims of Stalin and Hitler combined. And even today, the repressive power and policies of this government spill over its own borders to enable the morally bankrupt regimes of Iran, North Korea, Syria, and etc. to sustain. A government whose disdain for human dignity now openly challenges the very foundations of civilization itself.

Your recognition doubles my resolve to use all my God-given strengths to join with you in our common goal to confront lies with truth, dissolve tyranny with the power of nonviolent resistance, and to replace repression and divisiveness through the irresistible strength of compassion and understanding.

Though the struggle will be long, the outcome is certain. The voices of history speak to us over and over again. From Downing Street in London during the darkest days of World War II, to the dockyards of Gdańsk in Poland, to the voices of Gandhi, Martin Luther King Jr., Havel, the Dalai Lama and Aung Sang Suu Kyi, and the writings of Liu Xiaobo and Yoani Sánchez, all demonstrate to us the power of truth and individual courage to triumph over even the mightiest armies of repression. Though the languages are different, the message is universal:

The lust of power and greed is no match for the thirst for freedom. It is this universal and unquenchable thirst for freedom that drives humanity forward… away from darkness and into light.

Here I am reminded of Hans Christian Andersen's little match girl who lit matches to repel the cold and illuminate the sky. As she drew her last breath, the light from these matches carries her to heavenly love and peace.

As your honoree, and in the name of all the voices for freedom that CEPOS supports around the world, I embrace this award and hold close to my heart as I promise to light matches for freedom and justice until my very last breath.

Thank you and may God bless us all.

CHAPTER 62

Three Chinas, Liu Xiaobo, and the Rest of the World

Speech at the Fourth Annual Oslo Freedom Forum
Oslo, Norway
May 9, 2012

Dear friends,

Everyone asks: Why is China, a seemingly increasingly assertive world power, afraid of a single man like Liu Xiaobo? Why is it afraid of a moderate document like Charter 08, a manifesto authored by Liu Xiaobo and his colleagues demanding for political reform?

Liu Xiaobo and his colleagues recognize there are two Chinas. They have tried to bring together these two severely separated Chinas and construct a society based on universal values.

By "two Chinas," I am not talking about "Mainland China" and "Taiwan." Geographically, there is only one entity of Mainland China, but politically, economically, sociologically, and even sentimentally, it has largely broken into two societies.

Over the past twenty-three years since Tiananmen Square, the CCP regime has established a two-China structure and one of the two Chinas, which I call China, Inc., is formed by the marriage of China's political elite, economic elite, and co-opted intellectuals who monopolize power, capital, culture, and information.

Today, China, Inc. is dazzling the entire world with its wealth, might, and glory. It dominates the public discourse that outside observers believe that it represents China—the whole of China.

The truth is there is another society named China, the under China, a society constituted of over a billion Chinese who are virtually slave-laborers working for China, Inc.

There is an unprecedented wealth gap between the Chinas, and the citizens of the under China are severely exploited economically but without protection of constitutionally afforded civil and political rights. The two Chinas no longer speak a common political language and have no common political life, and the underclass have grown more and more discontent and distrustful of the elite.

It is, however, not enough to just see the severe division of the two societies of China. We must envision the emergence of a new, democratic China: the third China, which is represented by people like Liu Xiaobo.

Despite the division, there are two often overlooked consensuses among Chinese from both societies. The first is that the present China is not "normal." The second, agreed upon to a lesser degree, is that China will eventually become normal through democratic means.

In order to find a common ground to lay the foundation for the third China, we must create a political language based on universal values that can bridge the gap between the two Chinas. And that is exactly what Liu Xiaobo, and Charter 08, has been intent on accomplishing.

Change is unlikely to first happen from within the deeply entrenched CCP regime, which values stability above all. The persecution of Liu Xiaobo is evidence of this. Liu Xiaobo has repeatedly said, "In the people lies the hope for a democratic China."

The Nobel Peace Prize awarded to Liu Xiaobo has remarkable impacts on the hearts of the people, and over the past year, the civil movement has become increasingly mature, skillful, and resilient as evidenced by three cases: Chen Guangcheng, Ai Weiwei, and the Wukan villagers.

Charter 08 is our banner and Liu Xiaobo our standard bearer. Backed by large numbers of its real-name signers from diverse segments of society, the Charter will continue to transform individual protests into a long-lasting movement that demands across the board, systemic change.

As the people's forces grow and the civil protests escalate, power struggles within the CCP regime will become more pronounced. Once the external pressure reaches a critical mass, the rival factions within the CCP will have no choice but to take the voices of the people seriously and seek their support to survive. And the release of Liu Xiaobo will help signal the coming of that change.

When a large-scale movement takes place again, as it did in 1989, we will need leaders to play the roles that Mandela, Havel, Walesa, and Aung San Suu Kyi have played at the critical moments of political change in their respective countries. We will need a group of civil leaders who can disrupt the political order and establish itself as the legitimate voice of the people in negotiations with the state. Liu Xiaobo, as a widely accepted leader both at home and abroad, will surely play a unique role in forming such a group, which was most needed but lacking in our 1989 Tiananmen movement.

Therefore, working toward his freedom is vital for a democratic change in China. I am particularly encouraged by the strong support for Liu Xiaobo from world human rights activists. Aung San Suu Kyi was released from house arrest in November of 2010. For the first time, there is hope for reform in Burma. In seeking Liu's release, we hope and struggle for the same in China.

CHAPTER 63

There Must Be Universally Accepted Principles of Justice and Universally Condemned Violations of Human Rights

Acceptance Speech for the UN Watch Morris B. Abram Human Rights Award
Geneva, Switzerland
May 23, 2012

Ambassador Moses, Hillel, Arielle, Leon, all UN Watch friends, distinguished guests, ladies and gentlemen,

Thank you for this honor.

Indeed, it is a great honor to be recognized by UN Watch with its Morris B. Abram Human Rights Award. I gratefully and humbly accept this honor before this most impressive audience, not for myself, but on behalf of the great multitude of victims of human rights abuse in China and elsewhere, and equally on behalf of the many courageous souls who daily risk life and limb to aid, comfort, and defend them.

It is truly humbling to be put in the same company with such heroes as the past recipients of this award. Standing here, I am also cast in the long shadow of the glorious life of Morris Abram, whose many decades of service in the cause of human rights around the world is a shining example for us to try to follow.

In contrast to these towering figures, I am no more than a citizen of China, one of the 1.4 billion, nearly a quarter of humanity, ruled by a government who systematically and routinely imprisons, tortures, and exiles its best and brightest of us for no other reason than exercising the right to speak freely, who pursues cultural genocide on our Tibetan, Uyghur, and Mongolian brothers, and whose foreign policies and models of repression enable the morally bankrupt regimes of North Korea, Iran, and Syria to suck the freedoms and dignities from their people.

Tonight, I respectfully ask each of you, in your mind's eye, to look across the bridge created by Morris Abram between the world struggles against the horrors of the Holocaust and against today's assault on human rights. Look over that bridge spanning more than seven decades. Look across to the victims of the Holocaust, to the sixty-five million victims of WWII, and to many more lives lost at the hands of the Chinese communist regime. It is often said that those who do not learn from history are condemned to repeat it. So, what must we learn as we gaze across that bridge? We should learn at least two fundamental lessons:

1. Government that systematically deprives its citizens of human rights is inherently unstable.
2. If left unchecked, this instability inevitably destabilizes the world order with horrific consequences.

Therefore, there must be universally accepted principles of justice and human dignity and universally condemned violations of human rights that cannot be swept under the rug of international understanding or hidden behind a fig leaf of "cultural relativism." Unfortunately, all too often, the world leaders turn to that overused excuse for not confronting the perpetrators. Morris Abram knew that on such fundamental issues, there is a "right" and there is a "wrong." He established UN Watch to monitor the UN and require it to live up to the promises of its Charter and the Universal Declaration of Human Rights. UN Watch wisely and relentlessly insists on measuring what the UN and its members say in regard to human rights and justice against what they actually do.

Morris Abram knew, as we do today, that it is wrong for the UN to apply different human rights standards to different member countries;

it is wrong for the UN to allow citizen-abusing governments to pretend to represent their people in its mechanisms and even to bully the international community by virtue of veto power in its security council; and it is wrong for the UN to allow such world-leading human rights abusers as China, Cuba, Libya, Syria, and Saudi Arabia to be elected members of its human rights council.

As I stand here tonight as a honored citizen of China in the legacy of Morris Abram, I am rededicating myself to moving beyond talking about China's human rights record toward engaging all who recognize human rights as the key to world peace, to develop policies that produce real political reform in China, to make substantive political reform of the UN, and for the world democracies to enshrine human rights as a cornerstone of international diplomacy. This is for the good of the people of China as well as the people of the rest of the world.

Thank you, UN Watch. I will continue to look up to your leadership in the global cause of human rights.

Once more, I most sincerely thank you for this honor on behalf of all the victims of oppression and all those who seek to defend them.

Thank you.

CHAPTER 64

Be Strong and Be Supportive and Be Ready

Speech at AEI Forum "From Glasnost to the Arab Spring: The Moral Foundation of Anti-Authoritarian Revolutions"
Washington, DC, United States
June 13, 2012

It is an honor for me to speak here today at the American Enterprise Institute. I admire the AEI for the high marks it gets on policy analyses, solid reports, balanced panel discussions, and practical recommendations to policymakers. China would do well with a few AEIs in Beijing—provided they had First Amendment protections to "speak truth to power."

The first order of truth about China is that the people of China, too, want human rights. This sentence sounds a bit awkward with the word "too." I put it there because the truth—that the people of China want human rights—has not only been suppressed by the Chinese communist regime but is all too often overlooked by the world community.

"Given so much you have been through," I am often asked, "where does your confidence lie?" My answer is always, "My confidence lies in the simple fact that the people of China want human rights."

"Do you really believe so?" Some sound skeptical seeing the insurmountable China realities. Well, let me propose the following thought experiment for you to judge for yourselves.

Imagine that you visited China, taking with you a copy of the *Universal Declaration of Human Rights*. Arbitrarily choose any citizens on the street. Show the document, asking them with the language they understand whether they want the rights listed there. What would you expect them to say? Would you for a second believe they would say, "No, I do not want these rights"? Of course not. You understand the Chinese people through understanding yourselves: Nobody wants to be a slave. In this regard, the Chinese people are no different than other people in the world. The thirst for freedom and dignity is indeed universal.

The people of China have long ago begun the search for, using our dear host Leon Aron's term, "roads to the temple" of dignity, justice, goodness, fairness, equality, freedom, and brotherhood. They have produced a few major pushes toward these goals in this generation. In the 1989 Tiananmen democracy movement, the Chinese people courageously stood up against government corruption that in the words of Charter08 has "corrupted human intercourse." They stood up for democracy and freedom. The image of a lone man standing in front of a string of tanks has inspired the entire world, and our fallen brothers' spirits have been one of the greatest sources of inspiration for continued struggle for these noble goals in China.

But the Tiananmen Massacre created a strong sense of fear of political engagement among ordinary people. When fear, indifference, and cynicism soon became fashionable in China. Hopes for a public system of checks and balances against governmental abuse were swept away by the bloodletting of June 4, 1989.

But 1989 also created fear and crisis within the communist regime. Life was no longer the same for rulers who had to develop new tactics to meet its "overwhelming" need to preserve the status quo.

Then the Soviet Union disintegrated and the Eastern European Bloc opened up. This cast an even heavier cloud over the heads of Chinese communist officials. How long could the communists stay in power?

Shortly after Deng Xiaoping's famous Southern Inspection Tour in 1992, communist bureaucrats at all levels realized three realities:

First, the CCP's hold on power had nothing to do with communist principles.

Second, continued economic growth was the last, best hope to keep the ship afloat.

Third, the elite must be spoiled to retain their loyalty. Corruption was now accepted, endorsed—even demanded.

Understanding these realities, over the past twenty years, the CCP regime established a two-China structure. One of the two Chinas, which I call China, Inc. is formed by

1. Red Capitalists
2. Marriage between Power and Capital taking advantage of:
    - Low human rights standards
    - Low environmental protection
    - Low wages
    - Banning collective bargaining power
3. China, Inc. shares open to domestic and foreign capitalists
4. China, Inc. shares free to intellectuals

Today, China, Inc. is dazzling the entire world with its wealth, might, and glory. It dominates the public discourse so that outside observers believe that it represents the whole of China.

The truth is there is another society in China, a society of over a billion Chinese who are virtually slave-laborers working for China, Inc. I call this second China the under China.

Here is how these two Chinas diverge.

1. Unprecedented wealth gap between the two.
2. Citizens of the under China are citizens in name only. They are unable to enjoy basic benefits or constitutionally afforded civil rights.
3. The elite's monopoly over power, capital, and information makes mobility from one China to the other nearly impossible.
4. The two Chinas no longer speak a common political language.
5. The two Chinas have almost no common political life.
6. The two societies have grown more and more distrustful of each other.

Then how does the CCP regime maintain the two-China structure?

On top of the traditional lies and violence, which every autocratic ruler uses, the CCP regime has developed new tactics. It is comprised in the shape of a dragon:

- The body: sustaining economic growth at all costs to maintain the regime's ruling legitimacy
- Two wings: appeasing the elite with corruption and suppressing the powerless with rogue police
- Two claws: purging citizen advocates like Liu Xiaobo and blocking public opinion

Nevertheless, it is not enough to just see the severe division of the two societies of China. We must envision the emergence of a new, democratic China represented by people who have the moral courage and vision to cross the border, trying to integrate the two societies based on justice and universal values. Thanks to their arduous work and enormous sacrifices, the concepts of human rights and democracy have prevailed in the minds of the Chinese general public.

To find a common ground to lay the foundation for a more integrated China, we must create a political language based on universal values that can bridge the gap between the two Chinas. And that is exactly what Charter 08 has been intent on accomplishing.

A breakthrough for a democratic change will surely come from the people. Change is unlikely to happen first from within the heavily entrenched CCP regime, which values stability above all.

Despite the CCP's best effort to impose strict control over the media, the internet has allowed people to connect, to share information.

Following the release of Charter 08, grassroots support for the document was immediate and unprecedented, even though the CCP regime tried to block its spread. Those who signed the Charter with their real names came from diverse segments of society. Charter 08 is a banner that will continue to transform individual protests into a long-lasting movement that demands across the board, systematic change.

The Nobel Peace Prize awarded to Liu Xiaobo has had a remarkable impact on the hearts of the people of China. Over the past year, the civil movement has become increasingly mature, skillful, and resilient as evidenced by three cases: Chen Guangcheng, Ai Weiwei, and the Wukan villagers. All took place amid the latest round of heavy-handed crackdowns on dissent after the Arab Spring.

With a clear direction of the political resistance movement, the people will grow to exert greater and greater pressure on the communist regime. As non-governmental forces grow and civil protests escalate, the struggle for power among different factions within the communist regime will become more pronounced. Once external pressures reach a critical mass, rival factions within the CCP will have no choice but to take the voices of the citizens seriously and seek their support to survive.

When a large-scale movement takes place again, as it did in 1989, we will need leaders to play the roles that Nelson Mandela, Václav Havel, Lech Walesa, and Aung San Suu Kyi played in the political changes of their respective countries. We will need a group of strong civil leaders who can disrupt the political order and establish themselves as the legitimate voice of the people in negotiations with the state. Liu Xiaobo, as a widely accepted leader both at home and abroad, will surely play a unique role in forming such a group, which was most needed but lacking in our 1989 Tiananmen movement.

No one can predict with precision when the moment of dramatic opening for change will come in China. Virtually every one of the sixty-some peaceful transitions to democracy in the past few decades has come as a surprise to the United States. One reason is that diplomats, academics, and policymakers generally do not pay attention to what is happening with students, workers, and farmers—with the street level society and culture of the world's not-free countries.

The people of China are obviously experiencing revolutionary change. Above all else we must maintain our faith in my compatriots that we can and will join the vast majority of the world's people who now live in free or at least partly free countries. An opening for change could come in the next few months or it may take a few more years. Of course, it will never come without collective efforts, including those from the international community. So, we must persevere and be ready and keep the faith.

"Be watchful and strong in the faith, for the time draws near," exhorted St. Paul, a persecutor of Christians who converted to the faith. Ladies and gentlemen, our time draws near. We must watch and be strong and be supportive and be ready.

CHAPTER 65

To My Burmese Brothers and Sisters, I Say Two Very Happy Words: "Go Home!"

Speech at Farewell Party to Burmese Exiles
Washington, DC, United States
August 19, 2012

It is a unique welcome we extend today to these distinguished members of the Burmese 88 Generation. We wish them well as they begin their journey home from which they have been exiled for twenty-four years. To them I say, "Welcome to the beginning of your return!"

We, the Chinese democracy activists, have long admired the tenacity, nobility, and dignity of our Burmese brothers and sisters. There have been apparent parallels between their struggle and ours. I don't think I overstate matters when I say there is a certain kinship between the Burmese and Chinese democracy struggles—just as there is kinship between all movements seeking to dignify and ennoble mankind.

The Burmese democracy uprising of August 8, 1988, was met with violence by the state. Many of those who were not killed were imprisoned or sent into exile. The government refused to accept responsibility for the deaths it caused. Daw Aung San Suu Kyi was, for nearly twenty years, the only Nobel Peace Prize laureate kept in detention by her own government.

In China, our pro-democracy movement was met with a similar brutal crackdown—that of June 4, 1989. I was in Tiananmen Square when the tanks rolled in that day, and I saw my countrymen crushed beneath tank treads and felled by machine gun fire. I was among the lucky who escaped.

For us, it has been twenty-three long years of exile. During this time, we have seen the Chinese government refuse to accept responsibility for the deaths it caused in 1989—or for the ongoing repression that continues to this day. Now our leader Liu Xiaobo is the only Nobel Peace Prize laureate kept in detention by his own government.

Going home has long been a dream of exiled Chinese, Tibetan, Uyghur, and Mongolian freedom lovers, actually of all people for that matter. In the spate of the recent fifty-some Tibetan self-immolation protests, each and every one of the martyrs cried for the return of His Holiness the Dalai Lama who has been away from his home for more than five decades.

All of this has made our hearts very heavy.

And yet, when we look to the example of our Burmese brothers and sisters, we cannot help but be inspired.

They show us what is possible for their country, for China, and for the world.

Today, they begin their return to a Burma that is much changed since their exile began twenty-four years ago, changed because of their persistent and untiring efforts. While Burma is not yet the full democratic society they hope for, they—and we—have seen significant progress. The Burmese government has acknowledged the 88 Generation movement; Aung San Suu Kyi has not only been released from detention, she now serves in Parliament, and these brave Burmese leaders before us have at last been allowed to return home.

In short, we have seen an opening in Burma through which forces of freedom, democracy, and human dignity can more easily pass. This has shown all of us, once again, that repression—no matter how strong, no matter how entrenched—always has a fight on its hands. And it has given those of us fighting for freedom in China hope that, with enough effort, we too will soon see similar developments in our country.

And so, in tribute to the bravery and hard work of these inspirational Burmese leaders, let me close by saying words not typically associated with the warm welcome owed to distinguished guests, but in this case very fitting. To my Burmese brothers and sisters, I say two very happy words: "Go home!"

CHAPTER 66

Three Chinas and the Rest of the World

Speech at San Francisco Freedom Forum with Aung San Suu Kyi
San Francisco, CA, United States
September 28, 2012

Mr. Chairman, Daw Aung San Suu Kyi, dear friends,

You may well be puzzled by the title. Why three Chinas? Am I talking about Mainland China and Taiwan? No, that's two, not three. Or the Mainland China, Taiwan, Hong Kong, and Macau? No, that's four, again not three. Actually, I am talking about the Mainland China itself. The truth is geographically there is only one entity of Mainland China, but politically, economically, sociologically, and even sentimentally, it has largely broken into two societies. And we, the Chinese democrats, with the support and help from good people around the world like those at Human Rights Foundation, have tried to bring together these two severely separated Chinas and construct a society built upon universal values, that is the third China, a democratic China we are working on.

Over the past twenty-some years after Tiananmen Square, the CCP regime has established a two-China structure, and one of the two Chinas, which I call China, Inc., is formed by government officials, red capitalists, and co-opted business elite and cultural elite through the marriage between power and capital, shares open to domestic and foreign capitalists, and shares free to elite intellectuals.

Today, China, Inc. is dazzling the entire world with its wealth, might, and glory. It dominates the public discourse that outside observers believe that it represents China—the whole of China.

But the truth is there is another society named China, a society constituted of over a billion Chinese who are virtually slave-laborers working for China, Inc. I call this second China the under China.

There is an unprecedented wealth gap between the two Chinas. Citizens of the under China, constantly subjected to exploitation and persecution, are unable to enjoy basic benefits or constitutionally afforded civil and political rights. The two Chinas no longer speak a common political language and have no common political life.

To maintain the two-China structure on top of the traditional lies and violence every autocratic ruler uses, the CCP regime has developed new tactics. It is comprised in the shape of a dragon. Here you go.

- The body: sustaining economic growth at all costs to maintain the regime's ruling legitimacy
- Two wings: appeasing the elite with corruption and suppressing the powerless with rogue police
- Two claws: purging citizen advocates like Liu Xiaobo and blocking public opinion

Daw Aung San Suu Kyi has recently observed, "It is not power that corrupts, but fear. Fear of losing power corrupts those who have it." The China we view today reflects her wisdom.

The CCP regime's paranoid fear allows it to imprison and torture its best and brightest citizens. In considering this regime's record, we need look no further than these individuals, groups, events, and policies: The Tiananmen Massacre, Tiananmen Mothers, Charter 08… Liu Xiaobo and his wife, Liu Xia, Wang Bingzhang, Gao Zhisheng, Liu Xianbin, Chen Guangcheng, Ai Weiwei… Tibetans, Uyghurs, Mongolians… House Churches, Falun Gong, Forced Abortions, Forced Evictions, Forced Disappearances, Black Jails…

And this is the same regime whose foreign policies and models of repression enable the morally and philosophically bankrupt regimes like that of North Korea, Iran, and Syria to suck the lives, freedoms, dignities, and wealth from their people.

My earlier quote of Daw Aung San Suu Kyi about the fear of losing power was incomplete. Following what I quoted, she also said, "(And) fear of the scourge of power corrupts those who are subject to it."

This fear has not only worked in China but also gone beyond its borders. This regime, to use the words of a recent torture victim in China, is "spoiled" by the Western countries, particularly the United States. The world history tells us that no country that treats its own people harshly can be relied on to treat another country's people with compassion. This polarized two-China structure also poses a direct and real threat to the peace and security of all people everywhere. Are the collective wills of the world's great democracies so impotent that they cannot react? No, I don't think so.

Our confidence will be emboldened if we realize that the people of China, too, want human rights. This sentence sounds a bit awkward with the word "too." I put it there because the truth that the people of China want human rights has not only been suppressed by the Chinese communist regime but is all too often overlooked by the world community.

For those who are skeptical, let me propose the following thought experiment for you to judge for yourselves.

Imagine that you visited China, taking with you a copy of the Universal Declaration of Human Rights. Arbitrarily choose any citizens on the street. Show the document, asking them with the language they understand whether they want the rights listed there. What would you expect them to say? Would you for a second believe they would say, "No, I do not want these rights"? Of course, you wouldn't. You see, you understand the Chinese people through understanding yourselves: Nobody wants to be a slave. In this regard, the Chinese people are no different than other people in the world. The thirst for freedom and dignity is indeed universal.

The people of China have long ago begun the search for dignity, justice, goodness, fairness, equality, freedom, and brotherhood. They have produced a few major pushes toward these goals in this generation. In the 1989 Tiananmen democracy movement, the Chinese people courageously stood up against government corruption that, in the words of Charter08, has "corrupted human intercourse." They stood up for democracy and freedom. The image of a lone man standing in front of a string of tanks has inspired the entire world, and our fallen brothers' spirits have been one of the greatest sources of inspiration for continued struggle for these noble goals today in China.

We must envision the emergence of a new, democratic China represented by people who have the moral courage and vision to cross the border, trying to integrate the two societies based on justice and universal values. Thanks to their arduous work and enormous sacrifices, the concepts of human rights and democracy have prevailed in the minds of the Chinese general public.

To find a common ground to lay the foundation for a more integrated China, we must create a political language based on universal values that can bridge the gap between the two Chinas. And that is exactly what Charter 08 has been intent on accomplishing.

A breakthrough for a democratic change will surely come from the people. Change is unlikely to happen first from within the heavily entrenched CCP regime, which values stability above all.

Despite the CCP's best effort to impose strict control over the media, the internet has allowed people to connect, to share information.

Following the release of Charter 08, grassroots support for the document was immediate and unprecedented, even though the CCP regime tried to block its spread. Those who signed the Charter with their real names came from diverse segments of society. Charter 08 is a banner that will continue to transform individual protests into a long-lasting movement that demands across the board, systematic change.

The Nobel Peace Prize awarded to Liu Xiaobo has had a remarkable impact on the hearts of the people of China. Over the past year the civil movement has become increasingly mature, skillful, and resilient as evidenced by three cases: Chen Guangcheng, Ai Weiwei, and the Wukan villagers. All took place amid a latest round of heavy-handed crackdowns on dissent after the Arab Spring.

With a clear direction of the political resistance movement, the people will grow to exert greater and greater pressure on the communist regime. As non-governmental forces grow and civil protests escalate, the struggle for power among different factions within the communist regime will become more pronounced. Once external pressures reach a critical mass, rival factions within the CCP will have no choice but to take the voices of the citizens seriously and seek their support to survive.

When a large-scale movement takes place again, as it did in 1989, we will need leaders to play the roles that Nelson Mandela, Václav Havel, Lech Walesa, and Aung San Suu Kyi played in the political changes of their respective countries. We will need a group of strong civil leaders who can disrupt the political order and establish themselves as the legitimate voice of the people in negotiations with the state. Liu Xiaobo, as a widely accepted leader both at home and abroad, will surely play a unique role in forming such a group, which was most needed but lacking in our 1989 Tiananmen movement.

No one can predict with precision when the moment of dramatic opening for change will come in China. Virtually every one of the sixty-some peaceful transitions to democracy in the past few decades has come as a surprise to the United States. One reason is that diplomats, academics, and policymakers generally do not pay attention to what is happening with students, workers, and farmers—with the street-level society and culture of the world's not-free countries.

The people of China are obviously experiencing revolutionary change. Above all else we must maintain our faith in my compatriots that we can and will join the vast majority of the world's people who now live in free or at least partly free countries. An opening for change could come in the next few months or it may take a few more years. Of course, it will never come without collective efforts, including those from the international community. So, we must persevere and keep the faith and be ready.

Thank you.

CHAPTER 67

The Truth Will Set Us Free

Speech at the Closing Ceremony of the International Conference of Tibet Support Groups
Dharamsala, India
November 18, 2012

Dear brothers and sisters,

Nearly eighty Tibetans have set themselves on fire in the past three years for the cause of their people's freedom. This month alone, the world bore witness to fifteen more tragic and heroic self-immolations. We all have a strong sense that they will not stop. Even as I speak, there may be more actually happening.

The martyrdom of so many devoted and peaceable Tibetan people has overwhelmed me with grief. As a Chinese man, I stand before you shamed, embarrassed, and humbled. Shamed by the unspeakable suffering the Chinese government has systematically inflicted upon the people of Tibet. Embarrassed by the general apathy of the Chinese general public. Humbled because I am a proud man: a proud man brought to his knees by the weight of his grief, the force of his anger, and the unbearable feeling of helplessness in the face of such powerful evil. Yet I draw strength and inspiration from you, my dear Tibetan brothers and sisters; you inspire me through your endurance despite these grievous assaults on your language, your culture, your religion, your land, your spirit, and even your lives. And I draw strength and inspiration from good people like you, the participants of this international conference; your relentless efforts have kept the issue of Tibet alive and the worldwide Tibet support network snowballing. And I draw strength and inspiration from the words of His Holiness the Dalai Lama, *"Tragedy should be utilized as a source of strength. No matter what sort of difficulties, how painful the experience is, if we lose our hope, that's our real disaster."*

Yes, we must draw hope from these saffron flames of martyrdom. We must not lose hope. But hope alone cannot defeat this evil. We must have a tool more powerful than evil. His Holiness tells us, *"In our struggle for freedom, truth is the only weapon we possess."*

My dear brothers and sisters, the time has come to unite for a campaign of truth.

No evil, no matter how strong, can withstand the force of truth. Wherever the evil lurks, we must blind it with the light of truth. Wherever the conscience sleeps, we must awaken it with the sound of truth.

With the burning flames from Tibet, we should see the truth. These courageous martyrs sacrificed their lives in the most painful way; they did it in protest against Chinese rule. This rule has led to the killing of a million Tibetans, the destruction of thousands of temples and monasteries, the diluting and destroying of the Tibetan language and culture, the irreversible damage to the natural environment on the Tibetan plateau, and the more than five-decade-long exile of His Holiness the Dalai Lama.

Each time when tensions escalate, instead of showing concern and trying to address root causes, the Chinese regime responds with increasing force and oppression. The increased clampdown on the Tibetans, especially monks and nuns, stepped-up cultural genocide, and ever-growing ethnic oppression have made the situation in Tibet ultimately unbearable for the Tibetans.

Let's listen to the flames. Yes, there are voices in the flames: "Free Tibet!" and "Let the Dalai Lama Return Home!" When we hear the voices, our conscience permits us no alternative but to act as their transmitters and amplifiers, to awaken more people's moral conscience, to let more people know the truth about these tragedies, and to allow more people to experience these Tibetans' despair and desire to be reborn in the flames.

Brothers and sisters, the time has come for a campaign of truth.

We must press the Western governments to speak the TRUTH. The grassroots movement is very important, but it alone is not enough. The Chinese government generally does not respond if the world leaders remain silent because the only language it can understand is that of power. It does not understand that in democracies the power is ultimately with the people. We must take advantage of our democratic mechanisms to press our governments to represent our will in regard to the issue of Tibet. We must not let our governments base their policies on the wrong assumption—that CCP rule is permanent.

Power has passed to a new generation of leadership in China. It is the nature of tyrannical regimes that they grow weaker and less coherent with each successive generation. Already we see the cracks weakening the CCP. We must exploit these cracks by waving the flag of truth in their faces at every turn.

The question of Tibet is both a political issue and a moral one. All of humanity is challenged. Every world leader must take this test, and just like any other test, one either passes or fails. To our great dismay, many world leaders have so far either refused to take the test—or failed it. Too many of them looked the other way while our brothers and sisters were crying in flames. We should not let our governments continue to fail the test, politically or morally. We must insist that today silence is no longer an option. We must keep before us the words of Martin Luther King Jr., *"In the end, we will remember not the words of our enemies, but the silence of our friends."*

We must challenge the silence of our governments at every turn and press them to confront the lies of the Chinese government with the TRUTH. We must also give praise when a world leader does speak the TRUTH. We commend and support US Ambassador Locke's recent actions and the UN Human Rights High Commissioner Navi Pillay's recent strong statement and welcome these actions as a big step forward.

Brothers and sisters, the time has come for a campaign of truth.

We must empower the Chinese people to end their silence on Tibet. We should make special efforts to reach out to them to meet them with the TRUTH, to appeal to their conscience, and to let them realize that the suffering of the Tibetan people is the suffering of the Chinese people, and that the same government that brings such misery to the Tibetan people is the same government that is jailing their best citizens, robbing the land from the peasants, and controlling their right to speak and think freely. We must make the Chinese government feel the heat of the fires of martyrdom from all directions. My dear brothers and sisters, I promise with all my heart, all my physical being and spirit that I will commit myself to this campaign of TRUTH. With our combined help, the world will learn the truth. The world will know the truth. The world will speak the truth. And in the end, the TRUTH will set us FREE.

Thank you.

(At around 10:30 a.m. in the morning of November 17, 2012, the second day of the conference, while the participants of the conference were dividing into groups for photos with His Holiness, His Holiness and I held hands together. He asked me about China's new leadership and I briefly answered His question. Without wasting a second, I murmured to Him in grief, "Yesterday, three."

"I know, I know" said His Holiness: Of course, he knew what I was talking about, "I am helpless, I am helpless," He continued.

As we spoke, we were looking into each other's eyes. He poked my hand hard with his finger and said, "Even like this is painful... burning, burning." At that moment, I saw tears running in His eyes. Tears then ran down my face.

A few moments later, when He came to our group for the photo, His Holiness held my hands again. No words, we just looked into each other's eyes. Again, I saw tears pooling in his eyes and once again tears ran down my face.)

CHAPTER 68

We Are All Tibetans Today

Speech at Human Rights Day "Solidarity with Tibet" Rally
New York, NY, United States
December 10, 2012

Dear brothers and sisters:

Not long ago in Dharamsala—overwhelmed with grief while thinking of the sacrifices so many devoted and peaceable Tibetans have made for the cause of their people's freedom, but also enormously encouraged and strengthened by their spirit—I called for a global campaign of truth about the Tibetans' unspeakable suffering at the hands of the Chinese rule and about their remarkable struggle for freedom under the leadership of His Holiness the Dalai Lama.

Today I came to tell you another simple but deep truth:

I AM A TIBETAN.

Yes, I am a Tibetan.

For who can say that he is not a Tibetan today if he sees the burning flames in Tibet and is not numb to pain himself?

Who can say that she is not a Tibetan today if she hears the voices cry out from the flames and is still in possession of a heart to love and a mind to understand?

Today we are all Tibetans.

But dear brothers and sisters, please join me today in asking a question of the Secretary General of the United Nations. We all know that the UN Charter affirms the "faith in fundamental human rights, in the dignity and worth of the human person, [and] in the equal rights of men and women and of nations large and small."

Today we must ask, "Mr. Ban Ki-moon, are you a Tibetan today?"

Dear brothers and sisters, please also join me in asking this question of the President of the United States of America. We all know that its Declaration of Independence claims "All men are created equal."

"Mr. Obama, are you a Tibetan today?"

Dear brothers and sisters, please join me in asking this same question of the new leader of the People's Republic of China. We all know that its failed policies have rendered the life in Tibet unbearable for the Tibetans.

"Mr. Xi Jinping, are you a Tibetan today?"

I bring this question to these world leaders because, holding the powerful political positions they do, they can hamper or promote justice more easily than others.

My friends, I don't know what these Tibetan self-immolations will lead to in the near future, but I am sure that our children will learn about this unparalleled episode in their history textbooks. What they will also learn is whether these leaders, facing the human disaster now unfolding in Tibet, seized the opportunity to impede injustice and uplift humanity, or whether they squandered it—or what is worse, promoted policies that deepened the crisis.

Wise, mature, and powerful, these men don't need to be taught what is right and what is wrong. But they do need to be reminded of three characteristics that mark great leaders: courage, vision, and integrity. At the end of the day, the high court of history's judgment on each of them, in whatever office they are holding, will be measured by answers to these three questions: Were they men of courage? Were they men of vision? Were they men of integrity?

Dear brothers and sisters, let us say together, loud enough for these world leaders to hear:

We are all Tibetans.

Free Tibet.

Let the Dalai Lama return home.

Thank you.

SECTION VIII

NEW LEADERSHIP IN CHINA: THE CODE OF CORRUPTION AND CONTROL

December 2012—June 2013

"China watchers are struggling to figure out whether the new leadership will go about doing things differently. While Xi Jinping, after taking the party chief position, has said a lot of things and given some mixed signals, there is one constant: The party's resolve to keep its political monopoly… The Chinese communist regime is facing unprecedented pressure and challenges from all walks of life: Anger within the population is mounting over corruption, deepening inequality, official criminality, and constraints on freedom of expression. Looking closely, one can see that in order to soothe the anger and even unify Chinese society behind him, Xi Jinping has adopted two strategies: strong rhetoric on anti-corruption resolve and mobilizing nationalist sentiment by taking a bellicose stance over maritime territorial disputes with Japan and other East Asian countries."

CHAPTER 69

The Outlook on Democratization after the Recent Change of Leadership in China

Opening Remarks at Public Hearing "Prospects for Human Rights and Democracy in China after the Leadership Change; the Freedom of Expression, the Situation of Artists, Writers and Intellectuals" Held by European Parliament's Subcommittee on Human Rights (DROI)
Brussels, Belgium
December 6, 2012

Thank you, Madam Chair.

I want to first take this opportunity to congratulate the EU for its honor of winning this year's Nobel Peace Prize. But we should not forget that, as I speak, the winner of the 2010 Prize, Liu Xiaobo, is languishing in China's prison. Liu Xiaobo is the only detained Nobel laureate in the world.

Neither should we forget the human disaster now unfolding in Tibet. As of today, ninety-two Tibetans have self-immolated since 2009 in protest of the Chinese cultural genocide policies against the Tibetan people. Today silence on this crisis is no longer, indeed never, an option.

Today's hearing is intended to cover a few issues. I am here to testify on only one of them: the outlook on democratization after the recent change of leadership in China.

Before and after the Chinese Communist Party's eighteenth congress, people have been wondering about this one important issue: "whether the new leadership will start democratic reforms," and have embarked on an intense debate around this question.

From the speech given by the outgoing General Secretary Hu Jintao, we should have a clear answer to this question. That is, that communist China has decided not to abandon the one-party dictatorship in favor of democratic reforms. Hu's declaration of "never to take the evil road of changing flags and banners" unambiguously indicated this determination. The follow-up speeches given by the newly appointed general secretary, Xi Jinping, also struck the same cord. They both set the tone for the policy of the next generation of leaders, which based on past experience, has a tremendous binding power.

Nevertheless, the CPC is not the only factor that affects the future development of China. The reality is that the Chinese communist regime is facing unprecedented pressure and challenges from all walks of life that demand for democracy. The foundation on which the CPC regime has tried to mix a high-growth market economy and rigid one-party dictatorship is corroding.

For a period after "June Fourth," the CPC co-opted the intellectual elite economically and politically, and therefore successfully defused the regime's most direct legitimacy crisis. Terms like democracy, human rights, universal values, political reforms, etc. simply disappeared from the public dialogues. Today, however, these phrases and concepts increasingly occupy the center of the public discourse. They have essentially become the common theme of people of all social sectors.

The intellectual elite's renewed demand for democracy is mainly based on the understanding of the reality of China's national crony capitalism. This crony capitalism has sustained a long period of high-speed economic development, which has almost become the only source of legitimacy for the CCP's one-party dictatorship. However, such an economic system has carried an incalculable cost in the form of human rights abuses, environmental deterioration, and morality collapse. It has become insolvable.

The only positive achievement in the Chinese Communist Party governance is the establishment of the "two terms in ten years as a generation" term-limit system. Many observers stipulate that such a system will ensure long-term stability for the CPC regime, because they wishfully believe that this system found a way out of the pit of power discontinuity that has plagued all dictatorships in the history. The Bo Xilai event, however, mercilessly burst such a bubble. This "voluntary term limit" system may make do only temporarily. The unsatisfying undercurrent within CPC may erupt in the mid-term power shift five years from now and in the generation change ten years from now. The entire regime may collapse at the time.

Through long-term information control and neo-nationalist brainwashing, the communist regime somewhat successfully fed the Chinese public the idea that "democratization is a Western conspiracy to prevent the rise of China." However, the wide spreading use of the internet has started to break the information blockade. The Communist Party can no longer promote wholesale neo-nationalism. For example, there are substantial differences between today's public opinions in cyberspace to those as recent as 2008.

After "June the Fourth," corruption has become an important basis for stability of the communist system, because no Communist Party officials at any level will be loyal to the regime if they were not given the privilege to corrupt. Such a predatory regime is growing more and more mafia-like and has caused unprecedented infringement of the basic rights of the ordinary people, resulting in increasingly frequent protests on an increasing scale. At present, there are on average more than 500 protests EVERY DAY that involve over 100 protesters. That's once every three minutes. In order to keep these self-motivated protests from becoming a conscious pro-democratic movement that threatens the regime's power, the Chinese government has built a monstrous "Stability Sustaining System," which has an operating budget exceeding China's national defense budget. This gigantic SSS treats every citizen as a potential enemy: dissidents, independent intellectuals, landless peasants, victims of forceful demolition, victims of forced abortions, veterans, migrant workers, Tibetans, Uyghurs, Mongols, Christians, Falun Gong, you name it. Particularly, the SSS protocol mobilized an unprecedented 1.4 million strong professional police force and civilian "voluntary guards" to "defend" the Chinese Communist Party's eighteenth Congress. Against whom? No clue. What the communist ruling class does not know is the real enemy may actually come from the top leadership circle.

I am not saying that this regime is going to collapse or be forced to "change lanes" tomorrow. I am just pointing out the fact that there is a major crack within China's communist power structure and the public at large is accumulating enough power to seriously challenge the one-party dictatorship. These are the two most important factors leading to a democratic reform in a totalitarian country.

That said, we cannot forget that we still need an overall persistent pro-democracy movement to force the one-party dictatorship to crack open. A long-term resilient movement will reach critical mass when idealists like Liu Xiaobo join force with a self-motivated public who are unsatisfied with the status quo. One of the milestones would be the formation of a civic leadership group that possesses the following four characteristics: 1) represented and trusted by the general public, 2) powerful enough to at least partially alter the current political order, 3) able to catch the attention and support of the international community, and 4) able to carry out (and call off) effective negotiations with the government. What happened in Guangdong's Wukan village a year ago is a good example.

Such a group of civic leaders in China is taking form. So, my conclusion is there may not be significant change to the Chinese regime in the next one to three years, but there will be a major one in the next five to ten years. This major change will be caused by many factors, including international pressure, which will be a good topic for Q&A.

CHAPTER 70

The Significance of Liu Xiaobo for Democracy in China

Opening Statement at the Congressional-Executive Commission on China's Hearing on Liu Xiaobo
Washington, DC, United States
December12, 2012

Congressman Smith and Senator Brown:

Thank you for hosting this important hearing.

Liu Xiaobo and his wife's plight and the Chinese reactions to his winning the Nobel Peace Prize and the mounting international outcry for the couple's freedom are well known, and I won't repeat these facts today. Instead, I want to focus on the significance of Liu Xiaobo for democracy in China.

Liu Xiaobo's Nobel honor indicates the international recognition of the Chinese democracy movement represented by him. He has become the symbol of democracy in China. Simply because of such a symbolism, his continued imprisonment presents itself as a footnote to the vow made by Hu Jintao in his political report at the recent Party's eighteenth Congress that China's leadership would "never take the evil road of changing flags and banners"—code for abandoning one-party rule. This pledge dispelled any doubts about the party's resolve to keep its political monopoly.

But we must remember, the CCP does not have the only say about China's future. Liu Xiaobo represents another force that will also help shape the future of China, pushing China to take an alternative road, "the evil road" in the minds of China's leaders perhaps. And this force is becoming increasingly viable.

The most important sign is the recent intellectual awakening evidenced by the return of the democracy debate, which has occupied a central place in the public discourse around China's leadership change. More and more intellectuals, who were generally co-opted by the regime not long after Tiananmen and acted as its defenders for many years, have come to realize and acknowledge the value of Liu Xiaobo and his ideas and beliefs, which are embodied in Charter 08. The intellectual recognition that the status quo is unsustainable is always the first and vital step toward changing it.

The intellectual's renewed demand for democracy is at least in part based on the understanding of the reality of China's state crony capitalism. This state crony capitalism has sustained a long period of high-speed economic growth, which has become almost the only source of legitimacy for the CCP's rule. However, such an economic system has carried with it an incalculable cost in the form of human rights abuse, environmental deterioration, and morality collapse. It has become insolvable.

Another two important factors helping lead to a democratic change in an autocratic country, a robust plurality of disaffected citizens and splits in the leadership, are coming together in China.

Since the Tiananmen Massacre, corruption has become one of the CCP's important strategies for survival, because no party officials at any level would be loyal to the regime if they were not given the privilege to corrupt. Such a predatory regime has caused unprecedented infringement of the basic rights of the ordinary people, resulting in increasingly frequent protests. At present, there are on average more than 500 protests EVERY DAY that involve over 100 protesters. That's one every three minutes. In order to keep these self-motivated protests from becoming a conscious pro-democracy movement demanding an overall change, the Chinese government has built a monstrous "Stability Sustaining System," which has an operating budget exceeding China's national defense budget.

This gigantic SSS treats every citizen as a potential enemy and has successfully made them enemies: dissidents, independent intellectuals, landless peasants, victims of forced demolition and eviction, victims of forced abortion, veterans, migrant workers, Tibetans, Uyghurs, Mongols, Christians, Falun Gong practitioners—you name it.

Perhaps the only achievement in China's political system in the past thirty years is the establishment of its "two-term, ten-year, one-generation" term-limit system. Many observers stipulate that such a system will ensure long-term stability for the CCP regime because they wishfully believe that this system has helped the CCP find a way out of the pit of power discontinuity that has plagued all dictatorships in the history. The Bo Xilai event, however, mercilessly burst such a bubble. People within the Party have begun to challenge this power succession system. The cracks can only be widening.

As non-governmental forces grow and civil protests escalate, the struggle for power among different factions within the regime will become more pronounced. Once external pressures reach a critical mass, rival factions within the regime will have no choice but to take the voices of the citizens seriously and seek their support to survive.

That said, we cannot forget that we still need an overall, viable pro-democracy movement to force the one-party dictatorship to crack open. A long-term resilient movement will reach critical mass when idealists like Liu Xiaobo join force with self-motivated members of the public who are disaffected with the status quo. One of the milestones would be the formation of group civil leaders who are able to represent the general public to at least partially disrupt the current political order, to catch the attention and support of the international community, and to carry out (and call off) effective negotiations with the government. What happened in Guangdong's Wukan village a year ago is a good example.

Liu Xiaobo, as a widely accepted leader both at home and abroad, will surely play a unique role in forming such a group, which was most needed but lacking in our 1989 Tiananmen movement.

Therefore, working toward his freedom is vital for a democratic change in China. I am particularly encouraged by the strong support for Liu Xiaobo and Charter 08 from world human rights leaders and activists. Aung San Suu Kyi was released from house arrest in November of 2010. For the first time, there is hope for reform in Burma. In seeking Liu's release, we hope and struggle for the same in China.

Thank you.

CHAPTER 71

We Must Not Lose Hope

Speech at the Tibetan Rally Commemorating the Fifty-Fourth Anniversary of the Tibetan National Uprising
New York, NY, United States
March 10, 2013

Dear Tibetan brothers and sisters,

Tashi delek!

Ever since the 1989 Tiananmen Massacre, I have participated in each year's March 10 anniversary commemoration activity—in places from Boston to Dharamsala, from Taipei to Washington, DC, and from New York to Beijing. Yes, in Beijing too—in prison, from 2002 to 2007, each year during the five years of my imprisonment there, I gave a special prayer on that particular day, March 10, for His Holiness the Dalai Lama and my Tibetan brothers and sisters. In the darkest days of my life, I drew strength and inspiration from you, my dear brothers and sisters; you inspired me, as you do today, through your endurance despite enormous grievous assaults on your language, your culture, your religion, your land, your identity, your spirit, and even your lives, and through your extraordinary struggle for freedom under the leadership of His Holiness the Dalai Lama.

Today the fifty-fourth anniversary of the 1959 Tibetan National Uprising is being commemorated under heavy dark shadows. As I speak, my heart is agonized upon my thinking that another Tibetan or two in Tibet may set him or herself ablaze in the next moment and many more are to be incarcerated or will disappear.

Not long ago right here, I spoke at the Solidarity with Tibet rally on December 10 of last year. I asked you to join me in asking a question of the world leaders, including Secretary General Ban Ki-moon of the United Nations and President Barack Obama of the United States: Are you a Tibetan today?

I brought this question to them because I believed, as I continue to believe today, that nobody can say that he is not a Tibetan if he sees the burning flames in Tibet and is not numb to pain himself and that nobody can say she is not a Tibetan if she hears the voices cry out from the flames and is still in possession of a heart to love and a mind to understand.

I brought this question to them because I believed, as I continue to believe today, that these world leaders, holding the powerful political positions they do, can hamper or promote justice more easily than others.

Today, I want you to join me again in asking these world leaders more questions. Today we must ask them:

Mr. Ban Ki-moon, Mr. Obama,

After 109 Tibetans—monks, nuns and lay people—have set themselves on fire to protest the systemic and systematic repression, oppression, and cultural genocide of the Chinese government on the people of Tibet, how many more will it take for you to confront the Chinese government with truth telling them unequivocally that they must stop their repressive policies, which are the root cause of the crisis now unfolding in Tibet? How many more miles will the Tibetan people have to trudge in order to sound the international alarm, which we, the international community as a whole, have largely ignored both at their peril and our own? And how much more will they have to suffer before the world leaders like you realize this is not only a Tibetan disaster but a disaster of the entire mankind and take action to stop it?

I understand that the world leaders often find themselves in awkward positions where they feel that proclaimed principles must be compromised for the sake of short-term interests. But the question of Tibet is not only a political issue but also a moral one. All of humanity is challenged. Every world leader must take this test, and just like any other test, one either passes or fails. After all, the office of each world leader will ultimately be judged by the high court of history on his or her courage, vision, and integrity.

I do not know what will help stop the injustice most effectively, but I do know it will not be helped by silence. We must insist today that silence is no longer an option. Silence is indeed never an option. I call on the world leaders, on this global day of action, to stand in solidarity with the Tibetan people, to condemn the repression by Chinese authorities and to nurture dialogue with the Tibetan leadership with a view to protecting the human security and cultural identity of the Tibetan people.

I also appeal to the consciences of my Chinese compatriots on this day of global solidarity with Tibet. We Chinese must realize that grievances of the Tibetan people are many and genuine, that the suffering of the Tibetan people is the suffering of the Chinese people as well, and that the government that brings such misery to the Tibetan people is the same government that is jailing our best citizens, robbing the land from our peasants, and controlling our right to speak and think freely. We must not continue to look the other way while our Tibetan brothers and sisters are crying in flames.

In the face of such powerful evil, we may all feel powerless, but we should draw strength and inspiration from the words of His Holiness the Dalai Lama, "Tragedy should be utilized as a source of strength. No matter what sort of difficulties, how painful the experience is, if we lose our hope, that's our real disaster."

Yes. We must draw hope from the burning flames of martyrdom in Tibet. We must not lose hope. I am impatient with injustice. I don't think it will take another fifty-four years. We will see home and freedom in our lifetime. I am a great supporter of His Holiness the Dalai Lama's Middle Way Approach, which is upheld by the Tibetan government in exile. As a Chinese scholar, I believe the Middle Way Approach, full of kindness, compassion, courage, wisdom, and vision, will benefit both Tibetan and Chinese people. Let's unite and continue to fight the good fight. My dear brothers and sisters, I will continue to fight side by side with you, will walk with you every step on the road toward home and freedom.

Thank you.

CHAPTER 72

We Are Gradually Eroding the Fortifications of China's Ruling Regime

Speech at the Opening Ceremony of the International Conference
China's New Leadership: Challenges for Human Rights, Democracy, and Freedom in East Turkestan, Tibet, and Southern Mongolia
Geneva, Switzerland
March 11, 2013

Dear friends, dear brothers and sisters,

Thank you, Ms. Rebiya Kadeer, Mr. Dolkun Isa, and friends at the World Uyghur Congress for putting together this important conference. Many of us have traveled great distances to be here today, but all of us have traveled even further mentally to make this conference possible. The tension, distrust, and hostilities that have divided us are like so many open wounds on the body of our common cause. Only by healing these wounds will we march strongly toward the horizon where the dawn of freedom, truth, equality, and peace for us all will one day break. When I think of the distances, especially the psychological distances that we have traveled to be here, I am blessedly reminded that even with all the difficulties facing us which, sadly to say, may not have become less daunting than when we first tried to come together at the beginning of this century, so much has already been done to establish the foundational spirit of community that is essential to our labors in and on behalf of the future.

The Chinese Communist Party's rule is entirely based on a calculated combination of fear, violence, truth-suppression, ethnic tension and division and, most recently, a capitalism that trades wealth for silence, money for obedience. The Communist Party's more than sixty years in power testify to the effectiveness of these tools. But even with efficiency and ruthlessness at its disposal, it has no real future. Its ideals run so counter to the most fundamental human drives for freedom, truth, equality, and peace that it will always be beating back the tide in order to maintain its existence.

We ourselves are part of the crest of this tide, and we are gradually eroding the fortifications of China's ruling regime. Perhaps this is happening more slowly than we would like it to be, but we must not allow our occasional impatience to blind us to the fact that this very gathering is one more example of just how much of a failure the sixty-four years of communist rule in China have been.

In past years, we, all of us, have been committed to following the principles of respecting the differences between ethnic groups, embracing human rights as a universal value, uniting as one for the realization of a common democratic future, to nonviolence and overcoming evil with good. We have been committed to maintaining close communication exercising tolerance and forgiveness toward each other, eliminating hatred, resentment and misunderstanding, pursuing truth, accomplishing reconciliation and loving one another, and we have been committed to mutual concern for each other's human rights and to offering necessary assistance. I think in the following three days every one of us will be refreshed with these principles which, arduously established, should guide us today to move us forward together.

I wish the conference to be a great success.

CHAPTER 73

Ethnic Issues: A Test to China's New Leadership

Talk at the International Conference on China's New Leadership: Challenges for Human Rights, Democracy, and Freedom in East Turkestan, Tibet, and Southern Mongolia

Geneva, Switzerland

March 11–13, 2013

As the leadership change is yet to be completed, China watchers are struggling to figure out whether the new leadership will go about doing things differently. While Xi Jinping, after taking the party chief position, has said a lot of things and given some mixed signals, there is one constant: the party's resolve to keep its political monopoly, which strikes the same cord as Hu Jintao's vow at the eighteenth Party Congress: "Never take the evil road of changing flags and banners."

The reality, however, is that the Chinese communist regime is facing unprecedented pressure and challenges from all walks of life: Anger within the population is mounting over corruption, deepening inequality, official criminality, and constraints on freedom of expression.

Looking closely, one can see that, in order to soothe the anger and even unify Chinese society behind him, Xi Jinping has adopted two strategies: strong rhetoric on anti-corruption resolve and mobilizing nationalist sentiment by taking a bellicose stance over maritime territorial disputes with Japan and other East Asian countries.

I want to look at these two strategies in the context of China's ethnic policies, a policy field that has largely remained in obscurity in the debates around the leadership change.

Since the Tiananmen Massacre, corruption has become one of the CCP's important strategies for survival because no party officials at any level would be loyal to the regime if they were not given the privilege to corrupt.

In China, in each policy field and even with each policy, there is a huge interest group built up and the interest can only become more entrenched as time goes. As far as ethnic policies are concerned, there are twenty-four provincial/ministerial level institutions that assume "anti-secession" roles and deal with Tibet, Xinjiang (East Turkestan) and Inner Mongolia (Southern Mongolia) in China's bureaucratic system, which is a huge group with a considerable amount of power and resources.

These officials at different levels, mostly Han Chinese, have tremendous, entrenched personal interests in anti-secession related policies and economic development projects in these ethnic regions. Xinjiang's former party chief Wang Lequan, a widely hated hardliner, turned Xinjiang into not only his political base but his own personal business kingdom. These officials are the most important part of China's gigantic "Stability Sustaining System," which has an operating budget exceeding China's national defense budget. Nobody knows much money sinks to the bottomless structure and personal pockets.

To guard their own interests, they have to keep the secessionist movement alive and relevant, and oftentimes make it turn extreme, no matter how serious the outcome could possibly be. For example, on March 14, 2008, in Lhasa, there was a four-hour period when the armed forces occupying the peripheries took no action in the commotion area, allowing the degree of violence to escalate. A similar strategy was pursued on July 5, 2009, in Urumqi. This non-interference was made deliberately for "breeding" purposes. If the armed forces had taken over the situation at the beginning, the scale of events would have been much smaller. It would have been better off for the general situation but unfavorable to the bureaucrats.

One may wonder how the central leadership allows them to get away with letting or even making the tension escalate? Good question. There is a most convenient way to get excused that is to translate the burden of failure as a result of the "sedition and secession" efforts organized and carefully planned by overseas hostile forces, the "Dalai clique," in the case of Tibet, for example. This is invariably true in Eastern Turkestan and Southern Inner Mongolia. Why is this accepted and even demanded?

No matter what excuse is readily available, if it came from within, the top leadership would have to bear responsibility for the failure because everyone knows ethnic policies, which concern the core interest of the Chinese nation, like defense policies, is the top leadership's monopolized policy terrain. Each time tensions escalate, this kind of blaming immediately becomes the official statement by all "anti-secession" agencies. The lying statement became a model of language throughout the power structure from top down.

Despite his harsh rhetoric, if Xi does not want to dissolve the party's power base in favor of thorough democratic reforms, his effort to curb corruption is not sincere and severely limited. China's monstrous anti-secession agencies are part of the entire corrupt and abusive system, added with a layer of ethnic oppression. This layer is extremely important as far as the ethnic groups represented today in this room are concerned because it may well be tied to the nationalist policy Xi Jinping is taking pains to pursue now. While we must recognize the role of the anti-secession agencies and officials play in the making of the ethnic crises, we must remember that such roles have been acted on the stage where the entire government and a larger segment of the Han Chinese population, which make up nearly 92% of the people in the People's Republic of China, regard national unity as the paramount principle and believe the method of handling such crises is a crackdown, determined and unconditional. Xi Jinping does not want to be seen as weak on Japan, on other foreign countries, and on the minority groups, which they have never considered their own. The nationalist policy may well be directed inside to the ethnic issues which, again in their eyes, are concerning the core interest of the Chinese nation that Xi and his comrades are vowing to rejuvenate. Xi Jinping may well try to gain legitimacy and a mandate from the Han Chinese, further consolidating his power base, by continuing, if not intensifying, the failed hardline policy in Tibet, Xinjiang, and Inner Mongolia. And the officials in the anti-secession agencies, understanding Xi's need, may well continue their old way of going about business with the legitimacy bestowed from the top leadership and the Han Chinese populace.

This is the game that shows no sign of ending. This is my fear today.

As we all know, this is a very difficult time for our Tibetan, Uyghur, and Mongolian brothers and sisters. The wave of self-immolations in Tibet, intensified persecutions in Eastern Turkestan and Inner Mongolia have been immensely distressing and is an alarming sign of the worsening situations in these areas.

However, to me, I am not alone in seeing China's modern rise approaching a crossroads. And the issues of Tibet, Eastern Turkestan, and Southern Mongolia are a serious test to China's rise. I don't have time to elaborate on the perspectives of democratic transition in China, which does not seem that far anymore. I just want to emphasize that the CCP does not have the only say about China's future. After all, we are the most important factors shaping our own future. Now is not the time to despair. It is the time to take action and tip the scales of history toward freedom.

CHAPTER 74

It's Time to Begin Living in Light

Speech at the Opening Plenary of Global Conference on Human Rights, Democracy, and Fragility of Freedom
McGill University, Montreal, Quebec, Canada
March 21–23, 2013

Bonsoir! Good evening!

Dear friends,

Today we live in a land of shadows. Stark shadows cast by what is worst in us on what is best.

In 1948, shortly after one of the worst convulsions of violence in the history of mankind drew to a close, the Universal Declaration of Human Rights was adopted by the newly formed United Nations. This was a ray of light in a world still shrouded in darkness. This light of hope was emitted from the best human hearts and minds including that of John Humphrey, one of the greatest sons of McGill University. I feel honored and humbled to stand here today.

Dear friends, what is best in us, what is most hopeful about us, is beautifully articulated in the Declaration. These are the principles by which we should organize ourselves as a human family. These are the principles at the core of any meaningful democracy.

And yet, too many of our eyes have adjusted to the shadows that power and greed cast on the existence of our brothers and sisters around the world. Whereas brave and visionary people like John Humphrey could see a world beyond the catastrophe they had just endured, we live in an age where what has been gained in principle, what has been recognized in fact, has been eroded by an acceptance that it is better to accommodate the evil—and hope it changes on its own—than to seek to change it through pressure, denouncement, and direct confrontation.

We must ask today how is it that this Universal Declaration of Human Rights, which affirms the "faith in fundamental human rights, in the dignity and worth of the human person, [and] in the equal rights of men and women and of nations large and small" is so casually traduced by many of its signatory states including China?

We have gathered here, in the shadowy valley of our times, to summon the wisdom and the best heritage of mankind and remind the entire world once again that each one of us has an opportunity to act in a way worthy of the best of our humanity.

The other option is to adjust our eyes to the shadows.

But friends, I have seen firsthand what takes place in these shadows.

I was born three years before the Cultural Revolution. At an early age, the unspeakable sufferings that most families had at the hands of the communist dictatorship, including mine, made me disenchanted with the Communist Party. However, I was enticed into joining the party with the idea of reforming it from within. This all changed when I returned from my PhD studies in the United States to join thousands of my fellow students in Beijing as Chinese army tanks rolled across Tiananmen Square on the morning of June 4, 1989. Luckier than most of my fellow students, I narrowly escaped the massacre and the ensuing arrests and returned to the United States. While I continued my studies, I immersed myself in the work advancing human rights and democracy in China. In the Party's eyes, the former young communist star had now become a public enemy. I became persona non grata, a traitor, prohibited from entering the country. But in the spring of 2002, I decided to defy the ban. In China's industrial northeast, thousands of workers were taking to the streets, protesting the destitution brought on by government exploiting policies. Sensing an opportunity to forge bonds between democracy leaders and grassroots activists, I entered China using a borrowed passport and forged ID card.

For two weeks, I met with exploited construction laborers, expropriated farmers, and striking workers, documenting their grievances and the condition of their lives and helping them with nonviolent struggle strategies. But as I attempted to slip out of China across the Burmese border, my fake ID was spotted, and I found myself in the hands of the security police.

I was detained for five years. Much of those years I spent in solitary confinement. My mental condition deteriorated beneath endless isolation, repeated interrogations, and ongoing psychological and physical torture. I resorted to composing poems in my head and committing them to memory as a means of maintaining my sanity. Nearing a breakdown, I grasped onto my innermost resources of imagination, belief, and will to fend off insanity and find a reason to live. "Am I wrong?" I asked myself with a tinge of regret. But I repeated a thought experiment: imagining myself taking a copy of the Universal Declaration of Human Rights, arbitrarily choosing anyone on the Chinese streets, showing them the document, asking them with the language they understand whether they want the rights listed there. Would anybody say "no"? Of course not. Nobody wants to be a slave. In this regard, the Chinese people are no different than any other people in the world. The thirst for freedom and dignity is indeed universal. I drew strength and inspiration from this first order of fact.

I also thought of my fallen brothers and sisters in Tiananmen Square. I reassured myself that freedom is not free. Freedom must be earned. It was not free for those who paid with their lives. It is certainly not free for those of us who, while still blessed with our lives, have yet to complete the mission for which these brave students gave their lives and their freedom. I must not give up!

To make a long story short, in 2007, thanks to the overwhelming international support, I was freed, returned to the US, and recommitted myself to the hard work to advance human rights and democracy in China.

Today we are in a situation that is both more dire and more hopeful than that faced by the demonstrators of 1989. On the one hand, the

Chinese government has adjusted to new realities in order to maintain their hold on power. They have willingly jettisoned their ideology and allowed a distinctly undemocratic capitalism to supplant undemocratic communism in hopes that individual wealth will end demands for individual freedoms. But it will not. It cannot, because the desire for freedom is too great; it is too deeply rooted in all of the people who make up our common humanity.

Consider the number of people who engage in activities the Chinese government, with all of the resources at its disposal, aims to prevent—or actually cracks down on once they have begun. "Mass incidents" is the term the Chinese government uses to describe protests in which 100 or more people participate. Even underneath the ever-ready tyrant's baton, the number of these "incidents" has risen to 180,000 per year—which means that on average a new, large protest against the government's policies takes place every three minutes. Is it not logical to infer from this fact that no amount of violence or propaganda can ever suppress the desire for freedom?

But this does not mean that we in the West can sit back and wait for democracy to bloom. China is a dangerous and pernicious power, growing more so every day, and quietism or passive engagement are not an answer or an option. Before this regime is done—and one day it will be done—it has the capability of inflicting enormous damage on its own people and the people of the world. It is our responsibility to ensure that this does not happen.

Those people like John Humphrey in the middle of the last century rose to the challenge of their times in the midst of the worst the world had ever seen. Surely we, with their work as our foundation, can rise to the challenge of our own times. Surely, we can all see the shadows for what they are and say that it is time to begin living in the light.

Thank you.

Merci.

CHAPTER 75

Let Us Resolve upon Brotherhood as a Guiding and Uniting Principle for Our Work Together

Opening Speech at the Eighth Interethnic/ Interfaith Leadership Conference
Taipei, Taiwan
April 27, 2013

Good morning, distinguished guests, dear friends, my brothers and sisters.

And good day.

I say good day because any time friends of human rights from different ethnic, cultural, religious, and regional backgrounds join together to openly dedicate themselves to the collaborative work of advancing freedom, truth, equality, and peace is a good day. This is exactly what we, at this conference, are trying to do. And so, let me say again, good morning and good day.

Of course, although it is morning in this beautiful city, on this very good day, we know too that we are gathered in the shade of shadows—shadows cast by human rights abuses, shadows cast by human rights abusers, and shadows cast by what is worst in us on what is best.

But we must remember that we also live in the land of light, light shined by our best human beings, sometimes by the flames of their burning bodies. Twenty-four years ago, right here in this very city of Taipei, a man named Zheng Nanrong set himself on fire. The flames of his burning body forever changed the balance between darkness and light, and light has ever since been prevailing on this island.

And today, on this beautiful island, we are gathered in the spirit of Zheng Nanrong as well as that of the more than 110 Tibetan national heroes who have set themselves ablaze for their people's freedom in the past four years. But these rays of light are buried in a world still shrouded in thick darkness. This continued darkness is an embarrassment to common sense and to our common humanity. My soul is burning and, I believe, so are yours. We have gathered here to defy this darkness, to remind the entire world once again that each one of us has an opportunity to act in a way worthy of the best of our humanity and to summon the best heritage of mankind and the wisdom to let the rays of light shine through.

Many of us have traveled great distances to be here today, but all of us have traveled even further mentally. We are often shadowed by mistrust and hostilities that have divided us. Only by overcoming these shadows will we march strongly toward the horizon where the dawn of freedom, truth, equality, and peace for us all will one day break.

No matter whom you sit here representing, you have been victimized by the Chinese communist regime. Tibetans, Uyghurs, Mongolians, and Han; Christians, Falun Gong, Buddhists and Muslims, all have suffered, and all now suffer, at the hands of this regime. The people of Taiwan, Hong Kong, and Macau, their freedoms are being compromised by its political and economic intimidation.

My friends—and let us resolve that only in friendship will we find freedom, truth, equality, and peace—under the circumstances I have just described, we have no choice but to work together and avoid the divisiveness, apathy, fear, and hatred that will only play into the hands of the Chinese government and feed the darkness.

My friends—and let us resolve upon brotherhood as a guiding and uniting principle for our work together—we are each other's keepers, we are each other's freedom, we are each other's peace, we are each other's hope.

And it is in this spirit that I now officially open the eighth Interethnic/Interfaith Leadership Conference.

Thank you all.

CHAPTER 76

The Longer We Delay Our Actions, the Greater the Costs for All of Us

Acceptance Speech of the 2013 Harvard Kennedy School Alumni Achievement Award
Harvard University, Cambridge, MA, United States
May 11, 2013

Kennedy School alumni, distinguished guests and dear friends,

Good afternoon.

What a wonderful day! I am grateful to you for this award. This is recognition of the voice for democracy and human rights for one-fourth of the world's population which, as you asserted in your announcement letter, "must be recognized and amplified."

I can only accept this award with a deep sense of gratitude. In the aftermath of the Tiananmen Massacre, which I narrowly survived, I, a mathematician, decided to devote myself to the cause of democracy in China. When I made that decision, I understood my own need to study the democratic ethos and its concomitants in depth. I was lucky to be accepted by what I consider the best of all places to learn this knowledge—the Kennedy School, which is committed to both thought and action and provides an especially thought-provoking environment asking the question: "What You Can Do" to solve the greatest problems confronting our era.

I am enormously thankful to the Kennedy School. It provided for me a superb learning environment. But even more importantly, it was here that I was exposed to, and came to know well, faculty like Professors Richard Zeckhauser and David King, who are inspiring models of just, wise, and learned human beings who embody the values that I had committed myself to fight for.

Here I also found similarly motivated students, for example, Jared Genser, who has become a leading international human rights lawyer and worked to free me when I was imprisoned in China. Now Jared and I are partners in the struggle for the freedom of prisoners of conscience around the world.

During my five-year imprisonment in China, over 100 Harvard faculty members petitioned to the Chinese leaders for my release. They included Harvard President Professor Larry Summers and Kennedy School Deans Professor Joseph Nye and Professor David Ellwood. I also learned later, not surprisingly, that many staff members in the executive and legislative offices in the US government who worked tirelessly for my release are Kennedy School alumni. I thank all of you from the bottom of my heart.

I also accept this award with a deep sense of humility. I am here, enjoying this wonderful air of freedom that embraces this great country. But whatever I have done, whatever I have achieved, I have not done by myself. Whatever I have been able to do, I have done only because I am standing squarely on the shoulders of my countrymen who do not have the luxury of enjoying this wonderful air of freedom. I am standing on the shoulders and by the side of people who have knowingly traded their freedom, and in some cases their lives, to advance the cause of democracy in China.

You cannot see them, but they are here with me today. I speak of this noble to my left, Liu Xiaobo, author of Charter 08, recognized by the world as the 2010 Nobel Peace Prize laureate. And recognized by the government of China with an eleven-year jail sentence. To my right, Wang Bingzhang, recognized around the world as the founder of the overseas Chinese democratic movement. And recognized by the

Chinese government with a life of solitary confinement. Behind me are Zhao Changqing, Ding Jiaxi, Gao Zhisheng, Hada, Nurmemet Yasin, Liu Xianbin, Chen Wei, Yang Tianshui, Dhondup Wangchen, Chen Shuqing, Zhu Yufu, Tang Zuoren… the list can go on and on. All recognized around the world as men of peace and service to their fellow men but labeled as subversives by their government. Further behind me are the hundreds of thousands of ordinary Chinese citizens who risk their lives and their very fortunes every day to protest the corruption and the lack of the rule of law that defines life inside China today. It is on their behalf that I accept this gracious honor. It is on their behalf that I accept this honor.

This achievement award prompts me to exam what we have achieved. To be fair, we have done a lot. But this award comes as a reminder that we are still far from achieving our goal and so can only spur us to continue. I also take this award as a gesture of continued support for our cause from the Harvard community worldwide. Our Harvard motto is Veritas—the truth. No university, especially Harvard, should shy away from telling the truth about the dark side of the CCP's rule in China. We must fight together for human rights and democracy, not because they are noble abstract concepts but because they are the tools for achieving civilized societies and a peaceful world order.

To conclude, I want to share with you this quote attributed to the man whose name is affixed to this great institution. "There are risks and costs to a program of action, but they are far less than the long-range risks and costs of comfortable inaction." The longer we delay our actions, the greater the costs for all of us.

Thank you all.

CHAPTER 77

Let Us Learn from History

Acceptance Speech of Truman-Reagan Medal of Freedom
Washington, DC, United States
June 13, 2013

Dr. Edwards, distinguished guests, and dear friends,

Thank you for giving me this Truman-Reagan Medal of Freedom. I am honored even to be considered for an award that is named for the two great leaders of freedom and humbled to be included in the same company as such leaders and heroes as the past recipients of this medal.

Dr. Edwards, I stand in awe of your wisdom, your tenacity, and your passion, which gave birth to the Victims of Communism Memorial Foundation. I salute you for your prophetic vision in the selection of the Goddess of Democracy as the icon for this memorial park to more than 100 million victims of communism, this insidious form of government that, in the words of Charter 08, strips "people of their rights, destroys their dignity, and corrupts normal human intercourse." Dr. Edwards, you are indeed a conscience that keeps us sane in a world that could easily be characterized as its opposite.

In this world of moral ambiguity, human rights are the casualty of pragmatic diplomacy. So it is with China. It is a popular thinking in this city that, with China's embrace of trade, democracy will follow in due course. This is very naive thinking. It is as naive as I was in 1989 in Tiananmen Square. Never did it enter my mind or the minds of my fellow students that any reasonable, legitimate government would turn on its citizens with such brutality.

As the legendary defender of freedom Congressman Tom Lantos said of the 1956 Hungarian Revolution in his dedication speech exactly six years ago, "the 1956 Revolution was not crushed, its victory was only delayed," I stand here today, twenty-four years after Tiananmen, to tell you that democracy will and is coming to China. It will come through the continued struggle of the people of China.

But we must be reminded that it will be extremely difficult for democracy to come to China without the moral support from the international community.

Yes, communism was defeated in Europe and democracy prevailed over tyranny through the persistent will of people to be free. But the defeat of communism in Europe was possible only through the equally persistent pressure from the Western democracies led by the United States. From the Truman Doctrine to the Berlin Airlift to President Reagan's "tear down the wall," the brutality of communism in Europe had nowhere to hide in the eyes of the world.

But that is history. Today the Goddess of Democracy, which stood for one glorious moment in Tiananmen Square in early June 1989 and stands here as the icon of the Victims of Communism Memorial, tells the world that the scourge of communism continues to plague a good part of this earth and a big portion of the world's population and is a major patron of tyranny around the globe. This statue reminds us every day of the terrible costs of the communists' rule in China. The CCP has conducted the cruelest theft of private property in the history of the world and has been responsible for the bloodiest political turmoil, the most horrific starvation, and the greatest number of non-natural deaths, including one million Tibetans and another one million Uyghurs. It has created the most numerous cases of injustice and has perpetrated the most barbarous destruction of historic heritage, natural environment, and religious beliefs. The CCP has carried out the most notorious crackdown on a student movement, and it continues to produce the most widespread human rights violations and government corruption. The communist government that massacred its own citizens in the heart of its capital is the very same government who today continues to routinely imprison, torture, and exile its best citizens for no other reason than exercising the right to speak freely, who pursues cultural genocide on Tibetans, Uyghurs, and Mongolians and the religious purge on Christians and Falun Gong practitioners, and whose foreign policies and models of repression enable the morally bankrupt regimes of North Korea, Iran, and Syria to suck the freedoms and dignities from their people. Its paranoia and insecurity drive it to extend its tyranny beyond its borders. Its disdain for human dignity now openly challenges the very foundation of civilization itself.

Let us learn from history. The fight for democracy and the end of communism is not just the right thing to do, but a necessary engagement required for our own survival and security. Let us not forget that the persistent pressure of the United States ultimately freed Europe from the scourge of communism and in so doing preserved our own democratic way of life. We must apply that same tenacity with China. For China's peaceful transition to democracy is not only in the interests of the people of China but also in the interests of a peaceful and stable world.

I will leave you with the words of the Norwegian Nobel Committee as it awarded Liu Xiaobo the 2010 Nobel Peace Prize: "The Norwegian Nobel Committee has long believed that there is a close connection between human rights and peace. Such rights are a prerequisite for the 'fraternity between nations' of which Alfred Nobel wrote in his will."

I thank you again for this honor and dedicate this medal to all the victims of the Chinese Communist Party and all those who seek to defend them.

CHAPTER 78

In China, Communist Corruption Is Not a Legacy. It Is an Everyday Reality.

Speech at Week of Captive Nations Event Hosted by Victims of Communism Memorial Foundation at Heritage Foundation
Washington, DC, United States
June 13, 2013

In the first thirty years of the CCP's rule in China, it conducted the cruelest theft of private property in the history of the world and built a totalitarian central planning system, which resulted in thirty-six million deaths from starvation during the three years of great famine. The CCP constantly generated bloody political turmoil, including the Cultural Revolution, which resulted in another thirty million deaths. It created the most numerous cases of injustice and has perpetrated the most barbarous destruction of China's historic heritage, natural environment, and religious beliefs. Millions of families were thrown into unspeakable suffering and the entire country brought to the brink of collapse. In the late 1970's, not long after Mao's death, the CCP began the reform seeking to reverse the previous course. But people soon found that the CCP was conducting the other of the two diametrically opposed pieces of the devil's business. At first, the CCP had forced the Chinese people to surrender their private property to the state in order to establish a comprehensive planned economy, and now the CCP began, in the name of reform, to steal public property and to put it into the private pockets of party officials and their associates. This spawned the 1989 nationwide demonstrations to protest government corruption and demand for democracy and freedom. This movement ended in bloodshed with the Tiananmen Massacre.

Over the past twenty-some years after Tiananmen Square, the CCP regime has established a two-China structure, and one of the two Chinas, which I call "China, Inc." and the other is just consisting of everyone else. Let's see how this has come into being.

The Tiananmen Massacre created a strong sense of fear and dismay of general politics among ordinary people in China. Any room for a public system of checks and balances against governmental abuse of power was taken away.

It also created a sense of fear and crisis within the communist regime because it had brought unprecedented public awareness to human rights and democracy. The regime had to face a completely different domestic and international environment and had to resort to new tactics to meet its "overwhelming" need for stability.

The subsequent disintegration of the Soviet Union and the Eastern European Bloc cast an even heavier cloud over the heads of Chinese communist officials. "How long can the red flag continue to fly?"

Shortly after Deng Xiaoping's famous Southern Inspection Tour in 1992, communist officials at all levels realized three realities: First, the Chinese Communist Party's stay in power has nothing whatsoever to do with communist ideals. Second, "economic growth means everything;" that is, continued economic growth is the last, best hope to keep the CCP ship afloat. Third, in order to uphold the one-party dictatorship, it had to rely on capitalizing on the dark and evil side of human nature: spoiling the elite in exchange for their loyalty. Therefore, the corruption of the powerful elite now became accepted, endorsed, and even demanded.

With the understanding of these three realities, the communist officials developed an undocumented but almost unanimously accepted code of conduct—or rather, code of corruption. So, every piece of governmental power is on sale in the market and every corner of the market is invaded by political power.

As a result, the Communist Party elite, who used to label themselves "the vanguards of the proletariat class," have either turned themselves into get-rich-overnight capitalists or become brokers, patrons, and backers of domestic and foreign capitalists.

In such a political environment, political power was dancing a full-swing tango with capital operation. Low human rights standards, low wages, lack of environmental protection regulations and enforcement, and the illegality of collective bargaining all contributed to creating a golden opportunity for domestic and international speculative capitalists. As a result, "money" quickly courted "political power." In a sense, the Chinese Communist Party, which used to be China, Inc.'s sole shareholder, has now opened up its equity and offered its shares for capitalists to purchase.

The CCP's sixteenth National Congress published a new party charter that welcomed capitalists as party members.

While the shares of China, Inc. are open for domestic and foreign capitalists to purchase, they were offered to China's intellectuals as free, performance-related stock options. The regime knows that in addition to economic growth, there is something else that also means everything to its survival, that is so-called "political stability." In order to sustain such stability, the CCP regime offers all kinds of bribery incentives to buy off anyone and everyone of importance and influence in society. The policy of co-opting and buying off potential opposition is quite effective in conjunction with the high-pressure purges and persecution after the Tiananmen Massacre. The cruelty of political reality created terror in the minds of intellectuals as a psychological deterrent. As time went on, fear turned into the cynicism, becoming increasingly indifferent to what was right and what was wrong. Indifference and hypocrisy rapidly became a new fashion that all the modern Chinese intellect tried to follow. This, coupled with a piece of the action in China, Inc., made many intellectuals—who had once been independent and once been considered the conscience of the society—soften up their position against the post-Tiananmen status quo.

In summary, China, Inc. formed by

1. Red Capitalists, through
2. Marriage between Power and Capital taking advantage of:
    - Low human rights standards
    - Low environmental protection
    - Low wages
    - Banning collective bargaining power
3. China, Inc. shares open to domestic and foreign capitalists
4. China, Inc. shares free to intellectuals

In today's China, power (political elite), capital (economic elite) and "intellect" (social and cultural elite) are bonded together with corruption as the adhesive to form an alliance that maintains the existing political order. These shareholders also control all the channels of the information flow and dominate the public discourse. They can make their voices so loud that the outside observers believe that they represent China, that they are China—the whole of China.

The truth is there is another society named China, a society constituted of over a billion Chinese who are virtually laborers working for China, Inc.

Here is how China, Inc. and the under China diverge:

1. China, Inc. possesses all of the political, economic, and social and cultural resources in China.
2. The rules of the games at all levels in China are set by China, Inc., who also officiates the games. In just two decades, China achieved the polarization of the country with unprecedented speed. Data show that at present, 0.4% of China's households possess 70% of the national wealth.
3. Shitizens are by no means citizens, as they are unable to enjoy basic benefits or constitution-warranted civil rights. In China, discriminations against them are open, legal, institutionalized,

and all-inclusive, spreading into the fields of politics, business, culture, and education.

4. The elite's monopoly over power, capital, and information, and its insularity, makes mobility between the two Chinas nearly stagnant.
5. The two Chinas no longer speak a common political language.
6. The two Chinas have almost no common political life.
7. Emotional division.

To maintain the two-China structure, the Chinese government, over twenty-some years after Tiananmen, has built a monstrous "Stability Sustaining System" that has an operating budget exceeding China's national defense budget and established a gigantic stability-preserving system.

Let's see how it has been developed.

Since the Tiananmen Massacre, corruption has become one of the CCP's important strategies to survive because no party officials at any level would be loyal to the regime if they were not given the privilege to corrupt. Such a predatory regime has caused unprecedented infringement of the basic rights of the ordinary people, resulting in increasing frequent protests.

Currently in China, there are about 200,000 public protests with more than 100 participants each year—or once every three minutes. The government has no effective way to handle these other than increasing the police force to prevent the protests from becoming trans-regional.

But the Chinese government is afraid of the possible integration between the two societies based on justice. Such integration is against the current interest of the stockholders of China, Inc. That is why the CCP regime has always tried to contain and persecute those who (democracy advocates) believe and work for such integration. Some of them have been sent into exile overseas, others were put in jail. Still others were followed, monitored, or put under house arrest. It is a long-term strategy to guard against the democratization of China by eradicating, harassing, and eliminating citizen advocates.

Another strategy is to control, compress, and eventually block the space for public expression of opinions. Internet is on top of the government's hit list. Any forum of public opinions could serve as a launch pad to start a process of breaking the boundary between the two "Chinas," therefore eventually leading to the collapsing of the elite China. The CCP regime is fully aware of its significance and is making every effort to put a tight grip over the internet.

This is how I use the two-China analysis as the framework to summarize the Chinese communists' general strategies of maintaining authoritarian rule and resisting the democratization. On top of the traditional lies and violence, the CCP regime has developed new tactics. It is comprised in the shape of a dragon:

Here you go.

- The body: sustaining economic growth at all costs to maintain the regime's ruling legitimacy
- Two wings: appeasing the elite with corruption and suppressing the powerless with rogue police
- Two claws: purging democracy advocates like Liu Xiaobo and blocking public opinion

Nevertheless, it is not enough to just see the severe division of the two societies of China. We need to stand in a more elevated position to envision the emerging of a new, democratic China, the third China. Although this third China did not take shape, there are many signs indicating its coming.

It usually takes four factors to be present at the same time to change a country from an autocratic country to a democratic one: 1) the robust, general disaffection from people; 2) a split in the leadership in the autocratic regime; 3) viable opposition, viable democracy movement; and 4) international support.

Let me look at these factors.

First. CCP's dragon-shaped one-body, two-wing, and two-claw strategy has split China into two exclusive societies. This is what some experts called the rigid stable structure. But rigid human society never has a sustainable stability. If such a society is stable for the moment, it is only because a crisis is cooking and new opportunity is on the horizon.

China's Stability Sustaining System treats every citizen as a potential enemy, and it has successfully made them enemies—dissidents, independent intellectuals, land-lease peasants, victims of forced demolitions and eviction, victims of forced abortion, veterans, migrant workers, Tibetans, Uyghurs, Mongolians, Christians, and Falun Gong practitioners, you name it. The CCP regime does not lack enemies.

Second. Compared to the under China, which is more diversified, the elite China seem to have common and consistent interests. But the consistency is based on bribery and buy-offs of multi-faceted interest groups with an intrinsic flaw in the foundation. Fierce internal power struggles have never ceased since the founding of the communist party. Perhaps the only achievement in China's political system in the past thirty years is the establishment of the "two-term, ten-year, one-generation" term limit system. Many observers predicted that such a system would ensure long-term stability for the CCP regime, wishfully believing that this system helped the CCP find a way out of the pit of power discontinuity that has plagued all dictatorships in history. The Bo Xilai event, however, mercilessly burst that bubble. People within the party have begun to challenge this power succession system. The cracks are only widening.

Third. The concept of democracy has prevailed in the minds of the general public, thanks to the dozens of years of efforts made by the pro-democratic activists both in and outside of China. The most important sign of this is the recent intellectual awakening, evidenced by the return of the democracy debate, which has occupied a central place in the public discourse around China's leadership change. More and more intellectuals, who were generally co-opted by the regime not long after the Tiananmen Massacre and acted as its defenders for many years, have come to realize and acknowledge the Chinese democracy movement's contributions, ideas, and beliefs, which are embodied in Charter 08.

Recognition by intellectuals that the status quo is unsustainable is always the first, and vital, step toward changing it.

In the meantime, the ordinary people are becoming more mature, more skillful, and more aggressive in fighting for their own civil rights. China, Inc. can sure ignore the grievance of the society, but the people will eventually unite themselves to form organized rebellion if individual petitions yield no results. Among the people, there is a subgroup called the netizens, those who use the internet a lot, nearly 550 million of them. Although the Chinese authorities impose strict control over the media, the existence of the internet paved a way for the people's awakening and networking. In the cyberspace language, the communist regime is rapidly losing all its moral assets while the people are constantly seeking the opportunity to group together in a skillful way. The netizens constitute an "information elite" that cannot be all bought off. They will play a leading role in future organized activities. Generally speaking, as the non-governmental forces grow and the civil protests escalate, struggle for power among different factions with the communist regime will become public. Especially, once the external pressure reaches a critical mass, the rivalry factions with the CCP will have to take the citizen force into serious account and seek or use the latter's support. This means a decomposition of China, Inc.

That said, I want to emphasize that we need an overall, viable pro-democracy movement to force the dictatorship to crack open. A long-term resilient movement will reach critical mass when idealists like Liu Xiaobo join forces with the self-motivated public or the disaffected with the status quo.

A milestone to meet that objective would be the formation of a group of civil leaders able to represent the general public and to at least partially disrupt the current political order—a group that would catch the attention and support of the international community and carry out and to call for effective negotiations with the government.

Last but not least, international support. Many friends in the international community are skeptical about the Chinese people's demand for freedom and democracy. Let me propose the following thought experiment for you to judge for yourselves.

Imagine that you visited China, taking with you a copy of the Universal Declaration of Human Rights. Arbitrarily choose any citizens on the street. Show the document, asking them with the language they understand whether they want the rights listed there. What would you expect them to say? Would you for a second believe they would say, "No, I do not want these rights"? Of course, you wouldn't. You see, you understand the Chinese people through understanding yourselves: Nobody wants to be a slave. In this regard, the Chinese people are no different than other people in the world. The thirst for freedom and dignity is indeed universal.

The people of China have long ago begun the search for dignity, justice, goodness, fairness, equality, freedom, and brotherhood. They have produced a few major pushes toward these goals in this generation. In the 1989 Tiananmen democracy movement, the Chinese people courageously stood up against government corruption that, in the words of Charter 08, has "corrupted human intercourse." They stood up for democracy and freedom. The image of a lone man standing in front of a string of tanks has inspired the entire world, and our fallen brothers' spirits have been one of the greatest sources of inspiration for continued struggle for these noble goals today in China.

No one can predict with precision when the moment of dramatic opening for change will come in China. Virtually every one of the sixty-some peaceful transitions to democracy in the past few decades has come as a surprise to the United States. One reason is that diplomats, academics, and policymakers generally do not pay attention to what is happening with students, workers, and farmers—with the street-level society and culture of the world's not-free countries.

The people of China are obviously experiencing revolutionary change. Above all else we must maintain our faith in my compatriots that we can and will join the vast majority of the world's people who now live in free or at least partly free countries. An opening for change could come in the next few months or it may take a few more years. Of course, it will never come without collective efforts, including those from the international community. So, we must persevere and keep the faith and be ready.

Now, looking at what is happening in China, as I said in my opening remarks, the intellectuals are weakening, evidenced by the return of democracy debate around China's leadership change. The intellectuals' renewed demand for democracy is, at least in part, based on their understanding of the reality of China's state crony capitalism. This state crony capitalism has spanned the long period of economic growth, which has become nearly the only one source of legitimacy for CCP's rule in China.

However, such an economic system has extracted incalculable costs from its people by tolerating human rights abuses, environmental deterioration, and morality collapse. That system has come almost to a dead end. We all know from the news that the Chinese economy is taking a downturn. The slowing economy will lay bare the already-existing conflict between the people and the government.

Because of their evil deeds, the ruling elites have concluded that the political status quo is the only safe haven for them. So, their first political priority is to stall the democratization process as long as they can. The CCP's political paralysis has trapped itself and China in a vicious circle: Initial resistance to political reform only aggravates existing problems and gives rise to new ones. This sharpens tensions, which then increase the risks that any reform will get out of control. This, in turn, deters the CCP from undertaking any reform, further fueling state-society tensions as individual and collective grievances continue to mount, compounding the risks of future reform.

It is an impossible task for the CCP to convince people that the two opposite pieces of evil business are both right. In fact, the CCP has been unable to close its legitimacy gap despite all the theoretical bridges that it has tried to build—from Marxism to Mao Zedong Thought, from Mao Zedong Thought to Deng Xiaoping Theory, from Deng Xiaoping Theory to the Three Represents, and from the Three Represents to Harmonious Society and Scientific Development Concept.

Since the communists took over China in 1949, it has generated a legacy with a long-lasting impact—that is, the collapse of morality and humanity. China, therefore, has entered an unprecedented era of de-civilization and anti-civilization when barbarism is norm and a form of national pride. This barbarism preludes and underscores such social mentality and behaviors as populism and neo-nationalism.

Throughout the long history of China, there was no such concept of "citizen." The communism and materialism have made it worse. In today's China, few people have honesty, and few people have credit. Fraud is so ubiquitous among governments, organizations, and individuals that an occasional honest person is deemed more scarce and more near-extinct, and therefore more dazzling than a panda.

Communism has led to the most hypocritical form of theocracy—a theocracy without god but with idols. It has caused severe polarities: the polarity between ideology and public policies, the polarity between words and deeds, the polarity between what's official and what's unofficial, and the polarity between the ruling elite and the ruled society at large. These polarities completely destroyed both the ruling party's legitimacy and the traditional social values that had bonded Chinese society together for over two thousand years. As a result, everybody was flushed away by a runaway flood of materialism, and they feel like living in a doomsday every day.

In China, communist corruption is not a legacy. It is an everyday reality.

The rebuilding of China will have to start with re-sowing the seeds of basic humanity on ground zero that is filled with rubble.

SECTION IX

OPPRESSION OF ETHNIC MINORITIES: THE SAFFRON FLAMES

"I am a proud man. But a proud man shamed and embarrassed by the unspeakable suffering the Chinese government has systematically inflicted upon the people of Tibet and by the general apathy of the Chinese public. A proud man brought to his knees by the weight of his grief, the force of his anger, and the unbearable feeling of helplessness in the face of such powerful evil. Yet I draw courage from you, my dear Tibetan brothers and sisters; you inspire me through your unbelievable endurance. And I draw courage from good people like you, the supporters of free Tibet; your relentless efforts have kept the issue of Tibet alive and helped the worldwide Tibet support network gain momentum....When you run from fear, you'll run into fear wherever you go. But when you run toward hope, you'll find hope wherever you go. Let's run toward hope."

CHAPTER 79

None of Us Will Have Freedom and Human Rights until Others Do

Speech at the Uyghur Demonstration in Front of the Chinese Embassy Commemorating the Fourth Anniversary of the July 5th Incident
Washington, DC, United States
July 5, 2013

Dear Uyghur brothers and sisters:

Today we gather here to commemorate the July 5th incident that took place four years ago. Four years have passed, our memory is still fresh, and we are mourning those who died in that tragedy.

In the past four years, the Chinese regime's ruthless crackdown has not only failed to maintain stability and peace in the region but instead has created even deeper hatred. This is evidenced in the ongoing tensions, including the deadly incidents in Shanshan County and Hetian District that took place in recent weeks.

I am deeply concerned about the Chinese regime's war-like rhetoric and stance against the Uyghur people, dispatching thousands of police and special forces armed to the teeth, intending to ruthlessly suppress the Uyghur people as "terrorists."

This spate of tragic incidents was not isolated; they were a direct result of China's long-term policy toward Uyghurs and other ethnic groups. This policy can be summarized in five Ds: dominate, deceive, divide, dilute, and demonize. The internecine killings between Han Chinese and Uyghurs is the bitter fruit of the seed of hatred planted by the Chinese regime. We are all victims trapped in this vicious cycle of hatred. Now it is time to break this vicious cycle. We must stand up together against this evil policy and fight for freedom for all.

People across the People's Republic of China have all suffered at the hands of this Chinese regime, yet as a Han Chinese I must admit that our Uyghur brothers and sisters and other so-called minority groups have been subject to an additional layer of repression and have suffered more. We must, and hope my other Chinese compatriots do as well, look at the July 5th tragedy first and foremost as a human being and see the Chinese government's violence against the Uyghurs as a crime against humanity. We must realize that none of us will have freedom and human rights until others do.

I respect you as a people who have every right to determine your own future. Nobody but yourselves can represent you. Nobody but yourselves can tell whether you are happy or not. You cannot and shouldn't be forced to be happy. Yet there is a long and bumpy road ahead of you before your right of self-determination will be finally secured and, my dear Uyghur brothers and sisters, you must realize that you need me and many, many more Han Chinese like myself to walk alongside you. Let's join hands and walk side by side, shoulder to shoulder to our common democratic future.

Thank you.

CHAPTER 80

Truth, Compassion, Courage, and Hope

Speech at International Tibet Network's 2013
European Regional Meeting
Basel, Switzerland
September 27, 2013

Dear friends, brothers and sisters,

Tashi delek.

I am delighted to be with you again and feel honored to speak to you.

On the flight to come here, I asked myself: "What can I say to you this time after I have said so much on so many occasions in support of a free Tibet? What can I say that has not been said before? What can I say as we continue to be confronted with so many of my indifferent Chinese compatriots and, indeed, the motionless world?"

Then I felt the need of going back to listen once again to the voices in the saffron flames to search for my words, indeed, my moral compass.

The Tibetan writer Gudrub wrote before setting himself on fire:

We are declaring the reality of Tibet by burning our own bodies to call for freedom of Tibet. Higher Beings, Please see Tibet. Mother Earth, Extend compassion to Tibet. Just World, Uphold the truth. The pure Land of Snow is now tainted with red blood, where military crackdowns are ceaseless. We as sons and daughters of the Land of Snow will win the battle. We will win the battle through truth, by shooting the arrows of our lives, by using the bow of our mind.

From this heaven-and-earth-moving outcry, I hear four resounding words: truth, compassion, courage, and hope.

Let's begin with the truth we all know:

The truth is that, since the Chinese government occupation, over one million Tibetans have been killed through imprisonment, torture, executions, and mass killings.

In 2008, a United Nations report concluded that the use of torture in Tibet was "widespread" and "routine."

The Chinese government has destroyed more than 6,000 Tibetan monasteries.

Since March 2011, 130 Tibetans have set themselves on fire in protest of this oppressive occupation.

Tibetans are steadily losing their land, their language, and their culture through Chinese government programs that include a vast migration of Han Chinese into the Tibetan Autonomous Region. If not stopped, this oppression will soon make Tibetans a demographic and economic minority and ultimately a lost civilization.

This is the truth we all know. We must not let the truth be hidden from the world's conscience, nor that of China. We must be persistent in expanding our global campaign of truth and, in our dear brother Gudrub's words, we will win the battle through truth by shooting the arrows of our lives, by using the bow of our mind.

The Tibetan self-immolators' act of compassion would be unthinkable and pointless if they did not have a profound confidence in the conscience of man. We must carry their spirit of compassion forward to appeal to the conscience of the people around the world. Especially, we should make special efforts to reach out to the Chinese people with the truth about Tibet and empower them with compassion for them to recognize the truth and end their silence. I believe that the Tibetan selfless martyrs had a strong belief that compassion can clean conscience, including that of the Chinese, and clear conscience does not hide truth.

Dear brothers and sisters, you know I am a proud man. But a proud man shamed and embarrassed by the unspeakable suffering the Chinese government has systematically inflicted upon the people of Tibet and by the general apathy of the Chinese public. A proud man brought to his knees by the weight of his grief, the force of his anger, and the unbearable feeling of helplessness in the face of such powerful evil. Yet I draw courage from you, my dear Tibetan brothers and sisters; you inspire me through your unbelievable endurance. And I draw courage from good people like you, the supporters of free Tibet, your relentless efforts have kept the issue of Tibet alive and helped the worldwide Tibet Support Network gain momentum. We may seem few in face of the overwhelming indifferent many. But "one man with courage makes a majority," "they are the one to be afraid." We must not lose hope.

When you run from fear, you'll run into fear wherever you go. But when you run toward hope, you'll find hope wherever you go. Let's run toward hope. We draw strength and inspiration from the words of His Holiness the Dalai Lama who said, *"Tragedy should be utilized as a source of strength. No matter what sort of difficulties, how painful the experience is, if we lose our hope, that's our real disaster."*

Let's run toward the burning flames of martyrdom in Tibet because it is the burning of brave lives of compassion and love and because the martyrs committed the very act of self-immolation with the hope that the flames would shine for the world to see the truth and the truth would set us free.

I said loudly on many occasions that I am a Tibetan. I said so because I believed, as I continue to believe today, that nobody can say that he is not a Tibetan if he sees the burning flames in Tibet and is not numb to pain himself and that nobody can say she is not a Tibetan if she hears the voices cry out from the flames and is still in possession of a heart to love and a mind to understand.

But today I want to highlight my identity as a Chinese. I want to because I want to highlight the fact that, with your courageous efforts to meet the Chinese with compassion, more Chinese like myself will be awaking to the truth, will be set free of the bondage of bigotry and malice, and will even share your just cause for freedom. That is to say, with your courage, compassion, and your perseverance in hope, you can turn Saul to Paul.

Today I recommit myself to the cause of a free Tibet. My dear brothers and sisters, I will continue to struggle side by side with you and walk with you every step on the road toward home and freedom.

Thank you.

CHAPTER 81

If Each Democracy Says No, the Chances for China Will Be Zero

Speech at the Sixth Annual Briefing on Human Rights Council Candidates Hosted by UN Watch and Human Rights Foundation
UN Headquarters, New York, NY, United States
November 4, 2013

At about 9:00 p.m., September 24, I was on the phone with Ms. Zhang Jing in China, the wife of the street vendor Xia Junfeng. Four years ago, Xia Junfeng, acting in self-defense, stabbed two parapolice who were beating him and taking his things. She and their son had just had the last meeting with Xia Junfeng, who was that morning notified he was to be executed the same day. She cried to me for help. At the same time, the online community expressed its outrage over the imminent execution, yet nobody could figure out how to save Xia's life, which would be taken away in roughly an hour. I was in such a hurry to search for any clues from all the business cards of those parliamentary and executive leaders I knew in the world democracies, although I knew it would be almost impossible for any of them to do anything about it.

While it is debatable whether the world democracies should intervene in such controversial criminal cases in China as that of Xia, it is unacceptable for them to withdraw from their responsibility to press China on its human rights record when an opportunity arises for them to do so with the international lawful right and capability without risking being charged with "interfering with internal affairs." Such an opportunity will come up next Tuesday when the UN General Assembly will vote to choose new members on its Human Rights Council.

Before I continue, I want to emphasize that I am a citizen of China. As such, I am not a foreigner speaking to "interfere with China's internal affairs." Rather, I am voicing the concerns of a Chinese citizen, concerns that should be heard by the international community. If you will, I am a citizen of China trying to interfere with foreign affairs. But I am not alone. In my hand are a copy of nearly 10,000 names of Chinese, Tibetans, Uyghurs, and Mongolians who urge foreign governments to vote "NO" on China's membership on the UN Human Rights Council.

In the course of its affairs as a great nation, China has left large fingerprints on the canvas of human events. With regard to human rights, these fingerprints place China at the scene of so many activities, both domestic and international, that are so outside the norm of civilized nations that its membership in the United Nations Human Rights Council defies logic, reason, and common sense.

To put it simply, a country's qualification for UNHRC membership is based on how it treats its own people and how it helps promote the human rights of other people around the world. Unfortunately, China has failed on both accounts.

In considering China's record, we need look no further than these individuals, groups, events, and policies:

The Tiananmen Massacre, the Tiananmen Mothers; Liu Xiaobo and his wife, Liu Xia, Wang Bingzhang, Dhondup Wangchen, Gheyret Niyaz, Hada; Tibetans, Uyghurs, Mongolians; House Churches, Falun Gong, Forced Abortions, Forced Evictions, Forced Disappearances, Black Jails...

Almost a quarter century has passed since the Tiananmen Massacre, yet the Chinese government has never admitted its wrongdoing and has continually repressed any individuals and groups who have been working to expose the truth and commemorate the victims.

The government that massacred its own citizens in the heart of its capital is the very same government who today continues to routinely imprison, torture, and exile its best citizens for no other reason than exercising the right to speak freely. It is the same government who pursues cultural genocide on Tibetans, Uyghurs, and Mongolians and religious purges on Christians and Falun Gong practitioners, and whose foreign policies and models of repression enable the morally bankrupt regimes of North Korea, Iran, and Syria to suck freedom and dignity from its people. Its paranoia and insecurity drive it to extend its tyranny beyond its borders. Its disdain for human dignity now openly challenges the very foundation of civilization itself.

Some people have hoped and maybe continue to hope that the inclusion of China into the UN Human Rights Council will behave it. But China's track record from when it previously served on the Council was a dismal one. Thousands of instances of illegal repression happened from 2006 to 2012 when China was a member of the UN Human Rights Council. During that time, China became the only country detaining a Nobel laureate and its failed ethnic policies led to a series of deplorable incidents. There was the Lhasa incident on March 14, 2008, in Tibet, the July 5th Urumqi Incident in 2009, the May 25th Inner Mongolia Incident in 2011, and more than 100 Tibetan self-immolations.

In the most recent months, while China was bidding to become a UN Human Rights Council member, the government has intensified its suppression of online freedom of speech and of the citizen movement. It arrested and jailed about a couple hundred activists.

Therefore, voting to put China on UNHRC would be like picking the fox to guard the hen house—while he was still wiping the feathers off his mouth from his last meal.

We know that any candidate needs ninety-seven votes at UNGA to be elected to sit on UNHRC. If each democracy says no, the chances for China will be zero. Such a vote will test any democratic country's commitment to democracy and human rights. Therefore, we call on all democracies not to humiliate your great country and people and choose to cast a "No" vote on China. After all, how could democracies vote with a straight face to place China, the world-leading human rights violator on the body charged with protecting human rights? Unlike intervening with the case of Xia Junfeng, opposing China's candidacy for UNHRC is the kind of clear step that is needed. This is the least the world democracies can and should do.

CHAPTER 82

Walk Home Together

Speech at the New York Rally Commemorating the Fifty-Fifth Anniversary of the Tibetan National Uprising
New York, NY, United States
March 10, 2014

Dear Tibetan brothers and sisters:

Tashi delek.

As always, I am excited to get together with you and feel honored and humbled to speak to you on this solemn occasion to remember the Tibetan National Uprising that took place fifty-five years ago and to look forward. I am honored because I have become part of your extraordinary struggle for freedom, which has won worldwide respect. I am humbled because your unspeakable suffering has been at the hands of a government that is largely Chinese, my own people. Struggling together with you is a redeeming process for me; you have reached out your hands to me in forgiveness, in friendship and brotherhood. You hold your suffering close to your heart while somehow keeping a smile on your face. The wisdom and guidance of His Holiness the Dalai Lama have shown a path to justice paved with compassion and nonviolence for all to follow. I am indeed honored and privileged to follow the path of His Holiness and to walk with you and call each of you my brother or sister.

Today I want to talk with you about going home. This is the time of year when all of us feel a tug at our hearts for home. China's unjust rule in Tibet has led to the killing of a million Tibetans, the destruction of thousands of temples and monasteries, the diluting and destroying of the Tibetan language and culture, and the irreversible damage to the natural environment on the Tibetan plateau, and it has also resulted in the fifty-five years-long exile of His Holiness the Dalai Lama and produced nearly 200,000 Tibetan refugees, condemning them to a state of permanent exile. Scattered around the world as a minority among minorities, their existence is a constant battle for political recognition, financial survival, and cultural continuity. "There is no place like home." Returning home is an exile's greatest dream and being stranded in a foreign land his greatest sorrow.

For all the tragedies and hardships faced by the Tibetan people today, there is one constant root exacerbating or causing all the others in turn: China's block on the Dalai Lama and his people's right to return to their homeland. Let's listen to the saffron flames in Tibet. Through their heroic act of self-immolation, the nearly 130 Tibetan martyrs have expressed the great desire of all Tibetans, both in and outside Tibet, "Let the Dalai Lama Return Home"!

This voice, reverberating around all the time, often makes my heart burn and my eyes well with tears.

As remarkably kind, compassionate, tolerant, and patient as His Holiness may be, this need to return must burn hot on his heart as He faces this beloved new generation of Tibetans who either remain in their raped homeland without their spiritual leader or live with their spiritual leader in free lands that are not their own. This is a grave humanitarian emergency, which is getting worse day by day. It is disheartening that an emergency can be as old as fifty-five years.

I know the Dalai Lama and his people have traveled a long journey toward home but nobody knows when they might set foot on their homeland. Many good people seem to have been convinced that political realities make such an ultimate justice impossible. But the voice from the saffron flames has told us otherwise! The voice deep in our hearts is telling us otherwise!

If the past journey has taught us anything, it is that there is no shortcut or easy way home. We must battle every day to move forward.

We must battle against the hard hearts and iron arms of the Chinese rulers as well as the indifference of the world community and its leaders.

Now we must intensify our global campaign of truth and force China, a signatory of the Universal Declaration of Human Rights, and the international community onto the defensive about the right of return, which is enshrined in Article 13(b) of the UDHR: "Everyone has the right to leave any country, including his own, and to return to his country." The world community must recognize that the Right of Return for the Tibetans is a national, historical, and individual claim and that recognizing Tibetans' right to return home is not an option but a must.

Are you missing home?

So, I ask you, speak up about your plight. You should let everybody you meet know that you have been unjustly uprooted from your homeland. Let them know of your aching desire to return. You should educate the whole world that the roots of the Tibetans in Tibet are older than the roots of the British in Britain, and much older than the roots of most Americans in America.

The Tibetan self-immolators' act would be unthinkable and pointless if they did not have a profound confidence in the conscience of man. We must carry their spirit of compassion forward to appeal to the conscience of the people around the world. Especially, we should make special efforts to reach out to the Chinese people with the truth about Tibet and empower them with compassion for them to recognize the truth and end their silence. I believe that the Tibetan selfless martyrs had a strong belief that compassion can clean consciences, including that of the Chinese, and a clear conscience does not hide from the truth. I believe that with your courageous efforts to meet the Chinese with compassion, more Chinese like myself will be awaking to the truth, will be set free of the bondage of bigotry and malice, and will be particularly reminded of Confucius' teaching of *don't do to others what you don't wish for yourself* and realizing that our Tibetan brothers and sisters love their homeland and love living in their homeland, no less powerfully than we Chinese to our own homeland.

Many of the Chinese democracy fighters, including myself, have been forced into exile for nearly twenty-five years following the 1989 Tiananmen Massacre. We share the Tibetans' excruciating pain of homesickness. Not long after the massacre, I got to know Tibetan exiles and the nature of your struggle. I soon understood that we were at least thirty years late in coming to the aid of your cause. Yet we came together in brotherhood, and we have walked arm in arm. Today, on this painful anniversary, we recommit ourselves to continue to walk together toward freedom and home. With each step we take together in the path of truth, justice, and compassion, we are closer to our goal.

Let me close with a little story, which I have told many times and I think is worth being told again. On March 10, 2010, the fifty-first anniversary of the Tibetan National Uprising in Dharamsala, I led a group of Chinese freedom fighters in the audience with His Holiness. At the end of the meeting, we all stood up together. I noticed that His Holiness had a pair of shoes of very good quality. I whispered to His Holiness that he had a pair of very fine shoes, much nicer than mine. "Yes" His Holiness replied. "I will walk home in them." I replied, "Yes, your Holiness, I will walk with you." We suddenly found ourselves embracing each other.

Dear brothers and sisters, let's walk home together!

Free Tibet.

Let the Dalai Lama return home.

Thank you all.

CHAPTER 83

On the Five Factors Determining China's Future Political Direction

Opening Remarks Speech at the Ninth Interethnic/ Interfaith Leadership Conference
Taipei, Taiwan
April 24, 2014

Our distinguished guests, friends, ladies and gentlemen, good morning.

First, I would like to thank everybody for coming to the ninth Interethnic/Interfaith Leadership Conference. Particularly, I would like to thank those who have come a long way from across the world—from Mainland China, Hong Kong, Macau, India, Japan, Mongolia, the Americas, Europe, and Australia.

In fact, all of us here, including participants from Taiwan, are trekkers on a long and arduous journey. We represent groups of different regions and ethnicities with different histories, cultures, religions, and languages. But for a common goal, we are gathering here today with our sincerity, wisdom, determination, and hope. We are just like little sparks lighting and paving the way to equality, freedom, and democracy. For this common goal, all our groups have been working long and hard. Those from the People's Republic of China are fighting hard for their basic human rights; our Tibetan, Uyghur, and Mongolian brothers and sisters are fighting an even harder battle for ethnic equality and liberation, on top of fighting for their basic human rights; the citizens of Hong Kong and Macau are resisting the reality that their freedoms are being eroded, while at the same time struggling to advance the process of democratization; people from Taiwan are doing all they can to defend the freedoms and democracy they have obtained and to save Taiwan from the fate of a frog slowly being boiled alive. So, all of us are comrades on this long and arduous journey in pursuit of democracy, freedom, and equality, and our common enemy is the dictatorial regime of the Chinese Communist Party, which has become the biggest diehard standing in our way.

And how to get rid of it? This is a question we all have to answer, and this is exactly why we are here again.

After the Tiananmen Massacre, the Chinese communist regime gradually adopted a defensive position in terms of its political ideology, and in China the concepts of freedom and democracy have increasingly prevailed in the ideological battlefield and in public discourse. The CCP's so-called "Three Confidences" were proposed just out of their lack of confidence. However, the CCP's political tactics have become more and more active, flexible, practical, and aggressive due to the urgency of the political survival of the regime. In contrast, when we look back at our democratic forces, we find ourselves emphasizing political ideology too much and not focusing enough on political tactics. In China now, publicly talking about abstract concepts of democracy and freedom is no longer a taboo. Having an edge in political concepts but without seriously and systematically countering the CCP's political tactics, we tend to lack strength in our fight. Meanwhile, this regime is implementing its practical political tactics using the enormous resources it seized. Therefore, for all the groups represented here, the first and foremost task is to counter CCP's tactics of division and disintegration.

This kind of division is both vertical and horizontal. It comes in various forms: division between those in pursuit of political ideas and those of specific interests; regional division between Mainland China, Taiwan, Hong Kong, Macau, and macro-overseas regions; division between local areas within the Chinese Mainland; ethnic division between Han, Tibetan, Mongolian, Uyghur, especially between Han and ethnic minorities; religious division between Christians, Muslims, Buddhists, and Falun Gong practitioners; also division between different groups fighting for their rights on a wide range of issues, for example, land seizure, environmental pollution, and the one-child policy. All of these have contributed to an extremely complicated situation, which we must begin to take seriously. We must clearly understand these complex relationships in order to come up with a strategy to counter tactics of division and disintegration.

We, of course, do not deny that there is considerable suspicion, distrust, hostility, and even resentment between some communities, particularly between communities of different ethnicities, religions, and macro-regions, even between those who are fighting for freedom and human rights. We must constantly remind ourselves not to trip on these obstacles.

From a macro point of view, there exist five factors that determine China's future political direction.

First is the development of democratic forces. Second, the dynamics of the power structuring within the Chinese Communist Party, mainly the publicized struggle among the power-oriented factions or among the idea-oriented factions. Third, the uprising of Tibetan, Uyghur, and Mongolian ethnic minorities, as well as the development of their relationship with the Han people. Fourth, the development of Mainland China's comprehensive interactions with Hong Kong, Macau, and Taiwan. Fifth, the dynamics of China's relations with the international community.

All five factors are intertwined, with one influencing another. At least four out of the five are directly related to the communities we represent and the work we do. This is to say, what we are doing today and how we are doing it will affect China's political future, and therefore the very future of our communities is at stake. Among these five factors, the most fundamental one is the development of democratic forces, which includes forces within each community and collaboration and union with other communities. Democratic forces that are divided are not sustainable and thus will not lead to democratization. Therefore, how to unite to build viable democratic forces is at the top of our agenda. This is exactly the theme of the ninth Interethnic/Interfaith Leadership Conference.

I hope this conference will mark a new starting point toward a higher aim.

SECTION X

CHINA'S DARK AGE AND SECRET DOCUMENT #9: STRUGGLING IN THE SHADOWS

May 2014—April 2015

"China has now fallen into its own Dark Age. Not only has the party-state started a systematic, mafia-style campaign to silence any dissenting voice by physically removing pro-democracy and human rights activists through massive arrests, forced disappearances, and severe sentences, but more seriously it has launched an even bigger campaign to control the Chinese people's minds."

CHAPTER 84

China Has Now Fallen into Its Own Dark Age

Opening Remarks at the Hearing of the Committee on the House Foreign Affairs Subcommittee on Africa, Global Health, Global Human Rights, and International Organizations on the Topic "Tiananmen 25 Years Later: Leaders Who Were There"
Washington, DC, United States
May 30, 2014

Mr. Chairman Smith,

Thank you very much for hosting this timely hearing.

If I remember correctly, this is the fifteenth hearing you have hosted on human rights in China. Your leadership is remarkable. The statements you and other members just made have made clear once again that we have not been fighting alone. Today I will not repeat myself on my personal account of the Tiananmen Massacre twenty-five years ago, which I have testified multiple times before you; instead, I will try to provide you a window through which you may better see the overall political situation in China and the direction it is taking.

Twenty-five years ago, the Chinese students and citizens in Beijing and across China demanded a clean government and freedom of expression and media, but today the conditions in these areas are much worse than before in many ways.

For example, when the new leadership led by Xi Jinping took power in 2013, it issued a secret Document 9 which boils down to this, I quote:

"We must not permit the dissemination of opinions that oppose the Party's theory or political line, the publication of views contrary to decisions that represent the central leadership's views, or the spread of political rumors that defame the image of the Party or the nation."

It sounds like something from the Dark Ages. But it is happening today in China. China has now fallen into its own Dark Age. Not only has the party-state started a systematic, mafia-style campaign to silence any dissenting voice by physically removing pro-democracy and human rights activists through massive arrests, forced disappearances, and severe sentences, but more seriously it has launched an even bigger campaign to control the Chinese people's minds.

The Chinese party-state openly denounces the American and Western values and political system which we all cherish, and vows to eradicate the so-called "seven perils" that endanger the party-state's perpetual rule of China, including Western constitutional democracy, universal values of human rights, independent press and civil society, pro-market "neo-liberalism," and a few others.

This campaign to completely reject "Western ideas" is actually an essential part of Xi's "Chinese dream." It is much worse and further reaching than the anti-bourgeois spiritual pollution campaign during the mid-1980s, which the students in Tiananmen Square demanded to overturn twenty-five years ago.

Mr. Chairman, I have to sadly report to you that two activists have been detained and charged with leaking this infamous Document 9. They are Ms. Gao Yu, whom you may already know, and a gentleman, an author of several influential books and the highest ranking official detained in this round of crackdowns.

There was a chance for political reform and peaceful transition to democracy within the Chinese Communist Party in 1989, but with Xi's total rejection of universal value and democracy and his denial of free thought, the opportunity is now gone. The key question that the United States must ask is can a fascist party-state that ruthlessly kills its own people and continues to silence any opposition voice and ban people's intellectual freedom, can it rise peacefully? What danger does it pose to our society and universal values?

Finally, I ask to summit the Document 9 for the record. Thank you, Mr. Chairman.

Communiqué on the Current State of the Ideological Sphere

A Notice from the Central Committee of the Communist Party of China's General Office

Provinces, autonomous regions, municipalities directly under the Party committee, Central ministries and state organs, Party ministries, People's Liberation Army headquarters, major Party committees, and Party leadership groups of civilian organizations: This notice "A Communiqué on the Current State of the Ideological Sphere" has been approved by the central leadership, and is herewith distributed to you. Please thoroughly implement its suggestions.

April 22, 2013

(This document has been sent to local divisional levels)

Introduction

Since the Party's Eighteenth National Congress, under General Secretary Xi Jinping's strong central leadership, the nation triumphantly convened the National People's Congress and the Chinese People's Political Consultative Conference, the Party's and nation's various undertakings have made a good start, and the general mood of the Party and Government has been constantly improving. Cohesion among our nation's people has become stronger and our confidence in our path, our theory, and our system has become more resolute. Mainstream ideology is becoming healthier and more vigorous. The spirit of the Party's Eighteenth National Congress and General Secretary Xi Jinping's series of important speeches have unified the thought of the entire Party, the entire country, and the entire people enormously. The ideological foundation of our united struggle is unceasingly solidifying.

The new session of the central leadership group has: put forth a series of new principles for conduct in political administration, furnished an interpretation of the Chinese dream of the great rejuvenation of the Chinese nation, improved our work-style, maintained close ties with the masses, rigorously enforced diligence and thrift, opposed extravagance and waste, increased vigor in the fight against corruption, and won the widespread endorsement of cadres and the masses. We persist in upholding scientific development as the main theme, accelerating economic transformation as the main thread, and increasing the quality and efficiency of the economy as the core. The outlook for our nation's economic development continues to be favorable, and the people's faith in China's economic prospects has risen. In an effort to improve the people's livelihood, we are putting forth new measures to benefit the people so they may look forward to a better future: disseminating thought on the cultural front as the most important political task; studying, implementing, and advancing the spirit of the Eighteenth Party Congress; rapidly arousing mass fervor, proclaiming that socialism with Chinese characteristics and the Chinese dream are the main theme of our age; expanding and strengthening positive propaganda; strengthening guidance on deep-seated problems; strengthening the management of ideological fronts; promoting unification of thought; concentrating our strength and implementing the development of a positive atmosphere and providing spiritual strength to the party and nation.

Noteworthy Problems Related to the Current State of the Ideological Sphere

While fully approving of the ideological mainstream, we must also clearly see the ideological situation as a complicated, intense struggle. Currently, the following false ideological trends, positions, and activities all deserve note:

1. Promoting Western Constitutional Democracy: An attempt to undermine the current leadership and the socialism with Chinese characteristics system of governance.

Western Constitutional Democracy has distinct political properties and aims. Among these are the separation of powers, the multi-party system, general elections, independent judiciaries, nationalized armies, and other characteristics. These are the capitalist class' concepts of a nation, political model, and system design. The concept of constitutional democracy originated a long time ago, and recently the idea has been hyped ever more frequently.

This is mainly expressed the following ways: In commemorating the thirtieth anniversary of the enactment of the [Chinese] Constitution, [some people] hold up the banners of "defending the constitution" and "rule of law." They attack the Party's leaders for placing themselves above the constitution, saying China "has a constitution but no constitutional government." Some people still use the phrase "constitutional dream" to distort the Chinese dream of the great rejuvenation of the Chinese nation, saying things like "constitutional democracy is the only way out" and "China should catch up with the rest of the world's trend toward constitutional governance." The point of publicly proclaiming Western constitutional democracy's key points is to oppose the party's leadership and implementation of its constitution and laws. Their goal is to use Western constitutional democracy to undermine the Party's leadership, abolish the People's Democracy, negate our country's constitution as well as our established system and principles, and bring about a change of allegiance by bringing Western political systems to China.

2. Promoting "universal values" in an attempt to weaken the theoretical foundations of the Party's leadership.

The goal of espousing "universal values" is to claim that the West's value system defies time and space, transcends nation and class, and applies to all humanity.

This is mainly expressed in the following ways: [The people who espouse universal values] believe Western freedom, democracy, and human rights are universal and eternal. This is evident in their distortion of the Party's own promotion of democracy, freedom, equality, justice, rule of law, and other such values; their claim that the CCP's acceptance of universal values is a victory for universal values," that "the West's values are the prevailing norm for all human civilization," that "only when China accepts Western values will it have a future," and that "Reform and Opening is just a process of gradually accepting universal rights."

Given Western nations' long-term dominance in the realms of economics, military affairs, science, and technology, these arguments can be confusing and deceptive. The goal [of such slogans] is to obscure the essential differences between the West's value system and the value system we advocate, ultimately using the West's value systems to supplant the core values of Socialism.

3. Promoting civil society in an attempt to dismantle the ruling party's social foundation.

Civil society is a socio-political theory that originated in the West. It holds that in the social sphere, individual rights are paramount and ought to be immune to obstruction by the state. For the past few years, the idea of civil society has been adopted by Western anti-China forces and used as a political tool. Additionally, some people with ulterior motives within China have begun to promote these ideas.

This is mainly expressed in the following ways:

Promoting civil society and Western-style theories of governance, they claim that building a civil society in China is a precondition for the protection of individual rights and forms the basis for the realization of constitutional democracy. Viewing civil society as a magic bullet for advancing social management at the local level, they have launched all kinds of so-called citizen's movements.

Advocates of civil society want to squeeze the Party out of leadership of the masses at the local level, even setting the Party against the masses, to the point that their advocacy is becoming a serious form of political opposition.

4. Promoting Neoliberalism, attempting to change China's Basic Economic System.

Neoliberalism advocates unrestrained economic liberalization, complete privatization, and total marketization and it opposes any kind of interference or regulation by the state. Western countries, led by the United States, carry out their Neoliberal agendas under the guise of "globalization," visiting catastrophic consequences upon Latin America, the Soviet Union, and Eastern Europe, and have also dragged themselves into the international financial crisis from they have yet to recover.

This is mainly expressed in the following ways:

[Neoliberalism's advocates] actively promote the "market omnipotence theory." They claim our country's macroeconomic control is strangling the market's efficiency and vitality and they oppose public ownership, arguing that China's state-owned enterprises are "national monopolies," inefficient, and disruptive of the market economy, and should undergo "comprehensive privatization." These arguments aim to change our country's basic economic infrastructure and weaken the government's control of the national economy.

5. Promoting the West's idea of journalism, challenging China's principle that the media and publishing system should be subject to Party discipline.

Some people, under the pretext of espousing "freedom of the press," promote the West's idea of journalism and undermine our country's principle that the media should be infused with the spirit of the Party.

This is mainly expressed in the following ways:

Defining the media as "society's public instrument" and as the "Fourth Estate;" attacking the Marxist view of news and promote the "free flow of information on the Internet;" slandering our country's efforts to improve Internet management by calling them a crackdown on the Internet; claiming that the media is not governed by the rule of law but by the arbitrary will of the leadership; and calling for China to promulgate a Media Law based on Western principles. [Some people] also claim that China restricts freedom of the press and bang on about abolishing propaganda departments. The ultimate goal of advocating the West's view of the media is to hawk the principle of abstract and absolute freedom of press, oppose the Party's leadership in the media, and gouge an opening through which to infiltrate our ideology.

6. Promoting historical nihilism, trying to undermine the history of the CCP and of New China.

The goal of historical nihilism, in the guise of "reassessing history," is to distort Party history and the history of New China.

This is mainly expressed in the following ways:

Rejecting the revolution; claiming that the revolution led by the Chinese Communist Party resulted only in destruction; denying the historical inevitability in China's choice of the Socialist road, calling it the wrong path, and the Party's and new China's history a "continuous series of mistakes"; rejecting the accepted conclusions on historical events and figures, disparaging our Revolutionary precursors, and vilifying the Party's leaders. Recently, some people took advantage of Comrade Mao Zedong's 120th birthday in order to deny the scientific and guiding value of Mao Zedong thought. Some people try to cleave apart the period that preceded Reform and Opening from the period that followed, or even to set these two periods in opposition to one another. By rejecting CCP history and the history of New China, historical nihilism seeks to fundamentally undermine the CCP's historical purpose, which is tantamount to denying the legitimacy of the CCP's long-term political dominance.

7. Questioning Reform and Opening and the socialist nature of socialism with Chinese characteristics.

For the past several years, the discussion of reform has been unceasing, with all kinds of voices joining one after another. Some views clearly deviate from socialism with Chinese characteristics.

This is mainly expressed in the following ways:

Some blame the contradictions and problems of development on Reform and Opening. They say "Reform and opening up has gone too far" and that "we have deviated from our Socialist orientation." They question whether or not what China is doing now still truly is Socialism, or they just call it "Capitalist Socialism," "State Capitalism," or "New Bureaucratic Capitalism." Others say, "reform is still distant and hasn't be realized" or that "reform of the political system lags behind and obstructs reform of the economy." They bang on about how we should use Western standards to achieve so-called "thorough reform." Essentially, they oppose the general and specific policies emanating from the road taken at the Third Plenum of the Eleventh Party Congress and they oppose socialism with Chinese characteristics.

These mistaken views and ideas exist in great numbers in overseas media and reactionary publications. They penetrate China through the Internet and underground channels and they are disseminated on domestic Internet forums, blogs, and microblogs, They also appear in public lectures, seminars, university classrooms, class discussion forums, civilian study groups, and individual publications. If we allow any of these ideas to spread, they will disturb people's existing consensus on important issues like which flag to raise, which road to take, which goals to pursue, etc., and this will disrupt our nation's stable progress on reform and development.

Western anti-China forces and internal "dissidents" are still actively trying to infiltrate China's ideological sphere and challenge our mainstream ideology. Some of their latest major efforts include: Some people have disseminated open letters and declarations and have organized petition-signings to vocalize requests for political reforms, improvement of human rights, release of "political prisoners," "reversing the verdict on '6/4' [the Tiananmen Massacre]," and other such political demands; they have made a fuss over asset disclosure by officials, fighting corruption with the Internet, media supervision of government, and other sensitive hot-button issues, all of which stoke dissatisfaction with the Party and government. Western embassies, consulates, media operations, and NGOs operating inside China under various covers are spreading Western ideas and values and are cultivating so-called "anti-government forces." Cooking up anti-government publications overseas. Within China's borders, some private organizations are creating reactionary underground publications, and still others are filming documentaries on sensitive subject matter, disseminating political rumors, and defaming the party and the national leadership. Those manipulating and hyping the Tibetan self-immolations, manufacturing the violent terrorist attacks in Xinjiang, and using the ethnic and religious issues to divide and break up [the nation]. Accelerating infiltration of the Internet and illegal gatherings within our borders. "Dissidents" and people identified with "rights protection" are active. Some of them are working together with Western anti-China forces, echoing each other and relying on each other's support. This clearly indicates that the contest between infiltration and anti-infiltration efforts in the ideological sphere is as severe as ever, and so long as we persist in CCP leadership and socialism with Chinese characteristics, the position of Western anti-China forces to pressure for urgent reform won't change, and they'll continue to point the spearhead of Westernizing, splitting, and "Color Revolutions" at China. In the face of these threats, we must not let down our guard or decrease our vigilance.

Pay Close Attention to Work in the Ideological Sphere

Historical experience has proven that failures in the economic sphere can result in major disorder, and failure in the ideological sphere can result in major disorders as well. Confronting the very real threat of Western anti-China forces and their attempt at carrying out Westernization, splitting, and "Color Revolutions," and facing the severe challenge of today's ideological sphere, all levels of Party and Government, especially key leaders, must pay close attention to their work in the ideological sphere and firmly seize their leadership authority and dominance.

1. Strengthen leadership in the ideological sphere.

Party members and governments of all levels must become fully aware that struggles in the ideological sphere are perpetual, complex, and excruciating; you must strengthen awareness of the current political situation, big picture, responsibility, and risks. Leaders at all levels of government, you must strengthen your sense of responsibility-make work in the ideological sphere a high priority in your daily agenda, routinely analyze and study new developments in the ideological sphere, react swiftly and effectively, and preemptively resolve all problems in the ideological sphere.

2. Guide our party member and leaders to distinguish between true and false theories.

Forcefully resist influential and harmful false tides of thoughts, help people distinguish between truth and falsehood, and solidify their understanding. Party members, especially high-level leaders, must become adept at tackling problems from political, big-picture, strategic, and theoretical perspective. They must clearly recognize the essence of false ideas and viewpoints, both their theoretical falsehood and the practical political harm they can cause. We must have a firm approach and clear-cut stance toward major political principles, issues of right and wrong, what to support and what to oppose. We must uphold strict and clear discipline, maintaining a high-level unity with the Party Central Committee under the leadership of General Secretary Xi Jinping in thought, political stance, and action. We must not permit the dissemination of opinions that oppose the Party's theory or political line, the publication of views contrary to decisions that represent the central leadership's views, or the spread of political rumors that defame the image of the Party or the nation.

3. Unwavering adherence to the principle of the Party's control of media.

The [principle of the Party's control of media] stems from our political system and the nature of our media. We must maintain the correct political direction. We must firmly hold fast to the principle of the media's Party spirit and social responsibility, and that in political matters it must be of one heart and mind with the Party. We must persist in correct guidance of public opinion, insisting that the correct political orientation suffuse every domain and process in political engagement, form, substance, and technology. We must give high priority to building both the leadership and rank and file in the sphere of media work. We need to strengthen education on the Marxist perspective of media to ensure that the media leadership is always firmly controlled by someone who maintains an identical ideology with the Party's Central Committee, under General Secretary Xi Jinping's leadership.

4. Conscientiously strengthen management of the ideological battlefield.

When facing sensitive events and complex puzzles in the ideological sphere, we should implement the principle that the people in charge assume responsibility and use territorial management.

We must reinforce our management of all types and levels of propaganda on the cultural front, perfect and carry out related administrative systems, and allow absolutely no opportunity or outlets for incorrect thinking or viewpoints to spread. Conscientiously implement the "Decision of the Standing Committee of the National People's Congress on Strengthening Information Protection on Networks," strengthen guidance of public opinion on the Internet, purify the environment of public opinion on the Internet. Improve and innovate our management strategies and methods to achieve our goals in a legal, scientific, and effective way.

CHAPTER 85

It Is for Us the Living

Speech at Wreath-Laying Ceremony Remembering the Victims of Communism
Washington, DC, United States
June 11, 2014

Dr. Edwards, distinguished guests, and dear friends,

Thank you for your wisdom, your tenacity, your moral courage, and your passion that gave birth to the Victims of Communism Memorial Foundation twenty years ago. I salute you for your prophetic vision in the selection of the Goddess of Democracy as the icon for this memorial to more than 100 million victims of communism, including those heroes who died in Tiananmen Square twenty-five years ago.

As we gather here, I am struggling to find a fitting way not only to recognize the sacrifice of the Tiananmen victims but also to ask ourselves what pledge that remembrance requires of us today. I can think of no better words than Abraham Lincoln's famed Gettysburg Address. His call for renewed commitment might just as well be read today in Tiananmen Square.

Lincoln said:

"We have come to dedicate a portion of that field, as a final resting place for those who here gave their lives that that nation might live. It is altogether fitting and proper that we should do this. But, in a larger sense, we cannot dedicate … this ground. The brave men, living and dead, who struggled here, have consecrated it, far above our poor power… It is rather for us to be here dedicated to the great task remaining before us … that these dead shall not have died in vain…"

Today, twenty-five years after the Tiananmen Massacre, China's leaders remain obsessed to force amnesia about that cruel crime. They strive to erase it from all discourse and published history and, even as we speak, to imprison and torment those citizens who dare to remind China what took place and what it stands for.

But China's leaders will fail. The bipartisan events here in Washington a quarter century later—and similar events around the globe—make clear that, as Lincoln correctly predicted:

"The world ... can never forget what they did..."

The people of China are obviously experiencing revolutionary change. Above all else we must maintain our faith in my compatriots that we can and will join the vast majority of the world's people who now live in free or at least partly free countries. An opening for change could come in the next few months or it may take a few more years. As the legendary defender of freedom Congressman Tom Lantos said of the 1956 Hungarian Revolution in his dedication speech exactly six years ago, "the 1956 Revolution was not crushed, its victory was only delayed," I stand here today, twenty-five years after Tiananmen, to tell you that democracy will and is coming to China. It will come with our relentless collective efforts, including those from the international community.

Let us pray that all the people that still suffer under communist's rule—of whatever ethnicity, whatever faith, whatever region—shall have, in Lincoln's words "a new birth of freedom."

And let us commit our renewed efforts to that goal. "It is for us the living," our sacred duty.

CHAPTER 86

Communism Has to Be Guarded Against, Opposed, and Rooted Out

Speech at Reception for the Twentieth Anniversary of Victims of Communism Memorial Foundation
Washington, DC, United States
June 11, 2014,

Dr. Edwards and dear colleagues at the Victims of Communism Memorial Foundation,

I stand in awe of your wisdom, your tenacity, your moral courage, and your passion that not only gave birth twenty years ago to this monumental foundation, but that over the past two decades have served as a symbol of hope. Your work helps create a necessary place of remembrance in a world where many are forgetting the high price communists exacted from their captive people, as well as the free world. As a former political prisoner of communist China and as a Chinese citizen who lost his grandparents and a sister during China's three-year Great Famine, I want to express my profound gratitude to you on behalf of hundreds of millions of men and women in China who have lost their beloved ones and continue to live as everyday citizens under the oppressive communist regime, who have suffered or are suffering as political prisoners, and who have raised the banner of liberty as dissidents and are struggling to defend fundamental human rights and build a free China. Thank you!

To many people around the world, the Cold War is over; communism has largely been defeated and is no longer a threat. But as we celebrate the twentieth anniversary of the founding of this memorial foundation, we all understand that communism is never defeated, finally. It always makes a comeback in thoughts and words, as well as in deeds.

The 2014 Truman-Reagan Medal of Freedom was deservedly awarded to two leading Ukrainian human rights activists. This serves as a timely reminder of the rise of neo-Soviet imperialism, with the reanimation of the still-warm corpse of the Soviet Union as its ultimate goal. The specter is once again haunting Europe.

Communism is truly the death of the soul, but it itself has not yet died. People in China, Cuba, North Korea, Vietnam, and elsewhere still suffer under communist rule.

The Goddess of Democracy that stood for one glorious moment in Tiananmen Square twenty-five years ago and that now stands as the icon for the memorial to more than 100 million victims of communism reminds us every day of the terrible costs of the communists' rule in China. The CCP has conducted the cruelest theft of private property in the history of the world and has been responsible for the bloodiest political turmoil, the most horrific starvation, and the greatest number of non-natural deaths. It has created the most numerous cases of injustice and has perpetrated the most barbarous destruction of historic heritage, the natural environment, and religious beliefs. The CCP has carried out the most notorious crackdown on a student movement, and it continues to produce the most widespread human rights violations and government corruption.

The communist government that massacred its own citizens in the heart of its capital twenty-five years ago is the very same government that today continues to routinely imprison, torture, and exile its best citizens for no reason other than exercising the right to speak freely. It is the same government that pursues cultural genocide on Tibetans, Uyghurs, and Mongolians, as well as religious purges on Christians and Falun Gong practitioners. It is the same government whose foreign policy and models of repression enable the morally bankrupt regimes of North

Korea, Cuba, Iran, and Syria to suck the freedoms and dignities from their people. Its paranoia and insecurity drive it to extend its tyranny beyond its borders. Its disdain for human dignity now openly challenges the very foundation of civilization itself.

Some may argue that Putin and his government are not communist. They may argue China is ruled by communists, but without communism. But we must not forget they are all rooted in the very idea and organization of communism, which is committed to making tyranny universal. Whether the boot is red or covered with other colors, it's still a boot stomping on the human face. The world has to be ever on the alert against communism and its variations. There can be no resting on our laurels.

We must be resolved tonight that in this city, Washington, DC, human rights should no longer be the casualty of pragmatic diplomacy. Some believe that the United States cannot press China on human rights because it seeks Chinese cooperation on economic and national security issues. But even during the Cold War, Washington negotiated arms control and trade agreements with other countries, including the Soviet Union, while pressing for human rights reform.

Let us learn from history. The fight for democracy and the end of communism is not just the right thing to do but a necessary engagement required for our own survival and security. Let us not forget that the persistent pressure of the United States ultimately freed Europe from the scourge of communism and, in so doing, the US preserved its own democratic way of life. We must apply that same tenacity with China. For China's peaceful transition to democracy is not only in the interests of the people of China but also in the interests of a peaceful and stable world.

The lessons are clear. Americans of conscience should insist that their government confront China. They should demand that their government openly condemn China's violation of basic human rights and demand release of its "prisoners of conscience." They should express support for those in China bravely asserting or defending human rights. And they should support concrete action, including sanctions like those that the so-called "Magnitsky Act" now imposes on Russian human rights abusers.

All in all, communism has to be guarded against, opposed, and rooted out—all the time. That is how we can truly honor the victims of communism.

CHAPTER 87

The Thirst for Freedom and Dignity Is Indeed Universal

Speech at Civita Panel Discussion: Fellow Prisoners of Conscience and the Sixth Oslo Freedom Forum: Defeating Dictators
Oslo, Norway
October 28, 2014

I am truly honored and humbled to be put in the same company as Mr. Khodorkovsky and many other heroes at the Forum.

In contrast to these towering figures, I am no more than a regular citizen of China, one of the 1.4 billion, nearly a quarter of humanity, ruled by a government who systematically and routinely imprisons, tortures, and exiles its best and brightest citizens for no other reason than exercising the right to speak freely, who pursues cultural genocide on our Tibetan, Uyghur, and Mongolian brothers and whose foreign policies and models of repression enable the morally bankrupt regimes of North Korea and Syria to suck the freedoms and dignities from their people.

Today we are overshadowed by severe human rights violations around the world. Stark shadows cast by what is worst in man on what is best. One option is to adjust our eyes to the shadows. But friends, I have seen firsthand what takes place in these shadows.

I was born three years before the Cultural Revolution. At an early age, the unspeakable sufferings that most families had at the hands of the communist dictatorship, including mine, made me disenchanted with the Communist Party. However, I was enticed into joining the party with the idea of reforming it from within. This all changed when I returned from my PhD studies in the United States to join thousands of my fellow students in Beijing as Chinese army tanks rolled across Tiananmen Square on the morning of June 4, 1989. Luckier than most of my fellow students, I narrowly escaped the massacre and the ensuing arrests and returned to the United States. While I continued my studies, I immersed myself in the work advancing human rights and democracy in China. In the Party's eyes, the former young communist star had now become a public enemy. I became persona non grata, a traitor, prohibited from returning home. But in the spring of 2002, I decided to defy the ban. In China's industrial northeast, labor movements broke out. Sensing an opportunity to forge bonds between democracy leaders and grassroots activists, I entered China using a borrowed passport and forged ID card.

For two weeks I met with striking workers, documenting their grievances and helping them with nonviolent struggle strategies. But as I attempted to slip out of China across the Burmese border, my fake ID was spotted, and I found myself in the hands of the security police.

I was detained for five years. Much of those years I spent in solitary confinement. My mental condition deteriorated beneath endless isolation, repeated interrogations, and ongoing psychological and physical torture. I resorted to composing poems in my head and committing them to memory as a means of maintaining my sanity. Nearing a breakdown, I grasped onto my innermost resources of imagination, belief, and will to fend off insanity and find a reason to live. "Am I wrong?" I asked myself with a tinge of regret. But I repeated a thought experiment: imagining myself taking a copy of the Universal Declaration of Human Rights, arbitrarily choosing anyone on the Chinese street, showing the document, asking them whether they want the rights listed there. Would anybody say "no"? Of course not. Nobody wants to be a slave. In this regard, the Chinese people are no different than any other people on earth. The thirst for freedom and dignity is indeed universal. I drew strength and inspiration from this first order of fact.

I also thought of my fallen brothers and sisters in Tiananmen Square. I reassured myself that freedom is not free. Freedom must be earned. It was not free for those who paid with their lives. It is certainly not free for those of us who, while still blessed with our lives, have yet to complete the mission for which these brave students gave their lives and their freedom. I must not give up!

To make a long story short, in 2007, thanks to the overwhelming international support, I was freed, returned to the US, and recommitted myself to the hard work to advance human rights and democracy in China.

Today the people of China are in a situation that is both more dire and more hopeful than that facing us in 1989. The Chinese government has adjusted to new realities in order to maintain their hold on power. They have allowed a distinctly undemocratic crony capitalism to supplant undemocratic communism in the hopes that development will end demands for individual freedoms. But it will not. It cannot, because the desire for freedom is too great; it is too deeply rooted in all of the people who make up our common humanity.

But this does not mean that we in the West can sit back and wait for democracy to bloom. China is a dangerous and pernicious power, growing more so every day, and quietism or passive engagement are not an answer or an option. Before this regime is done—and one day it will be done—it has the capability of inflicting enormous damage on its own people and the people of the world. It is our responsibility to ensure that this does not happen.

Today we have gathered here at the Oslo Freedom Forum to summon wisdom and courage and remind the entire world once again that each human being has an opportunity to act in a way worthy of the best of our humanity. We must all see the shadows for what they are and say that it is time to begin living in the light.

Your valuable work represents the profound international community support for human rights in my country, China. It keeps us sane in a situation that could easily be characterized as its opposite.

Around the world, buried in prison cells, in sunless living graves, there are rights activists whose sole ray of hope is a beacon of freedom they only know about from the dedicated people at these human rights organizations.

CHAPTER 88

Lighting a Fire Is the Only Way That I Can Relate to the Surrounding Darkness

Speech at the Fifty-Sixth Anniversary of Tibet Uprising Commemoration in Front of the Chinese Embassy
Washington, DC, United States
March 10, 2015

Dear brothers and sisters:

Tashi delek.

I feel humbled, honored, and proud to stand with you at this solemn moment to commemorate March 10, one of the most significant days representing the Tibetan people's aspirations for a free Tibet. I am humbled because your suffering at the hands of the Chinese regime has been so great that I am afraid that I, as a Chinese, may never be able to properly understand it. I am honored and proud because your six decades of extraordinary struggle for freedom under the leadership of His Holiness the Dalai Lama has won worldwide respect and has long been part of this just cause, and you call me dear brother.

Although I have said so much on so many occasions in support of a free Tibet, before you, my dear brothers and sisters, I have a lot of strong feelings I want to share. But what I feel most strongly is to pay my homage to the 135 Tibetan martyrs who have set themselves on fire for the cause of their people's freedom, for which I would like to share with you an essay I wrote at the beginning of this new year:

At about 4 p.m. on December 22, 2014, in Aba County of Tibet, a twenty-year-old Tibetan girl, Tsepey, set herself ablaze. The beautiful girl's body creeping in the flames completely crushed me, and my tears rushed down my cheeks.

Tsepey was the 135th Tibetan martyr in a spate of self-immolations starting in 2009 in protest of the Chinese rule in Tibet. Such a high frequency reflects the overall deterioration of the human rights situation in Tibet, which has been caused by the ethnic oppression, economic exploitation, and cultural genocide committed by the Chinese government. No period in human history has witnessed such gravity of tragedy and scale of rebellion as in contemporary Tibet.

Many say that Tibetan self-immolations are out of their hopelessness. This is a sheer misinterpretation of the brave heroes. Indeed, a hopeless person might take her own life, but she would never do it in the form of phoenix nirvana with such breathtaking appeal. If one has lost her home, her freedom of belief, her freedom of expression, and her freedom of mobility, but she still does not give up her pursuit of freedom, the motivation of her self-immolation must be to inspire people at large and to let her extremely painful message be heard.

The Tibetan writer Gudrub wrote before setting himself on fire:

"We are declaring the reality of Tibet by burning our own bodies to call for freedom of Tibet. Higher Beings, Please see Tibet. Mother Earth, Extend compassion to Tibet. Just World, Uphold the truth. The pure Land of Snow is now tainted with red blood, where military crackdowns are ceaseless. We as sons and daughters of the Land of Snow will win the battle. We will win the battle through truth, by shooting the arrows of our lives, by using the bow of our mind."

The selfless Tibetan martyrs must have believed that compassion can cleanse human conscience, and a bright and clean conscience will reveal the truth. They must also have believed that everybody's conscience can conduct heat and can be awakened. That is why they resolutely set their bodies on fire to be the fire sticks.

If the Tibetan self-immolators had not had such strong confidence in human conscience, their great deeds would have been meaningless.

However, human evils often seem to dull human perfection and virtue, just as dark clouds cover the sun. Facing such enormous tragedies, the Chinese regime remains cold-blooded with its high pressure as ever, and our Chinese compatriots are almost as indifferent as ever. And there is little response from the international community.

This kind of silence is shocking and suffocating.

Have we all betrayed these martyrs who confided in our conscience? Shouldn't we have felt sorry for a young beautiful life ending in such a painful way, even if we do not know much about the Tibet issue, nor echo with Tibetans' demands or their approaches? Have we become so indifferent that we don't even bother to ask why all this happened?

In such silent darkness I felt so powerless and kneeled to pray to God. My life is too trivial for me to say Tsepey's martyrdom was unworthy, but I have come to better understand the significance of her lighting a fire in the darkness. "Lighting a fire is the only way that I can relate to the surrounding darkness," as my prison poem goes. I understand that not all have the courage to do what Tsepey did, but I believe, as Tsepey did, that most people's conscience is good enough to be lit up. My friends, let the burning body of Tsepey light up the conscience of each of us. Let us relay the torch to light up the moral intuition of more people so that they can see the truth, understand these Tibetan martyrs' desire and make their heroic voices heard: Free Tibet! Let Dalai Lama go home!

CHAPTER 89

Ours Will Be Remembered as One of the Greatest Moral Struggles of the Twenty-First Century

Opening Remarks at the Tenth Interethnic/ Interfaith Leadership Conference
Washington, DC, United States
April 27, 2015

Distinguished guests, friends, brothers and sisters:

Good morning. It is indeed a good morning to see all of you coming to the tenth Interethnic/Interfaith Leadership Conference. My special thanks go to those who have come a long way from across the world—from Mainland China, Taiwan, Hong Kong, Macau, Cuba, India, Turkey, Canada, and Europe.

Indeed, we have all traveled a long and difficult journey to come here.

As I prepared for this talk, I asked myself: "What can I say after I have said so much at the same conference year after year? What can I say as we continue, after so many years of struggle, to face the seemingly ever stronger diehard standing in our way toward freedom, justice, and equality?"

As these questions tumbled in my mind, I felt I had to go back in my memory to the time when this was just a dream, and everybody accepted it as just a dream—that of bringing people together to struggle for a better future for all—those of us from different ethnicities, faiths, and regions directly involved with China.

We can all remember the tensions, hostilities, and resentments that had divided us were like so many open wounds on the body of our common dream. The Chinese communist regime's "divide and conquer" strategy created these conflicts among us. The regime had maintained its iron rule largely on the basis of its ability to splinter those of us who were struggling for a better, more democratic future.

We represent groups of different regions and ethnicities with different histories, cultures, religions, and languages. We may not share blood, but we do share the air that keeps us alive, and even more importantly, we do share the spiritual air that not only keeps us alive but also nurtures and nourishes and preserves our dignity as human beings—that is our common desire for freedom, justice, and equality. But the air has long been overshadowed and polluted by the Chinese communist regime. Each and every one of us has felt our humanity denied or compromised by the mere existence of this regime.

We have been victimized by this same evil force. Tibetans, Uyghurs, Mongolians, and Han Chinese; Christians, Falun Gong practitioners, and Muslims; all have suffered, and all are still suffering today at the hands of this cruel regime. The people of Taiwan, Hong Kong, and Macau are suffering, too, from the political, economic, and even military intimidation radiating out from Beijing, whose very existence depends on the need to restrict and control and, wherever possible, to destroy the freedom of those its power can touch.

We realized we must come together; we must heal the wounds on the body of our common dream, and only by doing so will we march strongly toward the horizon where the dawn of freedom, truth, justice, equality, and peace for us all will one day break.

We came together not long after the Tiananmen Massacre with sincerity, wisdom, and most of all, with determination. We came together aiming to explore universal values and the common ground supporting a united front to advance democracy and human rights for all.

Up to this date, we have, together, walked a very long and difficult road.

In the past conferences and our work in between, we have been committed to maintaining close communication, exercising tolerance and forgiveness toward each other, eliminating hatred, resentment, and misunderstanding, pursuing truth, accomplishing reconciliation and trust, and loving one another. Today we can proudly say we have united as one in the vision for a democratic future.

But we must not underestimate the problems we face.

We are now well beyond six decades of oppression by the Chinese government. The Han Chinese people of the People's Republic of China have been fighting hard for their basic human rights; our Tibetan, Uyghur, and Mongolian brothers and sisters have been fighting an even harder battle for ethnic equality and liberation, on top of fighting for their basic human rights. The citizens of Hong Kong and Macau have been resisting the reality of their freedoms being eroded, while at the same time struggling to advance the process of democratization. People from Taiwan have been doing all they can to defend the freedoms and democracy they have obtained and to save Taiwan from the fate of a frog being slowly boiled alive.

The Chinese Communist Party's rule is entirely based on a calculated combination of fear, violence, truth-suppression, ethnic tension and, most recently, a capitalism that trades wealth for silence, money for obedience. The Communist Party's more than sixty years in power testify to the effectiveness of these tools.

Its recent emergence on the world stage, appeased by major democracies, has brought a tightening of the repressive political structure with an increase in political prisoners, a ruthless crackdown on ethnic and religious minorities, intensified censorship, and a most recent trend toward what can only be described as thought control.

We should also be aware of the fragility of our fledgling coalition, particularly given our past in which our divisiveness, apathy, fear, and hatred have played into the hands of the Chinese government and helped feed the status quo.

At this assembly, my dear brothers and sisters, I want to remind each of us of the difficult journey we have proudly traveled together. I want to refresh every one of us with the pledges we have sincerely made to each other and recommit every one of us to the principles we have arduously established. Let us continue to resolve upon brotherhood as a guiding and uniting principle for our work together—we are each other's keepers, we are each other's freedom, we are each other's peace, we are each other's hope. In light of the difficulty facing us today, we have no choice but to fight back equally strongly with our more strengthened and fortified unity. I cannot say it better than the English author J.K. Rowling.

"I say to you all, once again... we are only as strong as we are united, as weak as we are divided. [Evil has a] gift for spreading discord and enmity... We can fight it only by showing an equally strong bond of friendship and trust. Difference of habit and language are nothing at all if our aims are identical and our hearts are open."

To be sure, the tyrants of the world hate enlightened unity. They fear it. It is China's dictators' greatest fear because they see in our unity the seeds of their future demise. That is why they will do anything possible to prevent us from remembering our fundamental need of unity in idea and solidarity in practice.

But it is our belief that even with the resources and ruthlessness at its disposal, the Chinese communist regime has no real future. Its ideals run so counter to the most fundamental human drives for freedom, truth, equality, and peace that it will always be beating back the tide in order to maintain its existence. We ourselves are part of the crest of this tide, and we are gradually eroding the fortifications of China's ruling regime. Today we are united in our determination to succeed.

Dear brothers and sisters, by our relentless united struggle, we will solemnly honor the pledge we have made to ourselves and to the world; we shall redeem ourselves and thereby decisively widen the horizon of human freedom. And ours will be remembered as one of the greatest moral struggles of the twenty-first century.

Thank you all.

CHAPTER 90

To All Children of Prisoners of Conscience

Speech at the Tenth Interethnic/Interfaith Leadership Conference
Washington, DC, United States
April 29, 2015

Dear children,

I am most pleased and honored to see you all here. Today I speak to you as a father and as a former prisoner of conscience.

There are so many children, like you, children of prisoners of conscience who are not with us at the moment. We will not forget them. We will not leave anyone out.

It is a rather emotional moment.

When your parents were your age, they had already begun thinking about the hard questions and taking heroic actions. But, unfortunately, their actions, which were no more than exercising their basic rights as human beings, landed them in jail, and they became prisoners of conscience. The years they spent in Chinese prisons, no matter how long, were mostly their golden years. Their stories are incredibly moving, as well as tragic.

I want to ask you, if I may, all the children of those prisoners of conscience—whether or not you are here—to try to understand your fathers and mothers, try to understand what they have been through all those years. Their stories, as an important part of the history of China's human rights, carry many secret codes about today's China, the world, and even the meaning of life itself. I encourage you to learn to decode these codes. You will benefit greatly from doing so.

Your parents are the most fearless people in China. They are the people who have made the greatest contributions to, and greatest sacrifices for, the progress of Chinese society. Although such contributions and sacrifices have not been fully acknowledged by the world, you—the second generation—must give them credit and your sincere respect for what they sacrificed. Only by doing so will you carry on with their tasks and continue to support the noble cause of fighting for China's freedom. And this cause is the one that all young people should pursue. As the second generation of prisoners of conscience, you are bound to witness the most far-reaching change in China, the birth of a new and democratic China.

Today I want to also acknowledge the sufferings we, the parents and prisoners, have brought you. Your sacrifices are even greater. At the time when you were coming of age, we couldn't secure an environment of reasonable freedom and safety for you. Ever since you were born, you have faced all kinds of threats and persecutions. Many of you are still haunted by such persecutions. I must admit the suffering I have brought to my children is a wound on my heart that can never be healed. And I know there is an even deeper wound on your heart, which I have found in many cases, mine included, that we, the prisoners, can do little about it. That is the primary reason I have urged you and taken pains to help you to come together to form Children of Prisoners of Conscience, through which you can support each other as brothers and sisters.

While we apologize to you for all the hardships you have endured, I hope all the Children of Prisoners of Conscience, whether present here or not, will strive to be more understanding and committed. You should be confident that it was out of the love for their children and for your future that your parents never gave up their beliefs and ended up spending their prime years in prison. Indeed, if not for children, I would see little reason for us to come together and could not imagine we would have struggled so long and hard as we have.

Looking back at the sweep of history, we see those valuable beliefs are invariably passed down from generation to generation. This is universal, and China is no exception. Now, as parents, with our shared beliefs and commitments, we pass the torch of friendship into your hands. This torch is a symbol of the friendship among your parents, and this friendship should continue and grow among you. This kind of bonding is where the future of China lies. Please don't forget that it is you who drive us and make us more confident. Thank you for giving us hope. God bless all the Children of Prisoners of Conscience.

SECTION XI

CALLING FOR THE CHINA DEMOCRACY ACT: BRING DEMOCRACY TO CHINA

June 2015—October 2015

"We must abandon the delusion that economic growth will bring human rights and democracy to China in the foreseeable future. Instead, Americans of conscience should insist that their government confront China on human rights issues. They should demand that their government openly condemn China's violation of basic human rights and demand the release of its 'prisoners of conscience.' They should express support for those in China bravely asserting or defending the human rights of others and receiving brutal punishment for their good deeds. And they should support such congressional bills as the China Human Rights Protection Act… China's totalitarian regime has hijacked 1.3 billion Chinese people, imposing a political system on them by force and coercion, running the country like a slave owner of the past, obliterating their self-governance and controlling their life without their consent and denying universal values to justify its dictatorship. To support this regime is morally corrupt as well as strategically stupid."

CHAPTER 91

Congress Should Pass a "China Democracy Act"

Opening Remarks at CECC Hearing on China in 1989 and 2015: Tiananmen, Human Rights, and Democracy
Washington, DC, United States
June 3, 2015

Mr. Chairman and members of the Commission, thank you for hosting this important hearing on this anniversary of the Tiananmen Massacre.

Today we the panelists want to cover three distinct but related points: First, when it comes to Tiananmen, why we must "Never Forget" and why we must counter—as your Commission has persistently done—China's desperate attempt to infect both its people and the outside world with amnesia about those tragic events. Second, we want to stress the need to pierce the facade of President Xi Jinping's phony reforms and the CCP's PR campaign to portray Xi as the "Great Reformer" and a champion of the "Rule of Law." And third, we want to address the ultimate question of what the Congress and the administration can do to strengthen human rights and democratic values in China.

Since both my long written statement and my fellow panelists have covered the first two, I will focus on the third in the rest of my opening remarks.

After the Tiananmen Massacre, Americans of all political persuasions and faiths joined in protest of that slaughter of innocents. Their outrage showed that human rights are not partisan issues. But when it came to trade relations with China, there was a big debate. One side of the debate, led by Representative Nancy Pelosi, asserted that US trade relations with China must be linked to China's human rights record. This idea was embodied in Pelosi and Mitchell's legislation in 1993. When President Clinton reversed the policy in Representative Pelosi's proposal, he made a terrible mistake. The reversal was based on the theory, which was widely upheld by corporations, columnists, pundits, and policymakers, that trade would inevitably result in more political freedom and guaranteed basic human rights. In order to test that confident prediction, Congress established this Commission. Under its mandate, the Commission has annually examined just how much China's economic growth and interaction with the world has led to real civil liberty and political freedom for its citizens. And each year the Commission's clear conclusion has been "not very much." That finding is consistently echoed in the annual human rights reports of the State Department, US Commission on International Religious Freedom, international rights groups, and by the testimonies of my fellow panelists today.

In addition, although China's economic strength has continued to grow, the Xi Jinping regime, as you have already heard, has increased restraints on the civil liberties of the Chinese people.

The lessons are clear. We must abandon the delusion that economic growth will bring human rights and democracy to China in the foreseeable future. Instead, Americans of conscience should insist that their government confront China on human rights issues. They should demand that their government openly condemn China's violation of basic human rights and demand the release of its "prisoners of conscience." They should express support for those in China bravely asserting or defending the human rights of others and receiving brutal punishment for their good deeds. And they should support such congressional bills as the China Human Rights Protection Act that you, Chairman Representative Smith, introduced yesterday and the Global Magnitsky legislation that you and Representative McGovern introduced earlier this year.

We applaud and fully support these worthy initiatives. But in closing, I would like to suggest you carefully consider another proposal that is, at the same time, more fundamental. Congress should pass a simple, short, and sweet "China Democracy Act."

We, Initiatives for China, recently hosted our tenth annual Interethnic/Interfaith Leadership Conference. It was attended by a great many members of faith groups, ethnic minorities, and advocates in China and abroad of democracy, civil liberty, and human rights. At its conclusion, we passed a resolution that I want to expand on today. It calls on Congress to enact a "China Democracy Act," recognizing that advancement of human rights and democracy in China is in America's national interest and calling for an annual assessment of whether the American government is advancing or actually undermining those goals.

In the early nineties, I and many others believed that it would take only a few years and not much outside physical assistance from the US government to achieve those goals. But we overestimated how soon those bravely resisting in China could educate the people about the need for a peaceful transition when their voices were being silenced by prison and brutal torture, and their speech was blocked by modern technology.

At the same time, the Chinese government has tried to discredit the Chinese democracy movement with the claim of American policy to provide it with secret assistance. In fact, the US Congress has never passed something as simple as a China Democracy Act stating American policy to advance human rights, rule of law, and democratic values in China. It's shocking to me that there is no such law at the present time.

That brings me to the resolution proposed by our conferees a few weeks ago for a China Democracy Act. This would not be a nonbinding resolution. Instead, it would be binding legislation flatly stating congressional judgment that enhancing human rights and democratic values in China is decidedly in America's national interest. That would preclude the currently widespread but inaccurate claim that Congress must balance, on the one hand, its claim to support the universal value of human rights and, on the other hand, "America's national interest." Promoting human rights in China is clearly in the United States' national interest for several reasons.

History teaches that authoritarian dictatorships are more likely than democracies to be aggressors against other nations.

History also teaches that nations with freedom of speech, religion, and association are more likely to evolve peacefully into a government that respects the rights and rule of the people.

Finally, if America expressly commits to strengthening those ideals in China and visibly implements that commitment, it will enable the people of all nations to see that the words of Americans' proud promises to support liberty everywhere are fully matched by its deeds.

The bill also would require a report from the President to Congress every year on how any government program, policy, or action during the prior twelve months has strengthened human rights and democratic values in China and—equally important—how any program, policy, or initiative has weakened human rights and democratic values in China.

All federal departments of government—every single one—should have to report on what they're doing to bring democracy to China by advancing human rights and the rule of law there. The Act should also put them on notice to take no action, adopt no policy, and implement no program that would undercut the democracy movement or weaken human rights in China.

Such a "China Democracy Act" and an annual Presidential Report would give us a better idea of what successes we've had so far, what caused them, and how we should increase financial resources and deploy them to promote democracy and human rights.

Without such legislation, I very much doubt we will be on track and on course to succeed in what we dreamed of back in 1989.

CHAPTER 92

Suing Jiang Zemin Is a Laudable Move

Speech at LA-DC Ride2Freedom Culmination
Rally in West Lawn of Capitol Hill
Washington, DC, United States
July 16, 2015

Dear friends,

Good morning.

First, I want to thank my friend Keith Ware for his leadership in the wonderful project Ride2Freedom. You are my hero, Keith.

I salute you, the young people, and the members of the Ride2Freedom team, some of whom are as young as 11 years old. I tell you, if you were my children, I would be the proudest father in the world. I thank you for your heroic act of riding 3,000 miles to bring attention to the American public of the Chinese regime's oppressive, systematic torture of its citizens, men, women, and children, many of them prisoners of conscience, particularly the Falun Gong practitioners. I am proud to join you in the last ten miles of your journey to arrive at Capitol Hill, the center of democracy of the United States of America.

I also want to thank all the friends for coming today to protest the crimes against humanity that have now continued for sixteen years against Falun Gong practitioners across China.

Since July of 1999, the douzheng against Falun Gong by the Chinese Communist Party through mass imprisonment, torture, propaganda, and coercive "reeducation" has resulted in thousands of deaths. Numerous Falun Gong prisoners of conscience have been killed and their organs forcibly removed for transplant operations. Even today, many Falun Gong practitioners are held extra-judicially in forced labor camps where torture is routinely used. There is no neutral position to look at these atrocities. In front of such crimes, silence is simply the act of an accomplice.

Since the end of May of this year, more than 10,000 Chinese citizens have filed criminal charges against Jiang Zemin, the former head of the Communist Party. Jiang is being targeted in the lawsuits because he initiated the douzheng against Falun Gong in 1999 and saw that the entire Party and state apparatus was concentrated on the campaign.

Suing Jiang Zemin is a laudable move. I strongly support the action of Falun Gong practitioners, especially because it's initiated by practitioners inside China. The campaign will gain the attention of China's society and can lead to an outpouring of public dissatisfaction over the persecution, which has long been suppressed. But in order for this campaign to be viable and ensure its petitioners' safety, we must work harder to mobilize international support.

Dear friends, we are deeply outraged by the recent round-up of scores of human rights lawyers and activists in China and the senseless death of the prominent Tibetan religious leader Tenzin Deleg Rinpoche, who had served thirteen years of a life sentence based on politically-motivated charges and who had been repeatedly tortured and denied medical parole for his heart condition.

Dear brothers and sisters, let's unite in solidarity for those persecuted in China and for those daring to stand up to CCP's repression. We urge the US government and all governments around the world to do all they can to put pressure on China to end the persecution and not to allow their own economic and political interests abroad to rule over the fundamental human rights for Falun Gong practitioners, people of all faiths and ethnicities, indeed, all men, women and children living in the People's Republic of China. These are not American rights, nor Chinese rights. These are the universal rights we are defending.

Thank you all.

CHAPTER 93

China Democracy Act: Engaging China with Moral and Strategic Clarity

Opening Remarks at CECC Hearing on Urging China's President Xi Jinping to Stop State-Sponsored Human Rights Abuses
Washington, DC, United States
September18, 2015

Mr. Chairman and members of the Commission, thank you for hosting this important hearing.

Twenty-six years ago, after the Tiananmen Massacre, we came to Washington, DC, to plead with the US government to link China's most favorite nation (MFN) status with its human rights record. Without such a link, we argued, trading with China would be like a blood transfusion to the communist regime, making it more aggressive and harming the interests of both American and Chinese people.

But our warning fell on deaf ears. After a lengthy debate, the US government decided to grant permanent MFN to China contending economic growth would automatically bring democracy to the country.

With money and technologies pouring in from the US and other Western countries, with their free markets wide open for the Chinese-made goods, the Chinese communist regime not only survived the 1989 crisis, it has catapulted into the twenty-first century. The country's explosive economic growth has brought it from near the bottom of the world in GDP per capita to become the number two economy in the world; but democracy remains yet a far-fetched dream. Worse, Xi Jinping regime, as you have already heard, has launched numerous assaults against China's civil society on a scale and with a ferocity unseen in the past two decades, making Xi Jinping China's worst leader in twenty years in terms of human rights records.

China uses its economic power gained with the help of the West to build a formidable, fully modernized military that has reached every corner of the earth. With this unprecedented power, China is now forcefully demanding a re-write of international norms and rules. China wants to create a new international order with its dominance in the Asia-Pacific region as the centerpiece, threatening regional and world peace.

What went wrong with America's engagement policy?

In my view, the failure lies primarily in lack of moral and strategic clarity in its design and implementation.

The origin of the error can trace back to the early 1970s when then-Secretary of State Henry Kissinger claimed that by integrating Beijing into the international community economically and politically, China would behave responsibly, abiding by international norms and rules.

This amoral, geopolitical, and short-term pragmatic strategy fails to see the evil nature and hegemonic ambition of the communist regime as reiterated recently in Xi Jinping's "China Dream" of a great red empire, to replace Western civilization with the so-called China model.

Washington policymakers also fail to understand that economic growth may be a necessary condition but not a sufficient one for cultivating democracy. Consequently, this policy has fundamentally undermined America's national interests and security.

The alternative is to engage China with a moral strategic compass: China under the CCP's rule cannot rise peacefully, and its transition to a democratic country that respects human rights, the rule of law, freedom of speech and religion is in everyone's best interest, including China's own.

China's totalitarian regime has hijacked 1.3 billion Chinese people, imposing a political system on them by force and coercion, running the country like a slave owner of the past, obliterating their self-governance, and controlling their life without their consent and denying universal values to justify its dictatorship. To support this regime is morally corrupt as well as strategically stupid.

Like Frankenstein's monster, China is now seeking revenge against its creator—the West. It will destabilize and endanger the world, for the China model, better called the China disease like the black plague, has spread and infected the international community, but most people in the world are not aware of it, and many are even being fooled to believe it is the future. Now it is the time for the US to begin the era of engaging China with moral and strategic clarity.

To start, the Congress should pass a China Democracy Act.

It would be a binding legislation flatly stating congressional judgment that enhancing human rights and democratic values in China is decidedly in America's national interest. That would preclude the currently widespread but inaccurate claim that Congress must balance, on the one hand, its claim to support the universal value of human rights and, on the other hand, "America's national interest."

The bill also would require a report from the President to Congress every year on how any government program, policy, or action during the prior twelve months has strengthened or weakened human rights and democratic values in China.

All federal departments of government—every single one—should have to report on what they're doing to bring democracy to China by advancing human rights and the rule of law there. The Act also puts them on notice to take no action, adopt no policy, and implement no program that would undercut the democracy movement or weaken human rights in China.

Such a "China Democracy Act" would give us a better idea of what successes we've had so far, what caused them, and how we should increase financial resources and deploy them to promote democracy and human rights.

If America expressly commits to strengthening those ideals and visibly implements that commitment, it will enable the people of China, and indeed the rest of the world, to see that the words of Americans' proud promises to support liberty everywhere are fully matched by its deeds.

CHAPTER 94

There Is No Neutral Position When It Comes to Human Rights Violations

Remarks at the Freedom Week Organized by the Newseum
Washington, DC, United States
September 23, 2015

Good morning, everyone.

Gene, thank you again for the Freedom Week.

Yesterday, Xi Jinping set his feet on American soil beginning his first state visit to the United States. To prepare for the visit, the Chinese propaganda apparatus, as usual, has attempted to portray a China that is not only a far cry from reality but in many ways the opposite of what's true. But unfortunately for Xi Jinping, he is visiting a free country beyond the control of his communist mouthpiece media. The Newseum is exhibiting on the facade of its building the photos and stories of jailed journalists, human rights defenders, and dissidents of China, disclosing a China any people should not turn their eyes away from.

Yesterday, we put forward "64 Questions for Xi Jinping." These questions, concerning Xi Jinping, China, and its international relations might well be also considered by others worldwide, especially American officials, journalists, scholars, and citizens who are blinded by Beijing's propaganda.

Jim (Hoagland), thank you for your powerful message. I am glad you mentioned in your remarks the Tankman. Our Question 31 is: Where is the Tankman?

You can find these sixty-four questions on our website. It is our hope that people from different areas and with different particular concerns will find their questions articulated here and will directly or indirectly ask Xi Jinping to respond.

Xi Jinping wants the people of China and the rest of world to forget the infamous Tiananmen Massacre. I was there, Jim, you were there, and we cannot forget. Xi Jinping wants us to forget Nobel Peace Prize winner Liu Xiaobo, who, as we speak, is languishing in China's prison. I was in Oslo when there was an empty chair and cannot forget. The thousands of other brave men and women who have been imprisoned, tortured, made missing because they spoke up and sought a better China. Xi Jinping wants us to forget them. They are my brothers and sisters, and I know their bravery and cannot forget. We cannot and should not forget. Freedom-loving people around the world will not forget.

The Newseum will not forget. When you leave, please see the photos of those jailed on the front of the building.

I agree with the members of Congress who find it hard to understand why President Obama and Secretary Kerry seem to share that amnesia and are prepared to honor Xi with a state dinner later this week. That is the highest honor that America confers on a foreign leader. When you view the photos and explanations outside the Newseum, ask yourself if you think Xi should be honored with a state dinner.

But you can take some comfort in knowing that on Friday morning, the Tom Lantos Human Rights Commission of the US Congress will host a "stateless breakfast" instead of a state dinner. It will honor those who really should be honored. The representatives of the American people and that of the civil society of China will honor the members of persecuted ethnic, faith, and social groups and the other advocates for civil liberties in China, the lawyers, reporters, bloggers, and dissidents who have stood up for them and were imprisoned as a reward for their courage.

Dear friends, I want to thank you, American people, for this stateless breakfast, for standing up at this moment in solidarity with my brothers and sisters back in China.

And last, I would like to remind you that there is no neutral position when it comes to human rights violations in China and indeed anywhere on earth.

Thank you.

CHAPTER 95

Raise Our Glasses to Honor All Those Human Rights Defenders

Speech at "Stateless" Breakfast Hosted by US House of Representatives Tom Lantos Human Rights Commission to Honor Human Rights Defenders
Washington, DC, United States
September 25, 2015

Thank you, Chairman McGovern.

We raise our glasses to honor all those human rights defenders who have been brutally intimidated, imprisoned, tortured, and silenced by Beijing. They are far too many to name, but many in this room know a number of them, either personally or having learned their tragic tales. Their great misfortune is terribly sad, but it also is truly inspiring to everyone committed to human rights and human dignity.

As we toast their bravery this morning, it is ironic that last night, for most of official Washington, President Xi and his courtiers were the "toast of the town." While he and his retinue freely associate with America's highest officials, they brutally deny the basic right of "free association" to the Chinese people. President Xi's and the rest of the Communist Party dictators fear such freedom. Or as President John Kennedy well put it, years ago,

"THEY GLORIFY 'TOGETHERNESS' WHEN IT IS THEIRS, AND CALL IT 'CONSPIRACY' WHEN IT IS THAT OF OTHERS."

Yet the modern world has long recognized that allowing people to freely associate and exchange ideas benefits their society. For as US Supreme Court Justice Robert Jackson once observed:

"IT IS NOT THE FUNCTION OF THE GOVERNMENT TO KEEP THE CITIZEN FROM FALLING INTO ERROR… IT IS THE FUNCTION OF THE CITIZEN TO KEEP THE GOVERNMENT FROM FALLING INTO ERROR."

Increasingly, we see that the Chinese people are demanding freedom. Freedom of association, of speech, and of religion. And they are finding ways to win it, despite President Xi's determined efforts to deny them those universal rights.

In his pursuit of absolute power, President Xi ruthlessly ignored their thirst for freedom. But now he desperately fears its slow but steady growth. He has begun to appreciate the Chinese proverb that warns of pursuing one's aim so single-mindedly that one remains blind to larger dangers:

THE MANTIS STALKING THE CICADA DOES NOT NOTICE THE LURKING BIRD.

Xi is the stalking mantis. The Chinese people's demand for dignity, justice, and freedom is the lurking bird that will overcome his dictatorship.

Across town from here is the Robert F. Kennedy Center for Justice and Human Rights, which were two great concerns of its namesake. Robert Kennedy warned us that:

"Every time we turn our heads the other way when we see the law flouted, when we tolerate what we know to be wrong, when we close our eyes and ears to the corrupt because we are too busy or too frightened, when we fail to speak up and speak out, we strike a blow against freedom and decency and justice."

So even while President Xi is taking his final bows in Washington, let us urge our leaders not to turn their heads.

CHAPTER 96

Your Slavery Is My Servitude, Your Fight Is My Struggle, and Your Liberty Will Be My Freedom

Speech Presenting the 2015 Pedro Luis Boitel Freedom Award at Summit of Generations Hosted by Directorio Democrático Cubano Institute for Cuban and Cuban American Studies, University of Miami, Miami, FL, United States October 22, 2015

Orlando and John—our dear hosts, Carl and Barbara—two mentors of mine, respected human rights leaders from Cuba, distinguished guests, dear brothers and sisters:

I am very honored and moved to have the privilege of making these presentations of the 2015 Pedro Luis Boitel Freedom Prize. I am honored and moved because of the commitment and sacrifice made by the winners of the prize.

The first winner, Sirley Ávila León, an ex-delegate of the People's Assembly, fought valiantly when the regime wanted to shut down a school in the area she represented. When officials refused to meet with her and the press failed to report the issue, she appealed to the international media and joined the opposition. Her activism made her a priority target of the political police. They spied on her, tried to commit her to a psychiatric hospital, and gravely wounded her in a machete attack last spring. The attack deeply cut her neck and knees; she lost her left hand, and she could still lose her right arm. Her bravery is remarkable.

The second winner, the Forum for Rights and Freedoms, is not yet a year old. But it has already helped orchestrate the efforts of fifteen human right groups, various independent journalists, scholars, artists, and activists. The Forum works under the leadership of three general coordinators: Berta Soler from the Ladies in White, Antonio Rodiles from Estado de SATs, and Jorge Luis García Pérez (Antúnez) from the Orlando Zapata Tamayo National Front of Civic Resistance and Civil Disobedience.

The Forum advances on two fronts:

1. A road map or specific proposal for moving toward a free and democratic Cuba; and
2. Civic action in the public sphere.

Both paths are designed to resolve US-Cuba relations in a way that truly advances human rights and liberty in Cuba. Most importantly, the Forum is helping bring about unity among the Cuban freedom fighters, and in the unity, we see hope.

Tonight, we also honor the Ladies in White and its martyred leader, Laura Polan. Ladies in White is world famous as an opposition movement founded in 2003 by the wives and other female relatives of jailed dissidents. They protest those imprisonments by attending Mass each Sunday wearing white dresses symbolizing peace and then silently walking through the streets. The movement received the internationally recognized Sakharov Prize for Freedom of Thought from the European Parliament in 2005.

Laura Polan was a prominent Cuban dissident leader who helped found the group and then bravely led its marches in the face of insults and abuse from government supporters and even, on several occasions, during tornadoes. I couldn't help noticing that when the Ladies in White received the Sakharov Prize, Polan was not allowed to leave Cuba to attend the award ceremony just as, a few years later, Liu Xiaobo was not allowed to leave prison, let alone the country, to receive the Nobel Peace Prize he had been awarded. That vividly brings home the truly universal nature of human rights and of the bonds that unite all of us devoted to those fundamental principles.

Let's consider the unifying dynamics of this ceremony. Here I am, a Chinese dissident working to end denial of human rights in China, making this presentation in Miami, USA, to human rights champions in Cuba of an award named after a Cuban human rights forbearer, created by a Romanian dissident with the backing of several Eastern European nations who suffered under the yoke of Soviet Communism. This year's jury for the prize consists of five members from Canada, Mexico, Egypt, Ukraine, and China. And in the audience is the Syrian freedom fighter Moustafa.

These special circumstances demonstrate the bonds that unite all of us working to promote human rights, rule of law, and democratic values. They remind each of us to keep in mind not only the victims of human rights abuse in our own homelands but also to support and stand with those defending human rights in other lands. It is in this spirit that the heroism embodied in the Boitel Prize winners' spirits, words, and deeds will serve as an important source of inspiration, not only to the freedom-loving people of Cuba but also to the rest of the world, including my home country China. So, tonight, let's stand together in solidarity with all the oppressed people around the world and say to one another: Your slavery is my servitude, your fight is my struggle, and your liberty will be my freedom.

Thank you!

SECTION XII

WHAT IS THE WEST'S RECORD ON DEFENDING HUMAN RIGHTS?

November 2015—March 2017

"The reluctance and inaction on the part of the US and other major democracies to confront the world's dictators on human rights issues have emboldened the recent worldwide democracy recession, and that reluctance and inaction have in turn harmed the global security and national interests of these various democracies....Without China's democratization, a clash between the US and China is unavoidable because the two countries' strategic goals are on a clashing course, and their core interests cannot be compromised....I hereby call on the US to end the compartmentalization of human rights and begin to engage China with moral and strategic clarity."

CHAPTER 97

Propose an Index Ranking Democracies on the Basis of What Efforts They Make to Help Promote Human Rights in Autocracies

Speech at Victims of Communism Memorial Foundation's Truman-Reagan Medal of Freedom Award Ceremony for Chen Guangcheng
Washington, DC, United States
November 6, 2015

Distinguished guests, dear friends, ladies and gentlemen:

I am honored to speak at this Truman-Reagan Freedom dinner.

Let me first congratulate Chen Guangcheng, my hero and my hometown fellow. The Truman-Reagan Freedom Medal awarded to Chen Guangcheng is deserved and timely. Recent news reports attributed Beijing's relaxation of the "one-child policy" to demographic calculations. True. But world condemnation of that brutal practice was also a factor. Chen Guangcheng courageously challenged that policy in defending its victims. Worldwide publicity about his persecution and brave escape added to the embarrassing exposure of the policy. And now, even at the expense of hardship to his relatives in China, Chen Guangcheng continues to be a powerful voice insisting that China's human rights abuse should not be overlooked.

I greatly admire how the Victims of Communism Memorial Foundation's defense of freedom has far exceeded the expectations of its congressional creators.

Under Chairman Edwards' inspired leadership, the Foundation has vividly documented the horrors communism inflicted and reminded Washington, and indeed the world, that nightmare must not be repeated. It is critical because, as Harvard philosopher Santayana warned us: "Those who cannot remember the past are condemned to repeat it."

Today the Foundation is also a vital part of the coalition supporting the victims of communist China's current human rights abuse. Director Marion Smith's dynamic energy helps keep the Foundation at the center of every aspect of that effort.

The China Forum, which the Foundation is hosting, is the second event this week where I have witnessed both the bonds that unite everyone devoted to liberty and the growing focus on its repression in China. I just returned a couple of hours ago from the World Movement for Democracy conference in Seoul, Korea. There, Beijing's denial of fundamental freedoms was held up as a leading example of the current worldwide resurgence or continuation of authoritarianism. So, despite Xi Jinping's constant propaganda and efforts to downplay or sidetrack world attention from his war on liberty, the whole world is still watching and, more important, acting.

At the Seoul conference, participants from autocracies as well as democracies all recognized that the reluctance and inaction on the part of the US and other major democracies to confront the world's dictators on human rights issues have emboldened the recent worldwide democracy recession. And that reluctance and inaction have in turn harmed the global security and national interests of these various democracies. The participants committed to striving, through grassroots efforts of civil societies and academia as well as legislation and policymaking processes, to turn this situation around. Among many other action recommendations, I made a proposal which I would like to repeat tonight and respectfully ask you to consider.

I propose to build on the authoritative Freedom House Index of Freedom in the World, which rates countries on their upholding political rights and civil liberties for their citizens. Published annually since 1972, the survey ratings and their explanations have been used by policymakers, the media, international corporations, civic activists, and human rights defenders to monitor trends in democracy and track improvements and setbacks in freedom worldwide.

I propose that we all urge Freedom House to produce a second, parallel rating system, this time of the world's real democracies. The index could be called the "Freedom House Index of Nations' Efforts to Promote Freedom in the World." The index would rank countries on the basis of what efforts they make to help promote political rights and civil liberties in other nations—especially in the most flagrant abusers of those rights and liberties like China.

This may seem like a small step. To paraphrase a famous astronaut, if we could realize this proposal, I believe we would indeed be taking a giant step forward toward freedom for all mankind.

Thank you.

CHAPTER 98

Campaign to Inscribe the Tiananmen Massacre on the UNESCO's Memory of the World Register and Seek Truth about the Two Tiananmen Tank Men

Speech at the CECC Press Conference Commemorating the Fifth Anniversary of Liu Xiaobo's Winning the Nobel Peace Prize
Washington, DC, United States
December 9, 2015

Liu Xiaobo, how are you?

Thank you, Chairman Smith, and the CECC for holding this important press conference where we are standing together in solidarity with Liu Xiao and his fellow political prisoners of China. We are sending a clear and strong message to China and the rest of the world that we have not forgotten.

Nobel Prize anniversaries are usually happy occasions. But the fifth anniversary of Liu Xiaobo's winning of the Nobel Peace Prize is a solemn and sad one. He is still serving an eleven-year prison term imposed by the dictators of Beijing. What was the horrible crime that the CCP claimed deserved such harsh punishment? Liu coauthored Charter 08, a call for peaceful transition to democratic freedoms in China. Recognizing his courage and the importance of that document as well as his long-time commitment to nonviolent struggle for human rights and democracy, the Nobel Committee awarded him its coveted Peace Prize, placing him in the ranks of such esteemed leaders as Nelson Mandela, Aung San Suu Kyi, and Lech Walesa. But the Chinese government would not allow him, nor even his wife, to accept the award. He remains the world's only imprisoned Peace Prize winner.

China's rulers cannot hide Liu's bravery from the world. The images of his Empty Chair when the award was made in absentia went viral. He became, and remains, one of the leading symbols of the unquenchable human thirst for freedom.

We freedom-loving people around the globe today honor and demand his immediate and unconditional release.

My colleagues and I were struggling to find the best way to honor Liu Xiaobo on this occasion. We remembered that Liu Xiao, when first learning through his wife that he had been awarded with the Nobel Peace Prize, told her to dedicate it to the "Tiananmen martyrs." As the major leader of the Tiananmen protests and Chinese democracy movement, Liu Xiaobo has not for a moment forgotten the Tiananmen tragedy. We must not forget either. Indeed, the code to interpreting China's contemporary political history is embedded in the Tiananmen protests and the ensuing massacre, a key directing China to civilization charted by Charter 08 charts. To honor Liu Xiaobo, his contributions, and sacrifices, we, the dissidents of China around the world, come together to launch two worldwide campaigns. One is the Campaign to Inscribe the Tiananmen Massacre on the UNESCO's Memory of the World Register and the other is the Campaign to Seek Truth about the Two Tiananmen Tank Men.

It is important for China's future that we learn more about what led each of them to their brave actions. The "Tank Man" who faced down the tank already inspires those dissidents who learn about his bravery to stand up for their rights despite the danger. But the "Tank Man II," who drove the tank, also can be a model of decency, inspiring PLA officers and government officials to follow their conscience by refusing to be a cog in Beijing's machinery of repression. Instead, they can listen to their better nature, "raise their guns higher," or refuse to torture helpless prisoners, and earn the lasting respect of their countrymen.

I won't go over the details about the two initiatives, which are described in the documents distributed. Please take a copy with you when you leave. We will gratefully welcome your advice and support for our work.

Indeed, ideas cannot be massacred and neither can freedom be jailed. We come together today to recommit our determination that it is the duty of those alive and free to shoulder the responsibility left by the deceased and entrusted by the imprisoned to continue to fight the good fight for a free and democratic China.

Thank you!

Appendix. Announcement of the Launching of Two Worldwide Campaigns

Inscribe the Tiananmen Massacre on the UNESCO's Memory of the World Register and Seek Truth about the Two Tiananmen Tank Men

December 10, 2015, International Human Rights Day, 5th Anniversary of Liu Xiaobo's Winning the Nobel Peace Prize

Today is the fifth anniversary of Liu Xiaobo's winning of the Nobel Peace Prize. In honor of the occasion, we are launching two worldwide campaigns. One is the Campaign to Inscribe the Tiananmen Massacre on the UNESCO's Memory of the World Register and the other is the Campaign to Seek Truth about the Two Tiananmen Tank Men.

1. Campaign to Inscribe the Tiananmen Massacre on the Memory of the World Register

Open discussion about and understanding of the Tiananmen Massacre is a prerequisite for China's political civilization. It depends on two conditions. First, the Chinese people should have free access to the truth of the Tiananmen Massacre. Second, the Chinese people should have freedom in discussing the massacre. However, with the political pressure in today's China, these two freedoms have long been tightly clamped.

China's overall political reform can hardly depend on the communist regime taking the initiative. Neither can the urgently needed resolution of the case of the Tiananmen Massacre. Fortunately, ordinary citizens have been taking action. Over the past 26 years, people of all walks of life have been trying to expose through various channels what they know about the massacre. They include participants of the protests, journalists, eyewitnesses of the Tiananmen Massacre, the then-communist party officials, military officers, and soldiers.

We believe it is extremely important to comb through the collected pictures, videos, and text information in order to have more of the full truth exposed and, equally important, understood, in order to realize China's transition to democracy. To this end, it would be very meaningful and useful for Tiananmen Massacre documents to be registered on the list of UNESCO's Memory of the World, a depository of information about seminal historical events. The incident has had a major impact on world history. Its lessons should be remembered by the world forever.

Please widely circulate information about this project and provide our project coordinators with authentic materials about the Tiananmen Massacre.

While organizing materials that have been collected, we will lobby UNESCO for its official designation and prompt registration.

2. Campaign to Seek Truth about the Two Tiananmen Tank Men

The iconic image on Beijing's Chang'an Street bravely confronting PLA tanks is one of the most important photographs of the twentieth century. It represents ordinary citizens confronting the state violence, and it is not forgotten by history. Over more than two decades, the whole world has been asking: Where is the tank man? As of today, the background of the tank man "Wang Weilin" and his subsequent fate are still unknown to the world. At the same time, we should not forget that, despite the CCP's massacre order, the soldier in the tank chose not to shoot or run over his compatriot. The most logical explanation is that his conscience made him disobey the order. This soldier is equally a hero.

As *Time* magazine pointed out: "[T]he heroes of the tank picture are two: the unknown figure who risked his life by standing in front of the juggernaut and the driver who rose to the moral challenge by refusing to mow down his compatriot."

Nobody knows the fate of the two heroes, but it is our responsibility to know and to find them. For together, they symbolize that timeless truth that moral courage will triumph over cowardly cruelty.

We hereby launch the initiative of collecting signatures across the world to petition Xi Jinping for the identities, background, and the whereabouts of the two tank men (please see the attached open letter to Xi Jinping). Please sign your signature and encourage others to sign. There is no deadline for this project, and we will continue to collect signatures until the truth is obtained.

Ways to sign:

1. Go to http://tinyurl.com/finding2tankmen
2. Enter first name, last name, email, country, city or zip code.
3. If a street address is asked, and privacy is a concern, please enter N/A.
4. Click Sign.

CHAPTER 99

That Day Will Come Sooner with Our United Effort

Speech at the March 10 Tibetan Rally in Front of the Chinese Embassy
Washington, DC, United States
March 10, 2016

Dear Tibetan brothers and sisters, dear friends:

Tashi delek.

Today is March 10th, the Tibetan National Uprising Day. Ever since 1989, when I came to understand the plight of the people of Tibet through the Tiananmen Massacre, March 10th has become one of the most significant days in my life.

Fifty-seven years ago, the people of Tibet, who peacefully rose against the Chinese rule and sought freedom from the yoke of Chinese repression, were crushed violently by the Chinese military; their spiritual leader the Dalai Lama fled Tibet and began his long and arduous exile. Today, in 2016, Tibet is still a place of repression and fear. A place of blood and fire. The suffering the people of Tibet have had at the hands of the Chinese government in the past six decades is almost unparalleled in the history of mankind. So is their struggle.

Over these decades, the Chinese government has used everything to try to deceive the Tibetan people and the Chinese people as well; it has tried to sow seeds of division among Tibetans and between the two peoples, dilute the Tibetan culture, smash Tibetan monasteries, demonize His Holiness and his people, break the Tibetan spirit, and eventually destroy the Tibetan identity. It has failed. Today we stand together to declare its failure.

What we see today in Tibet is the new generation committed to fighting for Tibetan freedom at any personal sacrifice. Just last Tuesday, Kalsang Wangdu, an 18-year-old Tibetan monk, set himself on fire, joining in the company of more than 150 Tibetan self-immolating martyrs in recent years. He, like everyone else, called for the long life of the Dalai Lama, for His returning home, and for a free Tibet. This heroic act was soon followed by a solo protest by a Tibetan woman named Manga, 33. She held a portrait of his Holiness the Dalai Lama, shouting slogans against China's failed policies and crushing repression in Tibet.

These acts show incredible defiance to China's rule in Tibet. They are also a stark reminder of the dire situation in Tibet today.

China's false denials of all its human rights abuses are blatantly dishonest. But none of those lies are more outrageous than the stream of fairy tales seen in China's government-controlled media about how happy the Tibetans under China's rule are and how much they appreciate China's efforts to preserve their culture and traditions.

In response to China's propaganda, I have a simple question for Xi Jinping.

"Mr. Xi, if your rule of Tibet is so benevolent and appreciated, then tell me why so many Tibetans became so desperate about your rule that they have set themselves on fire?

"Rather than show a speck of remorse, your government has prosecuted grieving family members as accomplices to their loved ones in 'murder.' Even unrelated bystanders have been prosecuted as 'accessories to murder' for merely helping to load the victims' corpses into wagons so they could be taken to a decent Tibetan funeral.

"Mr. Xi, I have another question for you. Recent news stories in official Chinese media reflect your latest effort to build a cult of personality. They describe a handful of times when you shed tears over relatives, friends, or model officials.

"So, I ask you this. If you have any sense of decency or a real human heart, why have you not shed tears over the young Tibetan monks driven by China's persecution to set themselves on fire or over the young nuns sadistically tortured and imprisoned for many years?"

He may not want to answer my questions. But I am confident that the day will come when the Tibetan people as well as the Chinese public will hold the Chinese government and the individual perpetrators accountable, when the people of Tibet will use their right to self-determination to decide their own future. That day will come and will come sooner with our united effort.

Free Tibet!

Thank you all.

CHAPTER 100

The Best Use of Power Is to Help the Powerless

Speech at the March 10th Tibetan Rally in Front of the White House
Washington, DC, United States
March 10, 2016

Dear Tibetan brothers and sisters, dear friends:

Tashi delek.

Today marks the fifty-seventh anniversary of the Tibetan national uprising. I just spoke a few hours ago in front of the Chinese embassy. I won't repeat what I said there.

This summer, His Holiness the Dalai Lama will celebrate his eighty-first birthday, a wonderful occasion, as he continues to provide his unique spiritual and moral leadership. His strength, dignity, and wisdom have inspired not only Tibetans worldwide but also world leaders and all freedom-loving people. Sadly, however, 2016 also marks the fifty-seventh year he has spent in exile from Lhasa after the 1959 Tibetan uprising.

Today Tibet is still a place of repression and fear. Over the past decades, to ensure its control over the land, the Chinese government has used everything to try to deceive, divide, and demonize the Tibetan people, to dilute and eventually destroy their identity and spirit. But resistance in Tibet is as strong as ever. The heroic acts by more than 150 Tibetans who have self-immolated show incredible defiance to China's crushing repression. But they also are a stark reminder of the dire situation in Tibet today.

As supporters of Tibetans in Tibet, we know why we are here. Each of the 150-some self-immolations is one too many—we cannot afford to lose any more lives. And there is much we should and can do.

We must continue and expand the campaign of truth. When we hear the voices from inside Tibet, the voices in the flames, our conscience permits us no alternative but to act as their transmitters and amplifiers, to awaken more people's moral conscience and to let more people know the truth about these tragedies.

We must press the democratic governments to speak the TRUTH. We must take advantage of our democratic mechanisms to press the US government to keep Tibet on its agenda and make our elected representatives know that their voting base wants to see more proactive support for Tibet. The US is seeing another general election, which will decide who will lead this great democracy and the free world for at least the next four years. We must remind the US leaders that the best use of power is to help the powerless.

Tibet is both a political issue and a moral test. All of humanity is challenged. Every world leader, every US president, whoever occupies the place behind me—the White House—must take this test, and just like any other test, one either passes or fails. We should not let the next US president fail the test, politically or morally. We must insist that today silence is no longer an option. We must challenge the silence of the US government at every turn and press it to confront the lies of the Chinese government with the TRUTH.

In the face of such a powerful evil as the Chinese government, we may all feel powerless. But if we, all of us, are committed to fighting together relentlessly for our Tibetan brothers and sisters, contributing our time, energy, and skills to give voice to the voiceless and empower the powerless, then our hope is way more powerful than fear. I see a day when we meet freely in Golok, Labrang, Lithang, Lhasa, and Beijing!

Free Tibet! Free China!

Thank you all.

CHAPTER 101

Follow Dolkun Isa's Example to Continue Our United Effort

Speech at Victims of Communism Memorial Foundation's Human Rights Award Ceremony for Dolkun Isa
Washington, DC, United States
March 30, 2016

It is a great honor and pleasure for me to speak on this heartening occasion. I want to first congratulate my dear friend, brother, and human rights comrade, Dolkun Isa, for winning this deserved award. I wish to thank the Victims of Communism Memorial Foundation for recognizing three decades of Dolkun's struggle for the Uyghurs' freedom and his remarkable achievements. Under the leadership of Mr. Lee Edwards and Mr. Marion Smith, the Foundation is playing an increasingly important role in helping people around the world seek freedom from the yoke of communist dictatorships as well as other autocracies. It is most encouraging for the Foundation to expand its caring heart and dedication to include the Uyghur people, who are largely demonized by the Chinese government and whose miserable plight is often overlooked by the international community.

I first interacted with Dolkun in 1999. At that time, I tried to expand the Chinese-Tibetan dialogue that we had had for years to include Uyghurs and other ethnic and religious groups, but I found to my surprise and sorrow that no Uyghur out of control of the Chinese government would want to have any dealing with any Chinese. I made a determined effort to reach out. Long story short, a Mongolian friend introduced me to a Uyghur activist, Omer, who is also with us today. I was so excited that Omer wanted to give it a try and put me in contact with Dolkun, then-president of World Uyghur Youth Congress. I was thrilled hearing a calm voice from the other end of the phone. Why not? Soon thereafter in 2000, we had our first Interethnic/Interfaith Leadership Conference. I am proud to tell you that we—with our Uyghur, Tibetan, and Mongolian brothers and sisters, Christians, and Falun Gong practitioners, and activists from Taiwan, Hong Kong, and Macau, and with the encouragement and generous financial support from National Endowment for Democracy—will hold our eleventh Interethnic/Interfaith Leadership Conference in late April 2016 in Dharamsala, India.

I would be lying if I said that we, Chinese activists and Uyghur, have had no scuffles in the past years of dialogue or pretend that all the bitterness and distrust have disappeared. Looking back, my heart is filled with profound gratitude to Dolkun, my dear brother, who has provided undaunted visionary leadership at every difficult turn in the past twenty years. Dolkun, you have certainly been one of the few who has turned the impossible to inevitable. Thank you, brother.

When I think of the distances, especially the psychological distances, that we have traveled to be here, I am blessedly reminded that even with all the difficulties facing us, which, sadly to say, have not become much less daunting than when we first started, so much has already been done; and I believe, with the united effort of many brothers and sisters from both peoples following Dolkun Isa's example, we will establish the foundational spirit of community that is essential to our labors in and on behalf of the future, indeed, the freedom for all.

Thank you.

CHAPTER 102

Democracy for China: Missed Opportunities and Opportunities Ahead

Speech at the Congressional Defense and Foreign Policy Forum Hosted by Defense Forum Foundation
Washington, DC, United States
June 17, 2016

Thank you so much, Suzanne, for such a kind and generous introduction. The only problem was that, hearing the introduction, I thought I was dead. But I cannot and shouldn't think that, for my mission is not yet finished.

I am honored to be invited by the Defense Forum Foundation and specifically by its Chairman, Ambassador Middendorf.

I was impressed to learn that Ambassador Middendorf did such a good job as President Ford's Secretary of the Navy that President Carter paid him the unusual tribute of asking him to remain as Secretary.

I also admire the many years of efforts by DFF's President Suzanne Scholte to expose human rights abuses, especially in North Korea, which surpasses even China in the primitive brutality of its repression. Suzanne invited me to speak more than seven years ago about Charter 08, not long after it was published. Charter 08 is a manifesto led by Liu Xiaobo demanding a peaceful democratic transition in China, for which Liu Xiaobo was arrested and sentenced to eleven years in prison. And for his leadership role in Charter 08 and two decades of peaceful struggle to advance human rights and democracy, he won the 2010

Nobel Peace Prize. But I want to remind everyone that, as I speak, he is still languishing in China's prison.

Thank you, Suzanne, for inviting me back to talk about China's democratic perspectives. Can you think of any topic harder than this?

I personally think the three most difficult things facing humanity are making peace in the Middle East, democratizing China, and losing weight. Unfortunately, I am taking up two of the three.

Let's go back to the most important reference point in talking about Chinese politics—the 1989 Tiananmen incident, whose twenty-seventh anniversary we just commemorated less than two weeks ago.

The 1989 pro-democracy movement stood against government corruption and for democracy and freedom. This movement was widespread but ended in bloodshed. The Tiananmen Massacre created a strong sense of fear and dismay of general politics among ordinary people. Any room for a public system of checks and balances against governmental abuse of power was taken away.

It also created a sense of fear and crisis within the communist regime because it had brought unprecedented public awareness to human rights and democracy. Life was no longer the same for the rulers who had to face a completely different domestic and international environment.

The subsequent disintegration of the Soviet Union and the Eastern European Bloc cast an even heavier cloud over the heads of Chinese communist officials. "How long can the red flag continue to fly?" They all started to doubt.

To be sure, the CCP regime was struggling to survive the Tiananmen crisis, for which breaking international isolation was one of the imperatives facing the regime. Less than three weeks after the massacre, when China's leadership was least assertive and most susceptible to outside pressures, President Bush secretly sent his special envoy National Security Advisor Brent Scowcroft to meet with Deng Xiaoping and other Chinese leaders.

The meeting, later made public, did not seem to bring about any tangible results for either side. But this very gesture of President Bush's revealed America's weakness and assured China's leadership of the United States' intention to continue the recognition of and maintain the normal relations with the repressive regime, even if there was no indication of its willingness to admit or correct its serious mistakes or crimes. On July 28, three weeks after his special envoy returned to Washington, President Bush wrote a second, extremely carefully worded letter to Deng Xiaoping. "Please understand," wrote Bush, "that this letter has been personally written, and is coming from one who wants to go forward together. Please don't be angry with me if I have crossed the invisible threshold laying between constructive suggestion and 'internal interference'..." What could that imply? Judge for yourselves.

Democrats, especially Governor Bill Clinton on his campaign trail, harshly criticized Bush for "kowtowing" to China, while some conservatives saw Bush's move in the aftermath of the Tiananmen incident as premature in the absence of conciliatory gestures from Beijing. Different China views were reflected in the debate on whether and how to continue to grant China an MFN trade status.

One side of the debate, led by Representative Nancy Pelosi and Senator George Mitchell, asserted that US trade relations with China must be linked to China's human rights record. We, Chinese democracy activists, supported this idea because we understood that without such a linkage, continuing normal trade with China would be like a blood transfusion to the CCP regime, making it more aggressive and harming the interests of both the American and Chinese people. This idea was embodied in Pelosi and Mitchell's legislation in 1993. But one year after assuming presidency, President Clinton took a 180-degree turn and reversed the policy. The reversal was based on the theory, which was widely upheld by corporations, columnists, pundits and policymakers, that trade would lead to democracy because trade would inevitably result in economic growth and the growth of the middle class, which would in turn demand more political freedom.

This theory does not seem to apply to China, at least up to this point.

With money and technology pouring in from the US and other Western countries, the Chinese communist regime not only survived the 1989 crisis, it catapulted into the twenty-first century. The country's explosive economic growth lifted it from one of the poorest countries to become the number two economy in the world; but China remains firmly near the bottom of indicators on democratic development. Over the years, China's middle class have largely been acquiescent to its one-party dictatorship and its gross violations of human rights. What has gone wrong in China and the international community?

Let's look at China.

In 1992, when the Americans were heatedly debating about China policy and about to delink human rights from trade, Deng Xiaoping took the famous Southern Inspection Tour to further the economic opening up. Communist officials at all levels soon realized three realities: First, the Chinese Communist Party's stay in power has nothing to do with communist ideals. Second, "economic growth means everything;" that is, continued economic growth is the last, best hope to keep the CCP ship afloat. Third, in order to uphold the one-party dictatorship, it had to rely on capitalizing on the dark and evil side of human nature: spoiling the elite in exchange for their loyalty.

With the understanding of these three realities, the communist officials developed an undocumented but almost unanimously accepted code of conduct—or rather, code of corruption. So, every piece of governmental power is on sale in the market and every corner of the market is invaded by political power.

Officials in all government agencies spent most of their energy beefing up GDP, engaging in power arbitrage, bribing their superiors, and seeking luxurious personal perks. As a result, the Communist Party elite, who used to label themselves "the vanguards of the proletariat class," had either turned themselves into get-rich-overnight capitalists or become brokers, patrons, and backers of domestic and foreign capitalists.

In such a political environment, political power was dancing a full-swing tango with capital operation. Low human rights standards, low wages, lack of environmental protection regulations and enforcement, and the illegality of collective bargaining all contributed to creating a golden opportunity for domestic and international speculative capitalists. As a result, "money" quickly courted "political power." Business venture takers would go to any length to seek out someone in power to serve as backers so that they could grab market opportunities without fair competition. They also used political connections to shed any and all legal and social responsibility. In a sense, the Chinese Communist Party, which used to be China, Inc.'s sole shareholder, had now opened up its equity and offered its shares for capitalists to purchase.

This is very important for one to understand why "the middle-class prediction" has so far failed in China.

One. Given China's government-market relations, the middle class owed its success to privileged relations with the state. To expect such a state-dependent class to make bold political claims would have been fanciful.

Two. Trade and economic development were carried out as a matter of deliberate state policy, unlike the US and UK, and the fast growth did not give rise to a politically independent middle class but instead allowed the existing ruling structure to absorb into its own ranks the most talented and ambitious members of the business elite. The CCP's sixteenth National Congress, for example, published a new Party Charter that welcomed capitalists as Party members.

Meanwhile, the shares of China, Inc. were offered to China's intellectuals as free, performance-related stock options. In order to sustain stability, the CCP regime offered all kinds of bribery incentives to buy off anyone and everyone of importance and influence in society. The bribery list includes bureaucrats at every level, military officers, and business leaders as well as college professors, journalists, publishers, authors, art performers, high-profile athletes, and so on. The government pays all these people off in the form of salaries, bonuses, state-covered expenses, free medical insurance, subsidized housing, free pension plans, and so on. Laws and policies more and more favor this group of people in exchange for their recognition and acceptance of the political status quo. Their income and perks add up to wealth that is disproportionally higher than that of ordinary workers, farm workers, clerks, and small business owners. Such a policy of co-opting and buying off potential opposition was quite effective in conjunction with the purges and persecution after the Tiananmen Massacre. The cruelty of political reality created terror in the minds of intellectuals as a psychological deterrent. As time went on, fear turned into cynicism; they became increasingly indifferent to what was right and what was wrong. Indifference and hypocrisy rapidly became a new fashion that the modern Chinese intellect tried to follow. This, coupled with a piece of the action in China, Inc., made many intellectuals—who had once been independent and once been considered the conscience of the society—soften up their position against the post-1989 status quo.

Over the 1990s and the first ten years of the twenty-first century, in China, power (political elite), capital (economic elite) and "intellect" (social and cultural elite) were bonded together and formed an alliance that is maintaining the existing political order. This alliance owns and runs China, Inc., dazzling the entire world with its wealth, might, and glory. With China's vast geographic size and population, the shareholders of China, Inc. have impressed many observers with their prodigious wealth accumulation and astonishing growth rates, making those same observers believe that one-party dictatorship is good for economic growth. By the same token, these shareholders also control all the channels of the information flow and dominate the public discourse. They can make their voices so loud that the outside observers believe that they represent China, that they are China—the whole of China.

The truth is there is another society named China, a society constituted of over a billion Chinese who are virtually laborers working for

China, Inc. and whose basic rights are almost totally disregarded, the China that people sarcastically call "the China of shitizens."

This was China's two-China structure I often talked about before Xi Jinping took power. This was largely a two-player game.

During the same period, the US diplomatic establishment largely harbored the delusion that economic growth will bring about democracy in China. US presidents and other senior officials, deeming human rights issues inconvenient when engaging with China, would avoid them as much as they could. Faced with a rising China, the US gradually lost leverage. Now the Chinese leadership practically cares little about the pressure from Western public opinion because politicians and businessmen from around the world are salivating at China's immense purchasing power, investment, and markets. It's no exaggeration to say that today, Chinese leaders are the most well-received, honored guests in a majority of countries worldwide; China is the destination for many of the world's elite who thirst for gold.

Beijing tightly controls the freedom of the press. They could cut off Google and Yahoo anytime; they'd refused visas for *New York Times* journalists and critical scholars and blocked access to Twitter and Facebook. All without impunity. While at the same time, they can set up any media they would like in the US. Ironically, China, which screens, censors, and bans any print and electronic publication, has been invited to serve as the country of honor at book fairs in Frankfurt, London, and New York! Hollywood is the epitome of free American culture; filmmakers are free to ridicule, mock, and criticize American politicians and government officials such as senators, judges, and the president, without fear of persecution. But in their pursuit of China's box office dollars, Hollywood executives have consciously decided to steer clear of any criticism of the Chinese government. Despite this, American movies are still censored in China, and some are not allowed at all. Virtually all the American media are blocked in China. In the United States today, the Chinese government and its surrogates have wide access to universities, think tanks, and broadcast studios through which they can advance their opinions and rationalize their actions.

China is using the economic power it has gained with the help of the West to build a formidable, modern military. As its power grows, China is demanding a re-write of international norms and rules. China wants to create a new international order with China at the center of the Asia-Pacific region, bringing regional and world peace under threat. The current South China Sea tension is just a case in point.

In short, the failure of the US to proactively seek advancement of human rights and democracy in China has in turn harmed its long-term national interest and its democratic way of life.

Let's look at China again to examine opportunities ahead of us.

Despite his unprecedented high-profiled anti-corruption effort, Xi Jinping has largely continued the two-China structure and shown the world that he is more determined than his predecessors not to abandon the one-party dictatorship in favor of democratic reforms.

A subtle change, however, is taking place largely due to Xi Jinping's personality, anti-corruption campaign, and the unstoppable economic downturn.

Xi Jinping has concentrated power in his own hands and built a cult of personality. *The Economist* writes that Xi is now not the CEO (the chief executive officer) but the COE, the "Chairman of Everything." He's the head of state, the leader of the Communist Party, the commander-in-chief of the armed forces, the head of the security services, the head of the committee in charge of the so-called "comprehensive reform," and also the person in charge of the economy.

He has abolished the practice of "collective leadership," which was adopted in 1982 to prevent a return to the totalitarian terror of Mao's unchecked dictatorship, which produced such horrors as the Cultural Revolution. All this has undergone power struggles in the form of an anti-corruption campaign. In doing so, he has alienated his comrades at all levels, and they have remained in a "state of idle" to quietly protest.

One of the major reasons behind Xi's anti-corruption campaign is the two-China ruling model—co-opting the elite and exchanging corruption for loyalty has become increasingly costly and thus almost unbearable. But ending that model without granting people more liberties is an impossible task. The only thing it can achieve is to alienate the political, business, and intellectual elite, the middle class if you will. With the economic downturn, more and more members of the middle class are feeling insecure and seeking to leave the ruling structure and even the country.

At the same time, Xi, acting out of fear, has overseen the harshest crackdown on dissent since the Tiananmen Massacre, arresting lawyers, academics, workers, and civil society activists and tightening controls over the media and access to the internet.

Politically, the elite who are just beginning to turn their backs on the regime are caught between a ruling party above and a mass of workers and peasants below, with whom there is no mutual trust.

Xi Jinping is a game changer. He is unwittingly turning the two-player game into a three-player game, dissolving the power base that has helped the party stay in power to this day. This is the deepest crisis facing the Xi Jinping regime.

To be sure, growth is slowing; the party is in disarray because the rules it has established to limit internecine political warfare have collapsed; Beijing's foreign policy is driving the Sino-US relationship toward conflict; middle-class acquiescence is beginning to erode.

But I do not pretend that revolution will take place tomorrow.

It must be noted it usually takes four factors to be present at the same time to begin a real democratic transition in an autocratic country: 1) general robust disaffection from people; 2) a split in the leadership in the autocratic regime; 3) viable democratic opposition; and 4) international support.

Let me elaborate.

First. China's Stability Sustaining System treats every citizen as a potential enemy, and it has successfully made them enemies—dissidents, independent intellectuals, land-lease peasants, victims of forced demolitions and eviction, victims of forced abortion, veterans, migrant workers, Tibetans, Uyghurs, Mongolians, Christians, and Falun Gong practitioners, you name it. The CCP regime does not lack enemies. With slower economic growth, the grievances of the shitizens will be laid barer and social unrests can only be mounting.

Second. As I said earlier, the elite China is beginning to decompose. Party's leadership unity has also disintegrated, as shown by the purge of Bo Xilai, Ling Jihua, Zhou Yongkang, and their cronies since 2012.

Perhaps the only achievement in China's political system in the past thirty years is the establishment of the "two-term, ten-year, one-generation" term limit system. Many observers predicted that such a system would ensure long-term stability for the CCP regime, wishfully believing that this system helped the CCP find a way out of the pit of power discontinuity that has plagued all dictatorships in history. The Bo Xilai incident, however, mercilessly burst that bubble. Now it is Xi Jinping himself who is challenging this norm. The cracks within the party are only widening.

Third. The concept of democracy has prevailed in the minds of the general public, thanks to the dozens of years of efforts made by the pro-democratic activists both in and outside of China.

In the meantime, the ordinary people are becoming more mature, more skillful, and more aggressive in fighting for their own civil rights. Generally speaking, as citizen forces grow and the civil protests escalate, struggle for power among different factions with the communist regime will become public. Especially, once the external pressure reaches a critical mass, the rivalry factions with the CCP will have to take the citizen force into serious account and seek or use the latter's support.

That said, I want to emphasize that we need an overall, viable pro-democracy movement to force the dictatorship to crack open. A milestone to meet that objective would be the formation of a group of civil leaders able to represent the general public, integrating the middle class and lower class people in demanding for democracy, and to at least partially disrupt the current political order—a group that will catch attention and support of the international community and can carry out and call for effective negotiations with the government.

Fourth, last but not least, international support.

China under a one-party dictatorship cannot rise peacefully, and its transition to a democratic country that respects human rights, rule of law, and freedom of speech and religion is in everyone's best interest, including America. In other words, the US must push for a peaceful democratic transition in China. The reason for this is simple: To support China's regime, a regime that ruthlessly represses its own people, denies universal values to justify its dictatorship, and challenges the existing international order to seek its dominance, is morally corrupt as well as strategically unsound. Like Frankenstein's monster, China is now seeking to revenge against its creator—the West.

While many policymakers in Washington have now realized that it is time to get tough on China, some still believe that the present and future conflicts between the US and China can be managed. My view is this: Without China's democratization, a clash between the US and China is unavoidable because the two countries' strategic goals are on a clashing course and their core interests cannot be compromised.

I hereby call on the US to end the compartmentalization of human rights and begin to engage China with moral and strategic clarity.

To start, the Congress should pass a China Democracy Act that flatly states that enhancing human rights and democratic transition in China is decidedly in America's national interest and that directs the federal government and all its agencies to make democracy and human rights advocacy the core of all engagement with China. This would be binding legislation precluding the currently widespread but inaccurate claim that Congress must balance, on the one hand, its claim to support the universal value of human rights and, on the other hand, "America's national interest." The bill also would require a report from the President to Congress every year on how any government program, policy, or action during the prior twelve months has strengthened or weakened human rights and democratic values in China.

All federal departments of government—every single one—should have to report on what they're doing to bring democracy to China by advancing human rights and the rule of law there. The Act also puts them on notice to take no action, adopt no policy, and implement no program that would undercut the democracy movement or weaken human rights in China.

Such a China Democracy Act will give us a better idea of what successes we've had so far, what caused them, and how we should increase financial resources and deploy them to promote democracy and human rights.

Such an Act will serve as America's grand strategy toward China, setting a firm foundation that not only guides US activities with China in all spheres but also makes clear of the US intentions to the Chinese government and sends an unequivocal message of support to the Chinese people.

No one can predict with precision when the moment of dramatic opening for change will come in China. Virtually every one of the sixty-some peaceful transitions to democracy in the past few decades have come as a surprise to the United States.

Above all else we must maintain our faith in my compatriots that they can and will join the vast majority of the world's people who now live in free or at least partly free countries. An opening for change could come in the next few months or it may take a few more years. But it will never come without collective efforts, including those from the international community. So, we must persevere and keep the faith and be ready.

Perhaps, Suzanne, you will invite me to speak at this forum again in seven years. If so, it is my hope that by that time the China Democracy Act will have long been enacted and my topic will be Perspectives of Consolidating China's Nascent Democracy.

Thank you all.

CHAPTER 103

Report about China at the 2016 National Captive Nations Week Luncheon

Remarks at the Luncheon at Heritage Foundation Hosted by Victims of Communism Memorial Foundation
Washington, DC, United States
July 13, 2016

Thank you, Lee and Marion, and other colleagues at the Victims of Communism Memorial Foundation for inviting me to speak at this important annual event.

China has long been a one-party Leninist state with extensive censorship and perhaps the largest secret police establishment in the world. Xi Jinping became president in March 2013, having already assumed office as General Secretary of the Central Committee of the CCP four months earlier.

Initially, there had been hopes that he would be a reformer and that as China continued to open up economically, a new era of political liberalization would follow. It has become apparent, however, that the opposite seems to be the case.

Xi has overseen the harshest crackdown on dissent since the Tiananmen Massacre, arresting lawyers, academics, workers, and civil society activists, intensifying clampdowns on ethnic, religious, and regional groups, and tightening controls over the media and access to the internet.

Perhaps the most blatant example of the deterioration in human rights in China is the crackdown on lawyers and human rights defenders that began on July 9, 2015 (known as the "709 Crackdown"). Human rights groups recorded a total of 317 individuals affected by this crackdown. These included lawyers, their associates, paralegals, pastors, independent intellectuals, opinion leaders, and their relatives. After an initial period where hundreds were arrested, many were subsequently released, but at least twenty-one have been formally charged with specific crimes, including the very serious crime of sedition, and many others have been subjected to constant harassment, monitoring, interrogation, and threats.

The Xi Jinping regime has acted as it did not out of confidence, as itself claimed, but out of insecurity; the Chinese activists and intellectuals, people like those affected by the 709 Crackdown, have been in recent years making progress in broadening the social base of the democracy movement toward forming a viable democratic opposition, which is one of the four key necessary contributing factors for the erosion of the dictatorship and transition to democracy. The other three are general robust disaffection from the people, a split in the dictatorship, and international recognition of and support for the viable democratic opposition.

The CCP regime treats every citizen as a potential enemy and it has successfully made them enemies—dissidents, independent intellectuals, land-lease peasants, victims of forced demolitions and eviction, victims of forced abortion, veterans, migrant workers, Tibetans, Uyghurs, Mongolians, Christians, Falun Gong practitioners, you name it. The CCP regime does not lack enemies. With slower economic growth, the grievances of the powerless will be laid barer and social unrests can only be mounting.

The Party's leadership unity has also disintegrated, as shown by the purge of Bo Xilai, Ling Jihua, Zhou Yongkang, and their cronies since 2012. To be sure, growth is slowing; the party is in disarray, because the rules it has established to limit internecine political warfare have collapsed; Beijing's foreign policy is driving the Sino-US relationship toward conflict; middle-class acquiescence is beginning to erode.

At the same time, the concept of democracy has prevailed in the minds of the general public, thanks to the dozens of years of efforts made by the pro-democratic activists both in and outside of China.

As citizen forces grow and the civil protests escalate, struggle for power among different factions within the CCP regime will become public. Especially, once the external pressure reaches a critical mass, the rivalry factions within the CCP will have to take the citizen force into serious account and seek or use the latter's support.

That said, I want to emphasize that we still need an overall, viable democratic opposition to force the dictatorship to crack open. A milestone to meet that objective would be the formation of a group of citizen leaders able to represent the general public, integrating the middle class and lower class people in demanding for democracy, and to at least partially disrupt the current political order—a group that will catch attention and support of the international community and can call for and carry effective negotiations with the ruling regime.

The major impediment in the way of establishing a viable democratic opposition has long been the leadership issue, namely, that of forming such a stable and recognizable group of citizen leaders. The jailed Nobel Peace laureate Liu Xiaobo, as a widely accepted human rights and democracy champion both at home and abroad, will surely play a unique role.

Aung San Suu Kyi was released from house arrest in November of 2010, and that was the beginning of political reform in Burma. I believe Liu Xiaobo's case will have a similar significance in China. Therefore, working toward his freedom is vital for a democratic change in China.

Thank you.

CHAPTER 104

Steps to Make the United Nations Address China's Human Rights Situation More Effectively

Speech at the Forum entitled "Advance Human Rights: The United Nations and China" Hosted by Freedom House and the United Nations Association
Washington, DC, United States
September 27, 2016

There are many general steps that the US could take to improve UN human rights mechanisms. First, in order to faithfully back their words with actions, the US and other democracies should resolve to help mainstream human rights in the work of the UN, which, in turn, requires these democracies to first mainstream human rights in their bilateral diplomacy with dictatorships like China. Retiring UN Secretary-General Ban Ki-moon took a step in this direction by initiating the program designed to make every UN office and program take human rights considerations into account. But that effort has not really been implemented or embraced in an effective way. One fatal flaw is that UN personnel do not see member democracies integrating human rights policy in their own direct relations with other countries. Therefore, the US should internally establish a firm understanding that human rights advance in China is in the national interest of the US—including its national security interest. The US should end the more than two decades-long practice of compartmentalizing human rights and artificially isolating it from other diplomatic or economic interests and integrate China policy by linking human rights with other security, trade, environmental concerns, and so on and so forth.

After that, there are specific concrete steps to take that would make the U.N. a more effective international human rights governing and protecting body.

1. In my view, apart from thinking with changes to the existing UN human rights mechanisms, the least the US can and should do would be to use those mechanisms more vigorously and more effectively and establish collective actions to do so. A good example of unprecedented collective action at the Human Rights Council was the joint statement issued by the US and eleven other countries on March 10, 2016, condemning China's human rights record. We need more of this. The next day the US and Canada jointly hosted the Dalai Lama for a public event in Geneva. China was furious and reportedly urged many missions in Geneva not to attend the event. I don't think that effort of China was particularly successful, at least among the democracies.

Many countries are afraid of angering China. So, they don't push at all on human issues bilaterally, but the UN gives them a forum for confronting China collectively on human rights issues. The UN platform for collective action offers a solution to the I-FEAR-ABOUT-ACTING-ALONE, a dilemma that the democracies have been trapped in for years.

2. UNHRC-Open ballot

Despite the generally strong work of the experts in the "special procedures" machinery of the Human Rights Council, the credibility gaps of the old Commission on Human Rights have remained. The General Assembly has repeatedly elected countries known for major human rights violations to Council membership. Recall that, according to the establishing resolution, members elected and serving on the Council "shall uphold the highest standards in the promotion and protection of human rights and cooperate fully with its mechanisms." China is far from qualified, but it has been elected three times with high votes. NOT surprisingly, the result is selective investigation, bias, and reluctance to condemn such gross abusers as China. These embarrassments are still endemic in how the Council conducts business.

About 125 out of the 193 UN member states are democracies. If all democracies cast principled votes, namely, upholding their own human rights standard or the standard established in the founding resolution of the Council, countries like China, Cuba, Iran, and Russia would have no chance to get elected.

The UN resolution that established the Council envisioned competitive elections in which states with the best human rights records would be elected. To this end, a secret ballot was adopted. The past ten years of practice have proved the opposite. The secret ballot only helps dictatorships bargain under the table with democracies and makes it possible for democracies to compromise principles without risking scrutiny by people at home.

I strongly suggest an open ballot system for membership election for the Council. It is dictators that are afraid of light most, not the democracies. Open ballot will provide a lever to people of democracies to make democracies to cast just votes that are consistent with democratic principles.

This leads to another suggestion which I have proposed on a few occasions in the past year.

3. I propose building on the authoritative Freedom House Index of Freedom in the World, which rates countries on their upholding political rights and civil liberties for their citizens—that a second, parallel rating system be created. It would rank the world's real democracies on the basis of what efforts they make to help promote political rights and civil liberties in other nations—especially in the most flagrant abusers of those rights and liberties like China. The index could be called the "Index of Nations' Efforts to Promote Freedom in the World."

This index could be a mandate under the U.N.

Democracies' voting records in the U.N. should be a major factor.

4. Next, the US and other major democracies should lead efforts to strengthen and enlarge communication between the UN human rights mechanism and people oppressed by dictatorships. The U.N. is a world body of states. But a major problem with it is that many states, China, for example, do NOT represent the will or interests of their people in conducting business in the world body. The U.N. human rights mechanisms should be a more accessible platform to give voice to those who suffer human rights abuses at the hands of the Chinese government and other tyrannies. It is very important that their powerful voices be heard and their stories be reported at the UN—not least for the record they are creating.

5. Upgrade the Office of High Commissioner for Human Rights and expand its capacity. If mainstreaming human rights in the UN is our goal, we must make two structural reforms.

- Elevate its status so that the UN Secretary-General, or at least a Deputy Secretary-General, should also be the High Commissioner for Human Rights.
- Improve the current meager budget for the office.

6. Facilitating the flow of information about what is happening in Geneva to people in China is equally important. It is crucial. I think the US translated the March 10 joint critical statement by twelve member nations into Chinese, after which the US embassy in Beijing heard from hundreds of people words of thanks and appreciation for that. It's so important to let people in China's civil society know that we stand with them and are doing what we can to support them both bilaterally and at the world's government, the United Nations.

CHAPTER 105

Never Give Up

Speech at the Tibetan Rally in Front of the Chinese Embassy
Washington, DC, United States
March 10, 2017

Dear brothers and sisters,

Tashi delek!

Thank you for asking me to speak on this important occasion. Today marks the fifty-eighth anniversary of the 1959 Tibetan Uprising; it is a day on which we recall the struggle of the Tibetan people against Chinese occupation and oppression, and it is a day on which we draw the world's attention to our ongoing struggle for freedom in Tibet. I do not need to tell those of you gathered here just how dire the situation is in Tibet. You all know.

The recently released Freedom in the World Report for 2016 issued by Freedom House sums the situation up well: Tibet is ranked the second worst "Not free" country in the world; the only country worse in terms of lack of political and civil freedoms and liberties is Syria. Even North Korea is ranked higher than Tibet.

What is to be done? We, the Tibetans, Chinese, and the freedom-loving people around the world should be more united today than ever before in our worldwide truth campaign, exposing more and more Chinese to the truth, confronting the world democratic leaders with truth, urging them to collectively apply pressure on the Chinese government over Tibetan issues. As the Dalai Lama always says: "Never give up!"

Today, I do have messages to the US government and the Chinese government as well.

TO TRUMP/ADMINISTRATION

First, I want to echo Congressmen Smith and MacArthur in urging Secretary of State Rex Tillerson to help facilitate a US visit of a Tibetan women's soccer team to attend an international tournament in Dallas.

Appoint a Special Coordinator for Tibetan Issues, someone with relevant background and experience, as soon as possible and retain this position at the Under-Secretary level.

President Trump should meet with His Holiness the Dalai Lama in the White House as soon as possible to signal the United States' continuing support for Tibet and the cause of the Tibetan people and to underline the importance of religious freedom in Tibet for the stability of the region.

As soon as a Special Coordinator is named, he or she should continue working with "like-minded" countries on Tibet-related issues, including a multilateral effort to encourage the Chinese government to re-engage in a dialogue with the Dalai Lama or his representatives, without preconditions, as well as working toward the common position on HHDL's reincarnation that the decision regarding his reincarnation is reserved to the current Dalai Lama, Tibetan Buddhist leaders, and the Tibetan people.

Commit to continued engagement with the UN Human Rights Council (HRC). The US involvement has been instrumental in many advances in human rights and processes at the Council. The Council and its various mechanisms have played a key role in defending human rights and religious freedom in Tibet. The most recent example: A group of six Special Rapporteurs (representing different rights, including cultural rights, sustainable environment, peaceful assembly, freedom of religion, etc.) condemned China's violations of religious freedom and cultural rights in its demolitions and expulsions at Larung Gar and Yachen Gar in what is now Sichuan province.

When meeting with Chinese counterparts, the president and his administration should call for the release of Tibetan political prisoners, which number in the hundreds, if not thousands. These prisoners include the popular blogger and writer Shokjang, who was sentenced to three years in prison for "inciting separatism" in February 2016, and Tashi Wangchuk, an entrepreneur and Tibetan education advocate, who was detained in January 2016 and indicted in January 2017 on "inciting separatism" charges.

TO THE CHINESE GOVERNMENT

The Dalai Lama recently commented that the Chinese hardliners have parts of their brain missing. I hope they will regain the missing parts so as to look at the Tibetan issue with common sense and compassion. Here you are.

- Cease suppressing the right to religious freedom in Tibet and cease the demolitions of Larung Gar and Yachen Gar, and the expulsions of monks, nuns, and other Tibetan Buddhist adherents from these very important Buddhist centers of learning and worship.
- Stop vilifying the Dalai Lama and misusing "security" concerns to further trample on the rights of Tibetans. Cease restrictions on the right to freedom of movement of Tibetans both internally and internationally; return the passports of those taken from Tibetans who recently traveled to India for HHDL's teachings and were punished upon their return.
- Release political prisoners now, without delay, including Shokjang and Tashi Wangchuk, and allow an independent observer from an international organization to meet with the long disappeared Gedhun Choekyi Nyima, the Panchen Lama recognized by the Dalai Lama in 1995.
- Re-engage in the dialogue process with the Dalai Lama or his representatives, without preconditions, to negotiate a durable and mutually beneficial outcome for both sides.

Respect the right of the current Dalai Lama, Tibetan Buddhist leaders, and Tibetans to decide the issue of his reincarnation. There is no role for the Chinese Communist Party or Chinese government in this process.

SECTION XIII

THE DEATH OF LIU XIAOBO: HIS SEED WILL GROW

July 2017—October 2017

"Medical parole in China is a political, not a medical, decision. The denial of medical care led to Liu Xiaobo's advanced liver cancer, and at its core was a disguised death sentence....I believe the reason the Chinese regime denied Liu Xiaobo's wish and the world's appeal to allow him medical treatment abroad and to die in a free place is that it fears the truth of its ruthless persecution will come to light. The world media would focus on Liu Xiaobo and the regime's lies would be exposed. More and more people in China would see the true nature of this one-party state. The government would lose control....No doubt, the Chinese communist regime is responsible for Liu Xiaobo's death. However, the world democracies' appeasement policy toward China's human rights abuses has made them accomplices to Liu Xiaobo's slow murder. If the world continues to acquiesce to China's aggression against its own people, Liu Xiaobo's tragedy will repeat....But these cowards failed to understand that Liu Xiaobo is a seed. Where you bury him, there he grows."

CHAPTER 106

Preserve the Legacy of Liu Xiaobo's Struggle for a Democratic Free China

Opening Remarks at Hearing "The Tragic Case of Liu Xiaobo"
Hosted by the House Foreign Affairs Subcommittee on Africa, Global Health, Global Human Rights, and International Organizations
Washington, DC, United States
July 14, 2017

Chairman Smith and ranking members,

I had a sleepless night.

At this grievous moment, I would like to thank you for holding this critical hearing. It is critical for us to discuss how we can still lend a helping hand to assist Liu Xiaobo's family and how we can fight to honor the legacy of his courage and sacrifice.

Liu Xiaobo's tragedy represents the tragedies of many human rights activists in China, but it is also unique in its own way. In all of Nobel Peace Prize history, there have only been three jailed laureates. But among them, Liu Xiaobo is the most tragic one.

Liu Xiaobo had been held incommunicado since December 2008 until he became terminally ill and was eventually allowed a visit by a German doctor and an American doctor after the pleas to Xi Jinping from both President Trump and German Chancellor Merkel. During his entire imprisonment, he was not allowed even to talk about any current events with his wife, Liu Xia, during her visits, nor the persecutions Liu Xia and her family suffered. Even on his deathbed, he had no freedom to leave his last words. Now that he is gone, the world will never know.

Liu Xiaobo's cancer was diagnosed on May 23 during an emergency hospital visit because of internal bleeding, and since then he had been hospitalized in the First Hospital of China Medical University in Shenyang, Liaoning province. However, the news of his late-stage cancer was not leaked out until late June. During this time, his tumor enlarged from 5–6 cm to 11–12 cm.

It is reported that Liu Xiaobo had two CT tests last year. How can two tests fail to reveal Xiaobo's fairly large liver tumors? Many, including myself, suspect that the Chinese officials intentionally concealed this info from Liu Xiaobo and his family. This is why they have been withholding Liu Xiaobo's medical records. These records are classified as the top state secret.

I strongly believe that the Chinese regime deliberately chose not to treat Liu Xiaobo's cancer earlier. As early as 2010, Liu Xiaobo was suspected of suffering from hepatitis B. His lawyers had been petitioning the government to grant him medical parole, but the Chinese authorities never allowed him proper diagnosis and treatment. In China, it is not doctors but the Party officials who decide whether to grant medical parole. In other words, medical parole in China is a political, not a medical, decision. In Liu Xiaobo's case, it was up to China's top leaders to decide. The denial of medical care led to Liu Xiaobo's advanced liver cancer, and at its core was a disguised death sentence.

When Liu Xiaobo's worsening condition became public, human rights activists, 154 Nobel laureates, and world leaders called for Liu Xiaobo's immediate release and medical treatment overseas. Liu Xiaobo himself also expressed his wish to seek medical treatment abroad and to die in a free place. Unfortunately, the Chinese regime callously disregarded these requests. After persecuting him for so many years, the regime still didn't even hesitate to crush his final wish.

I believe the reason that the Chinese regime denied Liu Xiaobo's wish and the world's appeal to allow him medical treatment abroad and to die in a free place is that it fears the truth of its ruthless persecution will come to light. The world media would focus on Liu Xiaobo and the regime's lies would be exposed. More and more people in China would see the true nature of this one-party state. The government would lose control.

No doubt, the Chinese communist regime is responsible for Liu Xiaobo's worsening health and for his death. However, the world democracies' appeasement policy toward China's human rights abuses has made them accomplices of Liu Xiaobo's slow murder. If the world continues to acquiesce to China's aggression against its own people, engaging it without any moral clarity, Liu Xiaobo's tragedy will repeat.

Mr. Chairman, the US should do more to help Liu Xiaobo and his family. The Trump administration should make it a priority to urge China to grant Liu Xia full control of funeral arrangements for her late husband and help Liu Xia leave China for a country of her choosing. The US should implement country-specific and tougher sanctions against those personally responsible for Liu Xiaobo's death. The US can use the Global Magnitsky Act as a tool to sanction them, banning them from traveling in the US and freezing their assets in this country, and also encourage its allies to do the same. It should also consider trade sanctions. In addition, the US can honor Liu Xiaobo's life and legacy by passing legislation to permanently rename the street in front of the Chinese embassy in Washington, DC, as "Liu Xiaobo Plaza."

To fight for the ideals of human rights and democracy, Liu Xiaobo gave up his career, he gave up his liberty, he gave up his freedom, and now, he has given up his life. But we cannot give up on him. We have to seek justice for Liu Xiaobo's death at the hands of the Chinese regime, and we have to preserve the legacy of Liu Xiaobo's struggle for a democratic free China.

Thank you.

CHAPTER 107

Additional Remarks at Hearing on "The Tragic Case of Liu Xiaobo"

Hearing "The Tragic Case of Liu Xiaobo" Hosted by the House Foreign Affairs Subcommittee on Africa, Global Health, Global Human Rights, and International Organizations
Washington, DC, United States
July 14, 2017

Mr. Chairman, I have a few more points to make.

In life as well as in death, Liu Xiaobo represents the best of what China can ever be. He possesses a moral authority that his persecutors can only envy, and his legacy of love, justice, and sacrifice will surely far outlive the deeds of those who persecuted him.

Liu Xiaobo, then a young philosopher and writer, was a major leader of the 1989 democracy movement. He shouldered both moral and political responsibilities after the Tiananmen Massacre and continued to fight for constitutional democracy from inside China, while many others left the country and even abandoned the movement. He shared the sufferings of his compatriots and made great sacrifices for them. He is a saint. His spirit will be an uplifting and unifying force that will inspire more Chinese people to fight to realize his dream—indeed, the common dream of the Chinese people.

To the world, he represents the universal values that all democracies embrace, and he stands for the unwavering struggle of unfree people for freedom. Liu Xiaobo is a representative of universal ideas that resonate with millions of people all over the world.

It is a sad and disturbing fact that many leaders of the free world, who themselves hold democracy and human rights in high regard, have been less willing to stand up for those rights for the benefit of others. If this becomes a widely accepted approach and is continued, it will eventually jeopardize the democratic way and the security of free people.

I cannot help but ask: What kind government would callously refuse to grant the final wish of such a peaceful and kind man as Liu Xiaobo, a man who sincerely believes he has no enemies, to die as a free man—to die with dignity? What kind government would not even allow him in his final moments to be with his beloved wife without surveillance?

This is a totally morally bankrupt regime. Dealing with such a regime, one must have moral clarity. There is a lot of talk about engaging with China. Yes, no one can avoid engaging with China, but democracies must engage China comprehensively. Democracies must confront the brutal face of this regime and must not look the other way when human rights tragedies take place.

The Chinese government can never be considered a trusted peer on the global stage until it addresses its egregious human rights violations.

The tragic death of Liu Xiaobo gives us a stronger sense of urgency in helping the prisoners of conscience of China.

I believe there is clearly a pattern of the Chinese regime deliberately neglecting detained and jailed activists' health, mistreating them—including torturing them and forcing ingestion of harmful drugs, as reported by jailed activists' family members or released activists.

I am afraid that more human rights activists will languish and disappear in Chinese prisons.

Wang Bingzhang, Hu Shigen, Zhu Yufu, Ilham Tohti, Tashi Wangchuk, Wang Quanzhang, Jiang Tianyong, Tang Jingling, Wu Gan, Guo Feixiong, Liu Xianbin, Chen Wei, Zhang Haitao… the list can go on and on.

If American advocacy for human rights and justice is to mean anything at all, the US government must do more to support these political prisoners and to hold accountable the Chinese government and individuals who so brazenly abuse the fundamental rights of its people. One way of doing this is through the vigorous enforcement of the Global Magnitsky Act.

We all hoped that Liu Xiaobo would one day complete his unjust prison sentence and then have more time to share his passion and energy for human rights and dignity… and also perhaps one day to have time to enjoy for himself the fruits of his life's work: freedom. But instead, he is gone.

I want to share with you the beautiful words of Martin Luther King Jr., which he delivered in a speech in Memphis, Tennessee, on the evening before his own death.

"Well, I don't know what will happen now. We've got some difficult days ahead. But it doesn't matter with me now. Because I've been to the mountaintop.

"And I don't mind.

"Like anybody, I would like to live a long life. Longevity has its place. But I'm not concerned about that now. I just want to do God's will. And He's allowed me to go up to the mountain. And I've looked over. And I've seen the promised land. I may not get there with you. But I want you to know tonight, that we, as a people, will get to the promised land!"

CHAPTER 108

He Represents the Best of What China Can Ever Be

Speech at "Remembering the Legacy of Liu Xiaobo" Hosted by Victims of Communism Memorial Foundation
Washington, DC, United States
July 17, 2017

Tonight, we mourn the tragic passing of Liu Xiaobo, a great loss to the people of China, indeed, to all of humanity.

Liu Xiaobo was not only the best-known freedom and democracy fighter of China but, in life as well as in death, he represents the best of what China can ever be.

In April 1989, when the Tiananmen democracy movement just broke out, he returned to Beijing from New York and became the most important intellectual leader of the movement. After the Tiananmen Massacre, he shouldered both moral and political responsibilities and continued to fight from inside China while many others left the country and even abandoned the movement. He was in and out prison and spent half of the past twenty-eight years after the Tiananmen Massacre in incarceration. Never wavering in spirit, he shared the sufferings of his compatriots and gave his life for them. He is a martyr and saint.

Yes. Liu Xiaobo is a martyr and saint who possesses a moral authority that his persecutors can only envy. His legacy of love, justice, peace, and sacrifice will surely far outlive the deeds of those who persecuted him.

That is exactly why the leaders of China are so afraid of him, so afraid of his words and deeds, and so afraid of his legacy. They are afraid of the inevitable comparison between Liu Xiaobo's Chinese dream and Xi Jinping's; they are afraid of the unavoidable likening of the Chinese communist regime to the Nazi regime because Liu Xiaobo has been the first Nobel Peace Prize winner who died under confinement since Carl von Ossietzky, a German pacifist and an opponent of the Nazis, who died in 1938.

The CCP regime took pains to show the world it was strong and not afraid of Liu Xiaobo, yet its actions suggested otherwise. The CCP regime took pains to show the world that China is rising as a great civilized nation, yet its actions suggested otherwise. No nation that routinely persecutes, tortures, and murders its best people can ever be described as strong, as great; no nation that does not allow a man such as Liu Xiaobo to die as a free man is going to rise as a respected world power. Never.

In death, Liu Xiaobo has overcome the limits of time and space. The leaders of China wanted to bury him, trying make him disappear altogether. But these cowards failed to understand that Liu Xiaobo is a seed. Where you bury him, there he grows. He is everywhere and forever.

CHAPTER 109

Taiwan Out of the UN: Unfair to Taiwan and Harmful to Global Interests

Speech at the Rally "Taiwan Membership for the UN"
New York, NY, United States
September 22, 2017

Recently, the long detained Taiwanese citizen and human rights activist Lee Ming-che appeared in a bogus trial in Chinese courts and was forced to plead guilty to "subverting (Chinese) state power." Outraged family members and Taiwanese supporters might want to come to the United Nations' human rights mechanisms for help—but they can't. This is because they, as citizens of Taiwan, are not represented at the world governing body. With pressure from China, even Taiwanese tourists are routinely excluded from visiting the UN headquarters with Taiwanese passports. Egregious and ridiculous as such is the reality facing us today.

The only thing preventing Taiwan, a full democracy, from taking its rightful seat in the UN is China and China's aggressive posture on the international stage with respect to Taiwan. Allies of Taiwan such as the US and like-minded nations must stand up to China's bullying and intimidation and advocate for Taiwan to rejoin the UN, or at a minimum as the first step, to ensure that Taiwan is able to participate in a meaningful way in UN-affiliated organizations and meetings. Succumbing to pressure from China to exclude Taiwan from UN-related organizations and activities is tantamount to abandoning the beacon of democracy, human rights, and rule of law in Asia, and to depriving the twenty-three million citizens of democratic Taiwan their fundamental rights to participate in, and receive protections from, the mechanisms of global governance. This is as unfair to the people of Taiwan as it is harmful to the interests of the world.

Taiwan's participation in UN mechanisms not only benefits Taiwan but also the rest of the international community. Taiwan's absence from, for example, the World Health Organization, Interpol, the UN Framework Convention on Climate Change, and the International Civil Aviation Organization creates critical gaps in addressing borderless issues, such as the spread of disease, cross-border crime, counterterrorism efforts and global security, climate change, and aviation safety.

For the first time since 2009, as a result of pressure from Beijing, Taiwan was not invited to attend the World Health Assembly, the decision-making body of the WHO, which met in Geneva this past May. Beijing insisted that Taiwan publicly accept the "one-China" principle as a condition for retaining its observer status.

The importance of Taiwan's involvement in the WHO cannot be overstated. The SARS outbreak in 2003 is a clear example: WHO's delays in getting Taiwan critical information and timely assistance (because it wasn't a member of WHO and China said it would assist Taiwan and didn't) contributed to the deaths of over thirty Taiwanese citizens. As a leader in health care in Asia and a global leader in several medical specialties, Taiwan also has much to contribute to the international community.

Also in May, the Chinese delegation to a UN-affiliated conference called the Kimberley Process, which seeks to control the trade in conflict or "blood" diamonds, caused such a raucous scene at the meeting in Australia protesting the presence of delegates from Taiwan that the Taiwanese delegation was eventually asked to leave, even though Taiwan had received a formal invitation.

Similarly, due to Chinese pressure, Taiwan continues to be excluded from Interpol, which hampers international efforts to fight cross-border crime and terrorism. In November 2016, Interpol rejected Taiwanese participation in its general assembly.

Taiwan unsuccessfully sought observer status with the International Civil Aviation Organization, a UN-affiliated organization. While the ICAO invited Taiwan to attend as an observer in 2013, an invitation from the organization to Taiwan was not forthcoming for its meeting in Montreal in September 2016. Given Taiwan's bustling airports, economy, and the growing number of tourists (many of whom are from China), the absence of Taiwan from a key air safety regulatory body poses serious concerns for aviation safety.

China's relentless and increasingly aggressive tactics to exclude Taiwan from global regulatory bodies has only harmful consequences. Absolutely no benefit comes from Taiwan's exclusion; China's political machinations are cynical and detrimental to global interests.

And China's conduct contravenes the spirit and purpose of the United Nations, which includes: "to develop friendly relations among nations based on respect for the principle of equal rights and self-determination of peoples" and "to achieve international co-operation in solving international problems of an economic, social, cultural, or humanitarian character and in promoting and encouraging respect for human rights and for fundamental freedoms for all…" *UN Charter, Article 1.*

Taiwan has consistently acted as a responsible member of the international community. To name just a few examples: It was one of the few countries to voluntarily announce targets for reduction of carbon dioxide emissions, and Taiwan voluntarily adopted the two key UN human rights treaties (the ICCPR and ICESCR), incorporated their provisions into Taiwan's domestic law, and devised its own innovative review process since it cannot participate in the review process of the UN human rights treaty bodies.

Taiwan has much to contribute to world order, and the UN should open its doors to the vibrant democracy of twenty-three million people. The world needs Taiwan's involvement and contributions, and Taiwan's rights and interests must be protected.

CHAPTER 110

Liu Xiaobo's Shining Example and Stern Warning

Speech at Forum 2000
Prague, Czech Republic
October 8, 2017

Standing on this Forum 2000 stage created by Václav Havel, I cannot help but thinking of our Václav Havel, China's Václav Havel, my friend and hero—Liu Xiaobo.

Liu Xiaobo died a martyr's death less than three months ago. In this oblivious world, while many people are yet to know him, many others are pretending they've already forgotten him. Truly, as Milan Kundera wrote, "the struggle of man against power is the struggle of memory against forgetting." As a friend and supporter who represented his family at his 2010 Nobel Peace Prize ceremony and helped conceive the idea of Empty Chair at it, I think the meaning of remembering him is to embrace his legacy and follow his example in our continued struggle for democracy and freedom.

By the 1980s, Liu Xiaobo was one of the most provocative thinkers in China. His learning encompassed both Chinese and Western scholarship, particularly in philosophy and the humanities, and his genuine academic integrity enabled him to maintain independence and profundity in his thinking. An admirer of thinkers such as Václav Havel, Liu Xiaobo prided himself on his intolerance for hypocrisy, groupthink, and political pandering.

Compelled to live in a society that would not accept the public expression of dissenting views, Liu Xiaobo struggled with a dilemma: How could he stay true to his beliefs under such repressive circumstances? He particularly admired former Václav Havel as one of those rare human beings who, even while living in totalitarian circumstances, somehow found the strength in himself to step beyond "living within the lie," and manage to find a way "to live within the truth." Echoing the sentiments of Havel, Liu Xiaobo argued that "We need not demand of ourselves any extraordinary courage, nobility, conscience, or wisdom; we need not ask ourselves to risk prison or go on hunger strikes or carry out self-immolations. All we need to do is to eliminate lies from our public speech and give up the use of lies as a tactic of dealing with the threats and enticements of the regime... To refuse to lie in day-to-day public life is the most powerful tool for breaking down a tyranny built on mendacity."

When Liu Xiaobo flew back to Beijing from New York in late April 1989, the largest march of the weeks-old protest was in full swing. An endless crowd of peaceful protesters flooded the miles-long Chang'an Avenue—a true demonstration of people power. This march was a strong testimony and symbol for the Chinese people: that the pursuit of democracy was not the goal of just a few dissidents, but the common hope of millions of Chinese citizens, especially the youngest generation of students. From that point on, Liu Xiaobo undertook a twenty-eight-year-long journey from a scholar to a committed fighter for democracy. Before his fourth and final arrest, he was widely recognized as a political leader—a role which he never felt comfortable to play but a responsibility which his sense of mission drove him to shoulder.

He was last arrested in 2008 for being the lead author and organizer of Charter 08. Modeled after Charter 77, the declaration spearheaded by Václav Havel and Jan Patočka in 1977 that helped bring about the Velvet Revolution to end communism in Czechoslovakia, Charter 08 was published on the sixtieth anniversary of the Universal Declaration of Human Rights with the goal of spelling out the reforms necessary to end one-party domination and establish the rule of law in China. Since its release, this manifesto for democracy and constitutional government has been signed, at great personal risk, by more than 14,000 Chinese citizens. Liu's imprisonment only increased his stature and international fame, and in 2010, he was deservingly awarded the Nobel Peace Prize.

Through intense struggles, Liu Xiaobo came to the conclusion in his 2009 courtroom self-defense, "Hatred only eats away at a person's intelligence and conscience" and can "poison the spirit of an entire people (as the experience of our country during the Mao era clearly shows). It can lead to cruel and lethal internecine combat; it can destroy tolerance and human feeling within a society and can block the progress of a nation toward freedom and democracy… I hope that I can answer the regime's enmity with utmost benevolence and can use love to dissipate hate." As he acknowledged, June 1989 was a turning point, engendering a new philosophy, which he summed up in these words: "I have no enemies and no hatred."

Liu Xiaobo's unwavering commitment to bear such a burden as the misery of Chinese society shall live on and shine in history. Yet, his sudden death before our ultimate triumph brings tears and pain to everyone who shares his cause, values, and ideals. The international community stood helpless as the Chinese government ruthlessly shattered Liu Xiaobo's last wish by denying his request to seek medical treatment abroad and die as a free man. The free world's appeasement of the evil deeds of the Chinese regime will adversely affect global democratization, which is exactly what Liu Xiaobo warned against a decade ago. Liu feared then that the West might repeat the same mistake it made during the rise of the fascist Third Reich and the communist USSR. He warned that the international community must remain vigilant in the face of the rising Chinese communist dictatorship because the game for world dominance had changed. The Chinese communists had also morphed into a new beast—more adaptive, cunning, and deceptive than ever before.

And we are now witnessing an astonishing reversal of world history: Dictatorial China is gaining the upper hand. This constitutes the most serious threat to universal human rights and democracy since World War II.

From playing a pivotal role in Tiananmen Square in 1989 to suffering a lonely death under police guard, Liu Xiaobo's fate has become both a symbol of the plight of China's democracy and an urgent warning to the world. In Liu Xiaobo's own words: "To eliminate the adverse impact of the rise of China on world civilization, the free world must help this largest totalitarian country to achieve a democratic transition as soon as possible."

I hope that Liu Xiaobo's example will continue to shine on all freedom fighters and his stern warning will not fall on deaf ears.

CHAPTER 111

People of China, Too, Want Human Rights

Speech at Panel "Clash of Cultures, Values, and Principles: Right of the People or Human Rights?"
The 2017 Convention of the Nonviolent Radical Party Transnational Transparency
Rome, Italy
October 28, 2017

Thank you, dear friends at the Nonviolent Radical Party for inviting me to speak at this Convention of Transnational Transparency. It is truly an honor for me. I admire the Nonviolent Radical Party for its commitment to speaking the truth and promoting the rights to know.

The first order of truth about China is that the people of China, too, want human rights. This sentence sounds a bit awkward with the word "too." I put it there because the truth—that the people of China want human rights—has not only been suppressed by the Chinese communist regime but is all too often overlooked by the world community.

"Given so much you have been through," I am often asked, "where does your confidence lie?" My answer is always, "My confidence lies in the simple fact that the people of China want human rights."

"Do you really believe so?" Some sound skeptical seeing the insurmountable China realities. Well, let me propose the following thought experiment for you to judge for yourselves.

Imagine that you visited China, taking with you a copy of the Universal Declaration of Human Rights. Arbitrarily choose any citizens on the street. Show the document, asking them with the language they understand whether they want the rights listed there. What would you expect them to say? Would you for a second believe they would say, "No, I do not want these rights"? Of course not. You understand the Chinese people through understanding yourselves: Nobody wants to be a slave. In this regard, the Chinese people are no different than other people in the world. The thirst for freedom and dignity is indeed universal.

The people of China have long ago begun the search for roads to the universality of dignity, justice, goodness, fairness, equality, freedom, and brotherhood. They have produced a few major pushes toward these goals in this generation. In the 1989 Tiananmen democracy movement, the Chinese people courageously stood up against government corruption that in the words of Charter 08, has "corrupted human intercourse." They stood up for democracy and freedom. The image of a lone man standing in front of a string of tanks has inspired the entire world, and our fallen brothers' spirits have been one of the greatest sources of inspiration for continued struggle for these noble goals in China.

Charter 08 was published on the sixtieth anniversary of the Universal Declaration of Human Rights with the goal of spelling out the reforms necessary to end one-party dictatorship and establish a constitutional democracy in China. Since its release, this manifesto has been signed, at great personal risk, by more than 14,000 Chinese citizens.

The world is still mourning the death of the lead author and organizer of Charter 08, the 2010 Nobel Peace Prize laureate Liu Xiaobo. He died a martyr's death 110 days ago after nine years of imprisonment.

Thanks to the arduous work and enormous sacrifices by people like Liu Xiaobo, the concepts of human rights and democracy have prevailed in the minds of the Chinese general public.

A breakthrough for a democratic change will surely come from the people. Change is unlikely to happen first from within the heavily entrenched CCP regime which values stability above all.

Despite the CCP's best effort to impose strict control over the media, the internet has allowed people to connect, to share information.

Following the release of Charter 08, grassroots support for the document was immediate and unprecedented, even though the CCP regime tried to block its spread. Those who signed the Charter with their real names came from diverse segments of society. Liu Xiaobo and Charter 08 are a banner which will continue to transform individual protests into a long-lasting movement that demands across the board, systematic change.

With a clear direction of the political resistance movement, the people will grow to exert greater and greater pressure on the communist regime. As non-governmental forces grow and civil protests escalate, the struggle for power among different factions within the communist regime will become more pronounced. Once external pressures reach a critical mass, rival factions within the CCP will have no choice but to take the voices of the citizens seriously and seek their support to survive.

No one can predict with precision when the moment of dramatic opening for change will come in China. Virtually every one of the sixty-some peaceful transitions to democracy in the past few decades have come as a surprise to the West. One reason is that diplomats, academics, and policymakers generally do not pay attention to what is happening with students, workers, farmers—with the street-level society and culture of the world's not-free countries.

The people of China are obviously experiencing revolutionary change. Above all else we must maintain our faith in my compatriots that we can and will join the vast majority of the world's people who now live in free or at least partly free countries. An opening for change could come in the next few months or it may take a few more years. Of course, it will never come without collective efforts, including those from the international community. So, we must persevere and be ready and keep the faith.

"Be watchful and strong in the faith, for the time draws near," exhorted St. Paul, a persecutor of Christians who converted to the faith. Ladies and gentlemen, our time draws near. We must watch and be strong and be supportive and be ready.

SECTION XIV

SETBACKS TO FREEDOM: A CLEAR AND PRESENT DANGER

November 2017—April 2019

"The situation for Chinese human rights activists has drastically deteriorated since 2012 when Xi Jinping took power.... Xi believes that the regime security is in grave danger; all of these require the regime to take relentless and harsh measures to regain its control....Xi has taken a staunch position to resolutely oppose any Western ideals, such as 'universal values' and 'constitutional democracy,' which, according to Xi, have consistently infiltrated China to slander its socialist path. Under Xi's reign, the regime's growing sense of high insecurity and deepening alienation from its ideology and politics among young Chinese is pushing the party to put the entire population under total surveillance.

"Xi Jinping has forged a more offensive warfare with a grand strategy seeking to suppress any ideas that deviate from the CCP's thinking. Xi's recent suppression has become increasingly violent in order to keep every citizen in line with the regime's ideology."

CHAPTER 112

Overcoming Setbacks to the Advance of Democracy

Opening Remarks at the Twelfth Interethnic/ Interfaith Leadership Conference
Tokyo, Japan
November 14, 2017

Distinguished guests and friends:

Welcome to you all.

The twelfth Interethnic/Interfaith Leadership Conference has finally begun. In the course of preparing for this year's conference, we suffered the heavy blow of the tragic passing of Liu Xiaobo, and our work came to a temporary standstill. The emergence of a new dictator at the nineteenth National Congress of the Chinese Communist Party, the political left-turn of the Xi Jinping regime, its brutal suppression of freedom of speech, and its tightening control over civil society have caused this year's conference to face greater pressure than ever before.

Indeed, democracy is facing setbacks. This is not just a description of the suppressed democracy movement in powerful dictatorships like China, but also a description of the appeasing position and attitude of the world's democracies toward authoritarian regimes like the CCP.

Precisely because of this fact, the convening of this year's conference is more important than ever and poses additional challenges for us.

This is because the CCP regime—with its strong economic resources and military power, implausible political conservativeness, and determination to maintain its "Red Empire"—is implementing, both domestically and abroad, an overall strategy of divide and conquer, intimidation, and coercion; whereas, relatively speaking, our forces for freedom are scattered.

The forces for freedom that I'm referring to include, first of all, those of us who are directly promoting China's democratization, including those who are fighting for freedom for all the ethnic groups, regions, and religions that are directly related to China and represented by the participants of the Interethnic/Interfaith Leadership Conference. Faced with the powerful state apparatus of the CCP, we have no choice. Today, we must further eliminate the barriers between us through greater tolerance and understanding. We must accrue wisdom and enhance our capabilities with greater insight and determination. We must embark on an earnest path of helping each other, supporting each other, and working together in unity.

The forces for freedom to which I'm referring also include the world's democracies, especially democratic countries in Asia.

It is often said that the twenty-first century is the century of Asia. In fact, the twenty-first century is a century for everyone—whether it's good or bad will ultimately depend on each of us. The situation in Asia isn't as favorable as some prognosticators describe it. Perhaps just the opposite is true: In Asia, a tipping point of crises is nearing, which may engender global problems: North Korea's nuclear weapons program; disputes in the East China Sea, South China Sea, and Taiwan Strait; India-Pakistan tensions; the environment, population, and refugees; unpredictable political changes in China; and so on. Meanwhile, Asia lacks a multinational coalition to collectively respond to these crises, especially a coalition of democracies. We should see that the source of the most acute crisis that Asia is facing—or the difficulty of eliminating these crises—is the political tyranny in certain countries. Therefore, Asian democracies should form an alliance to fight against threats from authoritarian regimes. Japan, as Asia's most powerful democracy, should play a leadership role in the formation of such an alliance. Objectively, the formation of a regional alliance with democratic nations at its core will play a catalytic role in the democratization in China. Otherwise, an integrated Asia dominated by the CCP regime would be based on a completely different value system. Once formed, it would become a nightmare for Asian democratic countries and a further setback for the entire free world. It is no exaggeration to say that now is the critical moment that determines whether Asia is defined and triumphed by democracy or by tyranny.

Because China's growing economic strength has been used by the CCP regime to enhance, firstly, its military power, Japan faces the following reality: China is replacing Japan to become the most powerful nation in Asia, and the political philosophy of China's leaders is extremely regressive; whether domestically or abroad, it disregards any rules that are unfavorable to it. China has already become a real threat to peace in Asia. However, with China's massive size, simple military confrontation is unthinkable. Only by helping China to achieve modernization in the complete sense—i.e., political democratization—can Asia achieve real peace.

In preparing for this conference, I actively contacted and engaged in exchange with Japan's various political parties, groups, and factions. A friend of mine kindly warned me that Japan's leftist, centrist, and rightist parties each has its own position on China and that it would be wishful thinking to expect to be able to balance the parties. Admittedly, I have experienced these difficulties firsthand. However, I'm satisfied with the achievements that we have made to date. I will not give up on further efforts. While speaking at Meiji University this April, I proposed three points of China-related consensus that should be shared by each of Japan's ruling and opposition parties. Here, I want to reiterate these three points:

1. An expansive, undemocratic, and uncivilized neighboring regime is unfavorable to Japan's security and democratic lifestyle.

2. Japan's historical feelings of guilt are toward the Chinese people and should not be toward the CCP. Japan has never let down the Chinese Communist Party. Supporting democratization and the improvement of human rights conditions in China will eventually help to resolve the Chinese people's hatred toward Japan.
3. Japan is Asia's most powerful democracy and should have more self-confidence and a greater sense of moral responsibility to help democratize China.

I hope the three aforementioned points will get more people thinking.

Distinguished guests and friends, the theme of this year's conference is "Advancing Human Rights, Democracy, and Peace: New Tools, New Strategies, New Generation." In the twenty-first century, China, Japan, and Asia in its entirety need to promote the broad acceptance of human rights and democratic values in Asia and establish a permanent peace mechanism. This should be an integral part of the Interethnic/Interfaith Leadership Conference. I hope this year's conference can contribute, both in attitudes and actions, to overcoming setbacks to the advancement of global democracy.

Thank you.

CHAPTER 113

Let's Redouble Our Efforts for a Free Tibet

Speech at Human Rights Day Tibetans Rally in New York
New York, NY, United States
December10, 2017

Dear brothers and sisters:

Tashi delek.

I'm honored and humbled to have been invited to speak here today. Thank you.

Today, December 10, is Human Rights Day, a day that commemorates the anniversary of the adoption of the Universal Declaration of Human Rights by the UN General Assembly in 1948.

And it is on this date each year that the Nobel Peace Prize is awarded. In 1989, six months after the Tiananmen Massacre, the Nobel Committee bestowed the Peace Prize on His Holiness the Dalai Lama. We honor His Holiness today as a beacon of peace and for his commitment to nonviolence, religious harmony, human rights, and the Tibetan people.

His Holiness the Dalai Lama continuously reminds us to look at what unites us as human beings, not what divides us. This is also the message that the Tibetan people keep sending to the Chinese government. I deeply appreciate the fact that, despite the historical, cultural, linguistic, and ethnic differences, and despite decades of oppression, your message of His Holiness to the Chinese and indeed everyone in the world is still peace, tolerance, compassion, hope, and courage.

Despite these good-will efforts, the Chinese government ceased formal talks with the representatives of His Holiness the Dalai Lama in 2010 and continued its oppressive and cultural genocide policies in the Tibetan regions.

Just two weeks ago, on November 26, a 63-year-old Tibetan monk named Tenga self-immolated in protest of the Chinese rule. He was the 151st Tibetan to self-immolate in Tibet since 2009.

With the burning flames from Tibet, we should see the truth.

We must continue to empower the Chinese people in ending their silence on Tibet. We should make special efforts to reach out to them, to meet them with the truth, to appeal to their conscience, and to let them realize that the suffering of the Tibetan people is the suffering of the Chinese people and that the government that brings such misery to the Tibetan people is the same government that is jailing their best citizens, robbing the land from the peasants, and controlling their right to speak and think freely.

If we redouble our efforts to approach the Chinese people with tolerance, compassion, and truth, and to continue to build bridges and linkages between the two peoples, the Chinese people will be an integral part of the solution and not the problem.

We must press the democratic governments to speak the truth and commit their solidarity with the people of Tibet in words and deeds.

From my vantage point in Washington, DC, I would like to encourage those who are gathered here today to contact their representatives in the House and the Senate to urge them to cosponsor two pieces of Tibet-related legislation pending in both chambers—the Reciprocal Access to Tibet Act and a concurrent resolution on US policy toward Tibet, H.Con.Res.89.

The Reciprocal Access to Tibet bill, introduced by Representative Jim McGovern and Senator Marco Rubio, calls for access to Tibetan areas of China for US officials, journalists, and the average citizen. The bill also calls for restricting access to America for those Chinese officials responsible for blocking travel to Tibet.

H.Con.Res.89, introduced by Congresswoman Ros-Lehtinen, urges the US government to, among many other things, make the treatment of the Tibetan people an important factor in the conduct of United States relations with the People's Republic of China.

It's critically important to keep the Tibet issue alive in Washington when so many other problems and crises threaten to overwhelm it. Passage of these bills is a concrete step Congress can take to push the administration to take action, and you can play an important role by urging your members of Congress to support these bills, among other things.

The Tibetan issue is continuing to test the morality of the entire humanity, especially the world leaders' commitment to human rights. The picture has not at all been rosy. Let's continue to draw strength and inspiration from the words of His Holiness the Dalai Lama, "No matter what sort of difficulties, how painful the experience is, if we lose our hope, that's our real disaster."

Dear brothers and sisters, I draw hope from your compassion, courage, and audacity. Today, in front of so many Tibetan brothers and sisters who have gathered here, as a Chinese, I would like to announcement my recommitment to the Tibetan cause. I will continue to struggle with you shoulder to shoulder on the road to a free Tibet.

Thank you!

CHAPTER 114

Tyranny's Desperate Wars Against Fundamental Human Dignity Are Bound to Fail

Concluding Remarks at the Opening Session of Tenth Geneva Summit for Human Rights and Democracy
Geneva, Switzerland
February 19, 2018

It's wonderful to see so many old and new friends here at the tenth Geneva Summit for Human Rights and Democracy. I want to express my profound gratitude to Hillel and his terrific team for putting together just another important assembly of people's voices in the week leading to the opening of the annual session of the United Nations Human Rights Council. The camaraderie and the sharing of experiences and strategies at this summit has always given me hope, even during the darkest days for human rights when too many eyes have adjusted the shadows that power and greed cast on the existence of our brothers and sisters around the world and when what has been gained in principle, what has been recognized in fact, has been eroded by an acceptance that it is better to accommodate the evil—and hope it changes on its own—than to seek to change it through pressure, denouncement, and direct confrontation.

In this room today are human rights heroes coming from all over the world. They are brave defenders of the Universal Declaration of Human Rights (UDHR) whose seventieth anniversary this year will mark. What is best in mankind, what is most hopeful about us, are beautifully articulated in the Declaration. These are a distillation of all human experience, all the warnings and screams of our combined human history as well as the principles of light and hope by which we should organize ourselves as a human family.

But, sadly, we must ask again and again how it is that it is so readily ignored and even so casually traduced by some of its signatory states.

In the next two days, we will hear from our heroes from around the world and they will testify what becomes of us, of mankind, of our world, when these principles are ignored and how a handful of troublemakers can keep the boat of the entire humanity afloat. I think you will agree with me that they are not only defenders of the Universal Declaration of Human Rights but savers of humanity itself.

We should be grateful to these heroes for reminding us that tyranny's desperate wars against fundamental human dignity are bound to fail. History progresses and older methods of control are swept away as concentrated and illegitimate power faces increased opposition from more and more forces demanding freedom from domination, as has been most recently evidenced by protests in Iran and will surely be proved again and again by the people's struggle in China, Congo, Cuba, Iran, North Korea, Pakistan, Russia, Tibet, Turkey, Uganda, Venezuela, Vietnam, Zimbabwe, and other remaining world autocracies.

This is the promise of our time.

CHAPTER 115

Human Rights Defenders Wang Quanzhang and Yu Wensheng

Speech at the Tenth Geneva Summit for Human Rights and Democracy
Geneva, Switzerland
February 20, 2018

It's wonderful to see so many old and new friends here at the tenth Geneva Summit for Human Rights and Democracy, and it is an honor to speak at the gathering again this year. And I am proud that my organization, Citizen Power Initiatives for China, is a partner of the Geneva Summit. The camaraderie and the sharing of experiences and strategies at this summit has always given me hope, even during the darkest days of the Chinese Communist Party's (CCP) autocratic rule.

This year marks the seventieth anniversary of the Universal Declaration of Human Rights (UDHR), and the twentieth anniversary of China's signing of the International Covenant on Civil and Political Rights (ICCPR), which, after two decades, it still has not ratified. I have spoken several times in the past at this summit about the CCP's utter disregard for the human rights of people in China—the Han, Tibetans, Uyghurs, Southern Mongolians, and other ethnic groups—despite the government's rhetoric here at the UN Human Rights Council about how human rights are protected by the Chinese constitution along with many other laws and regulations. It's simply not the case. I've also spoken in the past about the CCP's relentless crackdown on human rights defenders, lawyers, and ordinary citizens who attempt to seek redress for rights violations. The CCP quashes them all, and thus demonstrates its utter disregard for international human rights domestically, as well as its own laws that purport to protect the rights of Chinese citizens.

As the CCP becomes bolder and more aggressive in the international arena, it is actively promoting its "human rights with Chinese characteristics" in Geneva and threatening the exercise and protection of human rights protections in other countries. Governments, NGOs, activists, the media, and concerned citizens must pay closer attention to what China is doing here at the UN and in countries around the world: from Australia and New Zealand, to Sri Lanka, Zimbabwe, and the United States. Its "sharp power" is being felt everywhere, and we must push back against it. If we turn a blind eye, we do so at our peril. Freedom and democracy are in crisis, and China is playing a key role in this global turn-away from human rights.

Nowhere is the CCP's attack on human rights more keenly felt than in China itself. Put simply, there is essentially no freedom left to peacefully advocate for change in China. In the latest example, in mid-January 2018, a Beijing-based human rights lawyer, Yu Wensheng, while walking his son to school, was seized by more than twelve police officers and surrounded by at least four police cars and a SWAT team. Yu had publicly called for political reform and criticized Xi Jinping and the CCP for its ongoing crackdown on human rights lawyers and defenders, which began in early July 2015. Chinese authorities detained him for exercising his fundamental human right to peacefully express his views on politics and reform and charged him with the serious crime of "subversion." Days before Yu was seized, authorities revoked his lawyer's license.

Among Yu's clients was another Beijing-based human rights lawyer who will be the focus of my remarks today—Wang Quanzhang.

Wang Quanzhang has been held incommunicado by the Chinese government for more than two and a half years. Authorities seized Wang on August 3, 2015, in a sweep of human rights lawyers and defenders that resulted in the detentions and interrogations of over 300 human rights lawyers and defenders. This unprecedented attack is called the "709 Crackdown" because the first disappearances and detentions occurred on July 9, 2015. Many of the 709 lawyers and defenders have since been released, and all of them have been accounted for, except one: Wang Quanzhang. On January 8, 2016, Wang was formally arrested and charged with subversion and subsequently indicted on February 14, 2017. He is reportedly being held at Tianjin No. 2 Detention Center. But his wife, Li Wenzu, an effective and fierce advocate for her husband, has not been permitted to see him despite countless trips to Tianjin to visit him. Nor have his lawyers been able to meet with him. As mentioned earlier, one of Wang's lawyers, Yu Wensheng, had also been unsuccessful in his efforts to meet with Wang despite repeated attempts and now, like Wang, is himself detained and similarly charged with subversion.

Wang has undoubtedly been put under immense pressure to publicly "confess" or otherwise admit guilt. He has steadfastly refused and remains detained, incommunicado, and without a trial date. Released 709 lawyers and defenders, or their family members, have given harrowing accounts of torture in detention. It is very likely that Wang is being tortured. We have no idea what his condition is. Indeed, we don't even know if he is alive. His wife, Li Wenzu, is constantly harassed and intimidated by the police, and she herself has been detained briefly. The couple has a young son, a toddler, who hasn't seen his father for over 900 days.

Born on February 15, 1976, in a rural area of Shandong province, Wang Quanzhang has represented a wide range of clients and taken on many "sensitive" cases since graduating from Shandong University Law School in 2000. He stayed in Jinan, Shandong, after graduation, working in legal aid and giving free lectures to villagers on Chinese law relating to issues relevant to their lives, such as rural land rights. Wang received many threats because of his work and eventually decided to leave Jinan. He moved to Beijing in 2008.

At the time of his detention in August 2015, Wang practiced law with the Fengrui Law Firm. Wang has been a particularly brave advocate in the rights defense movement, representing Falun Gong practitioners as well as other persecuted human rights defenders, such as housing rights activist Ni Yulan and the journalist Qi Chonghuai. In recent years, Wang focused increasingly on cases involving freedom of religion and belief and took on more and more clients who were practitioners of Falun Gong, a spiritual practice that is outlawed in China; such cases are known to be particularly "sensitive," and many human rights lawyers have steered clear of them because of the high risk involved.

Before Wang was detained in the 709 Crackdown, he had previously been harassed, beaten, and detained by Chinese authorities. In April 2013, for example, police took Wang into custody in a courtroom in Jiangsu province, while he was in the middle of providing a vigorous defense of his client, a Falun Gong practitioner, and given a ten-day term of "judicial detention." This was reportedly a first, and many human rights lawyers and rights defenders from around the country came to his defense, launching a protest outside the courthouse, which resulted in Wang's early release from "judicial detention."

In July 2015, before Wang was taken away, he wrote a letter to his parents in which he expressed his commitment to the work he had chosen to do—indeed, was called to do—and asked for their understanding and trust. He wrote: "I have never abandoned the qualities Father and Mother instilled in me: honesty, kindheartedness, integrity. In all these years, I have used these principles to guide my life. Even though I've often been steeped in despair, I have never given up thoughts for a better future."

Wang closed his letter to his parents with these words: "Dear Father and Mother, please feel proud of me. Also, no matter how horrible the environment is, you must hang on and live, and wait for the day when the clouds will disperse and the sun will come out."

Today, we meet on the eve of the first Human Rights Council session in 2018, a year marking the seventieth anniversary of the Universal

Declaration on Human Rights, the twentieth anniversary of China's signing of the ICCPR, and the twentieth anniversary of the Declaration on Human Rights Defenders. These human rights instruments, among others, protect the fundamental human rights of advocates like human rights lawyers Wang Quanzhang and Yu Wensheng—including their right to freedom of expression and freedom from torture and arbitrary detention. The Chinese government, in these cases and countless others, are making a mockery of the international human rights framework and system and are also violating its domestic laws that purportedly protect certain fundamental rights, including the right to freedom of expression and the right not to be arbitrarily detained.

China must be held to account. A submission has been made on Wang Quanzhang's behalf to the UN Working Group on Arbitrary Detention. We all eagerly await the Working Group's decision. And in November of this year, China will undergo its third Universal Periodic Review (UPR). For the UPR, I urge governments, NGOs, and citizen activists to raise the case of Wang Quanzhang and the other lawyers and defenders who were swept up in the 709 Crackdown and demand that China release them. Another point to stress during the UPR: It has been twenty years since China signed the ICCPR. China must be held accountable for the inexplicable delay in ratifying this key human rights treaty and should be urged to ratify it now.

Thank you very much for your kind attention.

CHAPTER 116

The Two Tank Men

TEDx Talk at Carnegie Mellon University
Pittsburgh, PA, United States
April 1, 2018

This photograph of the Tank Man is one of the most famous images of the twentieth century. It was taken during the 1989 Tiananmen Massacre.

Who was this Tank Man? No one knows. For nearly thirty years, people have wondered what became of him, but his identity and his fate are still a mystery.

This mystery lingers primarily because the Chinese government has made every effort to suppress the truth about what happened at Tiananmen. To this day, people in China who dare to remember face brutal persecution.

Just after the massacre, the Chinese government tried to use this photo as evidence that the military's response to the student demonstrators had been restrained. The regime praised the military's actions and called the demonstrators "thugs."

But the world was not fooled.

Part of the immediate power of this image was not just that it showed one man standing vulnerable in front of a column of tanks but also that the whole world knew about the events that had preceded this moment. The Tank Man had survived a massacre. And yet here he was, still risking his life.

I was a student protester in Tiananmen Square when the massacre began. A friend and I arrived in the square late on the night of June

3, just as the gunshots began. At one point, my friend and I were so close to the soldiers that we could shout up to them in their trucks and tell them not to shoot. We told them they had no idea what was going on here, and we tried to touch their hearts by singing songs that every Chinese would know. But when they received the order, they just opened fire.

I witnessed many people killed, including eleven students who were chased and run over by tanks on the morning of June 4th. I spent much of that day carrying bodies to the hospital with my friend.

The Tank Man photo was taken the next day, on June 5th, while the massacre was still going on.

By any measure, this picture is an image of heroism. But how many heroes do we see?

Nearly nine years after the picture was taken, the writer Pico Iyer said:

"The heroes of the tank picture are two: the unknown figure who risked his life by standing in front of the juggernaut and the driver who rose to the moral challenge by refusing to mow down his compatriot."

Not only did the second Tank Man, the driver, refuse to kill, he undoubtedly disobeyed orders and risked—and perhaps received—punishment in the service of a countryman's life.

Victimized by the same regime, these two heroic Tank Men remind us that those who stand opposite us are not necessarily our enemies. Common sense, conscience, and humanity can prevail, even under brutal circumstances.

I unfortunately lost sight of this truth during an extreme moment.

After watching troops kill people on June 4th, I saw a young soldier on Chang'an Avenue standing all by himself. He wasn't wearing a helmet, and he didn't have a gun. He looked just like a teenager.

The people I was with chased him because they were sad and angry. I gave him a punch. More and more people gathered around him and beat him. When the crowd knocked him to the ground, he yelled: "I didn't do it! I didn't shoot!"

I realized that a tragedy was taking place. But it was too late to stop the violence. I left the scene without looking back. A few minutes later, I knew from the loud shouts behind me that he'd been killed, and I began to cry.

Like all the other soldiers, that teenager had been *forced* to come to Beijing to massacre protesting students and civilians. Like us, he was powerless to stop the tragedy. Out of conscience, he had probably refused to kill, choosing instead to be a deserter. If so, he was a hero, too. A Tank Man in the opposite camp.

But I was not.

I let anger get the better of me. I had seen fellow students crushed beneath tanks. I had seen people whose only crime was calling for a democratic future shot and killed just three feet away from me. So, when I saw this soldier, I saw him *only* as my enemy, and I punched him. This might be the biggest sin of my life. I can't imagine the pain he suffered when he was dying or what was on his mind as he was being killed by an angry and frightened mob.

For nearly thirty years I have been mourning him. I think about his family, and I still look to a day when I find them and share my guilt.

Heroic feats often happen in moments that go unnoticed. In June of 1989, the streets of Beijing witnessed many Chinese like the Tank Man, standing face to face with soldiers who were killing. And on those streets, there were also some soldiers, like the second Tank Man, and like the deserter, who opposed the orders to kill.

Remembering this, I am convinced that no matter how difficult the road ahead, the direction of China's future must be toward freedom and democracy. The natural human desires for dignity and freedom that serve as the foundation of all democratic movements are not only present in dissidents. They exist in everyone.

Although the Chinese communist regime has become increasingly unwilling to reform, and although China's leader has recently assumed the role of "president for life," many within the system do not wish to stand in the way of history.

There are always those who will refuse to betray their consciences. Any police or military officer, anyone in the authoritarian state machinery, can be a hero if they are willing to "raise their guns an inch higher" when ordered to carry out an act of suppression. Their names may be unknown, but they, like the two Tank Men, and like the teenage soldier, will be heroes of the historical process.

I started by saying that we still don't know who the Tank Man is or what happened to him. And the same is true of the second Tank Man. But I don't think we should ever stop looking for any of them. Because there are always Tank Men all around us.

And if we know this, perhaps we might find it easier, when the times call for it, to aspire to what is best in us, to look to our own reserves of courage and compassion and try to be Tank Men ourselves.

CHAPTER 117

Red China and Red Notices

Opening Remarks at the Twelfth International Journalism Festival
Perugia, Italy
April 14, 2018

Human rights in China under Xi Jinping is the worst since the Tiananmen crackdown. The situation for the Chinese human rights activists is drastically deteriorating since 2012 when Xi Jinping took power.

Xi is convinced that the Chinese Communist Party is losing control over the Chinese people and the Chinese society, and particularly in the ideological front, despite numerous political campaigns to brainwash the Chinese people, particularly the young; Xi believes that the regime security is in a grave danger; all of these require the regime to take relentless and harsh measures to regain its control.

More than previous leaders before him, Xi perceives that the Western ideas and bourgeois liberalization spread via the internet eroded the minds of young people and that the foreign reactionary forces' peaceful evolution become a real threat, which has fundamentally undermined the Communist Party's rule.

Therefore, Xi has taken a staunch position to resolutely oppose any Western ideals, such as "universal values" and "constitutional democracy," which, according to Xi, *have consistently infiltrated China to slander its socialist path.* Under Xi's reign, the regime's growing sense of high insecurity and deepening alienation from its ideology and politics among young Chinese is pushing the party to put the entire population under a total surveillance.

In the past, the Chinese regime often took a defensive position against democratic values and ideas, but today, Xi Jinping has forged a more offensive warfare with a grand strategy seeking to suppress any ideas that deviate from the CCP's thinking. Xi's recent suppression has become increasingly violent in order to keep every citizen in line with the regime's ideology.

Xi targeted the country's liberal-minded leaders, public intellectuals, and university professors and later, Xi sought after human rights lawyers, who were subsequently rounded up, forced to disappear, detained, arrested, sentenced, tortured, and sometimes even killed. There is an emerging pattern of deaths of activists in prisons and released on medical parole. Retribution is also handed out to activists' family members. At the same time, Xi has launched a "content clean-up campaign" to remove and ban information the regime deems to be "harmful." Xi's repression against minority groups has also been ratcheted up. Today, there exists no space for dissenting voices or any rights advocacy NGOs in China.

While Xi is relentlessly repressing the dissent inside China, his offensive and overreach exceed far beyond China's border. The regime has been creating new international norms, such as "a Community with a Shared Future for Mankind," core socialist values, and subverting UN efforts to protect human rights, with the aim of globally expanding the regime's political and economic model.

China's rising global presence and aggressive expansion of commerce, grabbing global natural resources, and rapid military deployment has far-reaching implications for the post-cold war world order.

For example, China now bought and built forty-nine ports in nineteen countries with critical geopolitical locations, which include Greece, Myanmar, Israel, Djibouti, Morocco, Spain, Italy, Belgium, Côte d'Ivoire, Egypt, and other countries.

China exports corruption worldwide to gain foreign political and economic influence. For example, former Hong Kong Secretary for Home Affairs Patrick Ho Chi-ping was accused of offering bribes worth a total of US $2.9 million to prominent African leaders and ministers. A US federal court in New York has brought corruption charges against him, and he was arrested in January.

China has deeply infiltrated into the US to influence American policies. Investigative writer Peter Schweizer revealed in his new book, *Secret Empires: How the American Political Class Hides Corruption and Enriches Family and Friends*, that China is gaining influence over American policymakers by directly and indirectly funding thousands of free congressional trips to China using the legislative loopholes, one of which is the exemption of foreign-financed cultural exchange trips, making oversight of exchange trips for congressional staff fall into a bureaucratic no man's land. The regime often showers the congressional members and staff with gifts, cuisine food, entertainments, and more, while staying in luxury hotels.

Since the 1990s, China has been secretly funding US political campaigns, perhaps much worse than Russia.

The Chinese regime is gaining foreign influence by spying on the world. Examples include big data collected globally through Chinese companies and a huge espionage network. French newspaper *Le Monde* reported that China donated the African Union headquarters in the Ethiopian capital of Addis Ababa and also donated the AU's computer network at the AU, but it allegedly inserted a backdoor that allowed it to transfer confidential data.

China's global kidnapping campaign also shows its increasing global influence. This program has gone on for years under the disguise of anti-corruption. The regime has launched two programs, code-named "Skynet" and "Fox Hunt," supposedly to target corrupt Chinese officials living abroad, but in effect it aims at kidnapping Chinese citizens that the regime doesn't like.

The regime's Central Commission on Discipline and Inspection reported to have repatriated more than 3,000 individuals since Xi Jinping took power in late 2012. In 2016 alone, the Skynet caught and took

1,032 Chinese back to China, among them 134 government officials and nineteen people on the Interpol Red Notice.

In order to assert its global influence, China is actively seeking leadership in many international organizations. For example, China has been politicizing Interpol and using it to kidnap and repatriate Chinese citizens in the name of anti-corruption and anti-terrorism. In the past, Interpol's constitution has emphasized respect for human rights and the principle of political neutrality in its actions against suspected terrorists, criminals, and fugitives. But politicized decisions in recent years have seriously damaged its credibility.

Interpol is helping Beijing's dictators to repress and persecute political dissidents and human rights activists through issuing Red Notices, essentially international arrest warrants. Since Xi's coming to power in 2012, Interpol has issued about 200 Red Notices a year at the request of Beijing, and many of these Red Notices requested by China are "politically motivated."

In November 2016, Meng Hongwei, a deputy minister of China's Public Security, a notorious human rights abuser, became the first Chinese president of the Interpol, allowing Beijing to further manipulate and abuse the system from within the organization. There is no due process for appeals and for accountability, and no procedures to prevent wrongful arrests and extradition.

NGO Fair Trials' study shows that these politically motivated Red Notices have often led to the wrongful detention of many innocent victims who are at risk of torture and other ill-treatment. Victims of Red Notices have lost their jobs or their assets and bank accounts and face travel bans, greatly disrupting their life. However, Interpol's constitution prohibits any intervention or activities of a "political, military, religious, or racial character."

If the international community continues to allow the Chinese regime to use Interpol as a repressive tool, the organization will lose all of its credibility. We must demand a reform of this much abused and politically motivated Red Notice system. Credible evidence must be provided when requesting a Red Notice and fair process to challenge the Red Notice must be in place and accessible.

While Xi has become the most powerful leader since Mao Zedong, the country has fallen into one of the darkest and most expansionistic moments in its modern history.

CHAPTER 118

The Spirit of Tiananmen Continues to Change China

Speech at the Candlelight Vigil Commemorating the Twenty-Ninth Anniversary of 1989 Tiananmen Square Massacre
Washington, DC, United States
June 3, 2018

Thank you, Marion, for your kind introduction.

First, I want to express my profound gratitude to Dr. Edwards, Marion, and the entire VOC team for putting together this memorial.

I would also like to recognize the Tiananmen veterans and survivors of the Tiananmen Massacre who are present: Fang Zheng, Zhou Fengsuo, Li Hengqing, Wu Chaoyang, and Wang Dao.

Ladies and gentlemen, dear friends, I am honored and humbled to stand together with you tonight to remember our brothers and sisters who were killed in the Tiananmen Massacre.

In the spring of 1989, college students in China led a movement calling for freedom and democracy. They asked for more transparency and less corruption from their government. Their peaceful protest soon gained widespread support, attracting intellectuals, journalists, and labor leaders. Millions of people in Beijing joined them, and almost all classes of Chinese society—from all over China—sympathized with their aims.

On the night of June 3, 1989, PLA tanks and troops swept into the square and opened fire on students.

Tiananmen was an event that changed my life and the lives of many others. I was at Tiananmen when the tanks rolled in. I had been studying Mathematics at UC Berkeley when I went back to China to join the student movement. On June 4th, I saw my countrymen crushed beneath tank treads and felled by machine-gun fire. I was among the lucky who survived and escaped. I managed to avoid arrest and returned to the United States.

Since that day, I have committed my life to fighting for a China that will not ride roughshod over the fundamental human rights of its people.

The demonstrations of 1989 were an expression of a spirit that has always been present in the people of China—a spirit that is present in all of humanity. The struggle that began in Tiananmen Square twenty-nine years ago continues today. It gave birth to an era of the rise of human rights consciousness among the Chinese people. For the first time in history, the Chinese government faced massive international criticism for its human rights record. Rising dissent at home and pressure from abroad have together helped bring about significant developments in the area of human rights, though much work remains to be done.

Tonight, I ask you to help ensure that the spirit of Tiananmen continues to change China. The noble souls of the Chinese people who died in the crackdown are not yet fully honored—not because so many are unknown but because the goals of their sacrifice are still suppressed by the CCP regime. Those of us here know that honoring our fallen brothers and sisters with words alone falls terribly short if we do not bring those words to life by honoring them equally with deeds worthy of their sacrifice. We must persist in our efforts to replace lies with truth, atrocity with humanity, and tyranny with democracy. Let us stand together with those many, many individuals in China who bravely put themselves forward as obstacles against the forces of autocracy. Their fight is our fight, and we need only repay their courage with our love, support, and unified engagement to see their victory through to its rightful end: a just and free China.

Thank you.

CHAPTER 119

Jointly Counter Fascism with Chinese Characteristics

Opening Remarks at the Thirteenth Interethnic/ Interfaith Leadership Conference
Washington, DC, United States
December 10, 2018

Distinguished guests, dear friends, brothers and sisters:

Seventy years ago today, the Universal Declaration of Human Rights was born in the aftermath of World War II. It embodies our most cherished principles and aspirations. It recognizes that "the inherent dignity and the equal and inalienable rights of all members of the human family is the foundation of freedom, justice, and peace in the world" and that everyone is entitled to these rights, "without distinction of any kind, such as race, color, sex, language, religion, political or other opinion, national or social origin, property, birth or other status."

Today, along with people around the world, we reaffirm our respect for these principles and also our determination to ensure that all people can enjoy human rights and political freedom.

For the people represented at this conference, this is no joyous anniversary: For seventy years, the full life of the Declaration, the Chinese state has egregiously abused its principles, as fully one-fourth of mankind have been condemned to live under the yoke of the Chinese communist regime.

Over these seven decades, the loss and suffering at the hands of this regime has been unspeakable. But the people from all groups have never stopped struggling for the goals enshrined in the Declaration and have taken important steps toward these goals in this generation.

Ten years ago, a milestone in the struggle emerged—brave Chinese citizens led by Liu Xiaobo published Charter 08, which details nineteen specific recommendations for peaceful constitutional reform. Charter 08 is not only an indigenous and unequivocal call for democratic reform, it is also a roadmap for achieving it. It is the basis for dialogue among all societal groups, including the state.

This was a ray of light in a country shrouded in darkness.

But ten years later, this ray of light is covered by even darker clouds. China under Xi Jinping is showing all aspects of a fascist state. Xi Jinping's fascism is a real, clear, and present danger to free societies everywhere. Seventy years ago, the crimes of Nazi Germany led the international community to embrace the principle of universal human rights, but today similar patterns have emerged in China. A single, all-powerful party, one paramount leader, total control over all media, military aggression abroad, brutal suppression of dissent, creation of fictional external threats and enemies, and jingoism and strident nationalism masquerading as foreign policy. After the Holocaust of the Jewish people under Hitler we vowed "never again." But among post-war atrocities that belie that pledge, we today must add the "reeducation" concentration camps where more than one million people, one tenth of the Uyghurs, are detained. This is a mature fascism combined with communism, crony-capitalism, and an Orwellian 1984 digital totalitarianism. I call it the Fascism with Chinese Characteristics.

How can this have happened? There are, of course, many explanations. Allow me to emphasize two.

First, we, the freedom forces of various ethnic, religious, and regional groups, are not sufficiently united. As a result, we have not yet formed viable homegrown democratic movements, which has been a major goal of this Interethnic/Interfaith Leadership Conference ever since it started eighteen years ago. We must thus continue to build trust and solidarity through the joint efforts in our human rights and democracy work.

Second, too many world leaders, seeking security and economic benefits, have grown inured to the Chinese state's abuse of our brothers and sisters. And yet, there are still many democratic leaders who understand the Fascism with Chinese Characteristics is the biggest threat to world peace, the international economic order, and their own democratic way of life. So, it is in the interest of both the people under the yoke of the CCP regime and the world's democracies to push for a democratic transition in China.

But we must do more to energize this process. I hereby ask you to join me in calling on the United States to end the compartmentalization of human rights and begin to engage China with moral and strategic clarity.

In particular, I advocate that Congress pass a binding China Democracy Act flatly stating that enhancing human rights and democratic transition in China is decidedly in America's national interest and directing the federal government and all its agencies to make democracy and human rights advocacy the core of all engagement with China.

Such an Act will serve as America's grand strategy toward China, setting a firm foundation that guides US activities with China in all spheres. It will send an unequivocal message to the people there: We want you to enjoy freedom; that is our goal.

Seventy years ago, political leaders and civil society rose to the challenge of their times and promulgated the Universal Declaration of Human Rights. Surely, we, with their work as our foundation, with our united effort and with the support of the world's democracies like the United States, can rise to the most daunting challenge of our own times—that is to defeat the Fascism with Chinese Characteristics and ensure freedom for us all.

Thank you.

CHAPTER 120

To Tibetan Brothers and Sisters

Speech at Rally Commemorating the Sixtieth Anniversary of the Tibetan National Uprising
Dharamsala, India
March 10, 2019

Your Holiness the Dalai Lama, your Honorable Mr. President Lobsang Sangay, dear brothers and sisters:

Tashi delek.

What an honor to be with all of you on this special day.

Sixty years ago today, the Tibetan people rose up against the occupation of the Chinese communist regime at a time when their culture, religion, property, indeed, their very existence was being seriously threatened. His Holiness the Dalai Lama was forced into exile as the uprising was brutally suppressed. The CCP turned Tibet into a "hell on earth." The sufferings the people of Tibet have endured in the past sixty years at the hands of the CCP are almost unparalleled in the history of mankind.

But the Tibetan people, under the guidance of His Holiness both in and outside Tibet, have never given up hope. They have never stopped their struggle for beliefs, national identity, and freedom. Their courage, tenacity, and sacrifices have won them worldwide respect and admiration.

Despite being without land, army, or police, the 150,000 Tibetans in exile, under the leadership of His Holiness and the Central Tibetan Administration, have built dozens of settlements around the world. While maintaining their shared memories and beliefs, they have developed the miracle of a highly cohesive spiritual state, which includes all Tibetans. Going beyond mere survival, they have reached out to people around the world, presenting an image of tolerance, loving-kindness open-mindedness, and optimism while embracing universal values and implementing democratic practices, putting to shame those who rely on violence to pursue their goals.

Today, Tibet remains under occupation of the CCP empire. The dire situation in Tibet is a challenge to the conscience of mankind, especially that of the Chinese people. It is our privilege, as Chinese, to join you in standing united for Tibet.

As we commemorate the sixtieth anniversary of the Tibetan National Uprising, we reaffirm our gratitude to our Tibetan brothers and sisters for their long-term brotherhood, friendship, and spiritual inspiration. We recommit ourselves to respect and defend the Tibetans' right to determine their own destiny, supporting the Middle Way Approach advocated by His Holiness and passed by the Tibetan People's Assembly to resolve the Tibetan issue.

Today, we honor our brotherhood, friendship, and solidarity with the people of Tibet by redoubling our efforts on their behalf. We will walk every step together with His Holiness on the way home, and we will continue to fight side by side with our Tibetan brothers and sisters for their religious, cultural, and political freedom.

Free Tibet.

Thank you.

CHAPTER 121

Presentation Speech for Courage Award to Dhondup Wangchen

Geneva Summit 2019
Geneva, Switzerland
March 27, 2019

It has been an honor to be a part of the Geneva Summit over the past decade. Our annual assembly is a unique event, held in parallel with the UN Human Rights Council, which ensures that critical voices from oppressive regimes across the globe have a forum to stand up and speak truth to power.

Today we have heard inspiring testimonies by courageous men and women from around the world. They put their lives on the line to defend human dignity, freedom, and equality in their countries of origin.

We meet at a time when the Chinese government's repression is at an all-time high. And this month marks the sixtieth anniversary of the Tibetan National Uprising. It is fitting, therefore, that this year's award goes to a human rights hero who risked everything to shine a light on the abuses of the Chinese Communist Party in Tibet.

Dhondup Wangchen is a Tibetan filmmaker who showed extraordinary courage when he exposed the reality of Tibetan life under Chinese rule through his ground-breaking documentary, *Leaving Fear Behind.* This twenty-five-minute film was described by *The New York Times* as "an unadorned indictment of the Chinese government."

The story of Dhondup Wangchen began in 2006 when he and Golog Jigme thought to create a documentary. They interviewed ordinary

Tibetan people on their views of the Dalai Lama and of the Chinese government in the year leading up to the 2008 Beijing Olympics.

Anticipating potential reprisals by the Chinese government, Dhondup Wangchen moved his wife, Lhamo Tso, to India, together with their four children, before creating the film.

In the winter of 2007–2008, Dhondup Wangchen traveled through remote areas of eastern Tibet to conduct 108 detailed interviews. He collected thirty-five hours of footage over the course of five months. He did all of this with only a cheap video camera and no professional training in journalism or filmmaking.

After the footage was smuggled out to his cousin in Switzerland for editing and production, *Leaving Fear Behind* was released on August 6, 2008—days before the start of the Olympics.

But at that point, Dhondup Wangchen, along with Golog Jigme, had already been in secret detention since the end of March for subversion charges related to the documentary. After several interrogations and torture while in detention, Dhondup Wangchen was sentenced to six years in prison by Chinese authorities.

Following his release from prison, Dhondup Wangchen was kept under heavy surveillance. In December 2017, he finally fled Tibet for an "arduous and risky" escape to the United States, where he was granted asylum and currently resides.

Since he escaped from Chinese surveillance about one year ago, Dhondup Wangchen has continued to speak out against gross human rights violations committed by the government. He has said, "Tibet is a prison. Every year, the conditions get worse. More restrictions on traveling, practicing religion and culture, and severe limits on freedom of the press."

Against this backdrop, our honoree's critical efforts to expose China's abuses, despite severe risks for himself and his family, have become that much more important.

To so many Tibetans, Dhondup Wangchen's work allowed the truth of Chinese violations in Tibet to reach the rest of the world at a time when Beijing was in the international spotlight for the Olympic games. By giving a voice to the voiceless, Wangchen truly exemplifies the values of the Geneva Summit for Human Rights and Democracy.

For all of these reasons, I am proud to present the 2019 Geneva Summit Courage Award to Dhondup Wangchen. As the inscription reads: "For inspiring the world with your extraordinary courage in the defense of freedom, democracy, and universal human rights."

Dhondup Wangchen, please come forward.

CHAPTER 122

Supporting the Uyghur Human Rights Policy Act and UIGHUR Act

Speech at Rally Supporting Human Rights for Uyghurs
Washington, DC, United States
April 6, 2019

Dear brothers and sisters,

Today, we are gathering in brotherhood. Our Uyghur brothers and sisters are suffering severely under the yoke of Fascism with Chinese Characteristics. Seventy years ago, after the Holocaust of the Jewish people under Hitler, we vowed "never again." But among post-war atrocities that belie that pledge, we today must add the "reeducation" concentration camps where more than 1.5 million Uyghurs are detained.

Dear brothers and sisters, the 1.5 million are not numbers. They are human beings. They are not only human beings, they are parents; they are sons and daughters; they are husbands and wives; they are brothers and sisters. They are not 3146 and 4257, they are Aygul and Alim, a beautiful young Uyghur woman and a handsome young Uyghur man.

Today our conscience and morality are being challenged and judged, yes challenged and judged by our ability to see the suffering of others and do everything possible in our capacity to help end it.

In DC, there are a few places we must know. The Holocaust Museum is one of them. It speaks to the evil darkness into which we are capable of descending. But there are other places that, on the opposite, speak to the ideals of mankind: the Jefferson Memorial, the Lincoln Memorial and, of course, Capitol Hill. Today we look up once again to the highest palace of democracy, the US Congress, to demand its swift passage of the pending bipartisan legislations, the Uyghur Human Rights Policy Act and the Uighur Intervention and Global Humanitarian Unified Response (UIGHUR) Act.

We must not forget DC is the capital of the most powerful democracy on earth. I would like you to join me in urging the Trump administration to put on the sanction list, under the Global Magnitsky Human Rights Accountability Act, Chen Quanguo, the current Communist Party Secretary of the Xinjiang Uyghur Autonomous Region, also known as East Turkestan, for his gross violations of human rights.

Upon thinking of the Holocaust in today's context, I want to recommit myself, and would like to invite all of you to do so, that we will never be the next people to look away in the face of atrocity.

SECTION XV

CALLING ON AMERICA: SHINE THE LIGHT OF FREEDOM

May 2019—September 2019

"The trade deal under negotiation is not a deal between two similar systems seeking closer ties. Rather, this is a fundamental clash between two radically different economic models, which are deeply rooted in differing and even conflicting values and beliefs. Put it simply: Ultimately, it is not about money but value. The United States was built on the cornerstone of values. From the Mayflower Compact to the Declaration of Independence; from the Constitution to Lincoln's Gettysburg address to Reagan's 'Tear down this wall,' the United States of America was guided by ideals and faith every step of the way. These idealistic qualities have not only ensured stability and prosperity at the national level but also inspired the creativity and potential of Americans at the individual level. If the idealism and belief in American values were taken away, the United States would lose its soul, the fundamental driving force that made America great in the first place."

CHAPTER 123

To Make America Great Again: Lincoln and Reagan Standing as Shining Examples for President Trump and the American People to Follow

Speech at Skagit County Republican Party Lincoln/Reagan Day Dinner
Skagit, WA, United States
May 11, 2019

Good evening. Thank you, Jacquelin, for your kind introduction. What an honor to be in the company of you and Mr. Davidson speaking at this Lincoln/Reagan Dinner. Lincoln and Reagan are definitely among the American presidents I admire most. They are both liberators.

President Lincoln not only freed the slaves but saved the Union, not only saved the Union but saved it "in the purity of its principles," that is, in the principles of democracy, liberty, and equality.

On June 12, 1987, President Reagan stood just 100 yards away from the Berlin Wall and uttered some of the most unforgettable words of his presidency: "Mr. Gorbachev, tear down this wall." It also stood as a vivid symbol of the battle between communism and democracy that divided Berlin, Germany, and the entire European continent. His vision and guts helped the free world win the Cold War and defeated communism in Europe.

Few of you in this room know what it feels like to be blessed with freedom after living under the oppression of socialism and communism.

When the Venezuelan military vehicles drove into a crowd of civilians about two weeks ago, I was reminded of the horrors of the Chinese tanks running over students in the Tiananmen Massacre, whose thirtieth anniversary we will commemorate next month. The dictators have done in Venezuela all of the similar things that the dictators have done in China. Be it socialism with Chinese characteristics or Venezuelan characteristics. The results have been catastrophic. I have a first-hand understanding of these catastrophes.

I was born three years before the Cultural Revolution. At an early age, the unspeakable sufferings that most families had at the hands of the communist dictatorship, including mine, made me disenchanted with the Communist Party. However, I was enticed into joining the Party with the idea of reforming it from within. This all changed when I returned from my PhD studies in the US to join thousands of my fellow students in Beijing as Chinese army tanks rolled across Tiananmen Square on the morning of June 4, 1989. Luckier than most of my fellow students, I narrowly escaped the massacre and the ensuing arrests and returned to the United States. While I continued my studies, I immersed myself in the work advancing human rights and democracy in China. In the Party's eyes, the former young communist star had now become a public enemy. I became *persona non grata*, a traitor, prohibited from entering the country. But in the spring of 2002, I decided to defy the ban. In China's industrial northeast, thousands of workers were taking to the streets, protesting the destitution brought on by government-exploiting policies. Sensing an opportunity to forge bonds between democracy leaders and grassroots activists, I entered China using a borrowed passport and forged ID card.

For two weeks I met with exploited construction laborers, expropriated farmers, and striking workers, documenting their grievances and the condition of their lives and helping them with nonviolent struggle strategies. But as I attempted to slip out of China across the Burmese border, my fake ID was spotted, and I found myself in the hands of the security police.

I was detained for five years. Much of those years I spent in solitary confinement. My mental condition deteriorated beneath endless isolation, repeated interrogations, and ongoing psychological and physical torture. I prayed and prayed to God for understanding of his purpose on me and for spiritual strength to sustain. I resorted to composing poems in my head and committing them to memory as a means of maintaining my sanity. Nearing a breakdown, I grasped onto my innermost resources of belief, imagination, and will to fend off insanity and find a reason to live. "Am I wrong?" I asked myself with a tinge of regret. But I repeated a thought experiment: imagining myself taking a copy of the Universal Declaration of Human Rights, arbitrarily choosing anyone on the Chinese street, showing them the document, asking them with the language they understand whether they want the rights listed there. Would anybody say "no"? Of course not. Nobody wants to be a slave. In this regard, the Chinese people are no different than any other people in the world. The thirst for freedom and dignity is indeed universal. I drew strength and inspiration from this first order of fact.

I also thought of my fallen brothers and sisters in Tiananmen Square. I reassured myself that freedom is not free. Freedom must be earned. It was not free for those who paid with their lives. It is certainly not free for those of us who, while still blessed with our lives, have yet to complete the mission for which these brave students gave their lives and their freedom. I must not give up!

To make a long story short, in 2007, thanks to the overwhelming support from America, I was freed, returned to the US, and recommitted myself to the hard work to advance human rights and democracy in China.

We were asked by American friends after Tiananmen: "Yes, we believe in the universality of democracy and freedom, but other than that, why should we care about whether, and how fast, China becomes democratic?"

My answer was simple. "If China is allowed to continue its path of economic growth and military buildup under a one-party dictatorship, it will pose a serious threat to the security and economic interest of America and even its very democratic way of life."

Unfortunately, what I said nearly thirty years has become a reality today.

China has been waging economic war against industrial democracies ever since America allowed it a normal trade status, and now China has emerged as the greatest economic and national security threat the United States has ever faced. America is running the largest trade deficit with China, $350 billion annually. We must not forget China's human rights deficit has contributed largely to America's trade deficit with China. Low human rights is a big advantage for China in trading with free market economies just like the slavery system was an advantage for the South in trading with the North before the Civil War.

China is serving as a model for dictators and juntas. In fact, it is already a model and a leading supporter of these regimes. Pick a dictator anywhere on the globe—from North Korea to Venezuela, from Cuba to Iran—and you'll almost certainly find that the CCP is supporting it today.

In the United States today, the Chinese government takes advantage of our freedom and democracy to solidify its position at home. It, or its surrogates, has wide access to our universities, think tanks, and media through which they can advance their opinions and rationalize their actions.

The Chinese government has co-opted numerous American businessmen and academics by providing them with favorable business opportunities and all manner of privileges; in turn, they serve the purposes and interests of the Chinese government back in America as lobbyists for favorable policies toward China.

Make no mistake, the expansion of China's military power is also a significant and alarming development. Throughout the past decade, China's defense budget has increased at an annual rate double that of its GDP growth. The Chinese People's Liberation Army is acquiring more than enough power to intimidate surrounding East Asian countries, some of them America's allies.

President Trump's raising of tariffs on China's imports yesterday demonstrates the severity of this threat. Indeed, President Trump has been making the long-awaited right shift in China policy, beginning to treat China as what it is.

But I would like to remind you tonight: The trade deal under negotiation is not a deal between two similar systems seeking closer ties. Rather, this is a fundamental clash between two radically different economic models that are deeply rooted in differing and even conflicting values and beliefs. Put it simply: Ultimately, it is not about money but value. The United States was built on the cornerstone of values. From the Mayflower Compact to the Declaration of Independence, from the Constitution to Lincoln's Gettysburg speech to Reagan's "Tear down this wall," the United States of America was guided by ideals and faith every step of the way. These idealistic qualities have not only ensured stability and prosperity at the national level but also inspired the creativity and potential of Americans at the individual level. If the idealism and belief in American values were taken away, the United States would lose its soul, the fundamental driving force that made America great in the first place.

The United States faced many crises in history, including the Civil War, World War II, the Cold War, and the "9/11" terrorist attacks. History has witnessed that the United States has turned each crisis into opportunity for tremendous national growth. Why do crises become the driving force for growth? What is America's secret?

I think the secret lies in the democratic idealism and values that the US holds dear.

The threat from China that Trump is facing now is certainly quite different from what Lincoln faced then. However, if we draw a parallel between Lincoln's "North-South" dynamic and Trump's "America-China" dynamic, their situations are quite similar.

Here is an interesting case study. In the early nineteenth century, the slavery system in the South was on the decline. However, when the cotton plantations started to boom, there was a surge in slave trafficking.

In thirty years' time, the South accumulated tremendous wealth thanks to the free cotton market in the North and extremely low labor cost (slavery, human rights deficit if you will). As a result, the slave owners in the South developed "systematic confidence" toward slavery.

In the early 1990s, the disintegration of the Soviet Union and the Tiananmen Massacre nearly led to the collapse of communist ideology. The whole world optimistically assumed the (communist) history would "end." In about thirty years' time, China rapidly grew its economy by largely taking advantage of a human rights deficit. China not only stabilized its communist regime, but it has also become increasingly aggressive in its efforts to be the global hegemonic power.

Two hundred years ago, the internal low human rights condition and the external free market boosted the strength and confidence of slave owners. Similarly, in the past three decades, the internal low human rights condition and external free market has boosted the strength and confidence of the CCP authoritarian regime.

Lincoln had a choice: close the North's market to the South without caring about its slavery system or end the slavery system itself. We all know what Lincoln chose.

When dealing with an authoritarian regime like China, will President Trump follow the steps of President Lincoln with the South and President Reagan with the Soviet Union?

To conclude, I want to share a true story with you. A young prisoner in the same prison I was kept received a death penalty for a crime of stealing a couple of motorcycles. The night before his execution, he said to his inmates: "If there is a next life, I will make sure I want to be born again. I will refuse to be born again if I see the Chinese communist flag. I will agree only if I see the Stars and Stripes."

Dear friends, this is where the greatness of America lies. To make America great again, for President Trump and the American people, Abraham Lincoln and Donald Trump are shining examples to follow.

Thank you.

CHAPTER 124

Xi Jinping's Grave Threat to China and the World

Opening Remarks at #RightsCity Montreal 2019
Concordia University, Montreal, Canada
June 3, 2019

What is China up to and what should we do about it? Much current punditry focuses on the policy roller coaster of China's modern rulers: Mao, Deng Xiaoping, Jiang Zemin, Hu Jintao, and Xi Jinping. But step back and take a broader view. Since 1949, there has been scant change in the fundamental priorities of the Chinese Communist Party leadership. Hence, there has been scant real change in their strategy for dealing with China's population and with the surrounding world. CCP leaders have been obsessed with maintaining power and internal stability and paranoid about internal factionalism, separatist movements, and dissent of any kind.

Especially after the Tiananmen Massacre permanently exposed its fig leaf of communist ideology, the CCP has relied on two sources of legitimacy to maintain its rule: rapid economic growth and rising living standards (performance-induced legitimacy) and, to a lesser degree, distorted nationalism. The descent of China's economy, burdened by excessive corporate debt, global slowdown, and structural bottlenecks, became glaringly exposed after Xi took power. Additionally, his US trade war is hitting China's economy hard.

Xi faced widespread demonstrations of popular dissent, alarmingly emboldened doubt about his leadership among his official colleagues, business allies, and even noted silence about his performance by normal fawning state media. Xi had two choices. He could ease up or tighten up. It is widely known that Xi adopted de Tocqueville's advice that revolutions are most likely when harsh dynasties become tender and contemplate reforms.

Xi believes economic and political instability must be followed by even heavier-handed measures. When, for example, China's stock market precipitously fell in June 2015, Xi responded with the massive crackdown on civil society in early July (the "709 Attack").

Now, severe economic downturn seems unstoppable. Long-term economic hardship looms. Xi's desperate grasp for total control is inevitable. He wants to extend his Xinjiang model of 1984 Digital Totalitarianism to the entire country. His corrupt, dictatorial corporate-statist amalgam, beneath its flimsy facade of communist rhetoric, is now Xi's "Fascism with Chinese Characteristics."

His favored political slogans of "The Chinese Dream" and "the great rejuvenation of the Chinese nation" lie in tatters. In order to raise them aloft, to mobilize mass support, and to stabilize the CCP's rule, Xi must rely on his version of patriotic "nationalism."

For sure, Xi wants for his "Middle Kingdom" to become strong enough to form a "new type of major power relationship" with the United States. He changed Deng's policy of "keeping a low profile," and engaged in military expansion. He doubled down on government intervention to unbalance international trade to provide a "blood transfusion" for its regime, to force technology transfers, and to steal intellectual secrets from the United States. He uses debt traps and bribes to colonize underdeveloped countries through the Belt and Road Initiative and purchases China's influence in politics, academia, and show business in the world's democracies.

For Xi, China's nationalism, internally, means Han nationalism; the "true Chinese" must subjugate ethnic minorities (Uyghurs, Tibetans, Mongols), destroy their culture and traditions, and force total assimilation.

Patriotism, for Xi, means blaming those ills resulting from his lust for power, the CCP's greed and corruption, on external forces that threaten to thwart China's destiny—the West, especially the US, and now Canada, as well as Taiwan and Hong Kong dissidents.

For a long time, the world's democracies were not vigilant enough about this and let China continue unchallenged. The US-China trade war has shifted US-China policy toward countering China's influence in various fields. This has been described by some observers as the "New Cold War." The conflict is not merely about trade; it's comprehensive in nature. The deepest conflict is between values. Otherwise, it would be inexplicable as to why Canada, which is also involved in a fierce trade conflict with America, is siding with it in the so-called New Cold War. When Canada arrested Huawei CFO Meng Wanzhou upon America's request, China used tactics such as arbitrarily detaining Canadian citizens and illegally meting out the death penalty on a Canadian citizen to engage in crazy revenge.

The free world needs to be clear-eyed. It should recognize that Xi's need to respond to growing popular resistance stimulates his need for diversionary aggressive moves to create crises and permit calls for patriot support—from military moves in the South China Sea and efforts to subvert vulnerable governments beneath Silk and Belt Road glamor, to covert action in Taiwan's election and its increasingly blatant efforts to penetrate think tanks and universities in various democracies. In short, human rights abuse in China not only violates universal principles, it also has real consequences for the free world's security. The world's democracies must firmly challenge China's regime—a regime that ruthlessly represses its people, denies universal values, and challenges the international order to achieve its dominance. To do less is not only moral dereliction but also strategically unsound.

CHAPTER 125

Every Day, We Must Be Vigilant

Speech at the Candlelight Vigil Commemorating the Thirtieth Anniversary of Tiananmen Massacre
Victims of Communism Memorial Park
Washington, DC, United States
June 3, 2019

Tonight, we gather once again to remember our fallen brothers and sisters in Tiananmen Square and celebrate their courage that showed the world that the Chinese people desire freedom and justice above all earthly goods. We are here to reaffirm that, no matter how many days or decades have gone by, there will never come a time when we forget their sacrifices.

We can never repay the debts we owe to these heroes and their families, the Tiananmen Mothers.

The candles we light tonight remind us that we must all be the keepers of the flame once borne by our fallen heroes. The word vigil means, literally, "a period of purposeful sleeplessness." That is, in a sense, what we are here tonight to do: to refuse to sleep, to refuse to forget the heroes we've lost or their mission that remains undone.

It is up to all of us to bear true witness to the bravery and sacrifice made by these heroes we honor today by remembering that we all have a personal role to play in keeping the flame burning.

We must continue to do everything we can—with all that we have—to forge a world alliance to struggle to realize our shared dream—a free China.

Let us bring this light back to our cities, our neighborhoods, our streets, and our homes.

Tonight, we hold a vigil but, every day, we must be vigilant.

CHAPTER 126

"Go to Hell. I'm in America Now."

Remarks Accepting Honorary Citizenship of
Skagit County of Washington State
Washington, DC, United States
June 4, 2019

Thank you, Bill, for this great honor.

Being an honorary citizen of Skagit County is a big deal for me.

I want to take this opportunity to thank my team, Lianchao, and other team members; old friends from thirty years ago, Lao Wang, Anzhi, Rao Yu, Tao Ye, Tan Shi—you all deserve to share this honor. I am particularly happy that Mr. and Mrs. Golomb are present; your presence means a lot; thank you.

I visited Skagit and spoke at its Republican Lincoln/Reagan Dinner. I have fallen in love with Skagit where I found and got strengthened by its true American values. The people of Skagit cherish and nourish individual liberties more than anybody else and put serious efforts in defending them from any force in any form that may endanger them. They believe in and put into day-to-day practice the principle of "By the sweat of your face You will eat bread" (Genesis 3:19). This is also part of our traditional values in my home country China.

Moreover, they care for other people's freedom, and that is why they brought me to share the Chinese stories of our struggles against communism and socialist tyranny.

I have not been a citizen of any free country. America is my adopted home, which I love so much. Being an honorary citizen of Skagit County makes America more home than ever. The United States of America, for all its mistakes, remains the greatest country on Earth. Many oppressed and persecuted people around the world look up to the US as a beacon of hope. On a personal level, America is a God-blessed country where people like myself can find refuge and freedom.

Today I won't repeat the true story that I have told on many different occasions—the story of a young Chinese man I was imprisoned with saying, before executed, that he wanted to be born again under the Stars and Stripes. Instead, I want to tell a joke, which I reworked based on an old Soviet Union joke.

In the morning, Xi Jinping goes out in his yard and says, "Good morning, sun!" The sun says, "Good morning, Comrade Xi Jinping, President for Life of the People's Republic of China." After lunch, Xi Jinping goes out and says, "Good afternoon, sun!" The sun replies, "Good afternoon, Comrade Xi Jinping, our great leader." Later, as the sun is setting, Xi Jinping says, "Good evening, sun!" The sun says, "Go to hell. I'm in America now."

God bless America.

God bless Skagit.

God bless my home country China.

CHAPTER 127

Your Liberty Will Be My Freedom

Acceptance Speech for Order of Merit of Human Solidarity
Bestowed by the Assembly of the Cuban Resistance
Miami, FL, United States
June 18, 2019

This is a surprise but a humbling one. Thank you, Mr. Orlando Gutiérrez, and the Assembly of the Cuban Resistance for giving me this Order of Merit of Human Solidarity.

I feel lucky and honored to have a chance to get involved with human rights and democracy work for Cuba, fighting alongside my Cuban brothers and sisters against the tyranny of the Castro regime and for the liberation of the Cuban people. I have drawn tremendous inspiration from your courage, commitment, and sacrifice. Working with you is very rewarding; it reminds me every day that the ties that bind us make it possible for us to act in a way worthy of the best of our humanity.

This year marks the sixtieth year of the communist rule in Cuba, which has established and maintained an effective machinery of repression. Thanks to your relentless struggle, the Cuban democracy movement has in recent years been establishing "enclaves of civil society" within the totalitarian system. They are gradually eroding Castro's machinery of repression. The Castro regime is obviously trying to stop this process of erosion and promote deceiving changes to adapt. I think the regime sees a possible model for accomplishing this, that is, the China model of introducing economic liberalization while maintaining the communist system of control. The model has worked for CCP in part because the US and other world democracies allowed it to.

The nearly three decades of the US appeasement policy toward China was based on the theory, which was widely upheld by corporations, columnists, pundits, and policymakers, that trade would lead to political freedom. This theory does not seem to apply to China, at least up to this point, and I don't think it will apply to Cuba. Trade alone has not changed China, neither will it change Cuba. Trade must be linked with human rights. The free world policy toward such a communist dictatorship as Cuba must be an integrated one with human rights at its core. This is the lesson we have learned from the past three decades. This is the lesson I want to particularly share with you today.

Thank you again for this great honor. To be honest, I am not so confident that I deserve it. I take it as a spur to redouble my effort to serve the people of Cuba as well as my compatriots back in my home country China.

To conclude, I want to repeat what I said four years ago when I was invited by you to present the 2015 Pedro Luis Boitel Freedom Award: Let's stand together in solidarity with all the oppressed people around the world and say to one another: Your slavery is my servitude, your fight is my struggle, and your liberty will be my freedom.

Thank you!

CHAPTER 128

Washington Declaration on the Thirtieth Anniversary of the Tiananmen Massacre

West Lawn of Capitol Hill
Washington, DC, United States
June 4, 2019

Distinguished guests, dear friends of human rights, and my dear brothers and sisters,

We gather here to remember our fallen brothers and sisters in Tiananmen Square and celebrate their courage and sacrifice. We come here after thirty years to reaffirm that no matter how many days, years, or decades have gone by, there will never be a time when we forget the heroes we have lost and their mission that remains undone. On this important occasion, we are issuing a statement: *Washington Declaration on the 30th Anniversary of Tiananmen Massacre*. Time will not allow me to read the whole text. I will only read one paragraph.

"Thirty years ago, inspired by patriotism and idealism, deciding that we 'would rather disappoint our parents than not live up to our social responsibility,' we dedicated our youth, innocence, blood, and tears to the 1989 Democracy Movement. All the prices we have paid for freedom, independence, and democracy shall not be in vain; all the setbacks, sufferings, and loss of lives that were imposed upon us shall not be wasted. The sense of responsibility, morality and courage, the spirit of freedom, and the ideal of democracy demonstrated by the 1989 protesters blazed a rough but hopeful trail to freedom for the Chinese people who have been oppressed, exploited, and persecuted. Today, with deep conviction, we pledge to the heavens and the earth that as long as the tyranny and totalitarian rule by the CPC are not over, we will persist in our endeavor and sacrifice without regret. We are willing to work tirelessly like the legendary bird Jingwei to end the tribulations of our people—until the sun of freedom rises over China."

Thank you.

Appendix

Washington Declaration on the Thirtieth Anniversary of Tiananmen Massacre

Thirty years ago, the year 1989 marked the 200th anniversary of the French Revolution, the seventieth anniversary of China's May Fourth Movement, and the 40th anniversary of the founding of the People's Republic of China. In that year, stormy clouds gathered over the city of Beijing and an unprecedented confrontation between the spirit of freedom and the autocratic regime unfolded. Several million college students and citizens from all walks of life filled the vast Tiananmen Square and tens of millions more demonstrated in several hundred cities across China. Like sparks that quickly ignited a wildfire, a massive spiritual uprising in the form of peaceful petition, which had hitherto not been seen in the entire history of China, began to form. This democratic movement, which originated in Beijing but soon swept the entire country, marked the most significant turning point since the beginning of China's civilization. It was the prelude to the disintegration of the Soviet Empire, the collapse of the Berlin Wall, and the removal of the Iron Curtain that had confined Eastern European countries for decades. It also led to the end of the Cold War and the beginning of globalization.

After repeated setbacks for the promotion of political and social reform in China's modern era, a brand-new prospect, which was all the brighter, emerged from the horizon.

Despite the overwhelming support for the student protesters among the Chinese people, the octogenarian hardliners within the Communist Party of China (CPC) called in the People's Liberation Army. Hundreds of thousands of soldiers, armed with tanks, armored vehicles, and helicopters, rolled into Beijing from several directions and committed the horrendous massacre that stunned the entire world. In the wake of the atrocity, China's government-run TV station incessantly broadcasted the most-wanted list of student leaders, tens of thousands of protesters were arrested and imprisoned, and at least several hundred activists were forced into exile.

The light of freedom was brutally put out and the soul of democracy was once more banished from the land of China.

The visit of Mikhail Sergeyevich Gorbachev, the General Secretary of the Communist Party of the Soviet Union, focused the world's attention on Beijing at a time when the spirit of China's democracy movement was spreading rapidly across much of the world. Communist regimes in the Baltics, East Germany, Czechoslovakia, Poland, Hungary, Bulgaria, Yugoslavia, Romania, Albania, and Mongolia collapsed one after another. Eventually, the hammer and sickle that had been flying high over the Kremlin for more than seventy years came down in humiliation. The year 1989 proclaimed that communism is a shackle decorated with flowers and freedom trumps everything else. The peaceful demonstrations in China greatly encouraged the people of the communist countries; condemnation and sanctions from the international community shook the faith of panicking General Secretaries. Communism, both as a fantasy and as an existing social system, ended in a historic bankruptcy worldwide.

The 1989 democracy movement in China sounded the death knell for communism.

In 1989, to pay tribute to the Chinese people, France, the cradle of European Enlightenment, arranged for the Chinese parading squadron to march through the Arc de Triomphe at the head of the country's 200th National Day Anniversary parade, holding high gigantic signs of "Liberty, Equality, and Fraternity" in Chinese characters. In 2007, Washington, DC, witnessed the erection of the Monument to the Victims of Communism, a duplicate of the torch-holding Goddess of Democracy that student protesters put up in Tiananmen Square.

In the wake of the crackdown on June 4, 1989, the CPC kept a low profile while seeking to join the World Trade Organization in an attempt to reinvigorate the red empire by combining mercantilism and controlled market economy with political totalitarianism and opposition to human rights. As a result, a new and more ambitious communist power, supported by a greedy and arrogant red aristocracy, emerged on the world's stage.

As is described in an ancient Chinese poem, "Although the grass of the prairie is burned out by a wildfire, it will burst into life again when the spring breeze returns to the land." Having witnessed the tragic ending of China's pro-democracy protest, history will welcome the glorious homecoming of the Torch of Freedom and Beacon of Democracy. Today, we, the participants, witnesses, survivors, and international supporters of the 1989 Chinese Democracy Movement, solemnly gather in the capital of the free world to reaffirm our allegiance to the noble cause of democracy and freedom and jointly issue this "Washington Declaration on the Thirtieth Anniversary of the June 4th Massacre."

We pray for the hundreds and possibly thousands of massacre victims who laid down their lives for China's democracy and freedom.

We pray for "Tiananmen Mothers" whose courage and indomitable spirit are providing unremitting inspiration for the freedom-loving people of China and the world.

We thank the strong and unwavering support from the United States, Europe, Oceania, and free countries in Asia; we are grateful for the solidarity shown by the people of the former Soviet Union and Eastern European countries who had undergone the same ordeal under communist regimes before regaining their freedom; and we will never forget the love and brotherhood of our fellow Chinese descendants in

Taiwan, Hong Kong, Macau, and other parts of the world.

For us, having the opportunity to participate in the 1989 Democracy Movement was the greatest honor and the blessing of a lifetime.

Today, with our hands on our chests, witnessed by the heaven and the earth, we make a pledge that has been taking shape in our minds for thirty years.

We feel called upon to enter into a covenant with our motherland.

We are convinced that once the CPC's rule is over and the free Sun rises from Tiananmen Square, a brand-new China will come forth. This will be a free, democratic, and constitutional republic; a benevolent, courteous, magnanimous, and noble society; an oriental fortress of peace and civilization; a staunch ally standing side by side with the free world to overcome the world's challenges; and an industrious and indispensable contributor to the conscience and civilization of humanity.

We do wish to enter into a covenant with "the Tiananmen Generation."

Confucius said: "When a man reaches fifty, he will know his heavenly mandate." Our heavenly mandate is to continue to promote constitutional democracy by drawing lessons and experience from China's century-old transformation into a modern society, to end Marxism-Leninism's conquest of China and the rule by communist totalitarianism, and to establish the world's largest democratic republic that is a combination of traditional Chinese virtues and the universal values of humanity, a republic that is impossible to reverse and undermine.

We do wish to say a few words to today's college students.

We firmly believe that you are not only our next generation by blood, but also the logical successors of the spirit of the 1989 Democracy Movement. You will shoulder the task of building a free and democratic China. Your awakening will make China a new country. You will be directly involved in the fight to eradicate the last hegemonic empire of tyranny on earth.

We do wish to say a few words to China's intellectuals.

Without you there would not have been pro-democracy protests. Sadly, today's Chinese intellectuals have largely lost the courage and sense of responsibility demonstrated by the previous generation thirty years ago. You have been marginalized and now succumb to cynicism. The nineteenth century Chinese poet Gong Zizhen once said: "When all the intellectuals know shame, the country will never be subject to shame. If the intellectuals do not know shame, then the country should really feel ashamed." We would like to covenant with you to remember and live by these words.

We do wish to say a few words to China's workers and peasants.

In China you are the largest group of "the insulted and the injured" and find yourselves at the very bottom of the hierarchy established by the CPC. We hope that you will follow the example of the Polish working people to organize China's "Solidarity" trade union and we will be your faithful allies.

We do wish to say a few words to China's private entrepreneurs.

You know better than anyone else that you have never enjoyed legal protection and independence. Your assets are the most insecure assets under the sun. The Beijing regime, which aims at "eliminating private ownership," can take away all your assets overnight. Your most sensible choice is to leave the Communist China now and stay away until the establishment of a free, democratic China, which will welcome your return to the motherland.

We do wish to appeal to the military, the police, and others who serve in the communist state security apparatus.

In 1989, seven PLA generals, including Zhang Aiping, Ye Fei, and Xiao Ke, wrote a joint letter to the Central Military Commission of the CPC, which stressed that the military should not fire upon the people and become a tool in a massacre of civilians. Even more remarkable, the commander of the 38th infantry corps, major general Xu Qinxian, and some other military officers refused to carry out the order to fire upon unarmed citizens and set a shining example for fellow PLA officers and soldiers. In contrast, Liu Huaqing, Chi Haotian, Ai Husheng, and other commanders of the Capital Martial Law Forces will be tried at the tribunal of history. We appeal to you not to fire upon the people who nurtured you and, in answering the call of history, turn the muzzles of your guns toward the enemy of the people.

We do have a stern warning for the communist authorities.

You built the country under the guidance of Marxism-Leninism and established a Stalinist political system, which led to the enormous loss of innocent lives. You are the worst regime in Chinese history and have brought shame to the Chinese nation. The "June 4th Massacre" was one of the many heinous crimes you committed against China. Deng Xiaoping, Li Peng, Chen Yun, Yang Shangkun, Wang Zhen, Bo Yibo, Yao Yilin, and other 1989 Beijing Massacre perpetrators—dead or alive—shall not be allowed to escape justice.

The Xi Jinping clique is the reincarnation of evil. However, considering that Hu Yaobang and Zhao Ziyang were once leaders within the CPC and that after all we share the same ancestors, we want to warn you that with little time left, you must publicly admit to your crimes to the Chinese people by publishing a self-indictment and giving up your illegitimate rule, otherwise Nicolae Ceaușescu shall be your example.

Finally, we want to hold ourselves to the following pledge.

Thirty years ago, inspired by patriotism and idealism, deciding that we "would rather disappoint our parents than not live up to our social responsibility," we dedicated our youth, innocence, blood, and tears to the 1989 Democracy Movement.

All the prices we have paid for freedom, independence, and democracy shall not be in vain; all the setbacks, sufferings, and loss of lives that were imposed upon us shall not be wasted. The sense of responsibility, morality and courage, the spirit of freedom, and the ideal of democracy demonstrated by the 1989 protesters blazed a rough but hopeful trail to freedom for the Chinese people who have been oppressed, exploited, and persecuted. Today, with deep conviction, we pledge to the heavens and the earth that as long as the tyranny and totalitarian rule by the CPC are not over, we will persist in our endeavor and sacrifice without regret. We are willing to work tirelessly like the legendary bird Jingwei to end the tribulations of our people—until the sun of freedom rises over China.

Today, reflecting upon the 1989 crackdown and the CPC's records of the past thirty years, we cannot but conclude: the CPC has become the most corrupt, most predatory, most reactionary, and most hypocritical ruling clique in human history and China has become the center of dictatorship, barbarianism, and terrorism.

Therefore, we hereby solemnly declare:

The Communist Party of China has become a public enemy of the Chinese people and seriously threatens world peace and civilization.

The legitimacy of the CPC's rule has been depleted and to end its tyranny is our unwavering goal.

The free spirit and heroic dedication exhibited by the Chinese people in their pursuit of democracy have acquired a universal and historic significance.

Therefore, let us resume, arm in arm, the heaven-mandated journey to fulfill our arduous but glorious mission.

We shall prevail.

CHAPTER 129

Human Chain Against China

Speech at Global Anti-Chinazi Rally
Chinese Embassy, Washington, DC, United States
September 29, 2019

Dear friends,

Good afternoon. Thank you for coming to this rally on this hot Sunday afternoon.

Since the launch of the Anti-Extradition Legislation Protests in Hong Kong on June 9, the people of Hong Kong have waged a nearly four-month extraordinary struggle for freedom, democracy, and the rule of law. Their courage, endurance, wisdom, creativity, and unity have earned the world's admiration. We are joining a few dozen of the world's cities in rallying for Hong Kong. The struggle in Hong Kong is still ongoing.

#HongKongProtests have created #Chinazi, a wordplay hashtag of "China" and "Nazism." The protesters have also displayed a flag, which they designed by re-arranging the red stars in the CCP's national flag to form a Nazi swastika, naming it the "Chinazi Flag," in Chinese, the Red Nazi (赤纳粹) flag, symbolizing the fact that the totalitarian state under the CCP has become the "Nazism of the 21st Century" or "Fascism with Chinese Characteristics."

In two days, on October 1, the CCP will stage an unprecedented grand military parade in Beijing to celebrate the seventieth anniversary of the party-state and to show off its military muscle to the world. We, the people who have suffered under the yoke of the Chinese Communist

Empire, who have been bullied and threatened by its despotic power, who have suffered at the hands of the regimes backed by the CCP, and who try to support and give voices to the oppressed people, have come together in front of the CCP embassy to form a human chain against #Chinazi and condemnation of the CCP's seventy-year rule, and call for the end of communism and Fascism with Chinese Characteristics, and for a free Hong Kong, a free Taiwan, a free Tibet, a free Eastern Turkestan, a free Southern Mongolia, a free Cuba, a free Vietnam, a free North Korea and, indeed, a free China.

Let us roar for freedom.

SECTION XVI

WHY WE NEED A HUMAN RIGHTS NATO: THE NEW COLD WAR WITH CHINA

October 2019—November 2020

"The free world faces a new cold war with China under the rule of the Chinese Communist Party....The West's good-intentioned effort to help liberalize China by drawing China into the rules-based international order have not liberalized the regime but allowed it to corrupt international institutions, to bring many small nations under its thumb, and even to infect great democracies like the United States of America with illiberal ideas—to bully Americans into disavowing their most cherished ideals like freedom of speech....China is now the number one threat to world security and peace....Let us join hands in preventing Xi Jinping's long-term dream of a world-dominating Chinese Communist Empire from becoming a reality. Together, let us fight to preserve our freedom and extend it to all trapped in the CCP's oppressive yoke."

CHAPTER 130

A Human Rights NATO

Opening Remarks at Forum 2000 Panel: "China: Human Rights in the Twenty-First Century Digital Surveillance State"
Prague, Czech Republic
October 15, 2019

China's human rights situation is dire, as bad as anyone can imagine. In my opening remarks, I won't talk about it but will be ready to answer any questions regarding it later.

Instead, I want to raise a question and put forth a rough idea on how to answer the question.

I assume we all want to do something to help improve China's human rights situation if we can. But the question is: How much money is an individual, a business, or a country willing to or able to lose for standing up to China's authoritarian might?

It is probably too much to ask Norwegian fisherman—or Canadian farmers or Czech small businesspeople—to sacrifice their livelihoods on the altar of human rights.

There is a limit. We must be practically idealistic.

When the US left the UN Human Rights Council, I was interviewed by the media about whether it was a good idea, a sensible move. My answer was, yes, if the US had an alternative plan, and no, if not. I have no idea whether the US has one even today. The question we are seeking to answer is what kind of alternative we advocate for.

What has been in my mind is a human rights treaty organization of democracies, a Human Rights NATO if you will, that engages in both collective confrontation and collective defense on human rights issues.

1. Collective confrontation has three levels:
    - Each signatory country passes a Human Rights Act linking human rights with all fields of diplomatic ties with dictatorships—regular assessments and executive reports to Parliament or Congress, etc.
    - Collectively confront human rights violating countries for human rights issues on various world platforms.
    - Come up with united measures of punishment addressing individual human rights violating cases—economic sanctions, boycotting cultural events (exchanges, Games, etc.), Magnitsky sanctions, and so on and so forth.
2. Collective defense:

    This will help break the collective action dilemma all the democracies have been so far trapped in. It is very important for everyone, especially smaller ones. In the past, China, for example, has retaliated or threatened to retaliate against countries that confronted it for its human rights abuses.

    So, the treaty must be such that, if one member of the treaty organization is retaliated against economically by an undemocratic country for standing up for democratic principles, all other democracies in the treaty agree to come to its defense, helping ease its economic pain.

There are a lot of talks of democracy being on recess. If it is true, one of the major reasons is that democratic values routinely give way to economic interests. The Human Rights "NATO" will help turn around that trend; it preserves democratic values while protecting economic interests of democracies.

CHAPTER 131

Defeat Chinazi and Ensure Freedom for the People of Hong Kong and Us All

Speech at Rally Standing with Hong Kong
Catholic University, Washington, DC, United States
October 6, 2019

Since the launch of the Anti-Extradition Legislation Protests in Hong Kong in early June, the people of Hong Kong have waged a four-month extraordinary struggle for freedom, democracy, and the rule of law. Their courage, endurance, wisdom, creativity, and unity have earned the world's admiration. The struggle in Hong Kong is still ongoing. We must support HK, not only for the sake of Hong Kongers but also for the sake of safeguarding our freedom because Hong Kong is the front line of the new cold war between communist China and the free world.

Evidence shows that the Chinese communist regime has become the biggest threat to the US and the free world. This threat is real and very serious.

China under Xi Jinping is showing all aspects of a fascist state. Xi Jinping's fascism is a real, clear, and present danger to free societies everywhere. Seventy years ago, the crimes of Nazi Germany led the international community to embrace the principle of universal human rights, but today similar patterns have emerged in China. A single, all-powerful party, one paramount leader, total control over all media, military aggression abroad, brutal suppression of dissent, creation of fictional external threats and enemies, and jingoism and strident nationalism masquerading as foreign policy. After the Holocaust of the Jewish people under Hitler, we vowed "never again." But among post-war atrocities that belie that pledge, we today must add the "reeducation" concentration camps where more than one million people are detained. This is a mature fascism combined with communism, crony-capitalism, corrupting and colonizing diplomacy, Orwellian 1984 digital totalitarianism, and corruption-exporting internationalism (China virus). I call it the Fascism with Chinese Characteristics, or Chinazi, a term coined by the Hong Kong protesters.

Unfortunately, many people still haven't realized the magnitude, scope, and seriousness of the CCP's threat. The engagement and appeasement advocates continue to push for their failed China policy.

Therefore, it is our duty to inform and educate the American public and decision-makers what the Chinese Communist Party (CCP) really is, what it intends to do, and why it is so dangerous.

Nearly eighty years ago, American political leaders and young Americans like you rose to the challenge of their times and a few years later defeated Nazism, and seventy years ago, to the challenges of their times and forty years later won the Cold War. Surely, we, with their work as our foundation, with our united effort and with the support, can rise to the most daunting challenge of our own times—that is, to defeat the Chinazi and ensure freedom for the people of Hong Kong and us all.

CHAPTER 132

Arm Yourselves to Lead Change

Opening Remarks at the Fourteenth Interethnic/
Interfaith Leadership Conference
Capitol Hill, Washington, DC, United States
October 21, 2019

Dear friends and colleagues from around the world:

Welcome to the fourteenth Interethnic/Interfaith Leadership Conference. It is an honor to host this meeting, and we deeply value and appreciate your participation.

In all the years that we have organized the Leadership Conference, never have our challenges been more pressing, never have the moral and political choices forced upon the world by the inhuman and anti-democratic policies of the Chinese Communist Party been so stark and so consequential.

The theme of this year's Leadership Conference is "Arm Yourself to Lead Change." Let me explain.

Many people around the world resist this truth, but the free world faces a new cold war with China under the rule of the Chinese Communist Party. The regime in Beijing is trying to disguise its cold war with free societies. It is an ideological war with the ideal of freedom itself, with the very idea of democracy, human rights, and the rule of law, the ideas the regime fears more than any economic and military force.

In fact, this cold war is nothing new. It has been waged unilaterally by the CCP for the entire forty-year period of engagement and appeasement.

In fact, the anti-democratic policies of the CCP that began under Mao during the original Cold War period have never abated. Instead, they have been disguised or modulated for pragmatic tactical reasons from time to time.

The West's good-intentioned effort to help liberalize China by drawing China into the rules-based international order have not liberalized the regime but allowed it to corrupt international institutions, to bring many small nations under its thumb, and even to infect great democracies like the United States of America with illiberal ideas—to bully Americans into disavowing their most cherished ideals like freedom of speech.

But under Xi Jinping, the mask is off and the face of communist rule in China and toward Hong Kongers, Uyghurs, Tibetans, Taiwanese, Christians, Falun Gong practitioners and, indeed, all the diverse people that are directly related to China is being more clearly revealed for what it is: totalitarianism, ethno-nationalism, and fascism.

History has clearly shown that such regimes are threats not only to their own people but to people of other nations as well. The will and capacity to repress internally is positively related to the ambition and ability to expand externally. With no respect for the independence and sovereignty of others, the CCP turns its anti-human wrath against its neighbors and other countries and openly threatens world peace. Evidence shows that the Chinese communist regime has become the biggest external threat to the free world.

What can be done? What can we, as individuals, do in this decisive moment in history? How can we work together and combine our ideas and energies to build a movement for freedom and justice that is greater than the sum of its parts?

The ethnic, religious, and regional groups represented at this conference are on the front lines of the new cold war and live at the place where the reality of the Chinese communist regime shows itself. The participants include young leaders from these groups. I speak directly to you: You need and deserve moral and physical support from the US and other democracies. We want to help develop new international strategies and skills to help achieve it and to strengthen and sustain your leadership. This is exactly what this conference aims to achieve.

And we will not stop when this meeting is over. We will stay with you, because we are together. Arm Yourselves to Defeat Fascism with Chinese Characteristics. Arm Yourselves to Lead Change. We do not mean guns or other weapons. We mean ideas, principles, methods, solidarity, and courage.

May the spirit of the people of Hong Kong we just honored with our 2019 Citizen Power Awards inspire us to win the new cold war, to move forward toward the goal of peaceful change to democracy and respect for human rights in China.

Thank you.

CHAPTER 133

Opening Remarks at the Public Hearing: "Authoritarianism and Shrinking Space for Freedom of Expression, Press Freedom, and Human Rights Defenders, with Case Studies on China, Egypt, and Russia"

Hosted by European Parliament's Subcommittee on Human Rights (DROI)
Brussels, Belgium
February 18, 2020

Ms. Chairwoman Maria Arena,

Thank you for inviting me to speak at this timely and important hearing. It is timely because the coronavirus epidemic has helped reveal fatal defects of the Chinese Communist Party's totalitarian governance system under the leadership of Xi Jinping. This is deeply relevant to the theme of this hearing. The mishandling of the epidemic on the part of the CCP government, and its consequences for the entire Chinese society, has everything to do with Xi's totalitarian politics. Everything that is going wrong in this crisis could have gone wrong under the CCP rule without Xi Jinping, as we learned in 2003 when SARS plagued China, but it is significantly much worse under Xi.

Xi Jinping has grasped all the levers of power in the Party and the state, including the military and police. The Party has reclaimed the authority over economic policy that it delegated to the state starting in the 1980s. Within the Party, Xi acts as if he is personally in charge of everything. He chairs eight of the leading small groups. Xi's hold on the People's Liberation Army is even more complete than his hold on the Party and the government. Xi is preoccupied with shoring up loyalty to the Party and himself. Party officials in general are told to shun any "improper discussion" that questions central policies. These warnings serve not only to reinforce Xi's authority and keep the Party in line behind him but also to cripple the ability and power of other politicians and officials on various levels to do the governance job that any government should do.

Xi has also turned left ideologically, striking fear into intellectuals, journalists, and private businesspeople. Returning to Mao-style rule by terror, Xi is intent on controlling every aspect of people's lives. At the nineteenth Party Congress that kick-started his second term in power, Xi invoked a famous saying by the late Chairman Mao Zedong: "Party, government, military, civilian, academic; east, west, south, north, and the center, the Party leads everything." In addition to absolute control of political power, it ensures that the party-state will monopolize the key economic sectors.

Under Xi, the CCP's stability-maintenance machine has become more efficient and more totalitarian. Censorship was once fragmented across agencies, with cracks that nimble journalists and netizens could exploit to circulate information. Now the censors are more consolidated and centralized. A potent new Cyber Administration, run by a leading small group that Xi chairs, aims to win what Xi calls the "struggle for public opinion." Over 30,000 Chinese surveillance companies have more than 1.6 million employees. These firms are led by Huawei, Zhejiang Dahua, and Hikvision. They toil to perfect and export China's mass surveillance system. Their products, such as Hikvision cameras, are widely sold in the European market. Some of them, such as Alibaba and Tencent, use the EU free market to access capital and technology to develop surveillance products. Because thought control requires monitoring people's activities, mass surveillance is required. The CCP has spent lavishly to build a massive surveillance system that allows China to deploy its sophisticated network of social control. Just as with the Party in Orwell's Oceania, the reason is to preemptively eliminate any risks that could threaten the regime's security. In the CCP's phraseology, it is to "improve the three-dimensional, legalization, specialization, and smartness of social security." No doubt, China has become a high-tech digital surveillance superpower since Xi took power, and now its surveillance long arm is reaching out to the world.

The overriding grand goal of China's national rejuvenation and the China Dream allows the party-state to continue denying the political rights of Chinese people, as well as people of Hong Kong, and to continue to oppress the Tibetan and Uyghur Muslim minorities. Gross abuses of power in China are rampant. China's model of governance reflects Xi's regression to a Mao-style strongman rule—characterized by absolute party, dictatorship, violence and terror, and absolutely no mercy for any dissent.

All this has happened as the CCP itself and its apologists believed that Western liberalism as a mainstream global political ideology is declining rapidly, along with its governance system. They can no longer hold the world together, and the world is looking for China to provide an alternative ideology and governance model. That strategy evolved into actively participating in and pushing for global governance reforms, a euphemism for rewriting international rules, which further developed into "one world, two systems" by creating a dual international system to directly compete against the liberal democracy. Now the People's Republic of China has entered what Chinese official media have called the "inevitable stage of China's rise"—China will lead the world into the future, driven by the laws of history.

The CCP's grand strategy seems to avoid direct confrontation with the United States and to use global "rural areas" to encircle the United

States. It believes that the EU is the second world that can potentially form a united front against the US, a Maoist strategy. The EU is thus a main battleground in China's war for world dominance, a new cold war if you will.

The challenges posed by the CCP lie in the Party's lies and deception, its financial power, its propaganda apparatus, and its adaptation of the West's rules of the game in order to win the match. China is pretending to be a peace-loving, benevolent authoritarian ruler to get a foothold into the EU and expand its political and economic influence. Central Europe is a particular target because the CCP believes this area is a weak link in the chain where democracy has not firmly rooted, a region where China can achieve a breakthrough.

China wants to use the EU to establish RMB's dominance against the US dollar: another challenge. The export of Huawei's cheap 5G technology to control the EU communication network is still another strategy of domination.

What this means for the world is that China is on offense with the intention to lead through economic growth initiatives such as the Belt and Road Initiative, development via the Asian Infrastructure Investment Bank and, for a vision of united global future, China's "Community of Common Destiny for All Mankind," rhetoric that animates Chinese official documents and speeches.

Despite China's global governance ambition and aggressive propaganda campaign, the failure in containing the Wuhan pandemic shows its inferiority. The virus is shaking Xi Jinping's totalitarian system and his plans for global control.

Madam Chair, on December 6, 2012, a little more than seven years ago, I spoke at the public hearing held by this same subcommittee.

I predicted in my presentation that "(t)here may not be significant change to the Chinese regime in the next one to three years, but there will be a major one in the next five to ten years." I might have surprised many people by saying so. My prediction was based on the following analysis, which was also laid out in the same presentation. It usually takes four factors to be present at the same time to begin a real democratic transition in an autocratic country: 1) general robust disaffection from people; 2) a split in the leadership in the autocratic regime; 3) viable democratic opposition; and 4) international support. Plus, one triggering factor: crisis.

I knew the crisis would sooner or later come, natural and manmade, given the nature of the system; like the Soviet Union, PRC must have its Chernobyl moment.

Time does not allow me to elaborate on these factors, which are in the making in the epidemic crisis. I would like to talk about them in Q&A.

With regard to the factor of international support, I want to emphasize that the EU should soon come up with a contingency plan taking the leverage provided by this disaster to reshape China's future course, making sure the lives lost in the epidemic and the sacrifices many Chinese heroes have made in past decades are not, after all, in vain.

I do additionally have quite a few recommendations to make specifically to the EU, which I would reserve for Q&A.

Thank you all.

CHAPTER 134

Our Memory Concerns Life and Death

Speech at Victims of Communism's Tiananmen Square Massacre Candlelight Vigil
Washington, DC, United States
June 3, 2020

As the worst pandemic in modern history continues to plague the world, we once again observe the anniversary of the Tiananmen Square Massacre.

On this day, I have been thinking about the connection between the two seemingly isolated tragedies, thirty-one years apart.

The brave students in Tiananmen Square demanded political reforms to make the government more transparent and responsible. But the communist regime responded with machine guns and rolling tanks. As a result, political reform ceased, and the government has become even more blatant in its repression and corruption.

Today, thirty-one years later, it is a well-established fact that if, when the coronavirus first broke out in Wuhan, there had been any space in society and government to sound the alarm, if the government had not suppressed the truth and misled the world, hundreds of thousands of lives would have been saved.

By the same token, if the Communist Party, instead of slaughtering the Tiananmen protesters, had accepted their requests for political reform, the world would not have been plunged into the catastrophe we are experiencing today. This is an example of the principle that when a regime runs roughshod on its own people, it will sooner or later bring disasters beyond its border, one way or another.

Everyone should be reminded of this lesson: The difference made by freedom and democracy is not only whether we have a life of dignity and individual fulfillment but very often the difference between life and death.

The people of Hong Kong know it well. Carrying on the Tiananmen spirit, they are putting their lives on the line to defend their freedom and push for democracy. Under the cover of the pandemic, Beijing is intensifying crackdowns on the people of Hong Kong, aiming to kill their hope by suppressing the space for freedom of expression to zero, as it did thirty-one years ago in China.

But the people of Hong Kong will not give up. They will fight through to a free future. So will we. Today, there can be no better way to commemorate our fallen brothers and sisters thirty-one years ago than standing with Hong Kong.

Our memory today is not just a sad recollection. Our memory concerns life and death. Whenever we think of those young lives lost and of so many unnecessary deaths today, we need to challenge ourselves to ask how we can live so those sacrifices will not have been in vain. Let us work, together, to ensure that they were not.

Rest in peace, my dear brothers and sisters of Tiananmen. Rest in peace, our fellow human beings who died of the coronavirus.

CHAPTER 135

Breaking Up Xi Jinping's Long-Term Dream and Game of the Chinese Communist Empire

Speech at Virtual Side-Event Paralleling the Forty-Fifty UNHRC Session "China's Weapons of Mass-Subjugation: Surveillance, Camp, and Cultural Genocide"
Hosted by the Tibetan Office in Geneva
September 29, 2020

Good day.

The human rights situation under China has reached its worst level in thirty years.

My fellow panelists have just shared with you the atrocities that the CCP is perpetrating on their respective groups: the twenty-first century concentration camps, forced labors, Orwellian massive surveillance on people, and the cultural genocide of the Uyghurs and Tibetans, which is expanding to those living in Inner Mongolia.

There is sinicization of religions, annihilation of civil society, political cultural genocide on the people of Hong Kong, military intimidation to the democratic Taiwan. And the list goes on. All horror stories.

These stories are making international headlines, and America and other democracies are taking ever stronger measures to respond, which is good. But it is not enough.

We still need to ask the question harder. How can we help those inside to create the space needed to build a viable opposition? I believe that this is necessary in order to change conditions for the better.

Opportunities often present themselves as small cracks in China's dictatorial regime. We must unite to do things aimed at creating and enlarging and opening divisions in the CCP regime.

To that end, today, instead of repeating the stories we are familiar with, I would like to propose three joint actions. In short, they are:

1. Advocate for the world democracies to come together to hold the CCP accountable for COVID-19.
2. Advocate for the democracies to establish formal diplomatic ties with the Democratic Taiwan.
3. Advocate for a Human Rights NATO of the world democracies.

Let me explain each with some more details:

1. Advocate for world democracies to come together to hold the CCP accountable for COVID-19.

Citizen Power Initiatives for China produced a comprehensive report called "Examining China's Response to the COVID-19 Outbreak (September 2019–January 2020): The Catastrophe That Could Have Been Avoided," which documents how the CCP responded to the virus, especially day-by-day in the critical month between December 26, 2019, and January 25, 2020.

Six key conclusions have emerged in the course of this research:

1. The COVID-19 epidemic could have been stopped in its early state.
2. The top priority of the Chinese Communist Party was to maintain "social stability," i.e., its own control, at all costs.
3. The Chinese government deliberately suppressed information about the source and extent of the outbreak.
4. The Chinese government deliberately downplayed the threat of the epidemic.
5. The Chinese government deliberately misled the international community.
6. Chinese President Xi Jinping bears ultimate responsibility for ineptly handling the epidemic.

There are four main reasons why the world must hold the CCP accountable for COVID-19, whose death toll just passed one million yesterday.

1. Morality
2. Future of global governance (which has a lot to do with human rights issues)
3. Protecting against the next deadly pathogen
4. Helping crack open the CCP regime

I hope I will have time in the Q&A to elaborate on each of them.

2. Advocate for democratic nations to establish formal diplomatic ties with Democratic Taiwan. We need to strengthen Taiwan.

Taiwan is a shining democracy that deserves international recognition. In responding to COVID-19 and helping others in this crisis, Taiwan has shown the world it is a responsible, capable, and trustworthy partner.

Democracies must let the CCP, and other world dictators for that matter, understand that civilization and not barbarism will prevail.

The strategy has great potential to help split the CCP leadership, setting in motion a big internal fight in the Party, a wedge between the Chinese hyper-nationalists and the CCP leader, and emboldening our liberal democratic colleagues in China, including Tibetans, Uyghurs, Mongolians, and citizens of Hong Kong.

I say this based on my understanding of China's politics, as it is deeply rooted in the Chinese traditional world view of "middle kingdom," "imperial heaven." No ruler can afford to lose Taiwan.

3. And thirdly, advocate for a Human Rights NATO.

I think you all agree with me that democracies need to unite and confront China together on human rights more effectively and strongly.

A new idea would be to advocate for democratic nations to pull together and form a treaty-based Human Rights NATO!

A Human Rights NATO that will engage in both collective confrontation and collective defense on issues pertaining to human rights.

Collective confrontation has three levels:

1. Each signatory country implements a Human Rights Act, linking human rights to all fields of its diplomatic ties with dictatorships, including regular assessments and executive reports to its parliament or congress.
2. Member states collectively confront human rights violators.
3. Member states agree on a unified means of dealing with individual instances of human rights violations via economic sanctions, boycotting international cultural events (exchanges, Games, etc.), and so on.

Collective defense would help break the dilemma of collective action that all democracies have been so far trapped in. Such an accord is important for everyone, especially smaller countries, because in the past, states such as China have retaliated or threatened to retaliate against those that have confronted it for its human rights abuses. The treaty must be such that, if a member state of the treaty organization is retaliated against economically by an undemocratic country for standing up for democratic principles, all other democracies in the treaty agree to come to its defense, helping to ease its economic pain.

At the moment, there is a lot of talk of democracy being "on recess." If this is true, one of the major reasons is because democratic values routinely give way to economic interests.

A NATO for human rights would help turn this trend around; it would preserve democratic values while protecting economic interests.

These ideas I believe are concepts that translate into effective actions.

China thinks not in days, weeks, or years but in tens of years, hundreds of years. We need to do the same in our campaign, but at the same time, put all our energies into producing cracks in the CCP and start breaking up their longer-term game and dream of a Chinese Communist Empire.

CHAPTER 136

Preventing Xi Jinping's Dream of a World-Dominating Chinese Communist Empire from Becoming a Reality

Speech at the Rally "Global Resist the CCP Protests"
Capitol Hill, Washington, DC, United States
October 1, 2020

Seventy-one years ago the Chinese Communist Party (CCP) founded the People's Republic of China. But it is neither the people's, nor a republic.

Instead, it is a hell on earth. By even the most conservative estimates, the CCP's rule in China has resulted in the unnatural deaths of nearly 100 million people in the past seventy-one years. On average, that is more than 3,000 people dying tragic deaths every single day.

The victims include Chinese, Tibetans, Uyghurs, Mongolians, Hong Kongers, Christians, Falun Gong practitioners and people of other faiths, men, women, children, and the elderly. The CCP's hands are also tainted with blood for the lives of people around the world by extending its evil to embolden dictators in North Korea, Iran, Cuba, Syria, Sudan, Venezuela, and elsewhere.

Today, under dictator Xi Jinping—who is following in the footsteps of China's bloodiest dictator, Mao Tse-tung—the CCP is deploying an Orwellian mass control system, perpetrating the annihilation of civil society in China, the cultural and literal genocide of the Uyghurs, Tibetans, and Mongolians, political-cultural genocide of the people of Hong Kong, and military intimidation on democratic Taiwan. It has maliciously propagated the COVID-19 pandemic, which has killed over one million people worldwide with debilitating health and economic effects.

China is now the number one threat to world security and peace. The question now before us is this: Will we allow this threat from the CCP to continue for another seventy-one years, seventy-one months, or even seventy-one days?

Let us join hands in preventing Xi Jinping's long-term dream of a world-dominating Chinese Communist Empire from becoming a reality. Together, let us fight to preserve our freedom and extend it to all trapped in the CCP's oppressive yoke.

CHAPTER 137

This Is Not a United Nations Human Rights Abusers Council

Remarks at UN Watch Press Conference Contesting China, Russia, Cuba, Saudi Arabia, and Pakistan's Membership to the UN Human Rights Council
Geneva, Switzerland
October 9, 2020

On October 13, the UN General Assembly will be electing new members for the Human Rights Council's 2021–2023 term, and China is running for the fifth time. During the one-year period of time when China was waiting to be eligible again to run for the Council's membership, the Chinese government—under the increasingly draconian rule of Xi Jinping—has escalated human rights repression across the board, especially with its crackdown on critics of the government's handling of the COVID-19 pandemic, persecution of ethnic religious minorities in Xinjiang, Tibet, and Inner Mongolia, and annihilation of civil and political liberties in Hong Kong.

Nothing can be further from the truth than China's voluntary pledge for its current bid for Human Rights Council membership. It claims, for example, that "since the outbreak of COVID-19, the Chinese government has been giving top-most priority to people's lives and health" and that "China has acted with openness, transparency, and responsibility, updating COVID-19 information in a most timely fashion."

In July of this year our organization, Citizen Power Initiatives for China, issued a comprehensive research report entitled "Examining

China's Response to the COVID-19 Outbreak." Based on meticulous analysis of data, much of it directly from sources in China, the report establishes a day-by-day, objective record of the Chinese government's response to the virus outbreak, especially in the critical month between December 26, 2019, and January 25, 2020. The report concludes among other things:

- The COVID-19 epidemic could have been stopped in its early state.
- The Chinese government prioritized political stability over people's lives and health.
- The Chinese government deliberately suppressed information about the source and extent of the outbreak and the overall threat of the pandemic.
- The Chinese government deliberately misled the international community.

By any standard, China has grossly violated the Council's founding principles and does not measure up to its membership criteria. Any statement suggesting otherwise is as cynical as it is ridiculous.

We urge UN member states, especially the democracies, to seriously consider China's human rights record. If this were an election for a "Human Rights Abusers Council," it would be more than proper to vote for China, as it leads the entire world in violating human rights.

But sadly, I find it imperative and necessary to remind democratic governments around the world that this is an election for the UN Human Rights Council and not the UN Human Rights Abusers Council. The only choice that is commensurate with the values you claim to uphold is to vote "No" on China.

Although the vote next week will be cast in a secret ballot, I urge the people of democracies to ask how your governments vote. You and we, the victims of the Chinese government abuses and China's human rights defenders, deserve to know.

Thank you.

CHAPTER 138

Our Solidarity Must Become a Verb

Opening Remarks at the Fifteenth Interethnic/ Interfaith Leadership Conference
Washington, DC, United States
November 18, 2020

Dear friends from around the world,

Good morning! Good afternoon! Good evening!

I cordially welcome all of you to participate in the fifteenth Interethnic/Interfaith Leadership Conference.

China has been one of the campaign issues in the 2020 US election, but we have found a remarkable degree of consensus among the candidates. It was a bipartisan fantasy to believe that, as the PRC integrated into the global economy, the CCP would naturally loosen its grip on power. Both parties rightly recognize this as a problem, and there has been little partisan disagreement over, for example, targeted sanctions relating to CCP abuses in Hong Kong, Xinjiang, and Tibet. Nor have prominent Democrats criticized the current administration's aggressive responses to the threats to national security posed by the success of PRC-based technology companies beholden to the CCP.

By now, the need for principled solidarity should be obvious. Regardless of the election's outcome, we should urge everyone who cares about democratic values to deepen that sense of solidarity in the months and years to come.

Standing alone, even the United States has difficulty preventing the PRC from eroding democratic values. Dependence on the PRC, combined with financial incentives, bends everything—from domestic policymaking to the behavior of private institutions like Disney or the NBA to the tenor of discussions occurring in American universities—away from democratic principles.

In response to economically coercive statecraft that the CCP is practicing, a new kind of alliance like NATO, marrying economics with democratic principles, is needed. It is the best response to the CCP's own pursuit of a decades-long strategy of maintaining a united front with its allies and dividing and conquering its opponents.

What should members of a united, democratic front commit to doing? At a minimum, among many other things which I do not have time now to enumerate, they should credibly promise to assist each other economically if any member is retaliated against by the PRC—or any other country, frankly—for mere nonviolent advocacy.

Regardless of whether one favors Trump or Biden, regardless of whether a particular democracy leans center-left or center-right, so long as one claims to believe in ideals like the rule of law, human rights, and free speech, one should recognize that advancing those ideals requires putting aside our lesser differences. The CCP and other autocratic regimes would like nothing more than to continue dividing us along ethnic, religious, partisan, national, or various other solidarity-weakening lines. If we fall for it, those who will suffer most in the long run are the citizens of those regimes, few, if any, of whom really want to live in societies dominated by lies, fear, and violence. And while lasting democratic change ultimately depends on the organic efforts of those citizens, those of us lucky enough to live in freedom would do well to not undermine such efforts by letting increasingly powerful dictators play us against each other to the detriment of democratic values everywhere.

Our solidarity must become a verb.

Resources

Citizen Power Initiatives for China: A grassroots movement dedicated to advancing a peaceful transition to democracy in China. https://www.citizenpowerforchina.org

***Yibao*:** A Chinese-language online magazine providing op-eds and news articles focused on the human rights and rule of law situation inside China. https://yibaochina.com

64 Questions for Xi Jinping:
https://www.citizenpowerforchina.org/64-questions-for-xi-jinping/

Online petition: Tell Us What Happened to the "Tank Man":
https://tinyurl.com/finding2tankmen
or
https://www.change.org/p/xi-jinping-tell-us-what-happened-to-the-two-tank-men

About the Author

Dr. Yang Jianli is a world renown scholar, human rights activist, and architect and leader for China's democracy. Having narrowly escaped the 1989 Tiananmen Massacre, he immigrated to the United States to continue his human rights and democracy work. He is president of Citizen Power Initiatives for China, which he founded in 2007 on his release from his imprisonment in China. He was imprisoned there for five years, starting in 2002 when he returned to China to help the people of China with nonviolent resistance strategies. Dr. Yang firmly believes it is critical for a peaceful democratic transition in China that the world's democracies continue to hold China accountable for abusing the human and political rights of its citizens. He has won numerous awards, and holds several advisory positions in human rights advocacy organizations. He holds a Ph.D. of mathematics from U.C. Berkeley and Ph.D. of political economy from Harvard University.

Made in the USA
Columbia, SC
23 October 2023

24849312R00390